THE DEAL OF THE CENTURY

THE DEAL OF

THE BREAK

BY

NEW YORK   1986

THE CENTURY

UP OF AT&T

STEVE COLL

ATHENEUM

George Calhoun
October 5, 1986
en route to Tokyo

Library of Congress Cataloging-in-Publication Data

Coll, Steve.
    The deal of the century.

    Includes index.
    1. American Telephone and Telegraph Company—
Reorganization—History.   2. Telephone—United States—
History.   I. Title.
HE8846.A55C58   1986   384.6'065'73   86-47676
ISBN 0-689-11757-4

Published simultaneously in Canada by Collier Macmillan Canada, Inc.
Composition by Westchester Book Composition, Inc.,
Yorktown Heights, New York
Manufactured by Fairfield Graphics, Fairfield, Pennsylvania
Designed by Harry Ford
First Edition

*for **Susan** and **Alexandra***

Competition—effective, aggressive competition—means *strife*, industrial warfare; it means contention; it oftentimes means taking advantage of or resorting to any means that the conscience of the contestants or the degree of the enforcement of the laws will permit.

Theodore Vail
President, American
Telephone & Telegraph
Company
1910

Acknowledgments

This is a book above all about people, and thus it belongs first to my sources—the lawyers, executives, politicians, and government officials who opened their professional and sometimes their personal lives to me without any guarantees about my intentions or motives. To list the names of those who were especially helpful would betray their trust; they know who they are, and I am grateful to them. And of course, none of them bears any responsibility for what I have written.

This is also a book about institutions, and on that score, too, I count myself fortunate. Confronted with my requests for interviews and information, AT&T might easily have tried to deny me access. Instead, the company was courageous enough to open its doors, albeit cautiously and with one foot on the jamb. I found the professionalism and courtesy of its representatives, despite their concern about what I was after, to be exceptional among the large corporations I have dealt with as a reporter. Paula Horii in the media relations department was particularly helpful in arranging interviews and channeling information. Similarly, the Justice Department responded to my various inquiries, including a request for documents under the Freedom of Information Act, with speed and thoroughness unusual among federal bureaucracies.

I owe a great deal to the magazine and newspaper editors

who occasionally employed, always supported, and invariably taught me during the more than two-year life of this project. They include Scott Kaufer, Cal Fentress, Tom Bates, and Matt Smith at *California* magazine; George Gendren, Bo Burlingham, Gene Stone, and Steve Solomon at *Inc.* magazine; and Bob Thompson, Mary Hadar, Ellen Edwards, Janet Duckworth, and Len Downie at the *Washington Post*.

The late John Cushman, who once told me that he became a literary agent because he liked to "go home every night and clean the blood out of my teeth," favored this book with one of his last bursts of brilliance. Tom Stewart and Susan Leon at Atheneum made possible what Cushman began. And my current agent, Melanie Jackson, has done much to improve the quality of my professional life.

I was assisted in my research by the staffs at George Washington University's Gelman Library for telecommunications; the University of Southern California's Crocker business library; the University of California at Los Angeles' several business, law, and communications libraries; the AT&T legal document room in Washington, D.C.; the Library of Congress' law and periodical reading rooms; and by the staff at the National Archives. The clerks in the U.S. District Court filing room in Washington, D.C., went beyond the call of duty to locate missing documents and to arrange for copying services.

Chuck Jensvold, Martin Burns, Dan Leighton, Sue Horton, Rich Bonin, Anne Ball, Tensi Whelan, and Joel Kotkin helped me find materials I would otherwise have missed.

My family saw me through, especially my wife Susan, who for so long was the only one who understood what I was doing. Without her, I would never have finished.

Steve Coll
Gaithersburg, Maryland
March 1986

Contents

Cast of Characters   xiii
Local Operating Companies   xv
The Shape of AT&T on May 8, 1972   xvi

THE CASE

1 The Whites of Their Eyes   5
2 The First Shot   16
3 The New Trustbusters   27
4 The Decision to Decide   36
5 Legacy of a Scandal   53
6 "I Intend to Bring an Action"   63
7 Stillborn   73
8 McGowan's Gambit   83
9 DeButts' Last Stand   92
10 The Red and Blue Teams   101
11 Severed Limbs   113
12 The Answer Man   123

THE DEAL

13   The New Realism   135
14   Crimson Sky   147
15   Two Lawyers   161
16   The Sky Falls   172
17   Litigating to the Eyeballs   180
18   Connell's Deception   190
19   Saunders and McGowan   200
20   The Baldrige Proposal   211
21   The Disengaged Presidency   223
22   Escalation   230
23   Baxter's Finesse   239
24   A Judicial Temperament   254
25   Judgment Day   261
26   The Inter-Intra Split   268
27   Court of Last Resort   282
28   Fence with a One-Way Hole   291
29   The Two-Pager   303
30   Après Ski   312
31   January 8   324
32   "This Case Is History"   336

AFTERMATH

33   Congress Awakens   347
34   The Telecommunications Czar   357
35   An Imperfect World   365
36   Epilogue   375

     Notes and Sources   381
     Index   387

Cast of Characters

JUSTICE DEPARTMENT

Kenneth Anderson, *trial team lead attorney, 1977–1980*
William F. Baxter, *antitrust chief, 1981–1983*
Ronald Carr, *deputy to Baxter in antitrust front office*
Keith Clearwaters, *antitrust front office attorney*
Gerald Connell, *trial team lead attorney, 1980–1982*
Jim Denvir, *trial team attorney*
Loren Hershey, *antitrust front office staff attorney*
Thomas Kauper, *antitrust chief, 1972–1976*
Peter Kenney, *trial team attorney*
Richard Levine, *antitrust front office attorney*
Sanford Litvack, *antitrust chief, 1980–1981*
Hugh Morrison, *antitrust front office section chief*
Jonathan Rose, *assistant attorney general, office of legal policy*
William Saxbe, *attorney general, 1974–1975*
John Shenefield, *antitrust chief, 1977–1980*
William French Smith, *attorney general, 1981–1985*
Philip Verveer, *trial team lead attorney, 1974–1977*

AMERICAN TELEPHONE & TELEGRAPH COMPANY

Edward Block, *senior vice-president, public relations*
Charles Brown, *chairman, 1979–1986*

John Dulany deButts, *chairman, 1972–1979*
Mark Garlinghouse, *general counsel to deButts*
Charles Hugel, *executive vice-president, strategic planning*
C. W. Jackson, *business relations director*
Jim Kilpatric, *staff attorney*
Harold Levy, *staff attorney*
Robert McLean, *Sidley & Austin attorney*
Ian Ross, *president, Bell Laboratories*
George L. Saunders, Jr., *Sidley & Austin, lead trial attorney*
Morris Tannenbaum, *executive vice-president*
Howard Trienens, *Sidley & Austin attorney, general counsel to Brown*
Michael Yauch, *Sidley & Austin attorney*
John Zeglis, *Sidley & Austin attorney*

OTHERS

James Baker, *chief of staff to President Reagan, 1981–1985*
Malcolm Baldrige, *secretary of commerce, 1981–*
Vincent Biunno, *U.S. District Court judge, Newark, New Jersey*
Kenneth Cox, *senior vice-president, MCI*
Jack Goeken, *founder of MCI*
Harold H. Greene, *U.S. District Court judge, Washington, D.C.*
Larry Harris, *MCI staff attorney*
Senator Philip A. Hart, *chairman of Senate antitrust subcommittee, early 1970s*
Walter Hinchman, *FCC Common Carrier Bureau chief, mid-1970s*
William McGowan, *chairman of MCI*
Edwin Meese, *counselor to President Reagan, 1981–1985*
Kenneth Robinson, *Commerce department attorney*
Representative Peter Rodino, *chairman of House antitrust subcommittee*
Bernard Strassburg, *FCC Common Carrier Bureau chief, 1964–1973*
Joseph C. Waddy, *U.S. District Court judge, Washington, D.C.*
Caspar Weinberger, *secretary of defense, 1981–*
Rep. Timothy Wirth, *chairman of House telecommunications subcommittee*
Bernard Wunder, *assistant secretary of commerce, telecommunications*

The Shape of American Telephone and Telegraph Co. on May 8, 1972

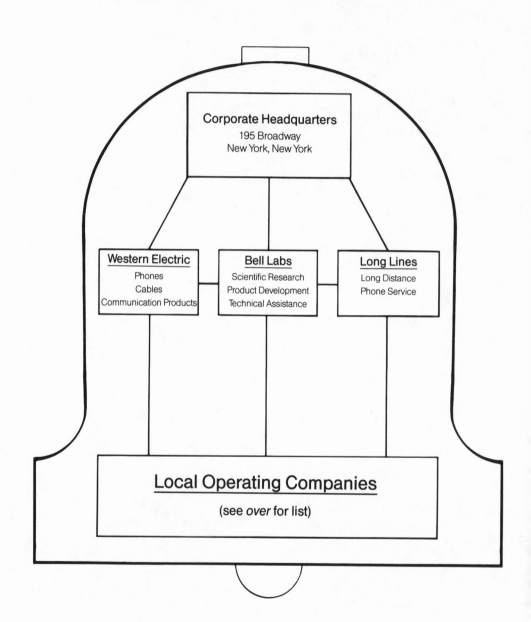

Corporate Headquarters
195 Broadway
New York, New York

Western Electric
Phones
Cables
Communication Products

Bell Labs
Scientific Research
Product Development
Technical Assistance

Long Lines
Long Distance
Phone Service

Local Operating Companies

(see *over* for list)

Local Operating Companies

Bell Telephone Co. of Nevada
Illinois Bell Telephone Co.
Indiana Bell Telephone Co.
Michigan Bell Telephone Co.
New England Telephone and Telegraph Co.
New Jersey Bell Telephone Co.
Northwestern Bell Telephone Co.
Pacific Northwest Bell Telephone Co.
Pacific Telephone & Telegraph Co.
South Central Bell Telephone Co.
Southern Bell Telephone & Telegraph Co.
Southwestern Bell Telephone Co.
The Bell Telephone Co. of Pennsylvania
The Chesapeake & Potomac Telephone Co.
The Chesapeake & Potomac Telephone Co. of Maryland
The Chesapeake & Potomac Telephone Co. of Virginia
The Chesapeake & Potomac Telephone Co. of West Virginia
The Diamond State Telephone Co.
The Mountain States Telephone & Telegraph Co.
The New York Telephone Co.
The Ohio Bell Telephone Co.
Wisconsin Telephone Co.
Cincinnati Bell Telephone Co.*
Southern New England Bell Telephone Co.*

*Partially owned

The Case

Chapter 1

The Whites of Their Eyes

ONE by one, in their rented luxury sedans, the executives of American Telephone & Telegraph Company crossed the Card Sound Bridge and drove east into the morning sun, toward Crocodile Lake. There was a warm, salty breeze wafting from the ocean; palm trees along the road bowed politely to the passing cars. It was Monday, May 8, 1972, the dawn of another dazzling week in the paradisiacal tropics of Key Largo, Florida.

At the stop sign where Card Sound Road meets the Overseas Highway, the cars turned north, along the peninsula, tracing the road as it sliced through a reedy everglade. A few hundred yards to the right lay the Atlantic, its crystal waters washing over the largest living coral reef in the world. Not far to the left was the still, blue deep of Card Sound.

Two miles on, the cars slowed at the security gate of the Ocean Reef Club, a lush and exclusive resort frequented by Jacqueline Kennedy Onassis and President Richard Nixon's close friend Bebe Rebozo. The AT&T executives were checked for identification and then ushered in. Beyond the gate, the manicured fairways of the club's several golf courses came into view, and beyond them, the gleaming masts of yachts docked in Ocean Reef's private harbor.

It would be an idyllic week for golf, or for sailing, but not all the AT&T executives arriving in Key Largo for the company's semiannual Presidents' Conference were in a playful mood. Though they were calm and patrician men, well-drilled in the manners and mores of corporate eminence, some of them were girding for a fight. The uncharacteristic outrage and emotion they would display over the next five days had been brewing inside them for months, even years.

Nearly all of AT&T's key executives had worked for the company for two decades or more, and only a few had ever been employed by anyone else. They were the guardians, many of them strongly believed, of one of the most important public trusts in America, "Ma Bell," which happened also to be the largest corporation in the world. And now that public trust was under attack, from within and without, and was in danger of being destroyed.

Some of the executives arriving in Key Largo could see parallels between the challenges their company now faced and other assaults on public institutions that were depicted each evening on the television news. That Monday night, for example, as they sat in their hotel rooms, some of the executives watched news reports about antiwar protesters who had forced the closure of the United States Capitol. Later that same evening, President Nixon delivered a somber, nationally televised address announcing that he had ordered massive air strikes against North Vietnamese targets and had also ordered the mining of all North Vietnamese harbors. "At this moment, we must stand together in purpose and resolve," Nixon urged. Even in those turbulent times, AT&T itself was not often faced with angry demonstrations by student protestors. Nonetheless, some of the company's top executives felt that it was precisely a lack of "purpose and resolve" that was the cause of AT&T's problems. The dissenters had come to the Ocean Reef Club to confront AT&T's new chairman of the board with their views.

And that was exactly what John Dulany deButts, the new chairman, wanted. He had taken over the company only six weeks before, and he, too, was dissatisfied with its state of affairs. Indeed, he believed that AT&T had reached one of the lowest ebbs in its century of existence, and he was determined to turn things around—quickly. The Key Largo conference was an important part of his plan. For too long, deButts felt, the presidents of AT&T's basic operating companies—the local phone companies across the country such as New York Telephone, Pacific Bell, Illinois Bell, Mountain States Bell, and so on—had been stifling their ideas and complaints, unable to convey them to AT&T's centralized corporate management headquartered in New York City. That was one reason why morale among AT&T's one million employees was disintegrating into malaise and dissension. By inviting the presidents to Key Largo, and by encouraging them to air their opinions with impunity in an atmosphere of free exchange, deButts hoped both to reassure the presidents that their views were being heard and to gain new insights about how to meet the challenges facing his company.

And he knew the challenges were plentiful. The most visible of them, and the most vexatious to AT&T's chairman, was a precipitous and unprecedented decline in the quality of AT&T's basic phone service to the public—what deButts liked to call "pots," or "plain old telephone service." By 1970, two years before deButts ascended to the chairmanship, the decline had reached crisis proportions in a number of major cities, including New York. The basic problem was one of supply and demand: too much demand for new phone service and not enough AT&T facilities to accommodate all the new customers. The result had been horrendous delays and breakdowns, especially in Manhattan, the nation's media and financial capital. Television networks, banks, securities underwriters, and publishing companies—all of which wielded great influence over how AT&T was perceived by investors and the public—had experienced long, aggravating delays in obtaining new phone service and in having their phone systems repaired. These peeved and powerful customers lashed back at AT&T, publicly criticizing, even ridiculing the giant monopoly for its apparent arrogance and incompetence. Such criticism fueled the public's own growing suspicions in the late 1960s about the motivations and priorities of large corporations generally. Ma Bell quickly became a favorite object of jokes and political satire. Lily Tomlin, the "Laugh In" comedienne, had developed a popular routine around an insolent telephone operator which seemed to capture perfectly the widespread unrest over deteriorating phone service.

John deButts also knew that, like most business crises, AT&T's telephone service emergency in Manhattan and elsewhere had been caused by the company's own shortsightedness. The cost of providing basic telephone service to the country was enormous. AT&T had to build, install, maintain, and replace hundreds of thousands of miles of cable and wire, millions of residential telephones and business telephone systems, as well as a sophisticated network of switching stations that directed every call to its proper destination. Just to maintain a system of that magnitude and diversity required huge expenditures by AT&T every year—$7.5 billion in 1971, more money than some large companies would spend in a decade on plants and equipment. And when customers demanded more phone service, as they had throughout the 1960s, AT&T's capital requirements became astronomical. But if AT&T cheated on its investment, if it failed to spend the necessary money to build new phone lines and switching stations to accommodate new customers, the disastrous results would become quickly apparent. That was exactly what had happened by 1970. Inflation during the 1960s had driven up AT&T's costs and had squeezed the company's profits. Rather than raising phone rates to cover inflation, the operating company presidents had decided to cut costs and to stop investing so heavily in the upkeep of the phone system. In the short term, the companies' profits rose, and the presidents were praised for frugality. But in just a few years, the neglected phone system, unable to accommodate the new demand for telephones, had collapsed under pressure.

So that was John deButts' first priority as he arrived at the Ocean Reef Club on May 8, 1972—to restore plain old telephone service and to redeem the Bell System's good name with the public. DeButts did not intend to approach this task with the cool detachment of a corporate turnaround artist; he regarded AT&T's service crisis as a kind of personal embarrassment. An

imposing, broad-shouldered figure at six feet, two inches tall
and weighing two hundred pounds, deButts seemed to embody
the spirit of the Bell System. Reared in a comfortable, Old South
railway family, he had taken his first job with AT&T more than
thirty years before, immediately after he graduated as a captain
from the Virginia Military Institute. Now in his fifties, deButts
still retained the bearing of a military man. He exuded leadership, power, and privilege. He was a self-styled captain of
industry, dressing in dark, conservative suits, flashing the
obligatory gold cufflinks and watch. When he met a man, he
shook his hand firmly and looked him in the eye; when he
spoke, deButts' southern drawl carried the authority of a general's wartime orders.

On his way up AT&T's long executive ladder, deButts had
worked in twenty-two different jobs and had seen every corner
of the company's vast telecommunications empire. He had
worked in the basic operating companies, starting as a traffic
manager with the Chesapeake and Potomac Telephone Company in Virginia and rising eventually to the presidency of
Illinois Bell. He had seen the Western Electric Company,
AT&T's multibillion-dollar manufacturing subsidiary, which in
May 1972 made virtually every telephone used in America, as
well as nearly all the cable, wire, and switching systems that
comprised the phone network. He had been involved, too, with
the prestigious Bell Laboratories, AT&T's research and development arm, which by the end of the 1970s would hold more
than 19,000 patents and which had been responsible since the
early 1900s for such seminal technological advances as radio
telephony, vacuum tube amplifiers, cable television, early digital computers, transistors, silicon chips, and lasers. For a time,
he had headed AT&T's "government relations" office, the company's powerful lobbying operation in Washington. And most
recently he had served apprenticeships in the New York–based
Long Lines department, which was responsible for long distance service, and in the company's financial department, which
had the unenviable task of raising billions of dollars in debt and
equity financing on the public markets each year.

By the time H. I. Romnes, a brilliant engineer but a relatively ineffective chief executive, announced his retirement as
AT&T's chairman at a February 1972 press conference, John
deButts was ready—the sprawling operations and the sacred
public mission of the Bell System not only had been drilled into
his mind, but had seeped into his soul. Like a king ascending
to a corrupted throne, deButts intended to reawaken the spirit
of AT&T's declining empire. In his first weeks on the job, he
made plans to travel around the country to deliver pep talks
to AT&T employees about the history of the Bell System's public
trust. He ordered emergency construction spending to restore
quality phone service in major cities. And he made it plain that
there would be no compromises on service—"pots" came first,
profits would follow, deButts said.

But there was one other problem facing AT&T as its executives gathered in Florida that May. And John deButts did
not appreciate just how large a problem it was about to become.

On March 30, in preparation for the Key Largo meeting,
deButts' executive assistant in New York had written letters to
all the participants asking if there were any special topics they
thought should be included on the conference agenda. The
response had been overwhelming. Many of the presidents of
the basic operating companies, as well as some top officers of
Western Electric, Bell Labs, Long Lines, and other divisions
that made up the Presidents' Conference, agreed that there was
one problem facing AT&T that demanded immediate and decisive action: competition.

John deButts understood why the presidents were upset.
The competition AT&T was facing in the telecommunications
industry made his blood boil. The new chairman, though, hadn't
yet decided what to do about it.

The competition came in two varieties. In 1968, in a landmark decision known as *Carterfone*, the Federal Communications Commission (FCC), the federal government agency
responsible for regulation of the communications industries,
had ruled that the "terminal equipment" market should be
opened up for the first time to companies other than AT&T.
"Terminal equipment"—or "CPE" (customer premises equip-

ment), as it was known inside AT&T—was really a bureaucratic euphemism for "telephones" or "telephone equipment." Before *Carterfone*, AT&T had owned virtually every residential telephone and business switchboard in the country, and it leased the equipment to customers. But the FCC, which was under political pressure to do something about AT&T's deteriorating phone service and rising profits, and which felt that AT&T was unable to keep up with the explosion in new telecommunications technologies, decided that independent companies making new communications devices like answering machines and mobile radio phones should be allowed to interconnect with AT&T's switched phone network, a privilege that had been previously denied them. Suddenly, phone users could buy non-AT&T equipment and plug it into the telephone lines at their homes or businesses.

But another, even more threatening kind of competition had been nibbling away at AT&T prior to the Key Largo meeting. It was referred to in industry jargon as "intercity services." And on that clear May morning when the presidents of AT&T's operating companies gathered in the Ocean Reef Club's Everglades Meeting Complex for their long-awaited free exchange with John deButts, it quickly became obvious that intercity services competition was the root cause of the executives' simmering discontent.

Richard Hough, president of the Long Lines department, began the meeting by briefing his colleagues on where the situation stood. In 1969, one year after *Carterfone*, the FCC had handed down another decision that had stunned AT&T's executives: The commission had granted the application of an embryonic, underfinanced, and aggressive company called Microwave Communications, Incorporated, to enter the intercity "private line" business between Chicago and St. Louis. MCI, which then had only about two dozen employees, would sell private long-distance lines to companies with offices in both the cities MCI served, but it would not provide long-distance service to residential or business customers. For a flat monthly rate, a company could connect the phones in its St. Louis offices directly to the phones in its Chicago offices, and it could save money by avoiding AT&T's switched long-distance network. AT&T was also in the private-line business, but MCI promised the FCC that its prices would be lower than Bell's because it would operate more efficiently. While AT&T had to pay for the nation's basic local phone network—made up mainly of expensive copper wires—MCI would employ a new and cheaper technology: microwaves. MCI proposed to erect a string of microwave towers between Chicago and St. Louis and to "broadcast" its calls on a microwave beam. The technology had actually been developed by AT&T, and Bell also employed microwaves on many of its long-distance routes. But since MCI's costs were not inflated by the upkeep of the basic wire-and-cable phone network, it could reap savings by using microwaves exclusively, and thus could charge less for its private-line service than AT&T. At least, that is what MCI claimed.

Preoccupied with major service crises such as the one in New York, AT&T's executives had paid little attention to MCI after its application was granted. There was a serious question as to whether MCI could ever raise enough money to get started with its ambitious microwave construction project. And even if it did, there were doubts about whether the company could find enough customers to support its limited network.

Three years later, as Hough reminded the assembled membership of the Presidents' Conference, MCI was still around, and it was beginning to steal away a startling number of AT&T's Chicago and St. Louis customers by pre-selling its service. (MCI had not yet even begun to construct its microwave towers.) Hough told the AT&T presidents why MCI was having such early success: its monthly rates were at least $100 less than AT&T's. And then he asked the crucial question: "What should our response be?"

There were two choices. The company could leave its prices alone and just absorb the loss of private-line revenues as AT&T's previous chairman, H. I. Romnes, had done. Or, the company could lower its private-line prices and go head-to-head with MCI. This was the strategy the operating company presidents intended to urge on deButts.

"There's been a change in MCI's position," one of the presidents pointed out as the discussion got under way. "Now they say that the viability of Chicago–St. Louis depends on inter-connections with other MCI routes."

The implication was clear: there might be no end to MCI's ambitions. The fledgling company might build on its Chicago–St. Louis route and create a national microwave network. That possibility outraged the AT&T presidents. AT&T's private-line and other long-distance prices, which were continually dis-puted and scrutinized by state and federal regulators, were set under a complex system referred to by AT&T as "nationwide average pricing" and "separations." In essence, AT&T priced some of its intercity services, such as private line, WATS, and regular long distance, relatively high in order to subsidize the enormous costs of building and maintaining the nation's wire-and-cable telephone infrastructure. If those costs were just passed on to local telephone users in the monthly bill, the price of residential phone service might double or triple. Instead, local service received a subsidy from long-distance revenues. How great that subsidy was, and what shape it actually took, was something regulators often disagreed about. But there was one thing everyone agreed on: AT&T's system of pricing kept the cost of basic phone service low for the average customer, as well as for the poor and elderly, who needed phones to obtain vital services. By jumping into just one area of the telecom-munications market—private line—MCI was just "creamskim-ming," as AT&T's executives put it. True, AT&T's private-line sales represented just a tiny fraction of the company's enormous revenues, and the FCC had said clearly that MCI would never be permitted to provide regular long-distance service. Still, any form of long-distance competition would inevitably drive AT&T's prices toward the company's costs: The price of local service, where costs were high, would rise dramatically, while the price of long-distance, where costs were lower, would decline. This possibility troubled AT&T's executives. What would happen to the Bell's delicate system of "public service" subsidies if MCI continued to grow? What would happen to AT&T's profits if it began to lose revenues in areas where AT&T's profit margins were high?

Or, as one of the presidents now put it, "How badly would we be hurt if we wait until we see the whites of their eyes?"

The anger of the local operating company presidents began to pour out. For months now, they had been forced to sit idly by while MCI went after some of their largest business customers. AT&T's New York management had done nothing to prevent it. "I would meet 'em or beat 'em," exclaimed T. S. Nurnberger, president of Northwestern Bell. "You bastards are not going to take away my business!"

"Shouldn't we act now, rather than wait until they have going businesses which regulators might not permit us to dislodge?" added A. W. Van Sinderen, president of Southern New England Telephone.

"If we're going to do this, we have to do it now," another president chimed in.

Nurnberger seemed ready to explode. "How many MCIs will proceed with construction plans if we file matching rates now? A big fat zero!"

"We must take account of the prospect of intrastate competition," said Charles L. Brown, who was at least as frustrated as Nurnberger—as president of Illinois Bell, Brown's territory was under direct attack from MCI. "There are large amounts of revenues that are vulnerable, which we can preserve if we choke off now. I think you have to hit the nails on the head."

It was a metaphor that Brown, already being groomed as a possible successor to deButts as AT&T's chairman, would later regret.

The meeting broke up around noon, and the executives wandered out of the conference room and onto the sunlit grounds of the Ocean Reef Club. DeButts had gotten the free exchange he had asked for—and then some. But what would the new chairman do? The presidents knew that deButts was as distressed by the FCC's piecemeal, procompetition decisions as they were. But deButts also appeared to believe deeply in the service traditions of the Bell System, including nationwide average pricing, from which he might be unwilling to deviate.

No direct answers from deButts were forthcoming. But in his closing remarks on Friday, AT&T's new chairman gave the presidents a glimpse of the strategy he was forming. Addressing the topic of terminal equipment competition, deButts told his lieutenants, "Why, then, is it not an altogether rational position to state that it will take time to resolve an issue of such far-reaching implications as this one? And why shouldn't we use that time in two ways: one, conveying our concerns in realistic terms to regulators and the public so that the long-term public interest implications are clear, and two, putting our own house in order?"

There would be no immediate changes. DeButts intended to wait.

On June 22, 1972, six weeks after the AT&T executives departed Key Largo, MCI issued a public offering of stock and raised more than $100 million for the company. In the prospectus that accompanied the offering, MCI announced plans to expand its Chicago–St. Louis route by constructing a network of microwave communications towers encompassing 165 American cities from coast to coast. When they learned of MCI's ambitious plans, it seemed to John deButts and hs angry presidents that a gauntlet had been laid down.

Chapter 2

The First Shot

WILLIAM MCGOWAN, the chairman of MCI, had for years been rich in potential but short on cash. So when his fledgling company became suddenly flush in the summer of 1972, one of the first things McGowan did was move its corporate headquarters some three blocks away, into a brand new, twelve-story building at the corner of 17th and M Streets in northwest Washington, D.C. He abandoned the rented office furniture that had cluttered his old headquarters and acquired for himself a large, oval desk with a center standard. The desk lent an air of authority and constancy to McGowan's new and spacious corner office on the ninth floor—and the impression of permanence was exactly what McGowan intended to cultivate in the months ahead. Though his company had leased only two floors, McGowan persuaded his landlord to affix three large, black letters to the building's exterior façade so that passing motorists and pedestrians on busy 17th Street would be reminded daily that MCI had arrived.

The touch was typical of McGowan, a man who believed in playing every angle, especially when there was money at stake. Once, vacationing on a Caribbean island and finding himself stranded by a local airline strike, McGowan had chartered a jet to the States and paid for it by selling tickets to frustrated tourists at the airport, rescuing his fellow travelers and clearing a handsome profit at the same time.

He had grown up in Wilkes-Barre, Pennsylvania, a bleak Appalachian coal town colored gray by smoke and soot from dozens of nearby anthracite coal plants. His father was a union organizer who worked with the men at Wilkes-Barre's bustling railyards, where tons of coal moved in and out of the city on five different railroad lines. McGowan knew early and profoundly the ethic of relentless hard work that drove Wilkes-Barre's smokestack industries, and if he was ever inclined to forget that ethic in adolescence, the corporal discipline meted out by the nuns in the Catholic schools he attended provided a painful reminder of his obligations.

McGowan seldom needed to be pushed, however. By the time he graduated from a local college, the coal fields were nearly depleted and Wilkes-Barre was in decline; and McGowan was determined to leave the city's encroaching despair behind him. After brief military service, he worked his way through Harvard Business School on the G.I. bill, graduating in 1954 in the top five percent of his class. His classmates went on to entry-level management jobs in America's largest corporations, including AT&T, but McGowan shunned such opportunities. He began to hustle, working for a multitude of small, entrepreneurial, start-up companies that were dabbling in new technologies. Five years out of school, McGowan launched the Powertron Corporation, a modestly successful company that made ultrasonic devices. He sold the company quickly and invested his cash in new ventures.

In 1968, a lawyer in Chicago told McGowan about a company called Microwave Communications, Incorporated, which was in desperate need of both management and financial assistance. MCI was a skeleton then—it had no full-time employees, and its principal asset was a five-year-old application that had been filed with the FCC to provide point-to-point private-line service over microwaves between St. Louis and Chicago. McGowan investigated the idea and decided to put his money behind it. Immediately, he was appointed the company's chairman and chief executive officer. One year later,

McGowan's gamble paid off—the FCC approved MCI's application.

By early 1973, aided by a $72 million line of bank credit, McGowan had taken MCI public, begun construction of the Chicago–St. Louis line, moved into his new Washington offices at 17th and M Streets, and laid plans for a national network of microwave towers. If all went well, Bill McGowan would soon be a very rich man, proprietor of the first independent, alternative long-distance telephone network in America.

But all was not going well, and that was why, on an unseasonably warm Tuesday in early January 1973, McGowan summoned six of MCI's key executives to the company's ninth-floor conference room.

The problem was AT&T. In order for MCI to pre-sell its new service to customers and to map out a business plan for its ambitious construction projects, the company had to make a deal with AT&T. MCI did not own any telephones, or local telephone lines, or any switching stations to connect them all together—nor did it ever intend to own such things. AT&T owned, maintained, and controlled the nation's basic phone network. What MCI wanted was to interconnect with that network in the major cities where it planned to sell its private line services. An MCI customer in St. Louis, for example, would still use his Western Electric–made AT&T-owned telephone to call Chicago on an MCI private line. When he dialed, his call would travel out of his office over AT&T-owned lines, through a few local AT&T switching stations, and finally to a larger AT&T switching station that served the St. Louis area. Without MCI, the call would then have been routed onto one of AT&T's Long Lines to Chicago, where once again it would be switched through the local exchanges and into the customer's branch office. What MCI proposed to do was to substitute its microwave system for the Long Lines part of AT&T's network. When its St. Louis customer's call reached the AT&T regional switching station, instead of traveling on an AT&T Long Line, the signal would be switched over to MCI's microwave towers and would be beamed all the way to Chicago. At the Chicago end, the call would again be switched over to AT&T's local lines, wending its way over the regular network into the branch office. This was the only feasible way for MCI to provide its service. It would be financially impossible for MCI to build its own labyrinthine local phone networks in St. Louis and Chicago simply to handle the long-distance calls of MCI's customers.

That meant that MCI had to negotiate to use AT&T's local phone networks in every city where there were MCI customers—and there was the rub. AT&T was not going to let MCI use its local networks for free. When the FCC authorized MCI to go into business, over the strenuous objections of AT&T's Washington lobbyists, the commission told AT&T that it had to allow MCI to interconnect with the basic phone network. But the commission didn't tell AT&T how much it should charge MCI for connections, or how fast AT&T should install MCI's lines, or how AT&T should calculate its own costs when determining an interconnection price for MCI. All of that was to be worked out in negotiations between AT&T and MCI.

The negotiations had not gone smoothly.

They had begun in September, four months after AT&T's secret discussion about MCI in Key Largo. Larry Harris, an MCI staff lawyer who had been hired by McGowan to handle the negotiations for the company, had traveled to New York to meet with AT&T's representatives. Less than a week after the talks began, AT&T told Harris that the company had changed its mind about how it would charge MCI for interconnections. Originally, MCI had planned to "rent" access to AT&T's local phone network on a monthly basis, and Harris figured the negotiations would center on determining a per-customer price, which MCI would pay AT&T. But that wasn't what AT&T had in mind. Mark Garlinghouse, AT&T's general counsel and one of John deButts' closest advisers, told Harris that AT&T had recently decided on a "capital contribution" plan under which MCI would be required to help pay for the maintenance and upkeep of the nation's basic phone system—its miles and miles of expensive wires and cables. In the months after Key Largo, and following MCI's successful $100 million stock offering, deButts had decided that AT&T wasn't going to let MCI get away with "creamskimming."

Harris and McGowan were surprised by Garlinghouse's new plan, but mainly they wanted to hear about the bottom line. Call it renting, or leasing, or capital contribution—what mattered most to MCI was the actual price it had to pay to interconnect with AT&T's local network. MCI's entire business plan depended on that price. But the negotiations stalled. The capital contribution plan would be complex, and time was needed for AT&T to work out the details, Garlinghouse said. By Tuesday, January 9, 1973, when the MCI executives met, McGowan felt that his company was at the brink of crisis.

What strategy should they pursue?

"If we wanted to buy, can we finance it?" asked Jack Goeken, referring to AT&T's alternative offer to actually sell independent lines in its local networks to MCI. Goeken was MCI's original founder, and his role in the company had been increasingly usurped by McGowan. During recent years, Goeken's relationship with McGowan had deteriorated.

"No, it would destroy us," answered another MCI executive.

"Do we have a study of the comparison between leasing and buying?" one of the vice-presidents asked.

"There's no comparison," McGowan said with finality. "Leasing is much cheaper. Bell loves anything that involves long negotiations. We should concentrate on our plan—building seven cities in four months, twenty-four cities in twelve months. Here are our only alternatives: we can deal with the local operating companies, and sue; we can deal with AT&T, and sue; we can complain to the FCC; or we can negotiate."

An antitrust lawsuit against AT&T had been much on McGowan's mind lately. He had consulted with a number of attorneys about the current negotiations with AT&T. McGowan knew a great deal about antitrust law himself. He knew, particularly, about something called the "essential facilities" doctrine in antitrust law. If one company—say, AT&T—owned exclusive facilities that were essential to the business of another company—say, MCI—then the first company was required to give access to the second company. McGowan carried that doctrine around with him like a concealed weapon, ready to pull it on AT&T whenever his back was against the wall.

"The threat of a suit against Bell has no impact," said Goeken, antagonizing McGowan.

"I like the threat of a suit against the local companies," McGowan responded. "It would break the company apart."

"Litigation takes too long," Goeken grumbled.

The discussion moved on, and a strategy began to take shape in McGowan's mind. Finally, he laid it out to his vice presidents.

"The first thing we should pursue is high-pressure negotiations with 195 Broadway," McGowan said, referring to the site of AT&T's corporate headquarters in lower Manhattan. "While this goes on, we should prepare an antitrust suit against AT&T, prepare an antitrust suit against the local operating companies, and send briefings to the FCC. And I would add another thing. We should maintain and increase the department of Justice's knowledge about this."

McGowan was aware that the Justice department's Antitrust division, which enforced the country's antitrust laws, could do more to move along his negotiations with AT&T than anyone else. Even an appearance of interest by Justice lawyers in the negotiations would worry AT&T, making it easier for MCI to get the kind of deal it was after.

MCI's chairman also had an idea about how best to pursue "high-pressure" negotiations with AT&T corporate headquarters. Perhaps McGowan should put the heat on AT&T himself, eyeball to eyeball with John deButts.

By the time Bill McGowan pushed through a revolving glass door into the lobby of 195 Broadway at about 9:30 A.M. on Friday, March 2, 1973, the MCI chairman had worked himself into a lather. He was ready to play hardball with his AT&T counterpart, and he was not going to be overmatched—as the son of a union organizer, McGowan had learned early in life about the use of threats and intimidation in business negotiations. John deButts, AT&T's patrician southern gentleman, was about to be introduced to a style of negotiation prevalent thirty years earlier in the smoky railroad union halls of Wilkes-Barre.

McGowan was now on AT&T's turf, however, and the headquarters building at 195 Broadway conjured up a culture far removed from the Dickensian milieu of an Appalachian coal town. The building was patterned after the Parthenon in Athens, and it was referred to as "a temple to the god of the telephone." There were 198 mammoth, fluted columns surrounding its white granite exterior, and there were forty more Italian marble columns in the lobby. On the roof was a large gold statue of a naked boy wrapped in wire, called "Genius of Electricity." The lobby interior was modeled after an Egyptian temple, containing a five-foot relief sculpture of Alexander Graham Bell and a marble floor inlaid with two bronze medallions, each eight feet in diameter. The medallions showed Mercury bearing the messages of the gods and were inscribed with the motto, "Universal Service."

McGowan crossed the lobby to a bank of elevators and rode to the twenty-sixth floor, where the offices of AT&T's top executives were situated. His relationship with AT&T had taken another turn for the worse since the January 9 MCI strategy session in Washington. At a February 26 press conference, deButts had announced that AT&T would finally break its decades-long policy of nationwide average pricing in order to compete with new companies like MCI. DeButts said that in November, AT&T would implement a new pricing system for its long distance services called "Hi/Lo." Prices for AT&T private-line services on the same routes serviced by MCI would be substantially reduced, which was precisely what the operating company presidents had urged deButts to do the previous May in Key Largo. With one fell swoop, MCI's $100-per-month price advantage over AT&T had been eliminated. The timing of the announcement, coming in the midst of crucial negotiations over MCI's interconnections with the local phone network, had made McGowan furious. When the elevator doors opened and McGowan stepped out, he was seething mad.

John deButts occupied a plush, gold-carpeted suite in the southwest corner of the building. There was an exterior office nearer to the elevators, and behind it was a sprawling sitting room filled with antique English couches and coffee tables. There were floor-to-ceiling windows on two sides of the room, protected by swirling wrought-iron railings.

DeButts greeted McGowan and introduced him to George Cook, an AT&T attorney who would be sitting in on the discussion. The trio moved into the sitting room and took places on the couches. Coffee was poured from a silver service.

"I presume you are familiar with the recent Supreme Court decision in the Otter Tail case," McGowan began ominously, referring to a government antitrust case that involved a utility accused of anticompetitive practices. "My lawyers are busy reviewing it."

"I look to my counsel on those things," deButts replied.

From that contentious opening, the meeting quickly degenerated into confrontation and accusation. DeButts was unprepared for McGowan's direct attacks, but the military school graduate was not about to back off from a game of brinkmanship once it began.

"My studies of this Hi/Lo filing show that a very large percentage of your customers are going to have their rates reduced by 30 percent," McGowan said. "That's going to cost me revenues. The timing is bad."

"I'm not going to get into a discussion of price levels, but the overall rate adjustments under Hi/Lo are a wash," deButts said.

"Not on the routes MCI plans to serve," snapped McGowan.

"You can't have it both ways," said the AT&T chairman. "If there's going to be competition, some of our rates are obviously going to go up, and some are going to come down. You can't have competition and expect the existing rate structures to continue."

"But if you're trying to beat competition with Hi/Lo, the rate filing is premature. We haven't even started," McGowan said.

"We can't wait until competition has taken our business away," deButts replied forcefully. "We lost 115,000 terminal equipment stations last year to the interconnection industry. Competition is real."

"We want cost justifications for those rates, and you won't let us see your costs."

"There will be cost references in our filing with the FCC."

"Well," McGowan said, "we're going to demand copius data and you had better be prepared to supply it. We're going to fight Hi/Lo at the FCC, and we have better relations with the FCC than you do. We also have a number of friends in Congress."

"What do you want us to do?" deButts asked. "Sit on our hands?"

As the debate moved on, deButts conceded that he would have liked to have filed Hi/Lo earlier, but that his staff had been unable to prepare the supporting documentation quickly enough. DeButts cited other examples of how the "one-family historical approach" of AT&T's management, which had been in place for nearly a century, made it difficult for AT&T to respond quickly to competitors and their complaints.

"That's completely understandable," McGowan said at one point, "as well as completely illegal. There is this historical practice in the Bell system where everyone in the operating companies, and in Long Lines, and corporate headquarters, thinks of themselves and act as one unit." McGowan tried to cite as many examples as he could muster of how that attitude was hurting MCI. He mentioned that MCI intended to offer an expanded private-line service known in the industry as "FX," which involved greater access to AT&T's switched phone network than the services MCI was now offering to customers.

DeButts pounced on McGowan when he mentioned FX service. "That's a good example. In no way do we think it's fair for MCI to compete in the switched telephone business. That is just wrong."

"What hat are you wearing when you say that?" McGowan asked acidly. "The hat of a local phone company, or the hat of Long Lines?"

"I am speaking for the Bell System," deButts said.

McGowan actually began to shout at deButts. "That's a

perfect example of what I was talking about with your antitrust problem! Here you are obviously using common control between Long Lines and the operating companies to prohibit competition, when the facts clearly indicate that the local operating company is simply being asked to install a business phone! And we're trying to install our private line to that phone in direct competition with Long Lines!... My antitrust lawyers have told me that your operating companies have to treat me just like Long Lines. There can be no distinction."

DeButts looked calmly at McGowan, nonplussed. "That sounds like a major shift from what the FCC decided. You started as an experimental company, became regional, then specialized, and before you are even in service on your new routes you seem to be attempting to push out the limits of the FCC decision."

"I have plenty of money," McGowan told deButts moments later. "I can spend it on litigation, or I can spend it on construction. I would prefer to spend it on construction."

"I've heard threats like that before," deButts said angrily. "I won't be coerced. If you have any specific grievances I'll be happy to have them looked into. As far as the local loops are concerned, it's our policy to treat them with the same dispatch we do for all our customers. We will do what we have to, but you will find that we won't be coerced by threats of lawsuits."

There was nothing left to discuss. After an awkward attempt by all three men to find a subject unrelated to business that might end the meeting on a cordial note, McGowan took his leave. When the elevator doors closed, deButts turned to George Cook and told him to brief four other top AT&T executives immediately about the meeting. "Nothing about MCI can be treated as business as usual," deButts said prophetically.

Shortly after he left 195 Broadway, an agitated Bill McGowan privately dictated a long memo about his impressions of the meeting with deButts. Afraid that the memo might fall into the wrong hands, he used a transparent code to identify himself ("W"), deButts ("B"), and Cook ("G"), and he referred to himself in the third person. The meeting had marked a turning point in McGowan's ambitious strategy for MCI. In deButts, McGowan had seen a man as determined and intransigent as himself. There was little doubt in the MCI chairman's mind, however, that he could eventually bring the largest corporation in the world to its knees.

"On the one hand," McGowan dictated, "they piously state a willingness to be fair and are willing to believe it themselves, while at the same time they interpret their mandate to compete hard by actions which they know result in a denial of their position on fairness. It is a little analogous to the pleadings of the defendants during war crimes trials. B is absolutely comfortable in living behind sloganism philosophy. . . . W stated that the specific actions by B in the last number of months have convinced him that W's staff is possibly right—that is, the only way to respond to the willingness of B to compete in the marketplace, and to B's insistence on competing through unfair means, would be for W to compete with all the tools available to him.

"It would be incorrect to be encouraged by the potential impact of antitrust action, although it might receive a very favorable reaction at 195 Broadway simply by having them spend more time being advised by counsel. B asked at one time—he seemed to be clearly defenseless if not obviously absolutely guilty—as to what should he do. W replied that the first thing he should do is to get competent antitrust counsel and lecture, in great detail, every person in all the operating companies and elsewhere who deals with us as to the realities of life. They should be extremely sensitive and overly pure in their response to us. He seemed, by his reaction and the note-taking of G, to accept this. If nothing else, we probably insured the unacknowledged gratitude of fifty lawyers."

McGowan's last remark was the most severe underestimation he had ever made.

Chapter 3

The New Trustbusters

M C GOWAN'S attempt to intimidate John deButts had done little to shake loose MCI's mired interconnection negotiations with AT&T, but the confrontational New York meeting had at least accomplished one thing: it had crystallized in McGowan's mind the strategy he would pursue for MCI over the next ten years.

The idea, which McGowan had been mulling over since the day he sunk his money into the company, was remarkably bold. If MCI were to realize McGowan's vast ambitions, if it were to become a national telecommunications network with billions of dollars in annual revenues, the company would have to do nothing less than tear down the existing order in America's telephone industry and reconstruct a new system based on competition, diversity, and decentralized ownership. If MCI simply tried to nibble around AT&T's edges, stealing a few customers in Chicago, a few in St. Louis, and so on, McGowan would never survive. Any telecommunications network—even a system of microwave towers connecting densely populated cities and supported by AT&T's local exchanges—would be too expensive to build and maintain if it relied, in the long run, on a narrow and specialized market such as point-to-point private lines. To slay a dragon as large and powerful as AT&T, McGowan would have to stop whacking the beast on its armored scales. Instead, he would have to risk everything in a daring lunge at its underbelly.

First of all, that meant he had to lure the giant monopoly onto a new field of battle: politics. And second, it meant that he must ruthlessly attack the delicate coalition in Washington that allowed AT&T to control the telephone industry. That co-alition argued that one centrally managed, closely regulated phone network provided the best way to serve the nation's communications needs. McGowan would have to change their minds.

In Washington, of course, the MCI chairman was perfectly situated to launch his political attack, and that was precisely why he had located his company's headquarters in the nation's capital. There were three governmental institutions that had to be persuaded to join McGowan's private industrial revolution against AT&T: Congress, the Federal Communications Com-mission, and the courts. No two of them would suffice—to rip apart AT&T's decades-old monopoly, McGowan would need the support, or at least the acquiescence, of all three. Congress was responsible for the broad policy decisions that shaped the industry, and it also legislated, through the 1934 Communi-cations Act, the specific laws that governed its structure and operations. The FCC regulated the day-to-day business of the telephone network. All of the long-distance rates AT&T pro-posed to charge customers, which were known in the industry as "tariffs," had to be filed in advance and approved by the FCC. So, too, did any new communications services that AT&T or MCI might want to offer the public. And finally, the courts would have to serve as McGowan's enforcer, arbitrating the many disputes engendered by his various assaults on the world's largest corporation.

To undertake this strategy, McGowan needed lawyers— an army of them. He needed lawyers to lobby Congress, law-yers to work with the FCC, lawyers to prepare his antitrust cases, and lawyers to advise him about how all his other lawyers were doing. And not just any lawyers would do: he needed specialists, insider Washington lawyers who knew FCC and congressional staffers by their first names; who dined at Washington power restaurants such as The Palm or Duke Ziebert's and waved to all the lawyers at the other tables; and who might, if the need arose, be able to resolve a crucial problem on the seventeenth fairway at exclusive Burning Tree Country Club, rather than in a courtroom. Early on, McGowan had worked assiduously to assemble such an army. When attorney Kenneth Cox, an FCC commissioner who had voted to approve MCI's application in 1969, left the commission for political reasons in 1971, McGowan hired him as a senior vice-president at MCI and assigned him to cultivate good relations with the FCC. He also spread his legal business around among Washington's top communications law firms, thereby creating conflicts of interest for the firms should AT&T ever try to retain them in a fight against MCI. McGowan held regular, early morning meetings with his lawyers at MCI's 17th and M Streets headquarters, where he briefed them on his plans and strategies and listened to their advice. Some of the attorneys jokingly referred to the meetings as "MCI prayer breakfasts," because of the young company's often precarious financial condition in the early 1970s. But as long as they were on retainer, the lawyers adopted the posture of true believers.

In McGowan, they were led by a capitalist proselyte possessed by relentless drive and energy. Just weeks after his meeting with John deButts in New York, McGowan set aside most of the routine company business that was piled on his desk. At home and in his ninth-floor office, he began to work on a document that would define his political platform of telephone industry competition—a platform that could make or break MCI in the months ahead.

Shortly before noon on July 30, 1973, Bill McGowan trained his squinty eyes on the hefty, typewritten statement lying on the table before him and said to Senator Philip A. Hart, Democrat from Michigan and chairman of the Senate Subcommittee on Antitrust and Monopoly: "As a businessman and competitor, I note three things about how AT&T actions relate to the

Industrial Reorganization Act. First, if Bell is violating the antitrust laws, and we have received definite legal opinions that they are, then there should be some way of stopping them.

"Second, I know that if MCI must—and perhaps we must—avail ourselves of recourse to the courts, we will be playing into AT&T's strength, that of long-drawn-out legal proceedings.

"Third and finally, I know that if I have shown the subcommittee that Bell has, in fact, attempted to stifle competition in the telecommunications industry, then this subcommittee will take the necessary actions to ensure free and fair competition."

McGowan's three-pronged political attack on AT&T—in Congress, at the FCC, and through the courts—had begun.

In Senator Hart's antitrust subcommittee, McGowan had probably chosen the best place to start. Hart was an aging, charismatic, New Deal Democrat who took a deep interest in antitrust law enforcement. Hart strongly believed that the country's principal antitrust statutes—the 1890 Sherman Act and the 1914 Clayton Act—had become inadequate in an age of multinational corporations and rapid technological change. With New Jersey Democratic congressman Peter Rodino, Hart had pushed through the first major new antitrust law in several decades, know as Hart-Scott-Rodino, which broadened the investigative powers of the Justice department's Antitrust division and made it more difficult for large companies to merge. And the senator had not stopped there. During the early 1970s, Hart hired an exceptionally large number of lawyers and economists to staff his prized antitrust subcommittee, and he instructed them to draft sweeping legislation that would restructure by fiat some of America's largest industries—transportation, computers, oil, and communications. The resultant bill, called the Industrial Reorganization Act, was one of the most radical economic proposals considered by Congress during the 1970s.

When he introduced the Industrial Reorganization Act on the Senate floor in early 1973, Hart made it clear that he viewed himself as a spiritual and political heir to the swashbuckling trustbusters like Senators John Sherman and Henry Clayton

Hardly!

and President Theodore Roosevelt, who had reshaped the American economy at the turn of the century. Hart even quoted Sherman, who had said on the Capitol floor in 1890, "If we will not endure a king as a political power, we should not endure a king over the production, transportation, and sale of any of the necessities of life. If we would not submit to an emperor, we should not submit to an autocrat of trade, with power to prevent competition and to fix the price of any commodity."

Such flourishing rhetoric conjured up for Hart a glorious era in the history of the U.S. Senate, a time when great populist battles were enjoined against "the greed and conscienceless rapacity of commercial sharks," as trustbuster Senator James K. Jones had put it on the Senate chamber floor in 1889. But the nostalgia also had a utility in the present: back in his home state of Michigan, Hart found that voters were easily excited in the early 1970s by talk of a "consumer revolution," and that voters of all kinds were suspicious of the mammoth corporations that dominated the nation's economic landscape. The country's liberal middle class could not stomach the methods of students and counterculture radicals who bombed banks and rallied against the "corporate state" during the late 1960s and early 1970s. But when Ralph Nader announced that American cars were unsafe because Detroit's "Big Three" automakers cared about profits first and people second, voters proved decisively that they shared Nader's cynicism about big business. The public's disaffection with large companies reflected the tenor of the times: it was half utopian, half populist, as suggested in the title of the best-selling economic treatise *Small Is Beautiful*. Senator Hart's interest in antitrust preceded this sudden consumer awakening, but the movement did offer convenient rhetoric for a subtle repositioning of the senator's old-style liberal views on antitrust. And in politics, nothing is so infectious as popular rhetoric. Soon, some of Hart's Democratic colleagues on the antitrust subcommittee, such as Edward M. Kennedy of Massachussetts and John Tunney of California, were adding their voices to Hart's call for tougher antitrust enforcement.

From his corner office perch in northwest Washington, Bill McGowan had watched all of this unfold. He cared little for partisan politics, except where it might affect his company. And in the passions of the new trustbusters, he saw an opportunity for MCI. Day after day in the spring of 1973, after the Industrial Reorganization Act was introduced, McGowan prowled the corridors of the Senate office buildings on Capitol Hill. For hours at a time, he educated Hart's staffers about the telecommunications industry.

"AT&T is an outrageous monopoly," McGowan told the young, liberal lawyers and economists, many of whom had been educated on the radicalized college campuses of the 1960s. "They're holding back technology. Maybe this system made sense thirty years ago, but today they're hurting my company and a lot of others. And they're doing it in complicity with the FCC. It's crazy!"

McGowan wanted the subcommittee to hold hearings on the Industrial Reorganization Act so that MCI would have a public forum at which to launch its political attack against AT&T. But some of the subcommittee staffers wondered if it was the right time to hold such hearings. Senator Hart's bill was highly controversial; it was the kind of symbolic legislative proposal introduced by congressmen when they want to influence, or reflect, the public mood. Hart's staff knew that the Industrial Reorganization Act was unlikely to become law—it was too bold, too far-reaching. But if the proposal received the right kind of publicity, it could have an important influence, as a sort of threat, on the behavior of federal law enforcement and regulatory agencies and large corporations. Thus it was important that the Act not be perceived as wild or quixotic. It might be better to work on the bill behind the scenes for a while, compromising with other senators and lining up support. Mc-Gowan, however, would not give up. He kept coming back to the subcommittee's office until hearings on antitrust problems in the communications industry were at last scheduled. He helped the staff line up other witnesses who were having trouble with AT&T. And he contributed questions that the senators could ask AT&T executives when they were called to testify.

"The notion is," Senator Hart said in a challenging tone when McGowan had finished reading his lengthy statement to the subcommittee that July 30, "that we have lost leadership in the telephone business. AT&T has indicated to me that they dispute your statement, and they say, as I have always assumed, that this country ranks first [in the world] with respect to communications.

"Now, are you telling us that it is in the narrower field that you are directly involved in, the specialized communications, that we run second or worse, or are you speaking of it in the sense of 'communications'?"

"I speak of it in the broader sense," McGowan replied, homing in on an argument that neatly transformed the self-interested needs of MCI into an appeal for national honor. "AT&T operates under a philosophy that not only should they supply all communications services but that communications services should be provided by a universal plan. They are extremely reluctant ever to have anything designed to deviate from that plan.

"Now, part of this you can understand in that they do not wish their plan to become obsolete, because they have some $60 billion invested in it.

"Now, that universal plan supplies satisfactory telephone service. That's a basic monopoly and, obviously, we get what we pay for. The average family in the United States, as you know, has invested $800 each in that system, so they should get pretty good service.

"So as far as telephone service—yes, they can supply that. But once you start leaving that one area of monopoly service, then you start getting to the point where we are in trouble and we are going to get more and more in trouble. The data processing industries, for example, have been before the FCC and have stated that unless they get better, more adaptable communications, their industries will be hurt bad."

MCI's private-line services, of course, were technically the same as AT&T's and did nothing to improve the quality of communications for high-tech data processors, but McGowan nonetheless went on: "And I can see the United States falling further and further behind. We are not making the progress necessary."

One of Senator Hart's staff members, Gerald Hellerman, intervened. "Are you recommending the separation of the local operating companies, setting them free, as it were?"

The question floated to McGowan like a slow-pitched softball, and he drove it hard. "I am recommending that somehow the Bell System be structured so that they cannot use the dual control they exercise over Long Lines and the operating companies when it comes to competitive business. We believe the local telephone company wants to serve us. We can be a very big customer of that local phone company. We are more than willing to pay a good rate of return for interconnections. But ...it would seem to me," McGowan finished "that if AT&T was no longer in a position to use the local phone companies to protect Long Lines, then they would no longer have the incentive to try to stop the local telephone companies from serving us."

"Does it take years for Bell's management to change its policies or decisions?" Hellerman asked, already aware of the answer, prompting McGowan to supply it.

"Obviously it does. Everybody in the industry tells me that it does. Bell has even admitted that it does.... We just don't have years, and the customer doesn't have years, and I don't see why it should take years."

"Do you find this is apt to change now? I am thinking of some of the statements made by John deButts, the chairman of AT&T, on competition, about how they are going to compete and direct more energy toward specialized common carriers."

"Yes," McGowan replied, "they are directing a significant amount of energy toward the specialized carriers. I would prefer that they direct a little less energy in that direction."

It was an amusing quip, but it was also a kind of smoke screen. It was true that MCI needed to negotiate fair interconnection agreements with AT&T in order to put its microwave system into profitable service. But it was also true in July 1973, when McGowan testified to the senators, that MCI's problems involved more than just stalled negotiations with the phone company. MCI's ambitious construction plans were becoming expensive—too expensive. McGowan had even decided recently to cut back on some of the building, and he was faced with the prospect of employee layoffs in order to save some of MCI's dwindling cash. A difficult time was ahead for his company. The more McGowan blamed his problems on AT&T before the Hart subcommittee and at other political forums, the easier it would be for himself, his employees, his investors, and his customers to survive the approaching hard times. If he kept punching furiously, perhaps no one would notice how badly McGowan himself was bleeding.

Of course, if the MCI chairman had known what move AT&T was going to make next, he might have relaxed a little.

After months of stoic resistance to McGowan's coaxing, John deButts was about to step boldly into politics. It was a decision that would play right into the MCI chairman's hands.

Chapter 4

The Decision to Decide

AT 2:30 P.M. on Wednesday, September 19, 1973, Larry Harris arrived at 195 Broadway for a meeting with C. W. Jackson, AT&T's business relations director. The negotiations, which would finalize MCI's arrangement to interconnect its private line system with AT&T's local exchanges, had dragged on for a year now. Harris was hoping for a breakthrough.

He had no idea that John deButts was about to declare war formally on MCI.

A few weeks after Bill McGowan's combative face-off with deButts the previous March, MCI had signed, under protest, an "interim" interconnection contract with AT&T. The contract set the access prices that MCI would pay to the Bell operating companies, and it also set certain restrictions on the services MCI could offer its customers. The interim agreement was necessary because after McGowan's meeting with deButts, it had been clear that no quick solution to the problem of MCI's interconnection demands was about to be reached. MCI needed *some* agreement—it was about to launch its private line network, and without a contract the network could not reach the phones of MCI's customers. So a temporary arrangement had been drawn up and signed by both parties. While it was in effect, Harris and Jackson were supposed to negotiate a long-term interconnection deal.

The negotiations had been unsuccessful. And on October 1, which was less than two weeks away, the interim contract was going to expire.

"We're probably not going to extend the contract," Jackson told Harris as the meeting got under way. "But don't worry. We'll continue to provide you local facilities even if the contract lapses and the new arrangements haven't gone into effect."

"What new arrangements?" Harris asked. The MCI lawyer had been trying for months to negotiate such arrangements. Had AT&T somehow decided to take matters into its own hands?

"I'm not in a position to tell you what it is now," Jackson replied. "But I'll try to let you know by Friday, and certainly by Monday or Tuesday."

Harris pressed Jackson—he had an idea about what AT&T might be considering. It was legally possible for AT&T to dictate unilaterally the terms of an interconnection agreement with MCI. Rather than sitting down at the bargaining table to hammer out a contract, as the two sides had been trying to do over the last year, AT&T could simply draw up the terms it wanted, in the form of a tariff, and submit them to state or federal regulators for approval. This was actually how AT&T handled most of its business and legal arrangements. Long-distance prices, telephone equipment prices, and proposed new telecommunications services were all submitted in advance by AT&T to the FCC, which had regulatory jurisdiction over interstate communications. Local prices and services pertaining to activity within a single state, such as the basic monthly phone charges paid by residential and business telephone users, were filed as tariffs with state utility commissions. Each state had its own system for approving local telephone tariffs, but most of them used a politically appointed commission, which regulated the phone company as well as other utilities such as electric companies, gas companies, and railroads.

Because the negotiations were going badly, Harris suspected that AT&T might try to submit its dispute with MCI to the state regulators. And he knew that if that happened, MCI would be in serious trouble. Over the years, AT&T, through its local operating companies, had cultivated very friendly rela-

tions with its state regulators. State utility commissioners did
not have large staffs to investigate the local prices and services
proposed by AT&T. Nor were the commissioners themselves
very sophisticated when it came to new telecommunications
technologies like microwave private line systems. The state regulators cared about two things: keeping the cost of local phone
service low and ensuring the Bell operating companies fair profit
margins. The first objective was a political necessity; if local
telephone users became outraged about high prices for basic
service, the state commissioners would immediately feel the
heat. Consumer groups would threaten electoral reprisals
against the governor who had appointed the state commissioners, and the regulators themselves would face mobs of angry consumers protesting that their "lifelines," their telephones,
were becoming unaffordable. The state commissioners knew
that revenues from AT&T's long-distance services, which were
used mainly by businesses, subsidized the costs of maintaining
the nation's local telephone networks. So when the FCC had
authorized long-distance competition by approving MCI's microwave application in 1969, the state commissioners had rallied
to AT&T's side, arguing that competition in the phone business
was not in the public's interest. If AT&T's long-distance revenues were eroded, or if AT&T was forced to drop its long-
distance prices to compete with companies like MCI, the cost
of local phone service would rise dramatically. The state commissioners would have no alternative but to raise local phone
rates too, and they would then find themselves in the midst of
serious political controversy.

   "We're worried about what will happen if October 1 comes
and we don't have any local distribution facilities," Harris said
to Jackson. "Are you going to go the tariff route? Is that what
is really going on here?"

   "We're looking at that possibility," Jackson said coyly. He
pointed out that when McGowan had taken this dispute public
in July by testifying before Senator Hart's antitrust subcommittee, the MCI chairman had said that he wanted to separate
control of the local operating companies from 195 Broadway.
Maybe AT&T would give McGowan some of what he asked for:

by filing state tariffs, AT&T would force MCI to negotiate separately with each of Bell's twenty-two different operating companies, before fifty different state utility commissions. Jackson and Harris both knew who would be the winner under such an arrangement: AT&T.

Jackson wouldn't admit to AT&T's plans, though, and the meeting ended. When he stepped out of the office, Jackson's secretary handed Harris a message asking him to call MCI's Washington headquarters.

Harris walked back into Jackson's office. "Can I use your phone?"

"Certainly," Jackson said, and he stepped out.

Harris walked behind Jackson's desk and picked up the telephone. Lying on the desk was an internal AT&T memo stamped "Company Confidential." Harris began to read. The memo was addressed "To All Vice-Presidents and Operations People." It said that in exactly one week, on September 26, AT&T intended to file state utility commission tariffs. The tariffs, if approved by the state regulators, would dictate the terms of future interconnection agreements with MCI. As he placed his call, Harris tried to memorize as much of the memo as possible. When he finished and left the office, Jackson said to him, "I'll do my best to call you on Friday to tell you how we're going to offer you local distribution facilities."

Harris shook Jackson's hand politely. The call wouldn't be necessary.

At the end of the Key Largo Presidents' Conference back in May 1972, John deButts had promised his operating company presidents that he would eventually make a comprehensive policy decision about how AT&T would respond to the threat of creamskimming competition from companies such as MCI. The promise became known among AT&T executives, who were furious about such competition, as "the decision to decide."

On Thursday, September 20, 1973, the day after Larry Harris' meeting with C. W. Jackson at 195 Broadway in New York, John deButts announced in Seattle, Washington, that he had finally made up his mind.

As was his style, deButts did not make the announcement meekly or modestly. When he stepped to the podium in the opulent ballroom of the old Olympic Hotel in downtown Seattle, on the last day of the annual convention sponsored by the National Association of Regulatory Commissioners, the commanding AT&T chairman appeared every inch a corporate regent. He was dressed in a dark suit, with a white handkerchief protruding from his breast pocket, and he carried in his hands a prepared text. His audience, a packed house of nearly 1,000 state utility regulators, AT&T executives, and reporters, rose to their feet to applaud him. DeButts motioned for silence. And then, in a powerful, steady voice tinted by his North Carolina drawl, John deButts delivered the most important and the most costly speech of his long Bell System career.

"It is a signal honor to have the opportunity to address this convention," he began. "I do not know how many of my predecessors as chief executive officer of the Bell System have been afforded this privilege. Perhaps only one—and that was back in 1927.

"When Mr. Walter Gifford came before this organization almost half a century ago in Dallas, he declared his intention to 'state very briefly the principles that guide the management of the Bell System.' What he said then has become a classic statement of our business' purpose.

"'The fact,' Mr. Gifford said, 'that such a large part of the entire telephone service of the country rests solely upon this company and its associated companies imposes on the management an unusual obligation to see to it that the service shall at all times be adequate, dependable, and satisfactory.' And he went on to say that in his view, the only sound policy that would fulfill this unusual obligation is 'to continue to furnish the best possible telephone service at the lowest cost consistent with financial safety.'

"How valid, and how viable, is that policy today? There is no question in my mind that down through the years it has served our business well. What is more to the point, it has served the public well.

"It has served the public well in terms of the quality, dependability, and availability of service. It has served the public well in terms of the efficiency and economy with which that service is provided. And it has served the public well in terms of continuously advancing technological innovation unmatched, to my knowledge, in any other industry. In short, I think it's fair to say that what Mr. Gifford called the 'unusual obligation' has been well met."

There was no applause to confirm deButts' hearty self-congratulation, so the chairman went on.

"From what, then, does this 'unusual obligation' arise? Almost unique among the nations of the world, this country has entrusted the development and operation of its communications resources to private enterprise. It has endowed these enterprises with the rights and responsibilities of common carriers, each solely privileged to purvey its services within its territory but all strictly accountable through regulation to the public they serve. In short, what gives rise to the unusual obligation that motivates our industry and inspires its accomplishments is what we have come to call the 'common carrier principle.'

"If there is no question that this principle has served our country well down through the years, there is no question, either, that not since the days of its inception has this principle been more severely challenged than it is today.

"Whence comes this challenge?" deButts asked rhetorically. The mood in the Olympic ballroom began to shift. The audience of state regulators knew the answer—they were as angry as deButts about the piecemeal competition that had been licensed by the FCC. The state commissioners considered themselves rivals to their federal counterparts at the FCC, and they resented the recent commission policies that, they believed, threatened to disrupt an effective system of telephone regulation which had been in place for more than fifty years.

"It comes from entrepreneurs who see opportunities for profit," deButts said disdainfully, "in serving selected segments of the telecommunications market and who, not unnaturally, want a piece of the action. It comes from newly authorized purveyors of communications services who, unburdened by any obligation to the whole body of customers, address their attention to those it costs least to serve and profits most.

"Admittedly, the challenge comes from some customers as well. Mostly, these are large businesses who see advantage to themselves in the new pricing arrangements competition will engender, but who have no obligation—and therefore no disposition—to reckon the cost of those new arrangements for the public at large.

"And the challenge comes, too, from some members of the regulatory community itself," deButts continued, in a thinly veiled reference to the FCC. "Doubtless some of it reflects a wariness of AT&T's sheer size and the potential for abuse that goes with it. Some of it may reflect the premise—to my mind insufficiently examined—that in all times and places competition is good and monopolies are bad.

"That this issue ought to be debated I can hardly deny and the Bell system wouldn't get very far if it did. All these topics, and more, figure in the current hearings of Senator Hart's subcommittee on antitrust and monopoly.

"At issue is the degree to which competition should obtain in a field that has been brought to its current state through the application of basic principles—end-to-end responsibility for service, the systems concept, the common carrier principle itself—that the doctrine of competition for competition's sake puts in jeopardy and could in time destroy.

"What concerns me is that, although debate over this issue has been going on with increasing intensity for some years now, the general public remains to this date very largely unaware of it or of its [the public's] stake in the outcome.

"The time has come to alert the public that regulatory decisions have already been taken in its name that, whatever advantages they may afford for *some* people, cannot help but in the long run hurt most people.

"The time has come for a thinking-through of the future of telecommunications in this country, a thinking-through sufficiently objective as to at least admit the possibility that there may be sectors of our economy—and telecommunications [is] one of them—where the nation is better served by modes of cooperation than by modes of competition, by working together rather than by working at odds.

"The time has come, then, for a moratorium on further experiments in economics, a moratorium sufficient to permit a systematic evaluation not merely of whether competition might be feasible in this or that sector of telecommunications but of the more basic question of the long-term impact on the public."

It had taken him more than a year, but deButts had not compromised on his decision to decide. The AT&T chairman was calling for nothing less than a public anointment of Ma Bell's right to exercise its monopoly in the national interest. If Bill McGowan was going to couch the economic self-interest of MCI in arguments about the public good, then so, too, would deButts. But where McGowan had only promises to offer, deButts had the historically superior service and dazzling technological accomplishments of the Bell System to support his position. The trouble was, and John deButts did not appreciate it on that rainy September afternoon in Seattle, the AT&T chairman had chosen an inauspicious moment in American history to launch a political campaign promoting the right of the world's biggest company to own a telephone monopoly.

As he sat in the rear of the Olympic ballroom watching John deButts exhort the state regulators to rise up in support of AT&T's "unusual obligation," Bernie Strassburg felt like a specter at a wedding feast. A bespectacled and modest man with thinning gray hair, Strassburg was not inclined to become emotional about his professional life. But when deButts finished his speech, and the crowd stomped and cheered in celebration of the AT&T chairman's bold pronouncements and challenges, Strassburg felt a profound anger and sadness welling inside him.

A clearly elated and exhilarated John deButts strode from the podium to the back of the ballroom, where he spotted Strassburg sitting alone. DeButts approached him and extended his hand. "Bernie, no hard feelings," the AT&T chairman said.

Dumbfounded, Strassburg shook deButts' hand.

As time passed, the image remained fixed in Strassburg's

mind: John deButts, one of the most powerful businessmen in America, having just delivered a blistering, personal attack on the FCC policies that Strassburg had for years developed and defended, had tried to dismiss the whole thing with a glib handshake. Maybe deButts meant what he said—that it was nothing personal—but on Strassburg the gesture had the opposite effect. To him, it was a clear example of deButts' overweening arrogance. It was as if the AT&T chairman was saying, "Only you, Bernie Strassburg, chief of the FCC's Common Carrier Bureau, are responsible for introducing this idea of competition into the telephone industry. Except for a few rip-off artists like McGowan, nobody else thinks it's a good idea. What this whole debate about competition comes down to, Bernie, is you, a myopic, restless federal bureaucrat, meddling with something you don't understand, on the one side, and me, the righteous chairman of a sacred American institution, on the other." Perhaps Strassburg was overreacting, but deButts' attitude appalled him. Competition was not some wild, radical idea—it was the American way. How could deButts fail to understand that at least *some* competition was inevitable in a dynamic, technology-driven industry like telecommunications? Did he really believe that the Bell System was like a sacred holy land?

Of course, Strassburg was feeling defensive because there was some truth to the views he attributed to John deButts. It was true that the FCC's Common Carrier Bureau, and specifically Bernie Strassburg, was the source of recent policy experiments in telephone industry competition. The bureau, which was the staff-level division of the FCC responsible for regulation of the telephone industry, had recommended that MCI's private line application be approved, and it had also introduced competition in the phone equipment business by recommending the 1968 *Carterfone* decision. Technically, the seven presidentially appointed FCC commissioners had voted to approve the bureau's recommendations, and it was their votes that gave the proposals the force of law. But in reality, the commissioners almost always went along with what the Common Carrier Bureau advised. To the politically appointed commissioners, regulating the telephone industry was dull, complex, and uncontroversial work. Much more exciting, especially during the late 1960s and early 1970s, was regulation of the broadcasting industry and arbitration of its controversial issues— violence on TV, sex on TV, children's programming, and so on. The FCC commissioners devoted to it the vast majority of their time and resources, fancying themselves as influential social critics of that new, pervasive technology. Conversely, everyone in the telephone industry knew that when it came to telecommunications policy, the commissioners preferred to rely almost entirely on the recommendations of the Common Carrier Bureau. Thus the bureau had become a kind of obscure, miniature regulatory agency, unknown to the public and largely unaccountable to Congress or the president.

Bernie Strassburg was the unassuming overlord of this domain. He had been the Common Carrier chief since 1963, and he had been a staff lawyer in the bureau for twenty-one years before that. The autonomous power he wielded had not gone to his head; he viewed government service as a serious and noble career, not, as was often the case with Washington lawyers, as a stepping-stone to lucrative private practice. As an American Jew in law school during the late 1930s and early 1940s, Strassburg had not enjoyed a wide array of career opportunities, and the federal government seemed an attractive choice. It was an exciting time for a liberal to join the government—Franklin Roosevelt's New Deal was in full bloom, and new federal bureaucracies were sprouting everywhere, each of them charged with improving, through regulation, one aspect of the quality of American life.

Throughout most of Strassburg's long career, the FCC's Common Carrier Bureau had an informal, friendly relationship with AT&T. Long distance and telephone equipment prices were regulated through direct, staff-level negotiation, persuasion, and compromise. If AT&T proposed prices that the bureau lawyers thought were too high, they would call in AT&T's lawyers, sit down, and work things out face-to-face. The New Deal lawyers in the bureau were suspicious of AT&T's monopoly, but they had to acknowledge that in its slow, steady way, the phone company was one of the world's most efficient utilities, and they regarded the nation's phone network as a natural monopoly. As Bell's technology advanced after World War II, long distance prices fell and service continually improved.

For reasons far beyond Bernie Strassburg's control, the Common Carrier Bureau's quiet methods of regulation, known in the phone industry as "continuing surveillance," broke down during the 1960s. Rapid technological advances in fields such as satellites and microwaves began to raise questions about how well the Bell System would keep up in an emerging "information age." More important was the political furor that erupted during the late 1960s, when AT&T's service crises in New York and elsewhere, together with the popular suspicions of the period about big corporations, led to an outcry in Congress that the FCC was not doing its job, that the commission was merely AT&T's servant. Such accusations provoked strong reactions in liberal bureau lawyers like Strassburg, who of course believed that the FCC was a strong and independent agency. To prove he was right, Strassburg put an end to the informal negotiations with the phone company, and the bureau launched wide-ranging investigations into AT&T's conduct. At the same time, companies like MCI were clamoring for a chance to offer what they called "new and innovative" services in competition with AT&T. And while Strassburg still believed that the phone network was a natural monopoly, he saw in limited competition a powerful opportunity to control AT&T and to vindicate the independence of his bureau.

Even at that moment in September 1973, when John deButts so angered Bernie Strassburg by shaking his hand and saying "No hard feelings," Strassburg would have been the first to admit that he had no clear vision of where his bureau's pro-competition policies were leading. He might even have agreed with deButts, in a less confrontational setting, that it was time to take a long, hard look at the implications of telephone industry competition. But by making that speech about AT&T's "unusual obligation," by trying to use sympathetic state regulators in a play to thwart FCC policies, deButts had changed, in Strassburg's mind, the whole equation of AT&T's relationship with the Common Carrier Bureau. Strassburg believed that deButts had declared, in effect, that AT&T was above the law.

And as he left Seattle on September 20, Strassburg decided he was going to do everything in his power to stop deButts from getting away with it.

What occurred in Washington, D.C., during the last week of September and the first weeks of October 1973, in the aftermath of John deButts' Seattle speech, would later become the center of a multibillion-dollar legal controversy. Millions of dollars would be spent by the U.S. government, by MCI, and by AT&T in an attempt to determine precisely whether MCI was authorized to sell "FX" and "CSSA" services to its customers. Several careers would be made and broken over the issue, and more than a few lawyers would become very rich resolving it. But at the time it occurred, the controversy was perceived as just another skirmish in the ever-widening war between Bill McGowan and the phone company.

To be sure, McGowan and his bankers considered the problem to be a serious one. MCI was scheduled to unveil its nationwide microwave network in October, but there was a serious question about whether the company would last long enough to see the system up and running. McGowan was in default on the line of bank credit he had secured to construct the system, and his bankers were pressuring him to expand the catalog of long-distance services that MCI could offer its customers. Revenues from point-to-point private lines had not been enough to cover the cost of MCI's ambitious network. Layoffs of many of the hundreds of employees who had been hired by MCI in the previous nine months appeared, by the end of September, to be inevitable.

But after five years of struggle, Bill McGowan was not about to fold up shop and go home. He had one play left, and if it worked, his company might turn the corner, escape bankruptcy, and even position itself for the kind of financial success McGowan had envisioned when he joined MCI in 1968.

The move depended on the foundation McGowan had laid at the FCC for the second prong of his three-front political attack on AT&T. And it depended, too, on the emotions John deButts had stirred in Bernie Strassburg in Seattle.

Strassburg was not a personal friend of McGowan's; in fact, away from the office, Strassburg was much closer to AT&T's general counsel, Mark Garlinghouse, whom he had come to know during the long Common Carrier Bureau investigations of AT&T during the 1960s. But Strassburg did feel a strong sympathy for MCI. After all, the company was in a way his child, his experiment. In the four years since MCI's application had been approved by the FCC, Strassburg had tried to nurture the telephone competition he had unleashed. MCI sometimes sent Strassburg blind copies of its contentious correspondence with 195 Broadway, and Ken Cox, the former FCC commissioner who now worked side by side with McGowan, stayed in touch with his former colleague, telling Strassburg in detail about MCI's difficult interconnection negotiations with AT&T. The intransigence displayed by Bell in those negotiations angered Strassburg, and he feared that MCI might fail, not because the market for a new long-distance company was soft but because AT&T was using its size and power to preempt competition. Until October, until John deButts' attack on Strassburg's policies, the Common Carrier chief had never directly intervened in the dispute.

From MCI's vantage, if there was ever a time it needed such intervention it was now. The company was bleeding cash, and to reverse the flow it needed to find a new source of revenues, a new market. There was only one realistic possibility: FX lines. An FX line was basically a private line between two cities, with one open end. An airline company, for example, would establish its national reservations center in Chicago. It would then lease a private line connecting the center to another major city, say, New York. A passenger in New York, wishing to make a reservation, would find a local phone number for the airline in his phone book. He would dial the call, without an area code, from his home or office. The call would travel

4 The Decision to Decide

from his telephone, through AT&T's local New York exchanges. But rather than being answered by an airline reservations clerk in New York, the call would then be switched onto an intercity private line, on which it would travel all the way to Chicago. The passenger would only be charged for a local call, but unbeknown to him, his call would actually be answered in Chicago. The long-distance price for the distance between New York and Chicago would automatically be charged to the airline company on a monthly basis.

The difference between a private line and an FX line, then, was that rather than connecting two private offices in two cities, an FX line connected one office in one city with all of the phones in a second city. Thus it depended much more on AT&T's local, switched telephone network. And that was precisely why John deButts had refused to provide MCI with FX lines. DeButts and other AT&T executives believed strongly that Bell's national switched network could not withstand creamskimming competition in regular, long distance services, what AT&T called MTS (message toll service). Private line competition was one thing, but competition in the switched network, deButts believed, would disrupt the structure of the phone system, leading inevitably to worsening service and higher prices. Moreover, the FCC agreed with deButts: the commission had stated clearly on numerous occasions that it never intended to allow MCI to enter the basic residential and business long-distance market. Even McGowan acknowledged publicly that MCI was not authorized to provide, and did not intend to seek to provide, regular long-distance service. The question, then, was whether FX lines were a kind of private line, which MCI was authorized to sell, or whether they were a form of MTS service, similar to basic long distance, which was outside the boundaries of MCI's franchise.

Considering all that was at stake for both MCI and AT&T, it was curious that the question had never been resolved before October 1973. AT&T claimed that MCI was not authorized to sell FX lines; MCI claimed it was. Angry letters had been exchanged between the companies over the matter, and Mc-

Gowan had discussed the problem with deButts at his March meeting with the AT&T chairman in New York. But neither side had asked the FCC to clear up the question, and it was the commission, after all, that had defined MCI's franchise in the first place. AT&T may well have feared what Bernie Strassburg, the father of telephone industry competition, would decide if he had the chance. MCI, on the other hand, probably worried that even if Strassburg ruled favorably on its position of FX service, the full FCC, under pressure from AT&T, might reverse its bureau chief and settle the question detrimentally once and for all. Faced with the possibility that MCI might lose, Mc-Gowan had good reason not to force the issue; as long as AT&T continued to refuse to provide MCI with FX lines, McGowan had grounds to file an antitrust suit for damages, a strategy that might prove even more profitable than a favorable decision from the FCC.

MCI's financial crisis and deButts' Seattle speech changed the picture, however. The time for swift action had arrived. MCI needed FX lines, and it needed them quickly.

The eye of the breaking storm was an important—though inscrutable—1971 FCC decision known as *Specialized Common Carriers*. Written by Bernie Strassburg, the landmark document had attempted to define precisely what services MCI was authorized to sell and what services it could not provide. The decision, which had the force of law, would later be described as a "mess," and worse, by lawyers and judges involved in the FX controversy. It was more than 100 pages long, and it had been written in the worst style of bureaucratic obfuscation: it was confusing, and in some places contradictory. The decision made no specific mention of FX lines; it referred only to MCI's "authorized services" and "private lines." But since it was so muddled and vague, the decision was open to interpretation.

Between October 1 and October 4, only two weeks after deButts' provocative Seattle speech, a series of meetings was held in Washington, D.C., between Bernie Strassburg, MCI's executives, other Common Carrier Bureau staff lawyers, and some executives from a new private line venture owned by the

giant Southern Pacific Corporation, which was cautiously following McGowan as he blazed into the private line market. At
those meetings, a strategy was developed to authorize MCI to
sell FX lines without ever bringing the matter formally before
the FCC.

On October 1, McGowan drafted a letter to Bernie Strassburg that said, in part, "MCI needs the FCC's clarification and
opinion regarding orders we have received from customers for
specific types of interstate services. It is our understanding that
we are authorized by the commission to offer, [that] we are
licensed to provide . . . FX services. We would appreciate your
confirming that we are entitled and obligated to supply these
services. We have orders for these types of arrangements and
are anxious to provide such services in accordance with our
rights and obligations under . . . the relevant law."

Two days later, Ken Cox, the MCI lawyer and former FCC
commissioner, met with Strassburg in his FCC office to discuss
the letter and what should be done about it. In a meeting later
that afternoon at a downtown hotel, McGowan told Cox and
some Southern Pacific executives, "We decided not to force the
issue in our Chicago–St. Louis line. We told AT&T we would
seek redress when we expanded. While they were saying in
negotiations we could have equality . . . it became clear they
were preparing for war. We are concerned about the commissioners, but the staff is strong."

That same afternoon, October 3, Bernie Strassburg walked
unannounced into a full FCC meeting and asked the commissioners to sign the letter of "clarification" McGowan had sent
him, thus giving the letter the force of law. The commissioners
were busy, and they put off Strassburg's request until the next
day. On October 4, they signed the letter. It was a routine
matter, but they had no idea what they had just done.

On October 15, McGowan wrote again to Strassburg and
said, in effect, "We understand that our letter, signed by the
commission on October 4, authorizes us to sell FX lines." Strassburg wrote back on October 19 and said, yes, that is correct.
No copies of any of this correspondence were sent to AT&T, as

was customary. John deButts had no inkling of what Bill McGowan had accomplished until MCI, armed with its FCC orders, demanded that AT&T immediately connect MCI's customers with FX lines.

On November 1, Bernie Strassburg, after more than four decades of government service, retired from his job as chief of the FCC's Common Carrier Bureau. He had sent a parting shot at John deButts from which the AT&T chairman would never fully recover.

AT&T, of course, was furious, and it ended up in court with McGowan. A federal judge in Philadelphia ruled that the FCC orders entitled MCI to sell FX lines. AT&T appealed, but it had no choice but to begin connecting MCI's corporate customers. The FCC, finally alerted to what had transpired under its nose, launched an investigation into precisely what services MCI was authorized to sell. Meanwhile, an appeals court ruled that the first judge was wrong, that the FX controversy was a "legitimate dispute" and that it was up to the FCC to settle the matter. As soon as that appeals court decision was handed down, it was ordered that all of MCI's FX lines be disconnected immediately. AT&T engineers worked an entire weekend unplugging the circuits, inconveniencing MCI's customers and infuriating McGowan. John deButts would later say that the decision to disconnect MCI's customers was one of the few he ever regretted. The FCC soon ruled that MCI was, in fact, entitled to sell FX lines, and AT&T was forced to reconnect all of MCI's customers. The damage, however, was already done.

Despite deButts' bluster in Seattle, McGowan had skated on the brink of bankruptcy and emerged with exactly what he had gone after. On March 6, 1974, MCI filed a sweeping antitrust suit against AT&T seeking hundreds of millions of dollars in damages. The third and most devastating phase of McGowan's attack on AT&T was under way.

Chapter 5

Legacy of a Scandal

W HEN Philip Verveer was in college during the 1960s, he traveled to Alabama to participate in the landmark civil rights demonstrations at Selma and Montgomery. It was there, in the heat of a historic struggle, that Verveer first decided he might like to work for the United States Justice department. The department's Civil Rights division lawyers who worked in the Deep South were romantic heroes in Verveer's eyes: they were young, very brave, and deeply committed to protecting blacks and enforcing the law against reactionary whites, despite threats and violence. The Justice attorneys were energetic, disciplined, driven by their moral beliefs—lawyers who could make a difference in the world. Verveer, a white, seriously religious Catholic from a comfortable, suburban Chicago family, wanted to be one of them.

He still felt that way four years later when he graduated from the University of Chicago law school, but by then Verveer was married and had children. When a Justice department recruiter arrived on campus, Verveer told him that he wanted to work for the Civil Rights division. "You don't want to do that," the recruiter told him. "It's too hard with a family. It would be really tough to work for Civil Rights and meet your family obligations." Verveer accepted the admonition; his family always came first. The recruiter suggested that Verveer consider a job with Justice's Antitrust division: it was safer, more stable, yet it was still a place where a politically committed young lawyer could accomplish good works in government service. Verveer agreed, and he accepted the offer.

"Socially Important Work in the Company of Good People" was Verveer's professional motto, and he even had the phrase inscribed on a plaque behind his desk. But he found that not all the attorneys at the Antitrust division in Washington shared his view of the division's mission. The lawyers at Antitrust came in all shapes and sizes, but they were roughly divided along generational lines. On one side were the older, "career" lawyers who had worked in the division for decades, rising slowly through its bureaucracy to supervisory positions. Over the years, these attorneys had tried hundreds of government antitrust cases, large and small. They had won many of them, lost a few, and settled the rest. They had seen political administrations and political movements come and go, and they had survived the tenures of politically appointed Antitrust chiefs of every ideological stripe. And through it all, they had acquired that salty, slightly world-weary, eminently pragmatic outlook peculiar to men of integrity who have spent their lives working in a bureaucracy. On the other side were the young, passionate lawyers like Verveer, most of them politically liberal and graduates of the turbulent 1960s campuses, who had come to Antitrust to combine a respectable profession with furtherance of the movement that had swept them up in school. As lawyers, Verveer and his contemporaries had been trained in caution and diligence, but they were also activists, and there was very little that was cynical about their approach to the legal profession.

Inevitably, these two generations within the Antitrust division met, clashed, compromised, and learned from each other. The younger lawyers acquired skills and patience from their supervisors; the older lawyers were reinvigorated by the energies and passions of the new recruits. And the result, during the early 1970s, was a period of activity and ambitious lawsuits unrivaled in the modern history of the Antitrust division.

Bill McGowan didn't know any of this when, in the fall of 1973, with his company in dire financial straits, he, Ken Cox, Larry Harris, and other MCI executives began an intensive lobbying campaign to interest the Antitrust division in AT&T. McGowan hoped to persuade the division to file a sweeping civil antitrust suit against AT&T, which would seek to break the phone company apart. Only the Justice department, the federal government's law enforcement agency, could seek such "structural" relief in a lawsuit; in its own antitrust suit against Bell, MCI was entitled to pursue only monetary damages to compensate for revenues lost because of AT&T's behavior. Even the threat of a structural suit by Justice could be useful to McGowan. Like Senator Hart's antitrust hearings and MCI's friendly relations with the FCC, a Justice investigation might serve notice to AT&T that MCI was a formidable political opponent.

As it happened, McGowan's initial complaints to the Antitrust division landed on the desk of Philip Verveer, who would soon prove that he, too, could be a formidable opponent of the world's largest corporation.

With the interconnection negotiations at a standstill because of deButts' Seattle speech and McGowan's FX ploy at the FCC, Larry Harris was free, late in 1973, to devote much of his time to educating Phil Verveer about MCI's plight. Harris had to start at the beginning; he spent hours at Verveer's office in the old *Evening Star* building, two blocks from the main Justice building at 10th and Pennsylvania in Washington, telling the young lawyer about how the telephone industry worked, about the history of competition decisions at the FCC, about MCI's fitful negotiations with AT&T, and about how AT&T had recently decided to call for a moratorium on "economic experiments" like MCI. The lectures roused Verveer's curiosity and his ire. The situation Harris described sounded like a classic example of a "bottleneck monopoly," where one company owned essential facilities—in this case, local telephone exchanges—that were required for a competitor's business. There was a long history of antitrust cases arising from such bottlenecks, particularly involving railroads, whose ownership of interstate tracks and local switching yards was in some ways parallel to AT&T's ownership of the switched phone network. (Bill McGowan, who had grown up in a railroad family, understood this parallel well.) And moreover, the stories Harris told about his negotiations with AT&T fueled Verveer's longstanding suspicions about the dubious motives of a huge, monopolistic corporation like AT&T.

After his conversations with Harris, McGowan, and Cox, Verveer sought and received permission to launch a sweeping investigation of AT&T to see if there might be a basis for a government antitrust suit. Verveer was put in charge of the inquiry. He subpoenaed tens of thousands of documents from 195 Broadway and the local operating companies, and he spent months sorting through them. Verveer and several division lawyers working for him traveled around the country seeking out and interviewing the executives of other companies, besides MCI, who had troubles with AT&T; Harris and other MCI executives had supplied the division with dozens of names. As early as April 1974, a month after MCI filed its own antitrust suit against AT&T, Verveer had decided that the government had a case, and he drafted the initial complaint for a lawsuit.

The complaint sought exactly what Bill McGowan wanted: complete separation of AT&T's local operating companies from 195 Broadway, as well as total divestiture of Western Electric, the phone company's mammoth manufacturing subsidiary. If successful, the lawsuit would reduce the size of AT&T by more than two-thirds.

Phil Verveer was not naive. In his three years with the Antitrust division, he had learned quickly that simply because a lawsuit had merit, that didn't mean it would ever be filed. Especially when a large and influential company such as AT&T was involved, the politics of a lawsuit were at least as important as the antitrust violations that were being alleged. And in April 1974, when Verveer sent his drafted lawsuit upstairs, political considerations were probably more important than merit.

The Justice department was at that time in a state of leaderless chaos. President Nixon was three months from resigning over Watergate, and attorney generals, assistant attorney generals, and special prosecutors were dropping left and right—some resigning in scandal, some being fired, and some quitting in protest. For months at a time, it wasn't clear to Verveer who in Justice's "front office," as the department's political leadership was called, had the power, never mind the inclination, to make a decision as controversial as this one. Once he had done his job by drafting the lawsuit against AT&T, Verveer could do nothing but sit and wait.

The irony was that scandal, far from paralyzing the department's political appointees, was precisely what drove them to move the AT&T suit along during the final days of the Nixon administration.

The scandal in question, however, was not a contemporary one. True, the fallout over Watergate, and particularly the perjury charges against Nixon's former attorney general, John Mitchell, had called into question the essential integrity of the Justice department. At Justice, there were career lawyers as well as political appointees who wanted to resurrect quickly the department's reputation for independence and objective law enforcement, and a lawsuit filed against AT&T would certainly help that campaign. But the real reason that the front office took seriously young Phil Verveer's recommendation that a suit be filed had to do with the legacy in the department of another scandal, now almost twenty years old, which had cast a still-lingering shadow over the Antitrust division's relations with AT&T.

The scandal had never acquired a clever moniker like Watergate or Teapot Dome, and the truth was that it was little remembered outside the Antitrust division. But within the division, it had taken on an almost mythical status among the career lawyers, because to them it was a classic example of how the political power of large corporations interfered with Justice's enforcement of the antitrust laws. Although Congress and the FCC had, for most of the century, informally blessed AT&T's telephone monopoly, lawyers in the Antitrust division had never

been comfortable with the exclusive telephone franchise of so
large a corporation. In the early 1900s, before the FCC was even
established, AT&T had built its basic network monopoly through
ruthless business practices that rivaled the tactics of such no-
torious ninteenth-century monopolists as John D. Rockefeller.
When a rival company built a new local telephone exchange,
AT&T would refuse to interconnect the exchange with its own
network, and it would pressure the upstart company until it
sold out to AT&T on favorable terms. Justice had sued the
phone company over its practices, and in 1919 a deal was struck
between Theodore Vail, then AT&T's chairman, and President
Woodrow Wilson. The deal was known as the Kingsbury Commitment. AT&T agreed to end its predatory feeding on small
telephone companies, and in exchange, the government agreed
informally to anoint AT&T as the nation's telephone monopoly—subject to federal regulation. For the next thirty years,
the arrangement had worked without major interruption. The
FCC was established during Franklin Roosevelt's New Deal,
and AT&T slowly transformed itself from an acquisitive monopolist into a steady, regulated utility.

In 1949, however, the Antitrust division had again been
aroused by AT&T's communications monopoly, this time because of the phone company's manufacturing subsidiary, Western Electric. The division lawyers saw that because AT&T's
operating companies bought all their telephones from Western
Electric, AT&T had a "captive monopoly" in the phone equipment business. Justice sued again, seeking to force the divestiture of Western.

The complex suit dragged on for years, and by 1956 it was
still not ready for trial. In the interim, the political circumstances
that had made the suit possible in the first place had changed—
fiesty Democrat Harry Truman had been succeeded by Republican Dwight Eisenhower in the White House. The economy
was in the midst of a long, robust expansion, and the lethargic
Eisenhower administration was enjoying a cozy relationship
with American business. Eisenhower's attorney general, Herbert Brownell, Jr., announced soon after his swearing in that
he would be examining all pending antitrust suits to see if they

ought to be dismissed. AT&T siezed the opportunity and hired a friend of Brownell's, businessman Bayard Pope, to persuade Brownell gently that the AT&T case should be thrown out. "A way ought to be found to get rid of the case," Brownell agreed in a private meeting with AT&T at a West Virginia resort. "AT&T could readily find practices that it would agree to have enjoined with no real injury to its business."

And that was precisely the deal that was struck: on January 12, 1956, a "consent decree" was filed in a New Jersey federal court settling the case. In exchange for being allowed to keep its giant Western subsidiary, AT&T agreed not to enter the computer business. At the time, it was a modest, even specious, concession; computers were in their infancy, and AT&T was not staking much of its future on them. Congress and the public were outraged. The House antitrust subcommittee held seventeen days of investigative hearings on the deal, and it used the forum to ridicule and embarrass the Antitrust division.

The wounds from that 1956 scandal never healed inside the Antitrust division. Many of the division's lawyers believed that AT&T had abused its political power, circumvented the legal process, and cheated the American public. Throughout the 1960s, the division maintained files about AT&T's activities, waiting for the right moment to go after Western Electric again.

The moment arrived, coincidentally, at the instant of Bill McGowan's desperate financial crisis in the fall of 1973.

While McGowan and his lieutenants were educating Phil Verveer late in 1973 about the state of competition in the telephone industry, a secret Antitrust division investigation of AT&T—unknown even to Verveer—was simultaneously under way. The investigation had been authorized by Tom Kauper, the assistant attorney general appointed by President Nixon to head the Antitrust division. Kauper was a brilliant Republican academic who had come to Justice on leave from the University of Michigan. It was an irony—telling of the incestuous relationships inevitable among America's elite lawyers—that prior to teaching at Michigan, Kauper had worked for the Chicago law firm of Sidley & Austin, whose largest client was AT&T. Howard Trienens, the Sidley managing partner who hired Kauper, would eventually spend more than seven years of his professional life, and earn more than a million dollars, fighting a government lawsuit filed under the Antitrust division reign of his former Sidley recruit.

Kauper and his Antitrust front office deputy, Keith Clearwaters, had been persuaded by some older career lawyers, who had been with the division during the 1956 scandal, that the FCC was incapable of regulating the phone equipment market and that it was time, once again, for Justice to consider suing AT&T over its Western subsidiary. The FCC had recently concluded a long investigation of Western by declaring, in effect, that it could not control Western's pricing policies. The career lawyers had pulled out the division's files on AT&T and had shown them to Clearwaters. They argued that advances in telecommunications technology had made the tainted 1956 deal even more of an embarrassment to Justice. Even AT&T was now unhappy with the deal, for computer technology was advancing with astonishing speed, and so was the interdependence between computers and communications. Because of the 1956 consent decree, AT&T had no choice but to stand on the sidelines while competitors such as IBM and Xerox raced into the future.

Clearwaters conducted the investigation for Antitrust chief Kauper, and what he found excited him. While Phil Verveer was following the Antitrust division's normal investigative procedures—subpoenaing documents, interviewing potential witnesses, filling out detailed reports—Clearwaters was holding a series of clandestine meetings at the White House and with Senator Hart's antitrust subcommittee staff. The White House's Office of Telecommunications Policy turned over to Clearwaters voluminous files it had accumulated on AT&T. So did lawyers working for Hart; they even gave Clearwaters typed transcripts of interviews with AT&T competitors who said they were afraid to testify in public before the antitrust subcommittee. Clearwaters organized the material and eventually handed it over to Verveer, who told Kauper he was "not amused" that a concurrent investigation of AT&T had been conducted behind his back. Kauper successfully mediated the dispute between Verveer and Clearwaters, and the two inquiries were finally folded into one. The findings were included in the lawsuit drafted by Verveer.

The Clearwaters investigation was crucially important because it captured the imagination of the Antitrust division's politically conservative front office. If Keith Clearwaters, during the winter and spring of 1974, had not daily described in urgent tones to Tom Kauper the promising results of his surreptitious meetings, Kauper might never have taken seriously the recommendations of young Phil Verveer, who, Kauper knew, was a committed liberal. Once the investigations were folded together, though, everyone in the division was happy: Verveer, who was still nominally in charge; the political appointees, who felt they had done the most important work; and the older career lawyers, who sensed that the evil spirit of the 1956 AT&T scandal was about to be exorcised.

By spring of 1974, the unlikely alliances had taken firm hold, and a united Antitrust division was prepared to recommend to the attorney general that a lawsuit be filed against AT&T by the U.S. government.

Fortunately for AT&T, there was no attorney general.

Elliot Richardson had resigned a few months earlier over Nixon's firing of Watergate Special Prosecutor Archibald Cox, and no one had been named to replace him. On August 9, 1974, President Nixon went on national television to announce his resignation. He was succeeded by Gerald Ford, a former congressman who had never been on a national ticket and who immediately promised to heal the nation through quiet, stable, and uncontroversial stewardship of the federal government.

Presumably Ford's cure for a nation in the midst of its worst political crisis in a century would not include the filing of a lawsuit seeking to break apart the country's biggest corporation. Shortly before he resigned, Nixon had finally appointed William Saxbe as attorney general. Saxbe was an aging former senator from Ohio and a man who, like the new president, enjoyed spending as much time as possible on the golf course. No one in the Antitrust division seriously expected that Saxbe would be interested in attacking AT&T. Phil Verveer, for one, assumed the matter of the lawsuit was over, and by the fall of 1974 he had turned his attention to other tasks that had piled up on his desk.

He was not the only one to be astounded by the brief but lively reign of U.S. Attorney General William Saxbe.

Chapter 6

"I Intend to Bring an Action"

THERE was something about William Saxbe that conjured the image of a wayward relative—an eccentric
uncle who vanishes for long stretches and then reappears at a
family reunion brandishing strange carvings for the children,
who sits on the porch spinning apocryphal tales of boom and
bust in African diamond country until, one morning, he dis-
appears again. Perhaps it was Saxbe's puckish blue eyes, so
alive with energy and mischief, or the elfin ears attached to his
round, balding head. Or maybe it was the wad of chewing
tobacco forever stuffed in his cheek, or the way Saxbe punc-
tuated his words by launching foul streams of amber juice toward the old spitoons in his office and in the attorney general's
conference room. Then, too, there were the convivial stories
he liked to tell about his hunting trips, his golf game, and his
days as a political roisterer in the Ohio legislature. When lawyers in the Antitrust division talked about Saxbe—even those,
like Phil Verveer, who disagreed with Saxbe's Republican politics and felt that he did not work very hard at his cabinet-level
job—they had to smile a little and admit, "He *is* a character."

As for his predilections about enforcement of the nation's
antitrust laws, Saxbe was considered a mystery, even by the
Republican appointees in the Antitrust division's front office.

There was an important reason, apart from his natural

playfulness, that Saxbe appeared to be detached from his job during the summer and fall of 1974, when the proposed lawsuit against AT&T came to his attention. Saxbe felt estranged from both the Nixon and Ford White Houses; before Nixon's resignation, Alexander Haig, the president's last chief of staff, had been Saxbe's only friend in the executive branch. The reason had less to do with Saxbe than with disintegrating morale and worsening crisis within the administration, which by 1974 had the White House senior staff in a state of distraction. After Ford took over, Saxbe's relationship with the White House deteriorated further because Saxbe tried to delay a series of domestic wiretaps ordered by Henry Kissinger's State Department. The ploy angered Ford, who was forced eventually to sign a personal order overruling Saxbe. By November, three months into the Ford administration, Saxbe was working short hours and was talking infrequently with the White House staff.

Saxbe was well aware, however, that there was a positive side to his poor relations with the White House: freedom. Whereas most attorney generals were constrained by the policy objectives of their president, Saxbe knew no such bounds. Nixon had abandoned policy-making during his last days, and Ford was a mere figurehead in the first months of his term, unable to put his own political team in place yet. Thus Saxbe could pursue the single goal he had privately set for himself when he took office: to reestablish the Justice department's integrity and independence. In sorting through the abuses of power uncovered during his renowned Watergate investigation, Senator Sam Ervin of North Carolina had suggested that perhaps the Justice department should be separated from White House control. It was an idea Saxbe opposed, but more important, it was a signal to him of the deep suspicion in Congress and among the public about Justice's integrity.

Saxbe knew there was only one way he could reverse public opinion about the Justice department—through bold, decisive, and independent action. The proposed lawsuit that reached his desk in November 1974 would do the job very nicely.

*   *   *

On Wednesday, November 20, 1974, President Ford was in Tokyo, Japan, in the midst of a goodwill tour of several Far East countries. In the morning, he attended a judo match. Later in the day, the president went sightseeing in the former Japanese royal capital of Kyoto.

Eight thousand miles to the east, in Washington, D.C., the morning broke foggy and rainy. At nine-thirty, in Saxbe's wood-paneled office on the fifth floor of the main Justice building at 10th and Pennsylvania, the attorney general met with several senior Antitrust division lawyers to discuss the AT&T case. Tom Kauper, the Antitrust chief, was at a White House economic policy meeting that morning, and he had sent Keith Clearwaters in his stead. Kauper had insisted that Clearwaters bring along Hugh Morrison, Phil Verveer's supervisor, a veteran division career lawyer who had an affection for Irish whiskey and cigarettes. Clearwaters and Morrison were supposed to brief Saxbe about a presentation to be made at eleven that same morning by Mark Garlinghouse, AT&T's general counsel. A few weeks earlier, Garlinghouse had been offered a personal meeting with Saxbe so that AT&T could attempt to dissuade the attorney general from filing the proposed antitrust suit.

No one in the Antitrust division was entirely sure why, but in recent weeks the proposed AT&T lawsuit had undergone an urgent revival. Earlier in the fall, AT&T had been invited by Tom Kauper to respond informally to the proposed suit. Garlinghouse and a flock of other AT&T lawyers had met with Antitrust division staffers and had attempted, using flip charts, graphs, and even a slide show, to persuade them that breaking up AT&T would not be in the public's best interest.

"Are you so damn sure you can do this to the benefit of the consumer in this country?" Garlinghouse had asked during one meeting.

But such protestations had no effect on Clearwaters and Kauper. Clearwaters, who like Tom Kauper was a moderate Republican, felt that the public interest argument was valid only in relation to splitting off the local operating companies from 195 Broadway, not in relation to the divestiture of Western Electric. And Clearwaters didn't care much about the operating companies part of the proposed lawsuit; that was Verveer's investigation, the one that had been developed in cooperation with MCI. Clearwaters never believed that the Verveer investigation was worth filing a lawsuit over, but he did believe in his own inquiry into Western and the 1956 scandal. His attitude was, as he put it later, "Just give me my little piece. If Verveer wants more chunks off, OK."

So although Garlinghouse didn't know it, he was wasting his breath with talk about AT&T's "unusual obligation" to manage the nation's telephone network. The front office of the Antitrust division, where the power to recommend lawsuits lay, was more concerned with the divestiture of Western Electric. Complaints about the operating companies had been included in the suit partly to keep Verveer and the division staffers from rebelling over Clearwaters' secret investigation of Western.

After AT&T's presentations to division staff, Clearwaters called Garlinghouse and told him, "We have made up our minds to recommend the suit to the attorney general. We are going to make that recommendation with the understanding that AT&T can meet with the AG before he makes up his mind and state its point of view. Also, we don't have any specific time frame as to when we're going to file the suit. You'll have your chance to have an audience with Saxbe and to try to dissuade him."

So now it was up to Clearwaters and Morrison to prepare Saxbe for what he would hear from Garlinghouse at eleven o'clock that morning. Saxbe sat in a high-backed leather chair facing the two Antitrust division lawyers.

Clearwaters suspected that the reason Kauper had insisted he bring Morrison to the briefing was that Kauper was afraid Clearwaters would not insist forcefully enough that Saxbe keep an open mind while listening to AT&T's presentation. Kauper had repeatedly told Garlinghouse, John deButts' chief legal adviser, that Saxbe had not yet made up his mind about the suit and that AT&T would have a fair chance to present its case to the attorney general. It would be a blemish on Kauper's honor if Saxbe did not live up to that commitment, if he did not treat Garlinghouse evenhandedly. No one in the Antitrust front office, not even Kauper, was certain of Saxbe's attitude about the case, but they had received the impression in recent weeks that he might be interested in filing it. And they knew Saxbe well enough to be sure that diplomacy was not one of the attorney general's personal strengths.

Another reason Kauper was worried about how Saxbe treated Garlinghouse was that AT&T was about to offer a public bond issue worth several hundred million dollars. Garlinghouse had pleaded with Kauper to consider the bond issue if Justice ever decided to file suit, since a poorly timed announcement of a lawsuit as sweeping as this one could cost AT&T millions in the market. Kauper had agreed to be especially careful.

Clearwaters began the briefing by presenting Saxbe with the legal arguments developed by his own and Verveer's investigations. He talked about "bottleneck monopolies" and Western Electric's captive control of the telephone equipment market. Then he told the attorney general about AT&T's presentations to division staff and repeated Garlinghouse's arguments about the public interest. He also mentioned the bond issue, and closed by emphasizing Kauper's admonition: "You must make AT&T realize that the staff has made this recommendation, and that you will consider AT&T's arguments."

Saxbe spit some tobacco juice and trained his eyes on Clearwaters. "Keith, they're going to try to stall us, aren't they?"

Clearwaters tried to hedge. He didn't want to agitate Saxbe. Even though he had Hugh Morrison as a witness, Clearwaters thought that Kauper would never believe he had tried to dissuade Saxbe from rash action. "Any company with lawyers as qualified as AT&T's is going to use any means available to avoid a lawsuit," he said.

"That means they're going to stall us, aren't they?"

"Yes, it does," Clearwaters conceded.

"Thank you."

Shortly before eleven, Kauper returned from the White

House and the AT&T lawyers arrived. Clearwaters said little to
Kauper about the Saxbe briefing. At the appointed hour, the
group gathered in the attorney general's conference room, which
adjoined Saxbe's fifth-floor office. It was a rich, august room
with a high, arched ceiling and studded, red leather chairs. In
the center was a twenty-foot walnut conference table. Saxbe
sat at the end of the table, beneath an arch painting by Leon
Kroll known as *Justice Triumphant*, which depicted a white-robed
woman and a black-robed judge assisting a group of destitute
field workers. On the other side of the room, in the arch above
the AT&T lawyers, was another Kroll lunette, called *Justice Defeated*, which showed the same workers being carried off to
slavery.

John Wood, a Washington lawyer retained by AT&T, stood
up to begin AT&T's presentation. Mark Garlinghouse, the company's general counsel, was seated beside him.

"Mr. Saxbe," Wood began, puffing on a pipe, "before we
start our presentation, I'd like to know exactly what your state
of mind is on this case. It might help me shape my arguments
to you."

Saxbe paused, spit, looked at Wood, and said, "I intend to
bring an action against you."

If the room had not been filled with a dozen controlled and
detached lawyers, it would have erupted in shouting. Clearwaters didn't know whether to laugh or cry, so he bit his tongue.
Wood did his best to appear unmoved, and he attempted to
proceed with his vain presentation. Garlinghouse shot a few
angry glances at Kauper and Clearwaters.

Kauper scribbled a note on a page from his yellow legal
pad, folded it, and passed it down to Clearwaters.

What the hell did you tell him? it read.

Clearwaters put the note in his pocket and scribbled on
his own pad, *Exactly what you told me to tell him.* He passed it
down.

Another note came back to Clearwaters—nobody was listening to Wood's arguments, not even Saxbe. *Shouldn't we notify
the SEC?* it asked.

They should. Whenever the Justice department filed a major suit against a company, it was required to notify the Securities and Exchange Commission (SEC) immediately so that trading in the company's stock could be suspended. The purpose of the rule was to prevent anyone with "insider" information on the lawsuit from speculating in stock and to prevent a sudden run on a company's stock before it had a chance to explain the lawsuit and reassure investors.

Quietly, Clearwaters got up from the conference table and excused himself. He stepped around the corner, then down the stairs to his office on the third floor, where he called Stanley Sporkin at the SEC. He told Sporkin about what had just happened at the meeting. "I'm just calling to be sure you're apprised of the situation," Clearwaters said.

"Well, are you going to sue them or not?" Sporkin asked.

"This is a very strange situation. I don't really know. I think that we'll try to talk to the AG in private after the meeting. But I'll tell you this, I know what the AG's state of mind is."

"OK," Sporkin said, "I'm going to stop trading in their stock."

Clearwaters trundled back up to the conference room. When he entered, he interrupted Wood's presentation to announce that the SEC had just suspended trading in AT&T's stock. The AT&T lawyers tried hard to maintain their composure, but it was clear now that someone was soon going to lose his temper.

"I think this might be an appropriate time for a recess," Tom Kauper suggested. "Let's reconvene in a few minutes."

Kauper, Clearwaters, and Saxbe crossed under the painting of *Justice Triumphant* into the attorney general's private office. They sat down, and Clearwaters began immediately, "General, you've put me in an embarrassing position. I know that's your prerogative, but I think the least we should tell these gentlemen is that we're going to go to lunch and consider their presentation."

"You do what you want," Saxbe replied nonchalantly. "I've got a luncheon engagement already. You and Tom can go out to lunch if you want."

Saxbe returned to the conference room and told Garling-house, "We will be in discussions. No final decision has been made. Clearwaters will call you after lunch."

Kauper and Clearwaters walked around the corner to Ham-il's, a favorite Justice department restaurant at 10th and E Streets. Both men liked Mark Garlinghouse, who had made it clear before the lunch break that he felt hurt and personally betrayed by Saxbe's preemptive announcement. Kauper and Clearwaters discussed the personal guarantees both had made to Garling-house and also talked about the problem of AT&T's bond issue. Antitrust chief Kauper was not backing down from filing a suit, exactly, but he was worried that Saxbe had not done the right thing.

They found Saxbe in his office after lunch, and Kauper repeated his concerns about the bond issue, the assurances that had been made to Garlinghouse, and the necessity that Justice at least appear to have considered AT&T's arguments seriously.

Saxbe, however, was losing patience with Kauper's pristine lawyering. "Look," he said gruffly, "I've backed you all the way. Do you want me to file the case or not file the case?"

Clearwaters, who was standing next to Kauper, thought that if the Antitrust chief said no, Saxbe would fire him on the spot. But Kauper turned up his palms. "File it," he said.

At 195 Broadway in New York, John deButts was in a meet-ing with his board of directors when Mark Garlinghouse sent in a message from Washington. It read, "They've filed the case."

DeButts happened to be chairman that year of the United States Savings Bond campaign. Later in the day, he called Wil-liam Simon, Ford's secretary of the treasury, to tell Simon that the bond-selling campaign had exceeded its objective two months ahead of time.

"Well, John, that's just wonderful," Simon told him. "What a tremendous contribution you've made to your country."

"Well, it's got a helluva way of showing its appreciation," deButts said angrily.

"What do you mean by that?"

DeButts told Simon that he had just learned Justice was going to sue AT&T in an attempt to break apart the Bell System and that trading had been suspended in AT&T's stock. Simon was surprised and upset. He told deButts that the lawsuit had never been discussed in a cabinet meeting. "Let me find out something about this."

Simon called the White House. No one there had heard anything about the filing of a sweeping antitrust suit against Bell. President Ford was sightseeing in Japan and obviously had not been consulted.*

Simon then tried to call Saxbe, but the attorney general had left his office for the day. He had gone pheasant hunting.

On Friday, two days after the suit was filed, John deButts held a press conference in New York to discuss his company's problems with the Justice department. "It just doesn't make any sense to me," the AT&T chairman told reporters. "I can't understand why Justice would take an action that could lead to dismemberment of the Bell System, with the inevitable result that costs would go up and service would suffer. And anybody who says that won't be the case is just plain wrong."

DeButts told reporters that the cost of a year's telephone service for the average American was seven times cheaper than in most European countries, and was less expensive than in any other country in the world. "Our service," deButts added truthfully, "is better today than it's ever been by just about any standard you care to use to measure it."

In Washington, Bill McGowan responded with glee to deButts' comments. "The fact that deButts said the suit is astonishing to him is in itself astonishing," the MCI chairman said. "The suit gives another statement of credibility to our industry."

*In an interview ten years later, Saxbe conceded that he never talked with Ford about the lawsuit while Ford was president. Saxbe insisted, however, that during a luncheon meeting with Ford in Saxbe's office, while Ford was still vice-president, Saxbe told him that he thought the lawsuit was a good one and that he would probably file it while he was attorney general. Ford and Saxbe never discussed the suit again until after it was filed.

His credibility in the nation's capital would be short-lived, but for the moment, McGowan was triumphant. He had lured AT&T onto his chosen ground—politics—and now the giant monopoly was reeling. For the next several months, McGowan would retire to his corner office in northwest Washington to plan MCI's final blow.

Chapter 7

Stillborn

PHIL VERVEER was sitting in his car on the campus of Georgetown University, where his wife had come for a doctor's appointment, when the news came over the radio: The government had filed its antitrust suit against AT&T. In a matter of days, the entire case would be handed over to him, but the political appointees in Justice's front office had not bothered to tell Verveer that they were planning to file. Verveer was just a staff lawyer; his job was to execute the policy handed down by Saxbe, Kauper, and Clearwaters. The Justice department's political appointees had decided that the Bell System should be broken apart, but from now on, the appointees would spend precious little time worrying about how to do it.

That was Verveer's concern. And while there was no question that Phil Verveer was a bright and highly capable lawyer, there was no doubt, either, that at thirty-two years old, he was vastly inexperienced in the management of complex litigation. He had never been involved, even peripherally, in any case as big as this one, where there was so much at stake, where the issues were so complex, and where the disputes that had given rise to the case were in a state of continuous flux. Of course, few others in the division had ever worked on such a complex case, either. Verveer was regarded as a rising star—his superiors were relying on his obvious potential. Still, it would be

years before *U.S.* v. *AT&T* came to trial, maybe as long as a
decade, and during that time the case could be won or lost,
depending on how the pretrial strategy was handled. Moreover, this was not some obscure legal dispute soon to be gathering dust in a dark corner of the U.S. District Court file room.
It was a political case, highly visible, one in which Congress,
the FCC, and even the White House were certain to take an
interest. Navigating the case through such treacherous political
terrain would require savvy, wit, courage, and experience.

Most lawyers in Verveer's position would have looked at
U.S. v. *AT&T* as the ultimate career litmus test, a case that would
make or break their professional reputation. But while Verveer
certainly considered the case to be a serious personal challenge,
he was motivated by much more than narrow, professional self-
interest. Indeed, he considered himself to be on a kind of mission of justice, a crusade against the nefarious practices and
stark arrogance of the Bell monopolists. As he grew older, Verveer's black-and-white world view would dissolve into shades
of gray. But in late 1974, there was nothing subtle about the
young, committed lawyer's assessment of AT&T: the phone
company was morally wrong, it was evil, and it was up to
Verveer to serve the public interest by enforcing the antitrust
laws against it. This was not just a job—it was a calling.

In the *Evening Star* building on 11th Street, where Verveer
set up shop under the general supervision of Hugh Morrison,
a team of government lawyers was hired who shared Verveer's
view of the case. Nearly all of the new staff lawyers were very
young and passionately liberal, and more than a few had been
campus activists in college during the 1960s. They had rallied
for Robert F. Kennedy in 1968 and for George McGovern in
1972, and they saw the AT&T case as a way to "bring focus"
to their political instincts. They were friends, too—some had
known each other in school—and they quickly developed an
unusual, emotional camaraderie. They considered Verveer, who
was older and seemed to them a man of extraordinary moral
and religious conviction, to be their leader, a kind of priest of
the liberal, Catholic, Kennedy cult so much in flower in America
during the mid-1970's. Under Verveer's guidance and because

of the benign indifference of Hugh Morrison, who had dozens of other lawyers in his section to worry about, the group soon became isolated from the normal, bureaucratic ebb and flow of the Justice department. They were happily on their own, unfettered by Justice's internal political squabbles and free to pursue the mission of "socially important work" that bound them together.

And immediately on the horizon appeared the enemy, in the person of George L. Saunders, Jr., partner in the Chicago law firm of Sidley & Austin, a man who would devote the next eight years of his life to defending AT&T against the courtroom attacks of MCI and the Justice department. If John deButts, AT&T's arrogant and aristocratic chairman, was in Verveer's eyes the king of Bell's evil empire, then Saunders was deButts' sinister counselor, the mastermind of court intrigue. To Verveer, Saunders stood for everything that was repugnant about the legal profession: amorality, calculated selfishness, and corporate greed. Saunders was a brilliant man, to be sure, and perhaps he even deserved to be called a genius, but Verveer and his team of lawyers believed that Saunders used his gifts not to make the world a better place but to enrich himself through the protection of AT&T's monopolists.

Saunders was in fact a warm and affable fellow, and later he would earn the affection of many of the Justice lawyers who opposed him. But in the winter of 1974–1975, when the case got under way, Verveer and his lieutenants detested him, mostly for what he represented.

Saunders was an unabashed fat cat, a smooth, luxuriant attorney who wore expensive suits, drank martinis like they were water, and smoked more than a dozen cigars a day. He had been born and raised in Birmingham, Alabama, the son of a house painter, and was the first member of his family ever to attend college. He went because even at age fifteen, when he graduated high school two years ahead of schedule, his extraordinary intellectual gifts were obvious—his mind was like some strange machine. He had nearly total recall of the most complex and obscure facts, and he could effortlessly organize knowledge in sophisticated, well-developed models. The lawyers who worked with him later tried to describe this capacity to others by saying that it was like Saunders had a giant flip-chart in his head that he could summon up instantaneously, search for the information he needed, and then flip forward to make his next point without ever skipping a beat. He could stand before a judge, without notes, and speak in eloquent paragraphs for three hours or more.

He was a tall man with long limbs, and usually he carried a pot belly from all the martinis and fine food he consumed. His face was strangely birdlike, beaked and quick with energy. When he talked, which was often, Saunders liked to stroll around a room, gesturing to emphasize his points, and so he seemed to soar like some great flying ostrich, born on the wings of his words. The deep pleasure he found in those words and in the warming of a good argument was often apparent on his face; it was an expression partly of satisfaction, partly of arrogance, but mostly of irresistible, unbridled joy.

Verveer and the government lawyers who worked for him were intimidated by George Saunders, and for good reason. Within just three months after the government lawsuit was filed, Saunders had sabotaged Verveer's mission to break up the phone company.

When the government antitrust suit was filed on November 20, 1974, George Saunders was in New York working on the MCI case with his mentor, Sidley & Austin managing partner Howard Trienens. Trienens was the liaison between Sidley and AT&T, and he had represented the phone company on various matters for more than a decade. Trienens was a brilliant though serious and reticent man, professorial in demeanor. He spent a lot of time with Saunders, whom he had hired and anointed as Sidley's star trial attorney. The contrast between the two lawyers was vivid: Saunders was gregarious and boisterous; Trienens was quiet and controlled and was very devoted to his wife and three children. Trienens frequently traveled on business with his wife, and Saunders often found himself at dinner with the couple. In the midst of one of his typically long monologues, Saunders would look across the table and see

Trienens with his head bowed in silence. Saunders would stop talking and look down, only to find that Trienens had a legal brief out and was quietly editing it under the table.

Saunders wanted desperately to be the lead attorney for AT&T on the government case. The MCI case, which Saunders was already in charge of, was, eight months after filing, just entering the discovery phase, in which both sides would spend years exchanging and cataloging documents to be used during the trial. Saunders could leave that work to others and thus be free to make the early arguments for AT&T against the government. Trienens, too, wanted Saunders to run the government case. Not only did he consider Saunders to be one of the brightest lawyers in the country but he also knew that if Sidley & Austin got the case, the firm would earn tens and tens of millions in legal fees from AT&T over the next five or ten years. As Sidley's managing partner, Trienens was one of the firm's key "rainmakers," lawyers who cultivate good relations with big-spending clients like the phone company. Only one thing stood in the way: the New York law firm of Dewey, Ballantine, Bushby, Palmer & Wood, which, until now, had been AT&T's principal antitrust counsel. The Dewey firm had defended AT&T against the government antitrust case that had ended in tainted settlement in 1956. During the last weeks of 1974 and in early 1975, Trienens and Saunders maneuvered to push Dewey out of the way, and by February they had succeeded. DeButts and Mark Garlinghouse put Saunders, under Trienens' general supervision, in charge of the government case. The coup left some partners at Dewey bitter for years.

Trienens, and especially Saunders, were itching to launch a counterattack against the government attorneys who had filed the antitrust suit, including Antitrust chief Tom Kauper, who years before had started his brief career at Sidley on the same day as George Saunders. Though they had not been involved in the discussions with Saxbe and Kauper—Dewey, Ballantine had handled those, before it lost control to Sidley & Austin— Saunders and Trienens knew well what had transpired. Saunders was infuriated. Many lawyers achieve a cool detachment about their clients' problems, so as to offer the most objective advice possible, but that was not Saunders' style. Like John deButts, Saunders believed passionately that AT&T was being victimized by greedy opportunists such as Bill McGowan, who used politics and the regulatory system to skim AT&T's profits, and by overeager government attorneys such as Verveer, who Saunders believed was carrying out a personal, political vendetta against the phone company simply because it was so large.

Saunders also believed, as did Trienens, that the Justice department did not have a legitimate antitrust case. How could a company violate the antitrust laws, they asked, when its every move—its prices, the services it could offer, the profits it could earn—was regulated by the FCC and dozens of state utility commissions? The same federal government that, through the FCC, strictly controlled AT&T's behavior was at the same time, through the Justice department, suing the company over the very acts it had sanctioned.

This argument—that all of the significant antitrust violations attributed to AT&T were really just attempts by the company to comply with confusing and conflicting FCC regulation—would become the heart of Saunders' defense for AT&T. But in the meantime, there was a way to use that argument to cut off Verveer and his young government lawyers at the knees. Saunders could argue, legitimately, that if one agreed that AT&T was subject to "pervasive regulation" by the FCC, then a dispute such as the one with MCI belonged at the commission, not in court. This was not an antitrust case, Saunders argued, it was a regulatory dispute. The FCC, after all, created MCI in the first place, and the commission should be responsible for solving problems that arose from that act. The FCC was an expert agency: it knew the telecommunications industry inside and out and was thus better equipped than a federal judge to straighten out industry problems. Saunders would argue to the court that it had no jurisdiction over the government suit and that the matter belonged at the FCC.

Even if this strategy failed, Saunders and Trienens knew there was no harm in trying. If they spent years arguing the point only to lose in the end, so what? They would have bought valuable time for John deButts, who was still trying to rally public opinion against competition in the phone business. And if they managed to postpone discovery in the Justice case while the jurisdictional question was resolved, they would have effectively shut down Verveer's Justice investigation, thus dashing McGowan's hope that the government lawsuit would pressure AT&T to give MCI what it wanted.

Even George Saunders conceded afterwards that what happened on the morning of February 20, 1975, was not Phil Verveer's fault.

Verveer was ill-prepared for the nine-thirty hearing before Judge Joseph C. Waddy, in the federal district court building in Washington, D.C., but that was mostly because no one was sure what was on the judge's agenda. Waddy had been assigned the government case when it was filed in November, and he had not yet met with lawyers from either side. He was an able, if undistinguished, black judge who happened also in February 1975 to be dying of cancer. The morning hearing had ostensibly been called by Verveer and his Justice superiors, though once it began, no one seemed sure what it was supposed to accomplish. The government lawyers were in a hectic state over a bit of gamesmanship concocted by Saunders earlier in the month. Purely for tactical reasons, Saunders had filed a motion with Waddy asking that the federal government be required to preserve every document in its possession that might be relevant to the AT&T case—not just at the Justice department and the FCC, where there was obviously a lot of paper AT&T was interested in, but at almost every other federal agency as well. There was no way the government could comply with such an order—there was too much paper about telephones in too many places—but if the motion was granted and the Antitrust division failed to abide by it, the government could be held in contempt of court. It was the sort of ploy a lawyer like Saunders used to shake up his opposition, to put them on the defensive early in litigation.

And this time, the ploy worked.

"Our concern is whether or not we need instruct the rest

of the federal government to retain the sorts of documents which their motion seeks to have preserved," Verveer told Waddy agitatedly as the hearing began.

"Well," Waddy asked, puzzled, "is that the rest of the federal government now or only those agencies that have been designated by AT&T? As I read it, the defendants have backed off from their broad concern and have now designated forty-four agencies that are involved."

"I believe that's correct," Verveer conceded.

"That's what it appears to me. If I'm wrong, correct me," Waddy said, suggesting that he didn't think Saunders' request sounded all that unreasonable.

Saunders, sensing a kill, approached the courtroom lectern.

"Let me get your name again," Waddy asked.

"Your Honor," Saunders drawled, "my name is George Saunders."

"Yes, Mr. Saunders."

"The government's position is quite simple. They want to continue to destroy on a daily basis any paper that is normally destroyed in the federal government. We say that ought to stop today. We think the law on this point is clear."

"The government hasn't filed a motion," Waddy said. "It has merely asked to come in, and I understood it was representing both Justice and AT&T when it asked to come in today."

"As I understand what the government asked to come in for today," Saunders replied, posturing boldly, "it was to inform Your Honor that they have problems complying with the law, and they would like to have the permission of the court not to comply with the law."

Saunders began to warm to his theme and continued. "What we are looking for in this case is not just the idle opinion of government employees who say that the Antitrust division made a mistake by filing this case. If that's what we needed, we have it in the newspapers all over the country, all the time. What we're looking for is hard evidence from government employees who recognize that what this case amounts to"—and here Saunders turned dramatically to point at Verveer and the group of young lawyers who had accompanied him to court—"is an adventure by a handful of lawyers in the Antitrust division who have decided that they would like to break apart the Bell System, and who now have what seems to me to be the *unmitigated gall* to walk into this court and say, 'You're not entitled to defend yourselves!' "

At that moment, with Saunders' finger pointed at him, Tom Mauro, a self-described "populist" who had been hired to work with Phil Verveer, decided privately that this hearing was about to become a major disaster.

Waddy was openly hostile to Verveer after Saunders' speech, peppering the young government attorney with accusatory questions, keeping him off balance, and preventing him from making any substantial points in response to Saunders.

And suddenly Saunders was on his feet again, this time thundering to Waddy that the case didn't even belong in his court at all, that it belonged at the FCC. "AT&T is regulated by the FCC," Saunders told him. "We are told what we must do. We are told what we cannot do. We are told who is permitted to compete in the communications industry. We are told the terms and conditions of that competition. We follow the orders of the FCC. If we don't follow those orders, the FCC has ample power to slap our hands. Basically, we believe this is not a proper case for the antitrust laws...."

Waddy was nodding his head; he was interested in Saunders' argument. He was so interested, in fact, that he told Verveer that he wanted to postpone discovery—in effect, shut down the case—until this jurisdictional question was resolved. Verveer was flabbergasted. Such a decision would play into AT&T's hands splendidly.

"I don't think it is necessary," Verveer said.

"Nonetheless, discovery probably should be postponed until after the court rules," Waddy answered.

"Your Honor, we'll undertake to..."

"That will be the order," Waddy snapped.

"All right, Your Honor."

Three months after filing, the case had been stopped dead in its tracks by Saunders and AT&T. Waddy's order meant, in effect, that neither side could develop any new evidence and that the case would be in a state of suspended animation until he decided whether it belonged in federal court or at the FCC.

That morning, neither Verveer nor Saunders could have predicted that, at least in part because of Judge Waddy's terminal illness, it would take three years to resolve the jurisdictional question. Far from restructuring the telecommunications industry, as Phil Verveer hoped, *U.S.* v. *AT&T* would be nothing but an inactive embarrassment to the Justice department for thirty-six long months.

"On a scale of one to ten, you get an eleven," an AT&T attorney told Saunders when the hearing was over.

The phone company's glee would not last long, however. In just a matter of weeks, it would be forced to confront a monumental and permanent restructuring of the telephone industry that was not ordered by Judge Waddy, the Justice department, Congress, or the FCC, but devised by the phone company's relentless opponent, Bill McGowan.

Chapter 8

McGowan's Gambit

ONE day in early May 1975, less than three months after the government antitrust suit ground suddenly to a halt, Walter Hinchman was visited in his FCC office in northwest Washington, D.C., by an AT&T lobbyist.

A telecommunications engineer with strong procompetition views, Hinchman had succeeded Bernie Strassburg as chief of the FCC's Common Carrier Bureau in the fall of 1973. He had perpetuated Strassburg's policy of "regulation by competition," and he had helped MCI consolidate its victories over AT&T at the commission, especially its controversial authorization to sell FX lines to business customers. Hinchman had little patience for AT&T's argument that FX service represented a sneaky encroachment by MCI into the switched telephone network. The new Common Carrier chief was highly suspicious of AT&T. He was more hostile to the phone company than even Strassburg had been during his last months on the job.

Hinchman knew, however, that FX service represented a line the FCC could not permit MCI to cross. The commission had said repeatedly that it would never allow competitors like MCI to enter the regular long-distance business, for to do so would wreak havoc on the delicate system of public interest subsidies and regulation that had been established in the telephone industry since World War II. Hinchman believed that even though FX involved open access to local exchanges on

one end of the line, the service should nonetheless be cate-
gorized as a "private line," since it was tied to a single point
on the other end—an airline reservations office or a company's
national customer service center, for example. For Hinchman,
FX was as far as the definition of "private line" could be
stretched.

The AT&T lobbyist knocked on Hinchman's door around
noon, without an appointment. "I want to show you this thing,"
he said, holding up a card that had a series of codes written
on it.

"What's this?" Hinchman asked.

"I want to show you a new service that's available from
MCI. Come on down the hall."

There was a Touch Tone phone near Hinchman's office.
The lobbyist gave Hinchman the card he was holding and said,
"Here, punch in these digits."

Hinchman obliged. He heard a pause, some connecting
clicks, a ring, and then . . . the Chicago weather. Hinchman was
starting to feel a little queasy. He had just dialed, apparently
over MCI lines, from a random phone in Washington to a random phone in Chicago, a regular long-distance phone call. How
could that happen? MCI was not authorized to provide switched
long-distance service.

"What do you think you just did?" the lobbyist asked in a
self-satisfied tone.

Hinchman became cautious; he knew that if this service
was what it appeared to be, it meant serious trouble. MCI might
even have violated the law. The Common Carrier chief did not
want to start discussing the matter in a hallway with an AT&T
lobbyist. Such a conversation could come back to haunt a government employee.

"You tell me," Hinchman said, backing away. "I don't know.
Maybe it was a local call. I don't want to speculate. I get the
impression that this is not an AT&T service and that you've got
a complaint. If you've got a problem, you know the procedures."

"Don't you think this is something the bureau should investigate?" the lobbyist asked.

"I don't know what this is. File a complaint."

Hinchman returned to his office and began to call frantically around the commission. He learned quickly that AT&T
lobbyists had held similar private demonstrations for a number
of FCC commissioners and that the commissioners were outraged. "My God! This is long distance!" one of them had
shouted.

Next, Hinchman tried to talk with his staff at the Common
Carrier Bureau, especially with those who were involved in
supervising and approving MCI's tariffs. No one was sure what
had happened. The service in question was called "Execunet,"
Hinchman discovered, and it had been filed with and approved
by the bureau staff the previous fall. MCI had been selling
Execunet since January. But how could this have happened?
Hinchman wanted to know. How could the bureau staff have
approved a service that they knew perfectly well MCI was prohibited from selling?

The answer, as it emerged over the next several months,
was that Bill McGowan had tricked and betrayed his supporters
at the FCC and in Congress.

In testimony before the Hart antitrust subcommittee, in
filings with the FCC, in speeches before industry groups, and
in dozens of private meetings with congressional and FCC staff
during the early 1970s, McGowan had said clearly that MCI did
not intend to enter the regular long distance market. That was
AT&T's territory, its natural monopoly. MCI's reason for being,
its authorized franchise, was not to duplicate AT&T's switched
telephone network but to offer "new and innovative services"
in private lines and business communications. This assertion
by McGowan—that he was not really a threat to AT&T because
no matter how successful he was, the phone company would
still reap billions each year from regular long distance—was a
key reason why MCI enjoyed widespread support in Congress
and at the FCC. If one accepted McGowan's word that MCI
would confine itself to private lines, then AT&T chairman John
deButts' apocalyptic warnings about the consequences of competition in the telephone industry sounded a little hysterical.

What harm could tiny MCI do to AT&T? Regular long-distance revenues were many times greater than those from private lines. Surely a monopoly as large as AT&T could afford to compete in a few specialized areas without jeopardizing the high quality and low cost of consumer telephone service.

McGowan claimed later that he was telling the truth when he spoon-fed regulators and politicians that argument, that he really *didn't* intend to enter the switched MTS (message toll service) long-distance market in the early 1970s. By the time the controversy over Execunet was resolved, there were plenty of telephone industry insiders—not all of them friends of AT&T—who were convinced that from the beginning MCI's publicly professed plans had been little more than a profitable lie orchestrated by Bill McGowan.

Whether McGowan had always secretly been planning to slip into the regular long-distance market will likely never be known. During the late 1970s and early 1980s, the MCI chairman spent tens of millions of dollars and hundreds of courtroom hours defending his company's conduct during MCI's and the government's antitrust suits against AT&T, and he always maintained that Execunet was a kind of happy accident, not a conspiracy, and that it had been properly authorized by the FCC even though the commission strongly believed otherwise. Despite extensive discovery of MCI's internal files by AT&T, McGowan's position was never conclusively contradicted in court. The evidence suggests, however, that as far back as October 1973, in the aftermath of John deButts' Seattle speech, and fully eighteen months before Walter Hinchman and the FCC commissioners learned what McGowan had wrought, the MCI chairman was planning his incursion into the switched long-distance network.

It was a risky strategy. McGowan's gambit, if successful, would make MCI a billion-dollar, *Fortune* 500–sized company within five years; if it failed, MCI would likely land in bankruptcy court.

The key to the strategy was cash. In the fall of 1973, McGowan had urged an angry Bernie Strassburg to authorize MCI to sell FX lines because McGowan desperately needed a new source of revenue for his company. MCI was in default to its bankers, it was laying off employees, and its microwave construction project was stalled. McGowan had hoped then that FX revenues would alleviate MCI's cash crunch. But the protracted legal fight over FX, and John deButts' decision after a court ruling in March 1974 to disconnect in one weekend all of MCI's FX customers, had squeezed the revenue flow.

Even after the legal fight was temporarily resolved and MCI was formally authorized to sell FX lines, the extra revenue was not enough. In the two years between March 1973 and March 1975, McGowan watched his working capital drain away at a rate of more than $1 million a month. If the company's negative cash flow continued much longer, MCI would be out of business. McGowan needed a way to bring in new revenues without investing another dime in construction projects, employees, or other start-up costs. And so, in the spring and summer of 1974, just when the FX fight was over and it appeared to AT&T that McGowan finally had everything he had asked for, MCI's chairman began to explore ways his company might enter the regular long-distance market—where the big money lay.

Execunet was an ingenious, if dishonest, solution to McGowan's cash problems. The challenge was to devise a "new service" tariff that would allow MCI to sell the equivalent of regular long-distance service to its customers without alerting staffers in the Common Carrier Bureau to MCI's real intentions. Those staffers would review any tariff filed by MCI. Late in 1974, McGowan settled on an approach called a "modular tariff." Essentially, MCI would take all the services it was authorized to sell, roll them up in a single package, and bring them down to the FCC. The company would tell the bureau staff that it wanted to sell to its customers new and different combinations of MCI's existing services. Then it would ask for approval of this "modular" package. The tariff might be vague, but MCI could argue that it was an innovative marketing technique: it had never been done before. A customer could take any available MCI service, combine it with any other service, and form an altogether new one.

For example—and MCI did not for a minute intend to lay

this example out to bureau staffers—a customer might choose to combine a series of FX lines. Before Execunet, an FX line looked like this:

Point A was a single office in one city, say, Chicago. Point B was the entire local exchange, all the telephones, in a second city, say, New York. A customer in New York could pick up any phone in his city, dial a local number, and the call would travel to the office in Chicago. But suppose a customer combined two FX lines between Chicago and New York, each with a different open end. Then MCI's "private-line" system would look like this:

A customer in Chicago could pick up any phone in his city and dial any number in New York. It would be exactly like a normal long-distance call over AT&T's switched network, except that the customer would have to dial some extra digits and the call would travel over MCI's microwave system. And, of course, the customer would be billed by MCI, not AT&T.

Execunet, as McGowan envisioned it, would extend this model even further. Instead of restricting a customer to calls between cities A and B, MCI would combine FX lines between all the cities in its nationwide network. In effect, MCI would instantly become a national long-distance network in competition with AT&T.

And if all went well with the tariff filing at the FCC, AT&T wouldn't know what MCI had done until it was too late.

The plan worked flawlessly. When they finally sorted it out in the summer of 1975, after the demonstrations by AT&T's lobbyists, Walter Hinchman and the FCC commissioners realized that they had been duped. When questioned, the bureau staffers who had approved the modular tariff sounded like dazed victims of a confidence scam: they remembered the tariff, and they recalled being confused by it, but they had no inkling of MCI's larger purpose. Some lawyers in the Common Carrier Bureau felt deeply angry and betrayed by MCI's manuever. More than anyone, the bureau staffers had protected and nurtured MCI during its treacherous early years in competition with AT&T, and in many ways the fledgling company had been their child. The staffers themselves freely used that metaphor when discussing MCI. Now their trust had been returned with scorn, and the staffers were hurt and humiliated. They felt they had been used and deceived by Bill McGowan.

Of course, McGowan himself was acting from a simple and powerful instinct of self-preservation. Without revenues from switched long distance, MCI would likely not have survived long enough to build its national network of microwave towers. And not all of the company's cash crunch during 1973 and 1974 was its own fault; AT&T's intransigence during the interconnection negotiations and deButts' ruthless stance in the FX fight had contributed mightily to MCI's plight. If McGowan had resorted to subterfuge to save his company in such dire circumstances, well, perhaps AT&T was only getting what it deserved. Free-market competition was not the sport of gentlemen.

The Execunet ploy did seem to confirm deButts' original assessment of McGowan and MCI. When the FCC had approved MCI's application and introduced competition in the private-line business in 1969, deButts and other AT&T officials had argued that such competition was impractical, not only because it threatened to disrupt AT&T's regulated profit and subsidy structure but because the economies of the telephone business were such that MCI could not survive simply by selling private lines. The telephone business offered a classic example of "economies of scale," AT&T argued. That is, the enormous cost of constructing a national telecommunications network made sense only if the builder could reap revenues from every telephone installed—return on investment rose as volume of traffic increased. Even if MCI were to capture 50 percent of the private-line market, an unlikely eventuality, the revenue would not be enough to pay for a national microwave network, AT&T argued. Inevitably, MCI would go broke, deButts said, or else it would try to expand its franchise into regular long distance. For him, the FX and Execunet controversies were outrageous confirmation of warnings made some six years before. McGowan, of course, argued otherwise with equal passion. And he intimated that if, by 1975, MCI needed Execunet to stave off bankruptcy, it was only because AT&T's antitrust violations had sabotaged the company's earlier plans.

After Execunet, though, the numbers began to speak for themselves. By the end of the 1970s, as MCI's annual sales began to approach $2 billion, more than 80 percent of its revenues came from regular long distance. At one point, MCI even stopped taking orders for private lines: they weren't profitable enough. In just a few years, deButts' worst fears about intercity telephone competition had been realized. The FCC's haphazard experiment had become, even in the view of some commission staffers, Frankenstein unleashed.

That realization, and the accompanying anger and embarrassment in Congress and at the FCC, offered deButts an opening. McGowan had built his company by outflanking AT&T in Washington, and it was McGowan who had shifted the field of battle from business to politics and law. With McGowan's credibility destroyed and his reservoir of political goodwill drained because of Execunet, perhaps now was the time for AT&T to turn the tables on MCI. The company took McGowan to court, hoping to have Execunet ruled illegal. At the same time, deButts turned his biggest guns on Washington. With one million employees, a strong labor union (the Communications Workers of America), and a lobbying network that reached across the country, the phone company was not without political clout. Perhaps McGowan's deceit would open Congress' eyes to the urgent need for a coherent national telecommunications policy. DeButts thought that perhaps Congress, in its wisdom, would solve AT&T's problems by crushing MCI and exonerating the phone company of any antitrust violations.

Such was the political agenda that John deButts began to draw up at 195 Broadway in the summer of 1975. He saw no reason to set his sights low. To save the phone company's monopoly, he intended to use every resource at his disposal. With Execunet, McGowan had abandoned all pretense of fair play. So, too, would deButts.

Chapter 9

DeButts' Last Stand

JOHN DE BUTTS called it the Consumer Communications Reform Act (CCRA) of 1976. Everyone else knew it as the Bell Bill.

Its formal title notwithstanding, the proposed legislation did not rely on subtlety to make its points. If it passed, long-distance telephone services of all kinds would become "utility" functions to be provided by a single, integrated system. The legislation suggested that since it was already built, AT&T's phone system should be selected as the country's official monopoly; MCI and other embryonic long-distance companies would be forced out of business. To be sure that the resultant hard feelings would not lead to nasty and lengthy court fights, the phone company would be immunized against all antitrust lawsuits and would be authorized to buy up any of its competitors. Regulation of telephones and telephone equipment would revert from the FCC to state utility commissions, thus vacating the FCC's 1968 *Carterfone* decision, which had introduced competition in the phone equipment industry. Answering machines and other devices—so-called "foreign attachments" regulated by local utility commissions—would be legal in some states, illegal in others. Competition in the telephone industry would be immediately and permanently choked off.

Upon learning of its contents, some telephone regulators in Washington considered the Bell Bill to be about as unassuming as Jonathan Swift's "A Modest Proposal," wherein the eighteenth-century author had suggested that the Irish solve their population and hunger problems by selling their children to the rich as meat.

The trouble was that, unlike Swift, deButts was not indulging in satire. Indeed, the AT&T chairman was deadly serious about the bill, so serious that in the six months after its introduction in early 1976, he spent millions of dollars lobbying for its passage and secured endorsements from fully 40 percent of the House of Representatives—although a general "endorsement," as deButts would discover, was far easier to obtain than a vote.

"We have decided the time has come to call the public's attention to its stake in the matter," deButts said. "Were the telephone companies deprived of . . . revenues from their more discretionary services, they would face the necessity of increasing the average customer's bill for basic service as much as 75 percent."

In response to deButts' round of speeches, Bill McGowan sounded rather shrill. He knew perfectly well what AT&T's chairman was up to, but he also knew that his own stature as a political mud-slinger was undermined by the controversy over Execunet. "After a decade of failing to prove any of its points to the federal government, the courts, and the marketplace, Bell now has gone to Congress in a do-or-die effort to deprive the communications consumer of the recognized benefits of competition," McGowan declared desperately. DeButts' speech-making about the Bell Bill amounted to a "bare-faced lie," McGowan said. But the irony of the MCI chairman's accusation was not lost on congressmen and staffers familiar with the recent chicanery at the FCC. For six years, McGowan had controlled his own—and AT&T's—destiny in Washington, but this time around, he would have to sit on the sidelines. If the Bell Bill was destined to pass, McGowan could not prevent it.

Fortunately for MCI, the heroics of its chairman would not be required. This time, McGowan would not have to outsmart

John deButts. When it came to legislative politics, AT&T's chairman was perfectly capable of defeating himself.

If a large corporation wants a special favor from Congress—a tax break, say, or a federal price subsidy, or a monopoly—there are a variety of strategies it can pursue to achieve its goal.

The most common and effective method, in the jargon of Capitol Hill, is to "attach a rider." The company persuades a congressman or senator, usually one who represents an area where the company has a large manufacturing plant employing thousands of voters, to "attach" quietly a special-interest bill as an amendment to completely unrelated and preferably popular legislation, such as a famine relief appropriation or an increase in social security benefits. Once attached, the fates of the two proposals become linked: if the president wants to veto the special corporate tax break, he will find himself in the embarrassing predicament of having also to veto the famine relief money. If the corporation and its congressman make their move at the end of a legislative session, when there is little time to detach amendments and when other congressmen are frantically trying to attach their own pet riders, the chances for success are excellent.

If the legislation sought is complex, however, the corporation may have to fall back on a committee strategy. Congressional committees are the body's "working groups," with specific jurisdictions: tax writing, energy issues, defense, and so on. The committees are relatively small and are dominated by strong personalities and Byzantine partisan politics. It is relatively simple for a large company to focus its lobbying on the one or two committees that have legislative jurisdiction over the company's industry. With a savvy understanding of the committee members' needs, ambitions, and weaknesses, a large corporation can quickly become a de facto committee member, helping to write legislation, plotting vote strategies, and worrying over election results.

Such winning political strategies depend on subtlety, fi-

nesse, and years of experience. More than anything, they require a certain blithe invisibility on the part of the corporation:
it is crucially important, long-time Capitol lobbyists know, to
let the congressman take credit for "hammering out a compromise," or "forging complex legislation," or however else he
wants to describe to voters his role in the pork barrel giveaway.
To have its way in Congress, a large corporation must walk
softly, lose graciously, flatter continuously, and gloat never.

All of which goes a long way toward explaining why the
Bell Bill quickly ran into trouble in 1976, despite the millions
of dollars spent by AT&T, despite the long days of grassroots
lobbying by phone company executives and employees, and
despite the thunderous "public interest" rhetoric from John
deButts.

Many of Bell's opponents regarded the phone company's
heavy-handed legislative strategy as a manifestation of John
deButts' blinding arrogance. After Execunet, deButts seemed
to assume that anyone who understood what had happened
at the FCC would share his outrage about it. In fact, many
congressmen and their staffs felt ambivalent about Execunet.
Perhaps McGowan had been underhanded, but if the result
was more competition then no real harm had been done, they
thought.

DeButts simply did not understand the tenor of his times,
or if he understood it he failed to come to grips with it. Deregulation was a Capitol Hill buzzword, and the idea was fast
gathering force among both Democrats and Republicans. Liberals wanted to deregulate because competition would lead to
decentralized ownership and a more diverse economy; conservatives just wanted the government off business's back. Together, they were an unstoppable coalition: airline, trucking,
natural gas, oil, banking, and other industries were all deregulated by Congress during the late 1970s and early 1980s.
DeButts saw this tidal wave coming, but he seemed to believe
that where the telephone industry was concerned, he could
restrain it singlehandedly and, indeed, reverse the flow. In an
era when Congress was legislating competition in one industry

after another, deButts insisted on nothing less than the right to swallow his competitors and preside over an officially sanctioned monopoly.

"You're all right when you get hired," an AT&T employee once observed, "but as the years go by, your head becomes more and more Bell-shaped." DeButts, a privileged man raised in the Old South, may have had little personal capacity to finesse his opponents in Congress. But it was really the institution he ran—its traditions, its size, and its power—that shaped his reaction to Execunet in 1976. When push came to shove, the phone company had always gotten its way with the federal government. DeButts believed that was because AT&T provided the best phone service in the world at the lowest possible price. With his back against the wall over Execunet, deButts asked, not illogically, "Why would Congress want to mess up the world's best phone system?"

The trouble lay with the way deButts phrased his question. Typical of AT&T's style, the Bell Bill did not say, in effect, "This competition thing has gotten out of hand over at the FCC. Why don't we sit down with you fellows in Congress and work out something that will best serve the American public, something we can all live with?"

No, the Bell Bill said something more along the lines of, "You bastards in Washington have made a mistake: you've gotten the phone company mad. Now we're going to come down to Congress and take what's ours. Either you're with us or against us. We're taking no prisoners."

DeButts' political strategy did have one thing to recommend it: it scared the daylights out of a lot of congressmen. More than two hundred of them signed on as cosponsors of CCRA in early 1976, and of those, probably less than ten fully understood the recent history of competition in the telephone industry.

The congressmen had good reason to be frightened. With a million employees spread around the country and a sizable political war chest at its disposal, the phone company was able to raise a terrible sound and fury about the Bell Bill. Its attack on Congress resembled a charge by Ayatollah Khomeini's Iranian army, for what it lacked in strategic planning, it made up for with waves of human flesh. Bell lobbyists, who became known on Capitol Hill as "shepherds" for the hovering attention they paid to their congressional flock, were flown into Washington by the planeload. They were unusual lobbyists. They shunned Italian pinstripes and fancy Washington bistros, and few of them were lawyers. The vast majority were employed not at AT&T's headquarters at 195 Broadway but by the local operating companies around the country. Unlike any other corporation, the phone company had employees in every congressional district, and this omnipresence became the key to the Bell Bill lobbying strategy.

A shepherd was selected from each congressman's home district. Often, the shepherd knew the congressman socially from the local Rotary or Kiwanis Club, where the congressman came to speak and raise campaign contributions. When the shepherd came to Washington, he brought with him a variety of AT&T employees from the home district—union members, middle managers, top executives—and then he spent weeks following the congressman around, talking with his staff, attending his committee meetings, and even fetching deli sandwiches when the legislator was hungry. Once during the Bell Bill fight, Representative Tim Wirth, a Democrat from Colorado and then a majority member of the House Communications Subcommittee, found himself at a crowded hearing where an AT&T executive was testifying. Wirth asked the executive to identify any of his colleagues who were in the room. After five minutes of introductions, only one small corner had been identified.

Wirth then asked in desperation, "Will everyone associated with AT&T just stand up?"

Everyone in the room stood, laughing nervously.

Other incidents were less whimsically amusing to the congressmen. An aide to one important senator was approached by an AT&T lobbyist early in 1976 to arrange a meeting between his boss and John deButts. The senator told his aide, "I don't want to see him," and the message was passed on to AT&T.

A few weeks later, the aide received a call from a friend, a fellow Irish Catholic with more than several children. "My job is on the line over setting up this meeting," the friend said. "My kids' livelihood is on the line." Grudgingly, the senator agreed to see deButts, but when the meeting was done, the senator worked harder than before to defeat the Bell Bill.

DeButts' lobbying blitzkrieg was ill-chosen for reasons beyond its high visibility and its undertone of political blackmail. Most importantly, the campaign inevitably persuaded only those congressmen who could do deButts the least good. Committed chairmanships were awarded on the basis of seniority, so the most powerful members were those with decades of service and electorally safe seats. Such congressmen were unlikely to be intimidated by AT&T's implied threat of reprisals at the ballot box; they could win reelection with or without the phone company. A weak congressman, with one or two terms of service and a tenuous grip on his district, might well agree to help the phone company in exchange for the votes of its employees, but he was unlikely to wield any real influence in committee or with his party leaders. So while deButts was able to rack up impressive numbers of cosponsors, it was clear by early summer that they were not the kinds of sponsors who could round up votes to move legislation quickly, if at all. The chairmen of both the House and Senate Communications Subcommittees were quietly opposed to the bill and hoped to smother it by inaction. And when the Bell Bill was formally introduced in the House, AT&T was unable to find anyone on the Communications Subcommittee to sponsor the legislation. The bill was finally submitted by Teno Roncalio, a Wyoming Democrat whose main interests were sheep, cattle, energy, and mining. Years later, Roncalio said that he still didn't know why AT&T had resorted to choosing "a little, lone congressman from Wyoming to carry their wash."

*   *   *

On the morning of September 28, 1976, a few days before
Congress' month-long election recess, the House Communications Subcommittee finally opened hearings on the Bell Bill.
No one present in the Rayburn Building hearing room that day,
including John deButts, expected that the bill would pass before
the close of the Ninety-fourth Congress, only three months
away. The hearings had only been called by the subcommittee's
chairman, Lionel Van Deerlin, a California Democrat, because
the scores of politically vulnerable Bell Bill cosponsors in the
House wanted to assure their shepherds that something was
being done before the November election. Without conceding
anything substantial to the phone company, the hearings were
a way to make deButts and his army of lobbyists feel that they
had accomplished something.

Once the questioning began, though, it became clear that
in the congressmen's minds the real issue had always been not
the merits of telephone industry competition but John deButts'
bludgeoning political tactics.

"Do you have an estimate," Congressman Wirth began,
"of what your lobbying activities for 1976 on this bill have cost?"

"From the introduction of the bill up until, I think, the end
of June, the total cost to the Bell system was something on the
order of $600,000," deButts said.

"Our estimate was that the one day in front of our committee came close to a hundred thousand dollars."

"We have a lot of people in Washington, Congressman,
who are not lobbying," deButts snapped.

"Like the day the president of Mountain Bell [from Wirth's
home state] came by to visit me with a copy of the bill."

"That would be included," said deButts.

"There were a lot of people from all over the country vis-
iting other members of Congress with a copy of the bill."

"That would be included."

"What was your original timetable for this legislation?"

"We had no timetable, sir."

"Have you been pleased with the efforts to date?"

"Yes, sir."

"Have you gotten the kind of support and sponsorship you would like?"

"I don't think we have enough," deButts said, "and I hope we will get more. The key thing here, Congressman, as I see it, is that we get this thing out on the table so that everybody knows what is going on. The problem is, these things are being done to the American public without the American public knowing anything about it. So we want you to know the facts."

"I agree with you," Wirth said sardonically. "A lot of things are done that the American public doesn't know about. Frankly, can you tell me how many people AT&T has working full time on this legislation?"

"I have no idea, sir, but it is very few—very few. Full time? I doubt if there is a single person in the Bell System that is working full time on this legislation."

With those words, John deButts' credibility in Congress reached its nadir. No one in the room believed that he was telling the truth—about his lobbyists, about his tactics, about anything.

The hearing room erupted in laughter.

The Bell Bill was dead, but deButts' political fiasco would have lingering repercussions for AT&T. It was as if, with McGowan reeling because of Execunet, deButts had tried to deliver a corkscrew knockout punch. But by swinging too hard, the AT&T chairman had missed everything and had hurled himself out of the ring. By the time he recovered, McGowan was off the ropes again, dancing and jabbing and looking for another edge against John deButts and the Bell System.

Chapter 10

The Red and Blue Teams

THE most important consequence of John deButts' Bell Bill debacle was that it confirmed, publicly and irrevocably, the suspicions and prejudices of AT&T's opponents in Congress. As a body, Congress was incapable of tackling an issue as technically complex and historically convoluted as telephone industry competition solely on the merits. Prior to 1976, even the expert staff lawyers on the two communications subcommittees paid scant attention to telephone issues. Like the FCC commissioners, they were far more interested in television issues such as violence and sex on TV, children's programming, and the concentrated power of the nation's three major networks. Lacking expertise, the congressmen and their committee lawyers relied on political instinct when judging telephone legislation. In 1976, in the post-Watergate era of *Small Is Beautiful*, that instinct urged skepticism and even cynicism when considering the motives and legislative proposals of AT&T, the ubiquitous phone monopoly.

DeButts' strong-arm lobbying tactics had transformed instinct into conviction. Congressman Tim Wirth, for example, who would ascend within four years to the chairmanship of the House Communications Subcommittee, never forgot that day in the House hearing room when 150 well-dressed Bell executives stood up in unison like so many programmed, corporate androids. Nor would his colleagues on the committee soon forget the Bell shepherds who always seemed to be sitting in their House office building reception areas, clutching copies of a bill that would legally permit AT&T to crush dozens of its competitors.

The fact was that behind the hyperbole of deButts' rhetoric there lay compelling arguments for Congress to restrain, or at least investigate, telephone industry competition, which had mushroomed during the preceding decade without any serious consideration of its consequences. Before Execunet, it was McGowan who had been the industry's proselytizer on Capitol Hill; in 1976, AT&T had the opportunity to right the balance. Not only had that opportunity been wasted, but new political life had been breathed into the procompetition forces. From the phone company's vantage, this was especially unfortunate because Congress, with its acute sensitivity to the public mood and the public interest, was easily the best arena for AT&T to make its arguments about competition. The two other arenas where McGowan had carried his fight, the FCC and the courts, were much less hospitable. A bureaucracy like the FCC would be unlikely to reverse competition policies it had itself originated, and besides, those policies had been initiated because commission staffers believed that AT&T's monopoly was out of control. And the courts, unlike Congress, were generally interested more in the rule of law than in the "public interest."

Within AT&T's corporate ranks, there was an even more sophisticated understanding of how the deButts strategy had wasted a crucially important opportunity. A new generation was rising in the company's management, younger executives who believed that if the phone company continued much longer to cling unyieldingly to its telephone monopoly, it might fall hopelessly behind its burgeoning competitors.

In the aftermath of the Bell Bill fiasco, staff lawyers on the House Communications Subcommittee began referring to the executives on either side of this emerging generation gap within AT&T as the "red" and "blue" team. The red ream was the deButts generation, and older hard-liners who believed deeply in the service traditions of the Bell System and who were de-

termined to fight as hard as possible against any and all competition. The blue team was the generation led by Charles L.
Brown, "Charlie" Brown as he liked to be called, the former
president of Illinois Bell who had suggested at the 1972 Key
Largo conference that AT&T respond to MCI by "hitting the
nails on the head." Since then, and for unrelated reasons, Brown
had risen steadily within the AT&T organization, serving apprenticeships in the financial department at 195 Broadway and
finally, in April 1977, being named president of the company
under deButts, the chairman. DeButts was not scheduled to
retire until 1981, but already it was clear that Brown was a
leading candidate to succeed him as chairman of the board.

To understand the important differences between the red
and blue teams, it is first necessary to appreciate the myriad
issues upon which they agreed, and the corporate culture they
shared. Brown had been a company man literally since his birth.
His parents were both mid-level Bell System employees, and
Charlie had taken his first job with the phone company at age
eighteen, digging ditches in the summertime. Apart from the
U.S. Navy during World War II, he had never worked for anyone else. Like deButts, he believed unquestioningly in the mission of the Bell System to provide high quality, universal
telephone service at the lowest possible price. He was especially
appalled by the advent of long-distance competition because
he believed it seriously jeopardized Bell's public service mandate.

Unlike deButts, however, Brown was an unassuming,
nearly colorless man. Of trim build and only five feet, eight
inches tall, with thinning gray hair and clear, gray-blue eyes,
he was almost invisible next to chairman deButts, the proud
captain of industry in his debonair suits. Brown had married
late, at age thirty-seven, and there were those in the company
who said that his wife, Ann, was his only close friend. Where
deButts was gregarious and emotional, Brown was reticent,
dispassionate, cool, rational. DeButts and many of AT&T's top
executives lived lives of corporate privilege in New York City,
replete with limousines, servants, and Upper East Side apart-
ments. But when he came to New York from Illinois Bell, Brown

moved quickly out of Manhattan to the quiet, isolated university town of Princeton, New Jersey. Though he was trained as
an electrical engineer, he fancied himself something of an intellectual, and he liked to attend humanities lectures and classical music concerts on the Princeton campus. The university
eventually awarded him an honorary Doctor of Laws degree.

Despite the contrasting sensibilities of their leaders, the
red and blue teams had no quarrel about the most important
challenge facing AT&T in the mid-1970s: MCI. Both sides agreed
that long-distance competition was impractical and undesira-
ble, both from the phone company's point of view and from
the public's. They also agreed that Bill McGowan was a con-
niving menace. Nor did they differ about the urgent need to
alert the public to its stake in the debate over competition. In
the aftermath of Execunet, Brown and his blue team had supported the idea of congressional legislation that would declare
intercity telephone service to be a natural monopoly and hence
revoke McGowan's franchise to do business.

But deButts, as he had from the day he took over the
company, insisted on going further.

The question was, should AT&T adopt the same hard-line
stance toward phone equipment competition that it took toward
long distance competition? The issue was not a trivial one, and
its resolution would help determine not just the fate of the Bell
Bill but the viability of AT&T's political and legal arguments at
the FCC and in antitrust court.

Back in 1968, when the FCC introduced phone equipment
competition with its *Carterfone* decision, the commission told
AT&T that it would have to let customers plug whatever equipment they liked into the AT&T switched network. AT&T argued
then, and deButts continued to argue afterwards, that this ruling would have grave consequences for the phone system. Unlike the phone company's response to long-distance competition,
AT&T did not object to *Carterfone* on economic grounds. That
is, it was impossible to argue seriously that ownership of phone
equipment was a natural monopoly or that competition would
jeopardize the system of cross-subsidies, which kept the price

of basic, local phone service artificially low. Telephones were readily interchangeable. True, if Western Electric was forced to compete (for the first time in its history) with other telephone manufacturers, it would inevitably lose its monopolistic control over the equipment industry. And true, some of Western's profits helped subsidize the price of local consumer telephone service. But the role of Western in the subsidy structure was far less significant than the role of Long Lines. And besides, the benefits to ordinary consumers of equipment competition were easily discernible. New computer technologies had rapidly advanced the potential uses and capabilities of telephones by introducing such features as memory, data communications, conference calling, and many others. The most efficient way to introduce these accelerating technologies was by competition. It seemed a simple enough idea.

Even H. I. Romnes, deButts' predecessor and the AT&T chairman at the time of *Carterfone,* seemed prepared to accept phone equipment competition. But when deButts took over, he reversed Romnes' procompetition decisions within months and made plans to fight equipment competition just as hard as he would battle MCI.

The argument advanced publicly by deButts, beginning with his Seattle speech in September 1973, was that equipment competition would lead to irreversible technical harm to the phone network. DeButts said, "The national, switched phone network is an interdependent, sensitive, highly sophisticated system. To work well, the system depends on technically compatible components. The phone network is not made of cans and string. It consists of intricate electrical switches and terminals, precisely configured, rigorously tested, and built to exact specifications. If consumers can plug anything they want into the network—any old piece of junk made who knows where—the system will break down. A faulty telephone in one house could conceivably disrupt service to an entire city. A system such as a switched phone network is only as good as its weakest component." To emphasize his point, deButts even referred to competitors' equipment as "foreign attachments."

He said repeatedly that Bell was unwilling to see its century-old network destroyed because of the FCC's underpublicized equipment competition policies. And because it lacked Bell's scientific expertise and resources, the FCC had no way to counter deButts' claims effectively.

And the FCC was not really in a position to argue with deButts. Certainly, the commission had no desire to destroy the phone network. Common sense, though, suggested that there were ways to alleviate deButts' concerns. One way would be for the FCC to set up a "registration" program, wherein new phone equipment manufacturers would submit their products to the commission to be sure they met certain technical standards. DeButts didn't like that idea—the commission wouldn't get the job done, he said. So AT&T's chairman suggested another method, called "protective coupling arrangements" or "PCAs." Each of the phone company's competitors would be required to attach to its products a protective device, manufactured and sold only by AT&T. The device would ensure that the competitors' products did no harm to the network. The phone equipment competitors were outraged, naturally. Many of them complained that AT&T was remarkably slow about providing the protective couplers to its competitors. More than a few sued AT&T for antitrust violations and won significant settlements. By 1976, when he was preparing for the Bell Bill fight, deButts' views on phone equipment competition had been completely discredited. Despite rapid proliferation of "foreign attachments," no harm to the network had occurred; AT&T had not a single example to back up its chairman's earlier predictions. By the end of the decade, the FCC had finally established a registration program, and use of the PCAs was discontinued.

The consequences of deButts' PCA strategy were serious. The chairman's views about harm to the switched network were sincerely held, and a number of Bell Laboratories' scientists had joined him in arguing for PCAs. Phone equipment competition was charting unknown technological waters. Since no one could be sure where it would lead, Bell's engineers were understandably proprietary about the phone network they had designed.

They did not want it jeopardized by experimentation. But since deButts' fears went unrealized, the PCAs seemed to be nothing more than a blatantly anticompetitive strategy pursued by an avowed monopolist.

One immediate result was that while discovery was stalled in the government antitrust case, Phil Verveer and his team of attorneys spent much of their time informally gathering evidence and interviewing potential witnesses about the PCA episode. They decided that in addition to the MCI case, the PCA story would become a major part of the government's prosecution of AT&T.

Despite such reversals, deButts stuck to his guns throughout the 1970s, and the more intransigent he became about phone equipment competition, the more trouble he created for himself and his company.

The real problem was that deButts had laid a trap for himself. He was a savvy businessman, and he recognized early in his tenure as chairman that equipment competition, in some form, was inevitable. He recognized, too, that AT&T was hopelessly unprepared to compete. The phone company had never been forced to sell its products in the marketplace: for a century, it had been the marketplace. If phones were soon going to be sold like televisions, bicycles, or soap, AT&T had to make rapid and wholesale changes in its structure and corporate culture. Until deButts arrived, the company didn't even have a marketing department. Its salesmen didn't work on commission. More fundamentally, the heart and soul of the phone company—its emphasis on service, its conservatism, its impenetrable bureaucracy—was anathema to the culture of a lean and mean competitive corporation. For a century, AT&T had been organized like a utility, and that meant it had no incentive to pare its costs—in fact, the reverse was true. The phone company's profit margin, its "rate of return," was a fixed percentage of its costs decreed by the FCC and state regulators, usually between 10 and 15 percent. If AT&T's costs, its "rate base," were $1 billion in a given year, its profits were between $100 and $150 million. Thus, as AT&T's costs rose, so did the dollar volume of its profits. Competition, which would require lower costs and lower prices, would force the company to alter the fundamental outlook of its employees.

DeButts did not shy away from this challenge, but he nonetheless felt ambivalent about it. "The service motivation has been bred in the bones of telephone people over the course of a hundred years," he said in one speech. "To supplant that motivation with a market motivation might make us a no less profitable business and a no less effective one, though by different standards. But we would be a different business surely, and I for one cannot help but feel that we would be the poorer for it, and so would the public we serve."

Still, when it came to profits, deButts' philosophizing gave way to pragmatism. Soon after he arrived, the AT&T chairman aggressively launched what he called a "marketing revolution" within AT&T. From IBM, the country's premier marketing corporation, he hired away Archie McGill to implement the sweeping changes. On the phone equipment side of its business, the company's structure was drastically reorganized so that it could better attack various market segments: residential customers, small businesses, large corporations, specialized industries, and so forth. A marketing plan was developed wherein AT&T's omnipresence in the phone market—the fact that almost everyone in the country owned an AT&T phone system—could be exploited against new competitors. The plan, called a "migration strategy" by McGill, called for AT&T salesmen to lock customers in with the phone company by leasing equipment on long-term contract. In part because of McGill's aggressive and antagonistic personality, all these changes were highly disruptive and controversial within AT&T. By and large, though, they were effective, and deButts made it clear to his executives that he considered change to be an urgent necessity.

But the political and legal dilemma deButts had created for himself was obvious. Out of one side of his mouth, he declared that phone equipment competition should be forestalled because it posed a threat to the quality of the switched network. Out of the other, he told AT&T's employees and executives to do all they could to prepare for competition. DeButts' use of the PCA strategy to resist equipment competition was seen not only as anticompetitive but as part of a calculated fraud. DeButts wasn't really worried about harm to the network, his competitors said. All he really was doing was trying to hold off competition for as long as possible so that AT&T could move its new marketing apparatus into place. The new equipment companies contended successfully in court that what deButts was really saying when he talked about "harm to the network" was that AT&T would compete only when it was good and ready.

AT&T's untenable position on equipment competition had reached its most exaggerated state by 1976, when deButts was preparing his Bell Bill agenda. Not only were the contradictions in the company's position utterly obvious, but deButts' scare stories about harm to the network had been proven unfounded, thus confirming the view of his opponents that the PCA strategy had been, from the beginning, a blatant lie.

And therein lay the seminal conflict between two generations of AT&T executives.

The blue team—the generation led by Charlie Brown—believed that responding to phone equipment competition and MCI's Execunet deception with equal amounts of public outrage would be a serious mistake. The company's position on phone equipment was far more difficult to defend in Congress and at the FCC. Besides, even deButts seemed to accept that equipment competition was inevitable. By insisting that long distance and equipment competition were the same, the red team threatened to blow AT&T's credibility on both issues. Brown and his colleagues argued that since McGowan's clout in Washington was diminished because of Execunet, AT&T had a golden opportunity to preserve, once and for all, the sanctity of its long distance network. Why jeopardize the opportunity by simultaneously attempting to turn back the clock on equipment competition?

That, of course, is exactly what deButts chose to do. When he introduced the Bell Bill, he told Congress that AT&T wanted it all: a legal long distance monopoly and a legal monopoly of the multi-billion-dollar phone equipment markets.

Early in 1976, after the bill was introduced and its congressional opponents were plotting ways to stall it, key lawyers on the House and Senate communications subcommittees began to talk with some well-placed AT&T executives about the bill's origins. For the first time, they learned about the vociferous debate inside AT&T between the red and blue teams. They were told that the decision to include equipment competition in the bill was made virtually at the last minute by deButts. The chairman had been supported by AT&T's chief lobbyist, John Fox, who argued that equipment provisions were necessary to enlist the whole-hearted lobbying support of the company's labor unions, which were involved in Western's manufacturing operations. The blue team, the congressional lawyers were told, let the equipment competition sections go into the bill for two reasons. First, deButts was the chairman, and there was only so much resistance that other executives could mount against him. Second, and most important, if the bill blew up in AT&T's face, then at least the red team's views on equipment competition would finally be discredited. As the Bell Bill fight wore on, and AT&T found itself in more and more trouble because of its lobbying tactics, the congressional lawyers came to believe, on the basis of conversations with top AT&T executives, that the blue team actually was content that the Bell Bill had become a major embarrassment. The deButts era of staunch, arrogant resistance to telephone industry competition had passed, the blue team believed, and perhaps the Bell Bill debacle would force the old generation to step aside. Charlie Brown and his cohorts believed the time had come to compromise, and that was something seemingly beyond deButts' capacity.

The congressional lawyers and many of the blue team executives agreed on one thing: If deButts had not chosen to include phone equipment in the Bell Bill, and if AT&T had not resorted to strong-arm lobbying tactics, there was a solid chance in 1976 that Congress would have taken action to control long-distance competition by MCI. And even if it hadn't, AT&T's credibility with Congress would have remained intact, and the odds that the two institutions could work successfully together in the future to shape telecommunications policy would have been greatly improved.

As it happened, Congress didn't pass a single piece of legislation dealing with telephone industry competition until the mid-1980s.

There was, however, no conspiracy to oust John deButts from the chairmanship of AT&T. He was well-liked and respected by many of the younger, blue team executives. Almost everyone within the top management of the phone company believed that during the early 1970s, a time of business crisis for AT&T, deButts had provided strong leadership. He had solved the two most pressing problems facing AT&T then: poor service and flattening profits. He had aggressively introduced marketing ideas and structures to a bureaucracy that was ill prepared to receive them, and he had stuck with the plan even when it threatened to unravel. And on the competition issues, well, at least there was no doubt about where he stood.

By the summer of 1977, however, when Appeals Court Judge Skelly Wright ended the Execunet controversy by ruling, in effect, that the FCC was too confused about competition to prevent it anymore, it was clear that an era was passing for AT&T. If it was to survive the rest of the century, the phone company could no longer be led by grand old Bell men like John deButts. Licensed to compete fully in the residential and business long-distance markets, MCI would grow in three short years to a billion-dollar corporation. Equipment competitors—mainly Japanese electronics companies—would take half of Western's market share in roughly the same period. The red team, the proud, emotional monopolists like deButts, had outlived their usefulness. It was time now for the cool-headed pragmatism of Charlie Brown's blue team.

More than two years ahead of schedule, John deButts told AT&T's board of directors that he intended to retire. Some AT&T executives suggested afterwards that the members of the board had pressured deButts to make that decision. DeButts denied it. Even if it was true, it made little difference. At a private dinner with the board at a Manhattan hotel in the fall of 1978, deButts wholeheartedly recommended that Charles L. Brown be named to succeed him. DeButts knew that a new era for the Bell System had begun. He didn't know, though, that it would be its last.

Chapter 11

Severed Limbs

WHILE the government antitrust suit was in deep freeze during the mid-1970s, the telecommunications industry had changed radically and permanently. Competition in the equipment and long-distance markets, once a stifled promise, was now an established fact. But despite this transformation, the commitment of Phil Verveer and his cadre of Justice lawyers to carry on their "socially important work" remained unabated.

Indeed, as the long period of stagnation neared its end in 1977, their enthusiasm was waxing. Since 1975, when attorney George Saunders had stopped the case dead in its tracks, Verveer had informally continued to develop and organize evidence to support the government's contentions. Two young law students working for Verveer—Tom Casey and Bill Barrett—had spent months traveling around the country interviewing potential witnesses. Casey and Barrett were so fond of Verveer that at times it appeared to other Justice lawyers that they were his disciples. Casey described himself as a "Kennedy-McGovern liberal," and like Verveer he had been a campus activist in college. Barrett was a Vietnam combat veteran and free-market conservative who believed strongly in the principles of antitrust law. All three of them were extraordinarily close, and while Barrett sometimes liked to bait his friends over their liberal politics, he nonetheless was fiercely loyal to the shared "mission," as they aptly described it, to break up AT&T.

From the start, the Verveer team had been somewhat isolated from the rest of the lawyers in the Antitrust division, but after the stay on discovery ordered by Judge Waddy in February 1975, the situation became extreme. They rarely talked to other Justice lawyers about their work, and even their supervisor, section chief Hugh Morrison, was kept largely in the dark. This was not a deliberate strategy pursued by Verveer; it was a by-product of the intense camaraderie that developed among the AT&T team. They were like a club: they had their own coded language, their own jokes, their own separate sensibility. They had no desire to participate in Justice's internal politics and thus advance themselves within the bureaucracy—theirs was a higher calling. And as long as the case was relatively inactive, Verveer's supervisors were content to let him run things entirely on his own. For nearly three years, there were no important strategic decisions to be made.

As it became clear in 1977 that the case was about to be reactivated—that AT&T's arguments that the government case belonged at the FCC, not in federal court, were not going to succeed—everything changed.

For one thing, Verveer's team found itself under the watchful eye of a new supervisor. Hugh Morrison had been promoted to the Antitrust front office as a deputy assistant attorney general, second in command to the Antitrust chief. When that happened, Verveer and his team were moved from the old *Evening Star* building into the main Justice building at 10th and Constitution. There they were to be supervised by Ken Anderson, chief of the Special Regulated Industries section.

By the summer of 1977, Verveer was gone, Anderson was running the case, and the government's entire approach to *U.S. v. AT&T* had been drastically altered.

Anderson, to begin with, was an unusual man. Short, stocky, profane, and pugnacious, he seemed more like a retired boxer than a lawyer—he was like Jake La Motta with a sense of humor. He had grown up in Connecticut, where his parents, Swedish Lutherans, were caretakers on a wealthy lawyer's estate. For a while, Anderson's father drove a Coca-Cola truck to earn money. With the help of a hockey scholarship and donations from an anonymous benefactor (Anderson never learned the benefactor's identity, but he always assumed it was the rich lawyer in Connecticut), Anderson attended Gettysburg College in Pennsylvania. He did well, graduating Phi Beta Kappa, and he won another scholarship to attend law school at Cornell University. Even after he got his law degree, Anderson wasn't sure what he wanted to do, and for a while he worked in construction jobs. Finally he took a position as a lawyer in the Federal Trade Commission's New York field office. "That place was a bag of shit," Anderson said later with typical succinctness, and so he transferred to the Justice department in Washington. There he made a name for himself by winning the Otter Tail utility case, a government antitrust suit similar in some ways to the one against AT&T (Bill McGowan had threateningly mentioned the Otter Tail victory to John deButts when the two met at 195 Broadway in March 1973). Afterwards, Anderson was promoted to section chief in the Antitrust division.

Anderson's approach to life and to the practice of law was somewhat unorthodox. Though he worked in the heart of the city, he lived on a farm in rural Virginia, and on summer weekends he liked to ride around on his big tractor under the hot sun, and then pull off his shirt and bale some hay with a pitchfork. When the day was done, he would tromp into town in his muddy work boots and buy himself a six-pack of Budweiser beer. He was a health food enthusiast, and when he rode into Washington on the train he often carried a large paper sack full of raw vegetables. He kept the sack on a shelf in his Justice department office, and during important meetings he would wander over, pull out a carrot stick or a piece of cauliflower, and take a large, loud bite.

His friends in the Antitrust division called him a "gutter-fighting litigator." Those who were uncomfortable with his methods called him a "loose cannon." And while it was hard not to like Ken Anderson—he was funny and surprisingly compassionate—he was a man who was unlikely to see eye-to-eye with Phil Verveer. To Anderson, there was only one thing that was important about any case: winning. He cared little about politics, or moral philosophy, or "socially important work." What moved him was the taste and smell of a good fight. His speech was littered with wild profanity and violent metaphors, as in, "I want to see those motherfuckers bleed all over the table." And since he looked on the practice of law as a kind of bloodsport, he did not lie awake at night worrying about whether his case was fair, or thorough, or well considered, or well rounded. What mattered to Anderson was the kill, not the efficacy of the chase. The cases he had tried during his career were uniformly complex, but Anderson had embraced litigating tactics distinctive for their expediency. He had no patience for drawn-out discovery of opponents' documents or for lengthy deposition programs. Such strategies, Anderson believed, tended to bog a case down and obscure its main issues. In Otter Tail, Anderson had used an innovative method that served as a substitute for the typical discovery program. Rather than "discovering" their own evidence, both sides "stipulated" to facts, entered them in the record, and then launched quickly into their arguments. The result had been a swift and sudden victory for Anderson.

Anderson's superiors in the Antitrust front office hoped to apply similar methods to the AT&T case. The division's other major antitrust suit at the time, against IBM, was being managed in the usual way—protracted discovery, numerous depositions, exchanges of millions of documents—and it had become a kind of legal black hole, as well as a serious embarrassment to the Justice department. The more lawyers Justice threw at the IBM case, the more hopeless it became. The suit had been filed on the last day of the Johnson administration in 1969, and eight years later, it was still not even close to trial. The department, and especially its Carter-appointed Antitrust chief, John Shenefield, was determined that U.S. v. AT&T not become a similar debacle. In Anderson's fondness for bloody expediency, they saw a solution.

In an odd and uncharacteristic way, Ken Anderson was intimidated by Phil Verveer when the AT&T team moved into his section on the seventh floor of the main Justice building. It was impossible not to be impressed with Verveer's character, to see the strength and moral commitment that so attracted the younger lawyers to him. And Verveer was not a self-righteous puritan: he was a self-contained man, principled but not priggish, articulate but not preachy. He commanded respect, and Anderson sensed this. "There's not anybody in this town who's a more honest guy," Anderson said later of Verveer. "And he is very, very dedicated. When you see him, you get a sense of him being almost priestlike—a highly moralistic sort of guy, somewhat self-effacing. He's aggressive in his own way, but he's not a rock'em sock'em kinda guy."

So Anderson mainly kept his distance. He was unhappy with the strategy that Verveer had developed for the case. He believed it was too academic, too broad, too much by the book. Verveer had hired a number of "expert" witnesses to develop complex economic arguments for the case—about utility prices, economies of scale, and so on—and Anderson considered these professors to be utterly worthless. No case like this was going to be won by some tweed-coated expert spouting interpretive economic theories. In Anderson's view, litigation battles were won or lost in the trenches, where the two sides wrestled over disputed facts like soldiers struggling for a bayonet. Verveer was not running the case like a ruthless field marshal; his approach was closer to that of a law school dean. Still, Verveer was in charge of the case day to day, and Anderson did not force his strategy ideas on him. Anderson felt that whenever he went near Verveer, the lawyer "got his nose out of joint."

Early in 1977, as part of the Antitrust division's routine budget process, Phil Verveer drew up a plan for expanding his team of attorneys, paralegals, and support staff once the stay on discovery was lifted and the case resumed in earnest. The plan reflected Verveer's approach to the lawsuit: expansive in scope, thorough, detailed, and somewhat unfocused. Verveer recalled later that it called for about twenty-five attorneys and perhaps 100 paralegals full-time; lawyers in the Antitrust front office remembered the numbers as being even higher. Either way, it was an ambitious program, and hauntingly similar in approach to the IBM case. Verveer sent the budget up through the division bureaucracy. He was nervous about the attitude of his section chief—he didn't think Anderson displayed much of a grasp of the factual and legal details of the case—but he assumed that Shenefield, the Antitrust chief, would approve the plan.

From a variety of sources—Hugh Morrison, Ken Anderson, front office lawyers Joe Simms and Bill Swope—Shenefield began to hear grumblings about Verveer's approach to the case and questions about whether Verveer was really the right lawyer to run it. Anderson had suggested cutting the large retainers earned by some of Verveer's expert witnesses, but no one told Verveer what was being contemplated.

One morning in early summer, Verveer was called to a meeting in Shenefield's office with the Antitrust chief, Morrison, and Anderson. For the first time, Verveer was told that he would have to pare down his plans and adopt the strategic approach advocated by Anderson. "You're not giving me enough support," Verveer argued. "Look, this is what you have to expect. There are millions of pages of documents. If we're right that there are millions of pages that have to be looked through, we're going to need these people to do it."

The front office lawyers heard Verveer out but did not answer his demands.

The next day, Hugh Morrison called Anderson and told him to report to Shenefield's office. "Here's what we've decided," Anderson was told. "Verveer's off the case and you're on." As section chief, Anderson would have to convey the bad news to Verveer.

"Phil, I didn't fuck ya," Anderson tried to explain when he saw Verveer. "Your friends fucked ya, or the guys who you thought were your friends."

Verveer didn't know how it had happened, and to an extent, he didn't care. Anderson, Morrison, Shenefield, Swope, and Simms were all involved, he thought. But it was the way it happened—the dishonest conspiracy behind his back, the cowardly failure to involve him in the strategy debate, the unilateral decision to put Anderson, who probably hadn't even read all the government's contentions in the case, in charge—

that led him to resign his job with the Justice department almost immediately. Within nine months, the core of the original team of attorneys that had worked to develop *U.S.* v. *AT&T*—notably Tom Casey and Bill Barrett— had also quit, partly in protest over how Verveer had been treated.

Alone in charge, Ken Anderson would have to manage one of the biggest antitrust cases in Justice department history on his own. Which, of course, suited Anderson just fine.

From Justice's point of view, the best thing to come from Verveer's resignation and Anderson's ascension was that it put the fear of God into AT&T. Anderson might be a loose cannon, but after so many years of quiet, professional stewardship by Verveer, perhaps it was time now to blast a few holes in the phone company's complacency.

At first, AT&T's lawyers saw the Verveer resignation as a welcome opportunity, and perhaps the end of their troubles with Justice. During the publicity that attended the Antitrust shake-up, lawyers on the Verveer team grumbled anonymously to reporters that the division's front office was throwing in the towel, that it was unwilling to pursue the AT&T case seriously. "We've been sat on too many times over the past few years to make us starry-eyed believers that the department of Justice is going to prosecute this case properly," one said.

The Bell attorneys seized the opening quickly. Only weeks after Verveer had quit, Hal Levy, the AT&T staff lawyer who was then working closely with George Saunders, arrived at Anderson's office wearing a white summer suit. Like Saunders, Levy smoked big black cigars, and he was more than a little overweight.

"Look, there's nobody on this case," Levy told Anderson, and he was right. Because of the spate of recent resignations, there was only a handful of Justice attorneys assigned to the suit. With all the fuss over Verveer, Anderson had barely been able to keep up with the paperwork.

"Maybe it's time to talk about a solution to this thing," Levy continued. Then he tried to sell Anderson on a vague, injunctive settlement. AT&T would agree to certain rules, negotiated with Anderson, governing interconnection arrangements with MCI and other long-distance carriers. The phone company would also take steps to buy more phone equipment from suppliers other than Western Electric. Otherwise, AT&T would be left alone and there would be no divestiture.

Anderson heard Levy out, and then he said, "I'll tell you one thing. This case is going to be a severed limbs case. We're going to have severed limbs, AT&T limbs, on the table dripping blood. That's the way this case is going to be settled. We're not going to settle this thing with injunctive relief."

"You can't expect me to go back to my board of directors and tell them something like that," Levy answered.

"That's exactly what I want you to do," said Anderson. "I want you to go back and tell them that the next time they send somebody down here to talk about settling, I want to see severed limbs on the table. In fact, if you want to come in the door, you've got to throw a couple of severed limbs in ahead of you, or you don't even get in the door."

Such bravado no doubt sounded desperate even to Levy, but it was effective. Levy dutifully carried Anderson's message to 195 Broadway. A few weeks later, Anderson received a strange phone call. An attorney for a private antitrust plaintiff suing AT&T told Anderson, "There's a group of people inside AT&T, high up, who really understand what this thing is about and who are willing to talk about a realistic settlement. Would you be willing to meet with them?"

"What do you mean?" Anderson asked. "Is this going to be one of these deals where I have to meet somebody in a parking garage?"

"I am talking about some people who are very highly placed in the company," the lawyer said. "I can tell you that there is a movement inside the company to be very realistic about this case. They want to talk to you."

"Well, then, why don't they call me? To arrange it like this, I'll have to talk with my supervisor."

Anderson told Hugh Morrison about the lawyer's call. Morrison told him, "Go ahead, see what they want."

The meeting was arranged not in a parking garage but in

a restaurant at 20th and L streets. The man who arrived from AT&T was Howard Trienens, the managing partner of Sidley & Austin, who had known Brown socially during the years when Brown was president of Illinois Bell. Eventually, Trienens would become vice-president and general counsel of AT&T under Charlie Brown. He would become a key member of AT&T's blue team, and he was laying the groundwork for a new approach to AT&T's antitrust problems even before John deButts' resignation. In his meeting with Anderson, Trienens never formally discussed a settlement. It was an informational session, a chance for Trienens and Anderson to feel each other out. The Sidley partner wanted to know from Anderson, "What is it that you have in mind?"

But Anderson felt that it was too early to discuss specifics. As he liked to put it, settlements of government antitrust suits don't work until "the other guy can taste a little blood in his mouth." At the moment, it was Justice that appeared to be negotiating from weakness, not AT&T.

Still, after his meeting with Trienens, Anderson continued on and off to meet with Hal Levy and George Saunders, mainly to talk about procedural issues having to do with the resumption of discovery early in 1978, when the United States Supreme Court finally ended AT&T's quest to have the case thrown out of federal court. (The courts accepted the government's argument that the FCC could not effectively regulate AT&T, and that the only way to resolve issues of phone industry competition was in antitrust court.) Anderson's occasional outbursts about blood and limbs actually had a strange effect on Saunders and Levy—they endeared Anderson to the AT&T lawyers. Here, at least, was a character far different from the devout Phil Verveer, who seemed to view the phone company and its lawyers as evil incarnate. Anderson made it clear that he had no "moral" view about the government suit; he only cared about tactics.

That was an attitude Saunders and Levy could respect. Anderson was a lawyer with a client. He had a job to do, and all his bellowing and ranting about goring the phone company was nothing more than the studied posturing of a well-trained litigator. Besides, Anderson had a sense of humor. Saunders

and Levy would sit in his sparse Justice office and fill the room
with smoke from their black cigars until Anderson would say,
"You guys are really disgusting. You're fat, smoking those cigars. The problem with you guys is that you don't have enough
roughage in your lives." Then Anderson would open one of
the brown paper sacks near his desk and pull out a handful of
string beans from his farm. After he passed them out, the three
stocky lawyers would continue their meeting, munching like
overstuffed rabbits.

They were the kind of lawyers who might enjoy trying a
case against each other. And that was a good thing, because
by the summer of 1978, one year after Phil Verveer's resignation,
it appeared that *U.S.* v. *AT&T* might move to trial faster than
any antitrust case of its size in many decades.

In part, that was because of Ken Anderson's expedient
methods. In part, too, it was because Charlie Brown's team of
executives, who would soon have full control over AT&T's policies and strategies, wanted to resolve Bell's antitrust problems
as quickly as possible. They could see that deButts' stand against
competition had failed: MCI was a billion-dollar company now,
and Japanese and other equipment makers were rapidly gaining
market share at Western Electric's expense. The challenge now
was to free the phone company from its Washington quagmire
and prepare for a competitive future, a future that Charlie Brown
frequently referred to as the "information age."

To arrive there intact, AT&T would have to win, or favorably settle, the government antitrust case with all possible speed.

Chapter 12

The Answer Man

ONE thing that John deButts, Charlie Brown, and other AT&T executives should have learned by the summer of 1978 was that it was difficult, if not impossible, for anyone in Washington to consider the largest corporation in the world to be, in any sense, a victim—whether of Bill McGowan's deceptive competitive strategy, or of overzealousness by young lawyers at the FCC and the Justice department, or of a rapidly changing telecommunications industry complicated by contradictory and confusing regulations. To the politicians and bureaucrats who ruled the nation's capital, AT&T would always be Ma Bell, the omnipotent and indefatigable matriarch of American business. (Charlie Brown hated the Ma Bell moniker, in part because it implied that the phone company was somehow invincible and immutable.) Thus it was only AT&T, not Congress, the Justice department, or the FCC, that viewed the assignment of the government antitrust suit to U.S. District Court Judge Harold H. Greene in August 1978 as the latest caprice of the fates in what by now had become, in the minds of the phone company's top executives, a full-blown Elizabethan tragedy.

George Saunders liked to say that Judge Joseph Waddy would have given the Justice department "the back of his hand" if he had presided over the trial of *U.S.* v. *AT&T*. As other events would prove, Saunders was not as good a fortune teller as he was a lawyer. Still, no one could disagree that, from AT&T's standpoint, Waddy was a far more attractive judge than Greene, who took over the case when Waddy finally succumbed to cancer in July. At least Waddy had expressed some sympathy for AT&T's position during the preliminary jursidictional arguments. About the only thing to recommend Greene to the phone company, it seemed, was that he was likely to move the case along with exceptional speed.

It was a standard practice of Sidley & Austin to research thoroughly the background of a judge who was assigned to a case handled by the firm. The theory was that a detailed profile of the judge—his personal history, his legal and political biases, his courtroom demeanor—could help an attorney make his case and presentation more palatable. Some trial lawyers regard such "psychoanalyzing" as a treacherous and ultimately disruptive endeavor, because it can cause a lawyer to ignore the strengths of his case while pandering to the supposed prejudices of the judge. George Saunders' attitude, though, was that in a case where there was as much at stake as there was in *U.S. v. AT&T*, it was important to play every angle.

The profile of Judge Greene assembled by Sidley's lawyers and researchers offered Saunders little encouragement.

There was no doubt that Greene was one of the hardest working, most intelligent judges in Washington and that he was an extraordinary and compassionate human being. A man of such depth and devotion, who had lived such a varied and interesting life, might be precisely the sort of judge who could not be psychoanalyzed easily. But there was no doubt, either, that on the surface, at least, Greene was exactly the wrong judge for AT&T. Indeed, Greene seemed akin in spirit to some of the young, idealistic Justice lawyers who had first developed the antitrust case against the phone company.

Like Phil Verveer, for example, Greene had learned early and profoundly that "politics," for some, was a matter of life and death, and the lesson had stayed with him. A Jew, Greene was raised in Germany during the 1920s and 1930s. His father owned a jewelry store, and in 1939, as the terror of Hitler's

Reich reached fever pitch, his family fled to Belgium, where it had relatives. Greene was just sixteen years old. When the Germans invaded Belgium, the Greenes fled again, this time to Vichy France. From there, they made their way to Spain, and later Portugal, before finally emigrating to the United States in 1943. Young Harold Greene was immediately drafted into the U.S. Army and was sent back to Europe with a military intelligence unit to work against the Nazis. He saw combat action in his former homeland, but he escaped injury. When the war was over he returned to Washington, D.C., where his family had settled.

As a civilian, Greene took to his new country with an extraordinary passion. At night, he attended law school at George Washington University in Foggy Bottom, near the State department. Though English was a new language for Greene, he did exceptionally well, graduating in 1952 at the top of his class. His first job as a full-fledged lawyer was as a prosecutor with the Justice department. In a few years, he had transferred to the department's Civil Rights division.

When a man or woman's talents, convictions, and ambitions coincide with the egress of an entire generation, there is the opportunity to make history, and such a blessing fell upon Harold Greene at the Justice department during the early 1960s. Robert F. Kennedy was attorney general, and for the first time in thirty years, the federal government was alive with energy and activity. Justice, especially, was invigorated with the vision of a Great Society to be forged by the rule of law. In the Civil Rights division, the hope and excitement was daily palpable, and most of it derived from Bobby Kennedy's personal style of leadership. Department lawyers who had served the government for twenty-five years without ever meeting an attorney general suddenly found themselves invited to Kennedy's expansive fifth-floor office for informal discussions over beer or coffee. The attorney general would wander through the old Justice building's cavernous hallways, stopping in randomly to compliment an attorney's work or inquire into one of his cases. The Civil Rights division was like Kennedy's favorite son, and Greene soon befriended the young attorney general and earned

his confidence. The promise of Robert Kennedy, his commitment and his oft-repeated vision of America made great through
justice and opportunity, was especially compelling to Harold
Greene, a man who did not take his country or its ideals for
granted. Greene was a pragmatist, not a visionary or an ideologue, but he nonetheless had a strong appreciation for the
theory behind America's system of checks and balances. As a
teenager in Germany, he had seen the consequences of a government devoid of such controls. He believed that the power
of the law, and its fair enforcement through the courts, could
mitigate a society's worst tendencies. And like Bobby Kennedy,
he saw the attempt by white southerners to preserve segre-
gation during the early 1960s as a kind of cancer on the nation.
Working closely with Kennedy, Greene wrote the Civil Rights
Act of 1964 and the Voting Rights Act of 1965, arguably the two
most important pieces of legislation passed by Congress in
twenty years. When Kennedy made his only appearance before
the U.S. Supreme Court to argue a civil rights case, Greene was
there with him, helping to put the finishing touches on the
argument. As Kennedy himself put it at Greene's Justice department going-away party, "Harold was the guy who had the
answers."

Onward and upward Greene went, seeking out new questions and new dilemmas, determined above all to make the
"system" work. Recommended by Kennedy's successor as attorney general, Ramsey Clark (Kennedy was now a senator),
Greene was appointed in 1967 as chief judge of the District of
Columbia's Court of General Sessions, Washington's municipal
court system. The court was then in a horrific state, plagued
by scandal: poor litigants were often not represented at all by
lawyers, cases were delayed for months, even years. Greene's
charge was to straighten out the system as quickly as possible.
With some help from Ramsey Clark, who helped appropriate
needed money from Congress, he accomplished the task mostly
through voracious hard work. When thousands were arrested
during the 1968 riots following Martin Luther King's assassi-
nation and the 1970 May Day disturbances, for example, most
municipal courts processed the defendants in groups of about

fifty at a time. Greene wouldn't have it. He ordered his court to remain open twenty-four hours a day, and he tried each case individually, advising everyone of his rights and providing public defenders when necessary. By the mid-1970s, the Washington, D.C., municipal courts were running smoothly, and Greene was being talked about in legal publications as "one of the best judges in America."

With the Republicans in power after 1968, however, there was no place for Greene to move, and so it was not until after Jimmy Carter's election in 1976 that he was plucked from the relatively obscure municipal courts and appointed for life to the federal bench in Washington. Technically, Greene was replacing Judge John Sirica, of Watergate fame, who had moved to senior judge status. But when he arrived at District Court in 1978, Greene also inherited cases from two other judges, including the late Joseph Waddy. Thus was Robert F. Kennedy's protégé, "the guy who had the answers," introduced to *U.S. v. AT&T*, a multibillion-dollar dispute between the federal government and the largest corporation in the world.

When they privately discussed the background and character of Harold H. Greene, some of AT&T's lawyers referred to him as a "liberal activist judge." It was a label that had come into wide use by conservatives in the late 1970s to describe some judges, mostly Democratic appointees to the federal bench, who seemed more interested in the political ramifications of their decisions than in whether those decisions were properly made under the law. One measure of whether a judge was more "active" than "judicial" was how often the judge's decisions were reversed on appeal, and some of the "liberal activist judges" were reversed quite frequently. But the label was really too simple to fit Judge Greene. Certainly Greene was a liberal. And it was also true that he was an activist, in the sense that he devoted great energy to his work and tried to effect political changes by it. But Greene's first commitment was to the fair working of the legal system itself, not to some scattered agenda of "liberal" issues. What he believed in, what he knew, what he cared about was the law. Clearly, what Greene meant by "the fair working of the legal system" was different from what a conservative meant. He believed strongly in due process and in the strict preservation of constitutional rights. Unlike some conservatives, he thought that a strong, independent judiciary was an important check on the excesses of Congress and the executive branch. Greene believed, for example, that if it hadn't been for the federal courts, the civil rights revolution which he had participated in might never have gotten off the ground. But the essence of his ideology was that the American system of law and government was a great one in theory, and that the first duty of a judge was to improve the way it actually operated, day after day, in his own courtroom.

And what better test could there be of Greene's commitment to the legal system than *U.S.* v. *AT&T*? In the summer of 1978, when Greene first began to read the briefs that had been filed in the case, a commission appointed by President Carter was reporting to the public that complex antitrust litigation such as *U.S.* v. *AT&T* was being hopelessly mismanaged by the federal courts and that unless judges developed new, innovative methods to expedite such cases, the danger existed that large companies would conclude that the nation's antitrust laws were basically unenforceable and might as well be disregarded. The president of the commission was John Shenefield, Ken Anderson's boss and the chief of Justice's Antitrust division. His report was well-received in Congress, where the judiciary committees in both the House and Senate were making considerable noise about the slow progress of Justice's two major antitrust cases, those against IBM and AT&T. Could Harold Greene do for major antitrust litigation what he had done for the Washington, D.C., municipal courts? Could he take charge of the AT&T case and prove, once and for all, that the government could sue large corporations and successfully bring them to account in court?

Greene was determined to do exactly that—he was going to find the answers. From the outset, he told both AT&T's and the government's lawyers that his overriding goal in the case was to prove that the federal courts could handle complex antitrust litigation. To do it, he said, he would develop new, expeditious methods to push the case to trial. In George Saunders and Ken Anderson, Greene was fortunate to have two lawyers willing to go along for the ride: Anderson, because he had won the Otter Tail case by using similar methods, and Saunders, because his client, Charlie Brown, wanted to win the antitrust suit quickly so that he could dispose of AT&T's phone industry competition problems.

For AT&T, though, there was a chilling aspect of Greene's brand of judicial activism. It came in the form of a question that lingered on the lips of the company's attorneys in 1979, as Greene pushed relentlessly to bring *U.S.* v. *AT&T* to trial. To make his point, to prove that the federal courts could effectively manage a major antitrust case, wouldn't Greene be more inclined to rule in the government's favor and break up AT&T? If he pushed the case to trial, and then agreed with the phone company that Justice's allegations were baseless, wouldn't his "example" be undermined? Judge Greene had declared that he was staking his reputation on this case. Would he use it to "make" a reputation, too?

Such nagging questions, as well as the natural suspicions aroused by the judge's background in Bobby Kennedy's Justice department, convinced some AT&T lawyers that Greene was going to be a very difficult man to persuade of the phone company's benign intentions during its disputes with MCI during the early 1970s. George Saunders, however, was not one of those lawyers. Saunders was a man who thought he could charm the skin off an alligator's back. He believed—no, he knew—that AT&T was right and that the company would be vindicated in court. The government's suit, Saunders said frequently, boiled down to the MCI story, particularly the controversies over FX lines and Execunet. And that story, Saunders drawled, was the tale of "the biggest rip-off of the century." Harold Greene was an intelligent man. He was a hard-working judge. When the case was laid out before him, Saunders believed, Greene would see the light, liberal bias or no liberal bias.

And to see the judge in court was to sense that Saunders might be right about one thing, namely that Harold Greene decided a matter on its merits. He was such a friendly and unassuming man that it was hard to imagine him in the van-

guard of a PTA revolt, never mind America's civil rights revolution. He was a short man, slightly rotund, with gray hair,
tortoise-shell glasses, and a prominent nose. His voice was
unabrasive, and it was still tinged by a distinct German accent.
His smile came quickly, and it expressed deep and unaffected
warmth. This was no shrill dogmatist determined to stoke the
embers of yesterday's political fires. Indeed, Greene was a typical, upper-middle-class Washington professional, a man who
lived in a comfortable home in the residential northwest section,
an "intellectual" who spent long hours watching escapist television shows, a sports fan who owned Redskins season tickets,
a gourmet who made a point to lunch at Washington's best
restaurants, a Jewish father who could be heard to say proudly,
"My son, the doctor . . ." George Saunders liked Harold Greene,
and soon Greene would come to like Saunders. Perhaps, Saunders believed, that would be enough to overcome the weight
of any biases the judge still carried with him, enough to right
the balance for AT&T.

In the meantime, though, the government's Ken Anderson
was getting the best of Saunders in the increasingly frequent
pretrial courtroom skirmishes before Greene. That was mainly
because Anderson and Greene had the same idea about how
to deal with the normal methods of pretrial discovery under
the Federal Rules of Civil Procedure: both wanted to throw
them out. Saunders said he did not want to hold the case back,
but he didn't seem sure about where Anderson and Greene
were going to take him with their "innovative" methods. While
discussing alternative approaches, the part-time farmer Anderson would explain concepts to Greene by saying things like,
"It is just like growing peas. If you want a good crop of peas,
you've got to really prepare the ground. . . ." Other times he
would talk about how he wanted to "truncate" and "shortcut"
the discovery process, and about how the government was
"taking a big risk" in order to speed the case to trial.

Greene, in turn, would occasionally make long speeches
about the necessity of swift action. "Some suggestions have
been made that the case be postponed," he said during one of
them. "I am unwilling to do that. The public has a right to have

this important case started with dispatch. There just is generally too much delay in complex antitrust litigation. I am unwilling to let this case fall into that pattern."

By 1979, between the expedient approach of Ken Anderson and the activism of Judge Greene, *U.S.* v. *AT&T* had been transformed from a moribund embarrassment to the Justice department into a case that might well be resolved in court before the IBM suit, which had been filed almost six years before the AT&T case. His delaying tactics now abandoned, Saunders narrowed his discovery requests for documents from government agencies—he was no longer trying to drown his Justice department adversaries in paper. Anderson had waived the usual document discovery in exchange for the right to look at all the documents in the private antitrust cases against AT&T filed by MCI and phone-equipment maker Litton. In effect, Anderson was saying that the government's effort to break up AT&T was going to be a piggyback ride on Bill McGowan's shoulders; the MCI case was now nearing trial in Chicago, and millions of documents discovered by McGowan's lawyers had become part of the record there. The same was true of the Litton "PCA" equipment case in New York. At the same time, Judge Greene had developed his own version of Anderson's Otter Tail "stipulation" system, wherein both the government and AT&T would be required to negotiate lengthy sets of agreed-upon facts for use at trial. The stipulations would eliminate the need for a great number of witnesses who would ordinarily be called to establish undisputed facts. The stipulations would also make clear exactly what the two sides agreed and didn't agree on, when it came to telling the story of the American telecommunications industry in the early 1970s. For better or for worse, *U.S.* v. *AT&T* was going to go to trial—soon.

Judge Harold Greene was going to make the system work.

The Deal

Chapter 13

The New Realism

ARLY in 1979, John deButts cleared out his personal belongings from his luxurious suite of offices on the twenty-sixth floor of 195 Broadway. Charlie Brown, the new chairman, was ensconced in a considerably smaller and less ornate office around the corner. Most people assumed that Brown would do what every new chairman had done before and move into the vacant suite. After all, deButts' office, with its spectacular view of Manhattan on three sides, its antique tables, couches, and silver service, was both an opulent perk and a potent symbol of authority and leadership. But weeks passed, and Charlie Brown stayed put. When some of his fellow executives asked him about the suite, he said that he liked his own office just fine. That was all there was to be said on the subject, too. Charlie Brown did not elaborate on his personal likes and dislikes, even to colleagues with whom he worked closely day-to-day. So for a time the plush deButts suite just sat there, unoccupied, like a didactic museum depicting the excesses of a renounced historical episode.

And very quickly it became obvious that the changes at AT&T under Charlie Brown's reign would extend far beyond the style of the company's new leader. The blue team was in control now, and its first objective was to end AT&T's rearguard battle against competition, especially in the phone equipment

135

business. Just weeks after formally taking office, Brown laid out his plans in a speech to a group of telephone executives. "Already it has been a decade since the *Carterfone* case opened the telephone network to equipment competition," he said. "But the world has not come to an end. Nor does the sky show imminent signs of falling. Competition is here and it's growing. As a consequence, there has developed in our business a 'new realism.'

"The new realism has changed the way we look at the world. No longer do we see the telephone industry as locked in mortal struggle with the equipment industry on the one hand and the specialized common carriers on the other. Rather, we see ours as a single industry encompassing all of us. . . .

"Ma Bell is a symbol of the past. No longer is a steady dividend sufficient. Today's investor looks to the prospect of improvement. Today's employees reject maternalism; they'll take care of themselves. Today ours is a business that knows that it is not we, AT&T, but the customer who knows best. Mother Bell simply doesn't live here anymore."

The central problem that Brown faced was that, while he might be willing to forget the past, Bill McGowan, Ken Anderson, and Harold Greene were not. Brown understood this well, and he knew that to disentangle his company from its sticky antitrust problems, he must be willing to pay a price. From his meeting with Howard Trienens, Ken Anderson already suspected Brown might be willing to make a deal—even a "severed limbs" deal—in order to extricate AT&T from the threat of the government's case. But Anderson was not yet ready to consider such a solution. With Greene now running the case, things were moving in Justice's favor. For his part, Brown still faced obstacles to a settlement within AT&T's corporate ranks. The biggest problem was that Mark Garlinghouse, deButts' chief legal advisor and a staunch red team holdover, had not followed the mentor's lead by retiring early. That meant Howard Trienens could not yet take full control of AT&T's legal strategy. For a decade, Garlinghouse had stood hard and fast with deButts against any compromises on the competition issue. Some lawyers with the Justice department felt that it was really Garlinghouse, not deButts, who was the root cause of the phone company's antitrust problems. If Garlinghouse had urged more caution during the early 1970s, the government lawyers thought, then deButts might have been able to get away with his "public interest" objections to competition. As it was, AT&T had made itself look foolish: it had gone way overboard when it did things like disconnect MCI's customers and insist that all "foreign attachments" be equipped with PCAs. The government lawyers believed that if Garlinghouse had thought through the antitrust implications of such actions, and if he had been able to persuade deButts that the actions were unwise, Justice might not have a case at all, and AT&T might still have held off some competition. In any event, the hard-liner Garlinghouse was about the last person at AT&T who was going to go looking to make a deal with the government. Until Trienens took full control of the legal department in January 1980, when Garlinghouse was due to retire, it would be difficult for Brown to pursue a settlement actively.

Just a few months before then, however, a series of events inside the government created an unexpected opportunity for AT&T to dispose of the antitrust suit. As would often be the case during the next three years, the settlement opportunity derived as much from the personal lives and internecine relationships of the government's lawyers as from the substantive economic and antitrust issues caused by telephone industry competition.

During the summer of 1979, Ken Anderson's vigorous and bucolic life on his Virginia farm took a turn for the worse. A child who lived next door to the Andersons died unexpectedly. Then, just a few weeks later, a neighbor was killed when he fell off his tractor. The events triggered some painful feelings in Anderson's wife, a woman who had known a very difficult childhood in the Bedford-Stuyvesant section of Brooklyn, New York. As the summer progressed, she began to have difficulty sleeping, and she felt anxious and depressed. Anderson tried to talk with her, but he was distracted by his heavy workload at the office: not only was he in charge of *U.S.* v. *AT&T*, he was also still chief of the Antitrust division's Special Regulated Industries section. Often he was unable to leave the city until well after dinner time. As the summer gave way to fall, the condition of Anderson's wife deteriorated. To pay for her medical expenses, Anderson began to borrow heavily from the Justice department's credit union. By November, Anderson was emotionally drained and deeply in debt. Perhaps irrationally, he felt that the long hours he worked at Justice had contributed significantly to his wife's problems. Most of Anderson's colleagues were unaware of his distress. Occasionally one of them would find Anderson standing bleary-eyed in front of the office coffee machine early in the morning and would ask how he was doing. When Anderson unburdened himself of his problems, he seemed a far different person from the tough-talking, gutter-fighting litigator his colleagues knew professionally. So when Anderson announced in November that he was resigning his Justice position to take a more lucrative, less demanding job in private practice, it was a decision that some of his colleagues understood and respected.

Anderson told the Antitrust division's front office that his resignation would be effective at the end of January 1980. What he didn't tell them was that in the interim, while they were searching for a new lawyer to run the AT&T case, Anderson was going to try to settle the lawsuit.

Among the small team of lawyers working on the AT&T case, various motives were ascribed to Anderson's secretive settlement attempt late in the fall of 1979. Some said that Anderson felt guilty that he was abandoning the case just as it was beginning to heat up again, and that the settlement initiative was therefore an attempt to atone for his sudden departure. Others described the effort as more of a selfish "swan song," an attempt by Anderson to take credit himself for the outcome of the case before he left the department.

Anderson himself claimed two different motives. First, he said the "taffy pull" over AT&T between the FCC, Congress, and Justice was probably not in the public interest. If there was a way to conclude the matter fairly, he was now in favor of doing so. Second, Anderson did not trust the Antitrust front office to prosecute the case vigorously after he left. The politically appointed Antitrust chief's slot was vacant at the time because of John Shenefield's promotion to associate attorney general. That meant the front office was run mainly by career lawyers, particularly an attorney named Don Flexner. Anderson and Flexner detested each other. Flexner was a leading advocate of the "Anderson is a loose cannon" school of thought within the division. He felt that Anderson had handled some aspects of the AT&T case in a sloppy manner, especially the question of relief. The telecommunications industry had changed dramatically since the lawsuit was filed in 1974, but Justice had never reconsidered its goals in the case. The original relief contentions seeking divestiture of Western and all the operating companies had been something of an internal compromise back in 1974, a way to reconcile two different teams of Justice investigators. With Judge Greene now pushing to take the case to trial, Flexner and others in the front office felt that it was time for a serious reevaluation of the case. What did Justice want from AT&T? Why? How would the arguments be presented in court? The front office felt that these were questions that Anderson, preoccupied with his expedient pretrial tactics, had grossly neglected. So Flexner had taken some lawyers from a different Antitrust section and had created a Relief Task Force, whose charge was to evaluate the case and make specific recommendations about what Justice should seek when the suit went to trial. The task force irked Anderson and his key lieutenants, especially since it had been created by Anderson's enemy, Flexner. To make his feelings clear, Anderson hung a Goya print on his office wall. The painting depicted a firing squad with their rifles aimed at a group of prisoners. One of the prisoners was already lying on the ground in a pool of blood. Someone on Anderson's team of lawyers taped a note to the painting that said, "Relief Task Force," though the note did not indicate whether the task force was supposed to be the firing squad or its victims. Anderson's private settlement proposal was a way to steal the task force's thunder and to preempt a more visible role for Flexner in the case.

The question for Anderson was, What should his offer to AT&T be? There was no doubt that without some divestiture by the phone company, no deal could succeed; an injunctive settlement would look like a sellout to both the Antitrust front office and the public. AT&T would have to sever a limb or two. So late in the fall, Anderson called Howard Trienens, who was by now working at 195 Broadway, waiting to succeed Mark Garlinghouse as Charlie Brown's vice-president and general counsel.

Anderson told Trienens that he was resigning for personal reasons and that before he left he thought the case should be settled. "The first question to you guys is, Are you prepared to accept divestiture of something? Because if you're not, I've got to go out and find a job. I've got other things to do."

Trienens said that he would have to talk with AT&T's chairman.

Not surprisingly to Trienens, Brown told his general counsel-to-be that he was willing to explore any realistic settlement framework. He instructed Trienens to meet with Anderson. Neither Brown nor Trienens, of course, knew that Anderson was acting on his own. They both assumed that the Antitrust front office had approved, and maybe even had insisted upon, Anderson's unexpected overture.

Within a few weeks, Trienens flew to Washington and met with Anderson and some of his staff at the Justice department.

Anderson's key lieutenants were two young government lawyers named Alexander Pires and Peter Kenney. Pires had been hired personally by Anderson, and he was similar to his boss in many respects. The son of Portuguese immigrants, Pires had been a boxer in Boston before entering law school, and he took a pugilistic approach to his profession. He was a large, barrel-chested man with a square jaw and curly black hair. Like Anderson, his specialty was litigation tactics, and when he talked about the AT&T case, he sometimes used phrases like "bloody limbs" or "knockout punch." Kenney contrasted sharply with the styles of Anderson and Pires. He actually had been hired by Phil Verveer just before his resignation, and he was more like Verveer than Anderson. Kenney was careful, detailed, and organized, and though he was no zealot about politics, he did have liberal views through which he filtered and measured the AT&T case. His thoroughness acted as a kind of counterweight to the urgent expediency of Anderson and Pires. Kenney was the one who had a firm grasp of the case's technical, economic, and legal details; it would be very difficult for Anderson to negotiate a deal without him. But neither Kenney nor Pires was entirely comfortable with Anderson's decision to fly solo on a settlement proposal to AT&T. The two lawyers were both going to be around after Anderson left, and they wanted to continue the case. Pires hoped to take over Anderson's job. Neither of them felt that Anderson, under the circumstances, was likely to get much divestiture from AT&T, and they knew that even if he did, there would be hell to pay when the front office found out what Anderson had done.

Howard Trienens knew none of this when he arrived at Ken Anderson's office that winter to discuss a settlement. If he had, he might very well have turned around and flown back to New York. But since Trienens believed that Anderson represented a united front at the Justice department, he took the negotiations seriously.

Anderson began by presenting Trienens with a document, undated and typed on plain white paper, that was referred to as "the menu." It was a list of ideas about how AT&T and the government might settle the antitrust case in the public interest. The menu was the brainchild of a lawyer named Ken Robinson, who had worked for a while in the Antitrust division under Anderson. Robinson had left Justice earlier that year to work for the Commerce Department's National Telecommunications and Information Agency (NTIA), the executive branch office in charge of telecommunications policy. Robinson was not well liked by most of the Antitrust lawyers who worked on the AT&T case. He was seen as a kind of impractical academic, a man more interested in ideas than law. Moreover, he was regarded as a closet AT&T sympathizer, someone who displayed no sense of outrage about AT&T's anticompetitive acts during the early 1970s. In fact, Robinson later made it plain that he thought the government's suit against the phone company was a serious mistake. When he arrived at NTIA in 1979, Robinson quickly began to develop ideas about how the suit might be settled, and he sent them over to Anderson, who happened not to be one of the Antitrust lawyers who regarded Robinson with suspicion.

When Anderson and Trienens looked over the menu together, they agreed that it contained some ideas that might form the basis of a realistic settlement. Ideally, any settlement would accomplish three things: it would enhance phone equipment competition, it would allow long distance competitors like MCI equal access with AT&T to the phone company's local exchanges, and it would not seriously disrupt the high-quality, low-cost telephone service enjoyed by the American public. From Trienens' point of view, that meant that while AT&T could accept some divestiture, a settlement would have to stop far short of the total breakup of Western Electric and all the basic operating companies, which the government was seeking in its lawsuit. Anderson, on the other hand, needed a couple of severed limbs both for their symbolic political value and as a means to ensure that AT&T did not revert to anticompetitive practices in the future. In 1956, after all, Justice had accepted a deal that contained no divestiture, and less than twenty years later it had been forced to sue AT&T again over many of the same competition issues.

There were three ideas on Ken Robinson's menu that seemed to fit both Trienens' and Anderson's criteria for a settlement. They were known as "the crown jewels," "the bellwether approach," and "the United Fruit approach." Combined, they would form the basis of a deal far more palatable to AT&T than the Draconian divestiture being sought in the lawsuit.

Among AT&T's twenty-two basic operating companies, there were four or five that were large and prominent enough to be considered "crown jewels": Pacific Telephone, Illinois Bell, Southwestern Bell, New York Telephone, and perhaps Southern Bell. All of them had assets worth more than $5 billion, and annual revenues greater than $1 billion. For starters, the menu suggested that AT&T divest itself of one of these "jewels." Among the four or five, there was one obvious candidate: Pacific Telephone. Considering its size, Pacific was easily the worst

performing operating company in the Bell System, mainly because of tough local regulations in California. The company
was burdened by a huge debt and its profit margins were low.
Trienens told Anderson that if AT&T was to sacrifice a jewel,
Pacific would be the one. Anderson agreed. Pacific's $14.5 bil-
lion in assets made it the largest of all AT&T's operating companies, and thus it would be a fine prize for the Justice
department.

The idea behind the crown jewel divestiture was called
"the bellwether approach." Bill McGowan had complained from
the beginning that the Bell operating companies discriminated
against MCI because they were owned by MCI's main competitor, AT&T. McGowan said that no matter how many rules
were written about equal access to local exchanges and no matter how many times AT&T claimed to have renounced its anticompetitive ways, MCI would still face a structural
disadvantage in competition with AT&T because the phone
company owned all the local exchanges. But rather than divesting all the operating companies and drastically disrupting
AT&T's centralized phone network, the bellwether approach
suggested that one company—especially a crown jewel—might
be enough. If a company like Pacific were made independent,
it could be used to measure the performance and compliance
of the other, AT&T-owned operating companies. If a dispute
such as the one over FX lines arose, independent Pacific's behavior would provide a legal test, a point of comparison for the
other operating companies. And to make sure that Pacific itself
did not try somehow to take advantage of its special bellwether
status, the menu suggested that AT&T also divest itself of two
relatively small operating companies in which it owned a partial
interest: Southern New England Bell and Cincinnati Bell. Though
they were not really as large as Pacific, they also could serve
as bellwethers.

In the opinion of both Trienens and Anderson, crown jewel
divestiture and the bellwether approach, together with some
negotiated rules about equal access to the local exchanges, would
effectively solve the problems raised by long-distance competition. Bill McGowan might not think it was enough, but it was

certainly more divestiture than a lot of lawyers—even some
working on the case for Justice—believed would result from a
trial of *U.S.* v. *AT&T.* To assess the reactions of McGowan and
the other procompetition forces in Washington, Anderson drove
over one night in the midst of his talks with Trienens to the
home of Walter Hinchman, the former FCC Common Carrier
Bureau chief, who was now a consultant to the Justice department as well as MCI and other new long-distance companies.
Hinchman told Anderson that he thought the proposal was a
good one.

But there was still the question of Western Electric and
phone equipment competition. On the menu, this problem was
addressed by what Ken Robinson had termed "the United Fruit
approach." In the early 1970s, as part of an antitrust agreement
with the U.S. government, United Fruit had agreed to take a
large portion of its own assets and spin them off, instantly
creating a new company large and experienced enough to compete with United Fruit in its own business. Robinson's idea was
that AT&T would do the same with Western Electric. Anderson
and Trienens talked about the idea, and Trienens expressed
serious interest. Losing one-third of Western would be a significant sacrifice for AT&T, but Trienens' instinct was that it was
an affordable price in exchange for having the government case
out of the company's way. It would certainly mean that the
1956 prohibitions on computer manufacturing would be lifted.
When Trienens talked to Charlie Brown about it, Brown agreed.

So there it was: a deal. Pacific, Cincinnati, Southern New
England, and one-third of Western, plus some negotiations about
equal access to the local exchanges. Enough severed limbs for
Ken Anderson. The national telephone network essentially preserved for Charlie Brown. A more favorable competitive en-
vironment for Bill McGowan. The uncertainty in the
telecommunications industry caused by the antitrust case over
with. And the public—well, probably only Wall Street would
even notice that anything had happened.

In January 1980, shortly before he left his job at the Justice
department to enter private practice, Ken Anderson finally told
the Antitrust division's front office about his talks with Tri-

enens. He told them that AT&T was seriously interested in the framework they had discussed.

"No commitment has been made," Anderson stressed. "All I want to do is give you an option."

To some of the key lawyers in the division's front office, an "option" from Anderson was like a Christmas present from a known terrorist: they assumed it was dangerous, and they were not about to open it up and look inside. A new Antitrust chief, Sanford Litvack, had just been appointed by President Jimmy Carter. Litvack was a well-known antitrust litigator with the prestigious New York law firm of Donovan, Leisure, Newton & Irvine. Don Flexner, whose enmity to Anderson went way back, told Litvack when he arrived that Anderson was not to be trusted. Anderson, for his part, let it be known inside the division that Flexner was "scared shitless" by the proposal because Flexner was the sort of lawyer who had to have a hundred economists "paw over" any deal before Flexner would feel safe in approving it. Litvack arrived just as the back-and-forth sniping was becoming intense. He told everyone involved with the settlement proposal to "slow down." Within weeks, Flexner had persuaded Litvack that the best way to proceed was to let his Relief Task Force finish its report about the department's goals in *U.S.* v. *AT&T*. In the meantime, Litvack told Anderson's team of lawyers he would not consider a deal with AT&T.

Howard Trienens and Charlie Brown, meanwhile, could not figure out what had happened. Trienens thought that he was moving close to a settlement. When Anderson left, he told Trienens that the matter had been passed up to the front office and that Trienens should establish contact with them to continue the negotiations. But no one in the front office would return Trienens' calls. In frustration, Trienens called Anderson at his new office to find out what was going on.

"What do I have to do?" he asked. "You have no idea what I had to do to get to this point within the company. This is a big step forward, if not a giant leap, and nobody in the division is even returning my calls."

"The moment's right," Anderson said. "You've got some momentum. Why don't you put this thing in a nice little package and take it up to Benjamin Civiletti, the attorney general? Goose 'em a little bit."

"I don't want to go over the front office lawyers' heads," Trienens replied. "That could cause a lot of problems."

So Trienens continued to wait. In March, shortly after Litvack took over as Antitrust chief, he put in another call. This time Litvack picked up the phone.

Trienens reminded him of the menu discussions AT&T had had with Anderson and said that he hoped to meet with Litvack to continue the negotiations.

"I think it's premature to discuss anything at this time," Litvack said abruptly. "I want a lot more than the menu."

And then Litvack hung up on the phone company.

Chapter 14

Crimson Sky

HOWARD Trienens and Charlie Brown, from their vantage at AT&T's corporate headquarters in Manhattan, never understood the internal turf wars, personality conflicts, and individual ambitions that caused the Justice lawyers in Washington to appear as uncompromising prosecutors one day and flexible negotiators the next. Even if they had understood, it is doubtful the knowledge would have done anything more than contribute to the mounting frustration and depression they felt about the phone company's ever-deepening entanglement with the U.S. government. Between regulation by the FCC, attempts to pass legislation in Congress, and the ongoing Justice antitrust case, Washington seemed to Charlie Brown like "a three-ring circus." Except neither Brown nor Trienens found amusement in the display. Justice's on-again off-again attitude toward the menu settlement deal seemed to be just another confounding side show.

So when Sandy Litvack called Howard Trienens in New York on Tuesday, December 16, 1980, offering once again to talk about a deal—it was now fully nine months since Litvack had unilaterally ended the menu negotiations—Trienens did not inquire about the reasons for Justice's most recent turnabout. He simply told Brown that the negotiations were on again, and he made an appointment to see Litvack in Washington on Friday.

Of course, Brown and Trienens could make an intelligent guess about why Litvack was suddenly willing to talk. Just as Ken Anderson had been when he initiated the menu discussions, Litvack was now a lame duck. In November, Ronald Reagan had been elected president over Jimmy Carter in a landslide. That meant Litvack would have to vacate his office when Reagan nominated his own Antitrust chief sometime after January. Trienens, Brown, and Litvack all knew that any Reagan nominee would likely be a conservative opponent of many of the Antitrust division's policies and practices and that the nominee probably would not be sympathetic to the AT&T case. If Litvack settled the case before Reagan could nominate his successor, then Litvack could take credit for the deal and prevent a conservative from undermining, or even abandoning, the case.

At the same time, there were reasons why Brown and Trienens were even more anxious now to make a deal than they had been a year ago. Six months before Litvack's call, on Friday, June 13—"Black Friday" as it was known by AT&T's lawyers—a federal jury in Chicago had returned its verdict in MCI's private antitrust suit against the phone company, the case that closely mirrored *U.S.* v. *AT&T*. Unimpressed with George Saunders' impassioned arguments on AT&T's behalf, the jury had found the phone company guilty and awarded MCI $1.8 billion in damages, the largest private antitrust award in American history. "Fully half of the Justice case is our case," McGowan told reporters when the verdict came in. "We've provided the government with a blueprint on how to conduct a trial." The MCI chairman could scarcely restrain his glee. And for good reason: just the yearly interest on the damage award, which would be withheld until all appeals were settled, amounted to $162 million, more than MCI's entire 1979 revenues ($144 million).

Howard Trienens was confident that there had been irregularities about the judge's instructions on damages to the jury, and that those irregularities would cause the $1.8 billion to be thrown out on appeal. But in many ways, that was beside the point. The verdict, together with all the publicity about the size of the damage award, had dealt AT&T a severe psychological blow. The working-level lawyers at Justice who were preparing *U.S.* v. *AT&T* for trial gloated about the verdict to the phone company's lawyers, and it was clear that the government, despite Ken Anderson's unexpected resignation, was now highly enthusiastic about its case. Judge Greene was continuing to push the suit toward trial, and he had set early January 1981 as a firm starting date. Trienens was not afraid of a trial— George Saunders assured him that AT&T's case was in better shape than the government's—but one could hardly be encouraged by events in Chicago. For his part, Saunders was feverishly anxious to bring the case to court, and to vindicate himself with a victory. "Another billion-eight and they may throw me out on the street," he joked to the AT&T trial team. So Trienens did not tell Saunders about the phone call from Litvack. It was better that the trial team continue to prepare as if there was no chance of settlement.

Another reason that Brown and Trienens were ready to deal was that their congressional strategy for settling the company's problems had also fallen apart the previous June. After two years of hands-on work by Brown, Trienens, and AT&T's government relations office in Washington, a comprehensive rewrite of the 1934 Communications Act had finally cleared the House Communications Subcommittee with AT&T's blessing. The bill would have ended the computer restrictions of the 1956 consent decree and would have solved the Western Electric problem by establishing a "fully separated subsidiary" company, still owned by AT&T, to sell phone equipment. But before the bill could be voted on and passed to the Senate, Peter Rodino, chairman of the House antitrust subcommittee, intercepted the legislation and killed it in his committee. Despite claims to the contrary by AT&T, Rodino said he was afraid that if the bill passed, the government's antitrust suit would be stopped cold because many of the competition issues would be resolved.

So even though AT&T's top executives assumed that the

election of Ronald Reagan augured well for their relationship with the government, Trienens was nonetheless seriously prepared to negotiate with Litvack when he flew to Washington on Friday, December 19. He also realized, however, that Litvack's lame-duck status offered AT&T at least some advantage in the talks; since Litvack had made the first overture, he must be somewhat eager to strike a deal. Sitting on Litvack's couch in the Antitrust chief's spacious fifth-floor office in the main Justice building, Trienens opened the discussion by listing for Litvack all the reasons why AT&T shouldn't be interested in negotiating with him.

"The next guy's going to be much more friendly," Trienens said. "There's no real reason why we should talk to you at all. . . . So you might be wondering why I'm here."

"Howard, the thought has crossed my mind," Litvack said.

"There *is* something that we'd be willing to talk about." Trienens reminded Litvack of the menu framework that had been worked out with Anderson nearly a year before: divestiture of Pacific Telephone, Cincinnati Bell, and Southern New England Telephone; divestiture and spin-off of 40 percent of Western Electric; and presumably, some injunctive rules governing AT&T's behavior to be negotiated with Justice.

"We have put that on the table before, and we'd be willing to talk about it again," Trienens said.

"What does that mean?" asked Litvack.

"I'm offering it now. What else do you need?"

"A framework for equal interconnection with the other long-distance companies," Litvack answered.

This was the big question mark. Unlike Ken Anderson, Litvack had taken great pains to be sure that he consulted with as many division lawyers as security permitted about his proposal to AT&T. If a deal was struck, Litvack wanted to be certain that it wasn't undermined by dissenting trial team lawyers who thought that they had been sold up-river by their politically appointed Antitrust chief. When Litvack discussed the menu terms with the Justice lawyers running the AT&T case—attorneys who, in some cases, had been poring over the details of telephone industry competition for half a decade—he heard loud and clear that "crown jewel," "bellwether," and "United Fruit" divestiture were not enough to make a settlement work. Also needed would be a set of strict, enforceable rules governing interconnection between AT&T and MCI. The division's Relief Task Force, which had been appointed a year before at the time Ken Anderson first approached AT&T about a settlement, had concluded that Justice's most important goal in the case should be to sever the structural conflict of interest faced by Bell's operating companies, which in theory were supposed to treat AT&T and MCI equally but which in fact were owned and managed by 195 Broadway. If the lawsuit was successful, the goal would be achieved by forcing the divestiture of all the operating companies, as well as Western Electric. The trial team lawyers told Litvack that there might be a way, short of the total breakup of AT&T, to reach the same end through negotiation. If the rules were strict enough, and if compliance with them was independently verifiable, then divestiture of only Pacific, Cincinnati, Southern New England, and 40 percent of Western would be acceptable. For Trienens and Brown, the obvious benefit of such terms was that the integrity of the nation's telephone network would be preserved. While the system of subsidies that kept the cost of local service low would inevitably be disrupted by competition with MCI and others, the quality of that service would not be seriously impaired.

Litvack told Trienens that the interconnection agreement would be the key to the deal. The terms of divestiture would not be an issue, since both sides agreed to the divestiture discussed by Anderson and Trienens earlier in the year. For the settlement to work, Justice and AT&T would have to negotiate quickly a document that laid out the rules for equal interconnection.

And time was of the essence for AT&T. The trial was scheduled to begin on January 15, less than four weeks away from Litvack and Trienens' Friday meeting. Once the trial began, the value to AT&T of any settlement might be severely diminished. There was a section of the antitrust Clayton Act which held that once evidence was entered in a case like *U.S.* v. *AT&T*, it could be used on a *prima facie* basis by other companies suing

AT&T for antitrust violations if the United States won its case or if the case was settled by consent decree. That meant that dozens of companies could piggyback on the government case without having to enter and prove their own evidence. The price to AT&T of such piggybacking, in the form of antitrust damage awards, would likely run to billions of dollars. There was some dispute among the AT&T and Justice lawyers about whether the rule applied in this particular case, but Trienens' view was that there was no reason to take chances. Once the trial began, it would probably be best for AT&T to abandon settlement talks and try to win the case, thus preventing piggybacking by private litigants.

Equally important was secrecy. If word leaked out that AT&T and Justice were close to a deal, all kinds of problems could ensue. Companies such as MCI and the phone equipment manufacturers, who by 1980 had banded together in a procompetition Washington lobby group, might fear that the settlement wouldn't go far enough to protect their interests, and they could put pressure on Congress to intervene. Also, AT&T did not want its settlement discussions disclosed either to its employees or to Wall Street. Disclosure might dampen morale, hamper the company's bond market offerings, or spark a run on AT&T stock. The secrecy problem was not an unusual one in the Antitrust division, where government lawsuits were frequently settled by consent decree, but the size and scope of the AT&T case made it especially important that leaks be prevented. As they concluded their Friday meeting, Litvack and Trienens agreed that they would restrict knowledge of the negotiations to as few lawyers as possible, and that they would hold the talks, at least at first, some place where they were not likely to be discovered. The Antitrust lawyers who would be working on the negotiations set up a protected file in the division's computer system so that only a person who knew the proper password could review the consent decree as it was drafted and revised. Luin Fitch, the lawyer who set up the file, chose the passwords *crimson sky*. Fitch had just finished reading the popular historical novel *Shogun,* and in the book Crimson Sky was the code name for a general's plan to take over the Japanese empire in the event of war. The name stuck, and for years afterward the Justice lawyers used it to refer to their December 1980 negotiations with AT&T.

Litvack and Trienens scheduled the first meeting for Monday, December 22, in a private suite rented by AT&T at the Four Seasons Hotel on Pennsylvania Avenue, ten blocks from the White House. Several lawyers from each side were present, and they concentrated immediately on devising the rules for equal interconnection. One side would offer a draft, and the other would revise it and identify unacceptable passages. The teams worked separately over Christmas and met again at the Four Seasons on Saturday, Sunday, and the following Tuesday. Litvack and Trienens were not directly involved in the detailed discussions since each had appointed "point men" from his trial staff. By Wednesday, New Year's Eve, the teams of lawyers had agreed on two things: they had devised a general framework acceptable to both sides, but they had also agreed that they needed more than two weeks—when the trial was due to start—to hammer out the specific language of the decree. When he talked to Litvack, Trienens would say, "Look, we can't start trial. If we start trial, it's all over."

On New Year's Eve, Litvack was on vacation in Vermont. After talking with his "point men," he called Trienens. "OK," Litvack conceded. "We've got a concept. We'll go in with you to see Greene and ask for some time."

It wasn't until the next Monday, January 5, that everyone who mattered was able to get back to Washington. It had been a deadly holiday for the lawyers on both sides. Few of them had taken more than Christmas day off from work. Throughout the two weeks, the weather had been cold and overcast with periodic sleet and ice storms. When they gathered late Monday afternoon in Litvack's office, the sky they saw through his southern windows was not crimson but a disheartening gray. The temperature outside was falling into the twenties.

After a review of where the talks stood, Litvack picked up his phone and dialed Judge Greene's chambers, only to find out that Greene had gone for the day.

"Can we call him at home?" Litvack asked. No, and the

clerk wouldn't give out the judge's number. (It happened that Greene was one of the few federal judges in the country whose home number was listed in the phone book, but Litvack naturally assumed it was unlisted.) So Litvack left a message, and the clerk promised to pass it on to Greene. A few minutes later, the call came back: Greene would meet them in his chambers at eight o'clock that night.

After dinner, Litvack, Trienens, and some of the other lawyers piled into their cars and headed over to the courthouse seven blocks away. Greene's chambers were on the second floor of the building. The chambers were a richly decorated, comfortable place. There was an exquisitely detailed, red Bokhara rug on the floor, and red leather chairs with brass studs were placed before the judge's polished desk, which was modeled after one used by George Washington. On the wall nearby was a framed copy of the first draft, in Greene's handwriting, of the 1964 Civil Rights Act.

"I apologize for the phone call," Litvack began.

"I do have a reporter here," Greene said, referring to the stenographer who had set up his machine on a nearby conference table. "There was some mention on the phone about confidentiality. I don't know about confidentiality. As of the moment, so far as I am concerned, it is a matter of public record. Go ahead, Mr. Litvack."

"As I said, we do apologize, and I would not have bothered you, as you know, unless we thought it was extremely urgent. At the outset, I am concerned a bit about the nature of the record which we make. With your permission, at the end I may move to ask you to seal the record, if that seems appropriate to you at that time."

"These are my law clerks and my secretary," Greene said, motioning. "So there is no outsider here. We do not have the *Washington Post* here."

Litvack continued. "The purpose of our asking to get together with you so promptly was because we have been having conversations between and among ourselves, sort of on and off—really more off than on—over a relatively long period of time, and more recently and more concertedly over the last week or eight days, with a view toward trying to determine whether or not we could reach any kind of agreement that might resolve the litigation.

"Those conversations have sort of come to a head, and we are now in a position where I think both sides can report to you that we have what I will call an agreement on a concept and a framework for the settlement. . . . One, we want to tell you that we do have that kind of understanding. And two, as I am sure you can guess, we think under the circumstances both sides would like to request that the trial be put off for a sufficient time to enable us to try to put together for the court a decree."

"I should say," Trienens chipped in, "that so far as the telephone company is concerned, strategically and as far as litigation, we are ready to go. We are ready to go to trial on the fifteenth. It is probably better for us to start now, if it has to be tried.

"On the other hand, we have the government of the United States coming at us from at least three different directions: Mr. Litvack's forces; the FCC, which is endeavoring to restructure this industry in fairly major ways; and the rest of the executive branch coming at us from quite a different direction. It has been very difficult for our client to determine how to plan for the future, with all of these things going on, and with fast-moving technology, and with this uncertainty for some period. An opportunity to deal with the United States government speaking with one voice, as this would be, is a thing we have to take very seriously."

But Greene wasn't persuaded. After years of pushing and pushing to bring to the case to trial, to prove that the courts could manage complex antitrust litigation, he was not going to postpone the case because of a "framework" for a deal. "You obviously do not have a settlement today, and you are not going to have a settlement in two weeks," he told Litvack. "With all due respect, somebody else is going to be in your position in two weeks or two months, or whenever."

"Surely," Litvack admitted. The Reagan transition team was already at work.

"And we do not know anything about any of that, do we?"

"Yes and no. Yes, you are right. We do not have a settlement today and we are not going to have one in two weeks, in terms of a signed document to submit to anyone. But we do have some very key, specific principles that the two parties have agreed upon. It was not just a 'It would be nice to resolve this matter' kind of conversation.

"And this is an institutional thing," Litvack continued. "This is not me out on a frolic. I mean, I realize the controversy that this may ultimately cause. We are prepared to do it. And if I am there at the end to take the credit or the blame, then so be it. And if I am not, then someone else will deal with that."

"What you want me to do, in effect, is postpone everything in the hope that all of this is going to fall into place. Is that what it comes down to?" Greene asked.

"Obviously, that is a way of putting it," Litvack said.

"Why is this all coming up now?" Greene asked impatiently. "Why didn't it come up a year ago, or six months ago, or three months ago? Why is it coming up ten days before the trial?"

"Well, I can't answer you as to a year ago. I can answer you as to the limited time..."

Greene cut Litvack off. "Why is it coming up today?"

"Well, your honor, I..."

"At eight-thirty on the 5th of January?"

"I can't give you an answer to that, except to say that the parties have talked on and off for some time. We find ourselves here."

"And you really don't—I don't know if you want to put this on the record or not—but you do not really know whether your successors in the Reagan administration are in agreement with this."

"Oh, no, I clearly don't know that. I mean, I don't even know who my successors are, let alone whether they are in agreement. But..."

Again, Greene interrupted. "We are fifteen days from the new administration taking over. To be blunt about it, how can you talk about settling a case sixty to ninety days from now when that is about to happen?"

"I guess the best answer I can give you is that this is a settlement proposal and a proposition which, again, is not a personal one to me. It is institutional. Now, can someone come in and replace me and repudiate the whole thing? The answer is yes. Of course they can. Is that likely to happen? And I feel a little awkward saying all of this . . . I have no reason to believe, if I may say this without getting political, that the next administration is going to be any tougher on antitrust than I am."

"No, I don't want to go into all of that," Greene answered. The diminutive judge, slumped in his high-backed swivel chair, was typically self-effacing. "I only point this out to indicate the uncertainties. Now, you have heard me. I have talked again and again about how everybody, and particularly the department of Justice, has been preaching and beating on the judiciary to get these cases going and for dealing with these complex antitrust cases. And here we are on the verge of trial, and here you are saying, 'Well, now, we are thinking of settling the case. . . .' Why can't we just start the trial? If somebody wants to settle it, we are always here. We are always open."

Litvack and Trienens tried to bring up the piggyback problem again, but Greene would not change his mind. Furthermore, he said, he was not inclined to keep the meeting secret.

"You have not told me what the framework and the format is, so I can't tell the newspapers," Greene said. "So as far as there was a discussion and that this has been mentioned, I am not so certain that I want to be a party to keeping it confidential or secret. I don't know what is secret about it. I don't know what the public can't know about it, except that somebody thinks it may be inconvenient." Clearly, the circumstances of the 1956 settlement scandal were vivid in the judge's mind, as they would remain in the weeks and months ahead.

Two days later, on Wednesday, January 7, Judge Greene issued a public order denying Litvack and Trienens' request for a trial postponement and disclosing that Justice and AT&T had agreed on a "framework" for settling the case. Suddenly, news of a possible deal was all over the newspapers and trade press. Speculation about divestiture terms was rife, and some elements of the Crimson Sky framework leaked out. The trial lawyers for both AT&T and Justice who had not known about the talks assumed now that the case they had slaved over for so long was finished. In a few weeks, as a memorial, one of the lawyers in the Antitrust division had printed up a T-shirt that said, "Reach Out, Reach Out and Crush Someone. *U.S.* v. *AT&T.* 1974–1981." There was an elephant drawn on the shirt with a phone wrapped in its trunk and a bell on its chest.

In the week following Greene's order, Litvack and Trienens redoubled their efforts to convince the judge that the settlement talks were serious and that the trial should be postponed. They decided to draft a specific document, resembling a consent decree, that would lay out both the divestiture terms and a specific outline for equal interconnection rules. As soon as possible, they would bring the document in to Greene and show him that they had moved far beyond a settlement "concept."

On the morning of Wednesday, January 14, the day before the opening of *U.S.* v. *AT&T*, while snow was blowing on gusty winds across Washington's wide avenues, Trienens and the government lawyers trudged back over to the courthouse to visit Greene in his chambers. They found the judge once again behind his George Washington desk. He seemed in a better mood than he had been the week before. Perhaps they had taken him by surprise at the first meeting.

"We have worked on the settlement last week, over the weekend, and through last night, and we do have a concrete, detailed proposal for settlement," Trienens began. "We have a tangible, concrete agreement. We have no complex or controversial features waiting to be resolved. But we do have last-minute technical drafting problems.

"The major question," Trienens continued, "is the factor of the incoming Reagan administration. I am not here to conjecture on their relative eagerness to break up the Bell System. That is not for me to conjecture about."

"I don't know anything about it one way or the other," Greene said. "What do you want me to do?"

"Specifically, I think we are not going to ask you for what can be characterized as an indefinite postponement. I am not concerned about whether the trial starts tomorrow in terms of opening statements. I would like to recommend a two-week postponement of taking of evidence. Why two weeks? Because I think the biggest problem which none of us can address is that we have to get ahold of and get the attention of the incoming administration starting on the afternoon of January 20, when they take over."

"I am obviously not unsympathetic to the idea of settling this case if it can be settled," Greene said. "I am not a masochist and don't want to be sitting for years listening to this testimony, but the question is: Are we any more definite today than we were a week ago? I don't know."

"Let me clarify one thing," Trienens added moments later. "I want to say that the 'ground up' features of this agreement are unique. I was told by some very learned hands around this town a year ago that the way to get a case settled is you go and sweet-talk the top people who don't know much about it, and then the people at the bottom who do not want to settle, they have it imposed on them. This is exactly the opposite of the traditional learning, if that is what it is. This does come from the trial staff and it is relevant because these are the institutional people, not the people at the political level."

It was an argument worth stressing to Greene, who had been an "institutional level" staff lawyer at Justice for more than a decade.

"Let me think about it," the judge said. "I will try to let you know this afternoon, but in any event we will go ahead with the opening statements tomorrow. So if I don't let you know this afternoon, I will let you know Monday when the taking of evidence would begin. I am not rejecting it out of hand and I am not accepting it out of hand."

That was about as much as Howard Trienens and Charlie Brown could hope for from Greene. Less than twenty-four hours before George Saunders would deliver his opening argument in *U.S.* v. *AT&T* to Judge Greene, AT&T's top executives were as optimistic about the company's antitrust problems as they had been in months, even years. President Reagan had said occasionally during his campaign in 1980 that he thought the government's suit against the phone company was silly. With a little help from Reagan, and from Greene, the debilitating controversy over phone industry competition would be over in a matter of weeks, and while AT&T would have made a sacrifice, the Bell System would be preserved.

As snow descended on Washington that night, Charlie Brown's "new realism" seemed like an idea whose time and place had finally come.

Chapter 15

Two Lawyers

THE weather had worsened by early the next morning when Gerald Connell steered his Plymouth Horizon onto the George Washington Parkway and headed north toward Washington. Snow was still falling and fog clung to the icy Potomac River on Connell's right. He crossed over the river on the slippery 14th Street Bridge and merged onto the Southwest Freeway. At 12th Street he went north to E Street and then turned into the FBI garage where the government provided him a parking space. For almost two decades now, Connell had made this twenty-minute morning trip with blind regularity, had listened to the news and the comic disc jockeys on WMAL AM-63 radio, had seen the cherry trees along the Potomac blossom and fade and blossom again, had endured the traffic and the rain and snow. The sameness of his commute must at times have seemed a stark metaphor for the life of a career government lawyer with a handful of children and a mortgaged house in the Virginia suburbs. But this morning, the drive represented something else entirely. It was a new beginning, an opportunity for personal and professional renewal rarely available to a settled husband and father nearing fifty years of age. And already, Gerry Connell felt vaguely ill at ease.

There were those in the Antitrust division who questioned

whether Connell had been the right choice to succeed Ken Anderson as the lead attorney on the government's case against AT&T. Connell was a capable trial lawyer, they said, but hardly the sort of firebrand leader that this large, complex, and important case demanded. A hot-shot trial lawyer like AT&T's George Saunders might chew Connell up and spit him out. Connell had never worked on a case as big as this one; of course, no one else in the division had, either. He had been in charge of twenty lawyers in the division's General Litigation section, where he supervised trials, occasionally tried a case himself, and increasingly handled a lot of paperwork. He was a sleepy, even-tempered man, the sort of fellow you might say hello to on the elevator for twenty years without even knowing his name. He looked older than he was and always seemed to be weary or overworked. His face was like a basset hound's, with droopy eyes and jowls and a prominent red nose. He reminded some people of an aging Irish politician from Boston, an assessment that wasn't far from the truth. His mother and father were both Irish Catholics, and his father had been active in New England politics. Connell was perhaps best known inside the Antitrust division for the Saint Patrick's Day party he threw every year. It was a rough and ready affair, and at it Connell could be seen wandering blithely about with a half-empty bottle of Paddy's Irish whiskey, pouring generously to keep his guests' glasses full.

Sandy Litvack had offered Connell the AT&T job for several reasons. When Ken Anderson first told the front office that he was leaving, Litvack had considered looking outside the government—because of the prestige that would accrue to him—for an experienced trial lawyer willing to come in and run the case. Quickly, however, Litvack realized that it could take months to conduct such a search, and that even if it was successful, such outside talent might never blend with the younger department staff lawyers who would inevitably do much of the work during trial. Once the decision was made to look inside the division for Anderson's successor, Connell's name quickly arose. Morale in Connell's General Litigation section was generally high, and Connell himself had an exceptional winning record on cases he tried or supervised. He was steady and thorough, qualities that contrasted sharply with Ken Anderson's style. And Connell was experienced, even if he had never handled a gargantuan case like *U.S.* v. *AT&T.* The big question was whether Connell had the energy and desire to transform his professional life by hurling himself, eighty hours a week, fifty-two weeks a year, into a litigation battle against the largest corporation in the world. To some, it seemed that Connell had retired on the job in the General Litigation section. Was he capable of a professional metamorphosis? After talking with his old Antitrust drinking buddy Hugh Morrison, and even though he told himself that the case might be a "killer," figuratively if not literally, Connell had decided that he was. A few days after Litvack called with an offer in January 1980, Connell accepted.

The questions about Connell's desire and stamina had really not been answered by the morning of Thursday, January 15, 1981, when he arrived at the U.S. District Courthouse on Constitution Avenue to present the government's opening arguments to Judge Harold Greene. Some of the lawyers on Connell's staff still talked about that time the previous March, soon after Connell took over, when, during a Saturday meeting at the height of intense stipulation negotiations with AT&T ordered by Judge Greene, a blood vessel had spontaneously burst in Connell's nose. Connell tried to stop it, but he bled profusely, and some of the lawyers had to half-carry him to the hospital for surgery. Connell had missed several weeks of work, and more than a few of the lawyers on his staff wondered whether the incident was a foreshadowing of how their leader would hold up under the tremendous personal pressure ahead.

The scene at the courthouse as Connell arrived that morning was enough to make any jaded trial lawyer nervous. As wet snow fell, newspaper photographers snapped pictures of Connell entering the building. Inside, the wide hallways were crowded with lawyers, reporters, and industry executives. Several of AT&T's executives had flown down from New York to hear Connell and Saunders summarize their respective cases. The floors were wet from all the snow that had been tracked in, and the air was hot and steamy. Judge Greene's courtroom was on the second floor, and it was a windowless, airless room with wood paneling on every wall, wooden spectators' pews, a wooden jury box, a wood bench for the judge, wood-colored carpeting, and even a wood clock on one wall. It felt like a coffin. Even though word about the Crimson Sky settlement talks had leaked out, the atmosphere inside the courtroom was akin to the opening of a sensational murder trial. There were more spectators than available seats, and tickets were issued so that the working lawyers and reporters could find a place to sit. Since this was a bench trial—there was no jury, and Judge Greene would decide every aspect of the case—the jury box had been converted into a makeshift press headquarters. There was even an artist poised to sketch Connell's profile once he began to present his argument.

Just after 9:30 A.M. and slightly more than six years after Attorney General William Saxbe had decided to "bring an action" against the phone company, Judge Greene rapped his gavel and called the trial of U.S. v. AT&T to order.

What Gerry Connell noticed more than anything else as he stood behind the lectern and prepared to begin his speech was the heat. It was not just warm inside the courtroom, it was hot. Connell was sweating, and he felt uncomfortable. Under the circumstances, though, he couldn't be sure how much of his discomfort was simply nervousness. In front of him was a large notebook that contained an outline of Connell's argument. Most of the work had been done by Connell's key lieutenants, notably Peter Kenney, who had stayed on the trial team after Ken Anderson left, Michael McNeely, Jeff Blumenfeld, Jim Denvir, and Alan Silverstein. The outline had been literally cut and pasted together from various briefs and drafts prepared by Justice in recent months. It was organized by sections: opening statement, the MCI case, the phone equipment case, a few other topics, and a conclusion. Connell clung to the notebook because the last thing he wanted to do was stand in front of an audience this large and forget what he had to say. In the more than two hours it took him to present his argument, he never once moved from behind the wooden lectern directly in front of Judge Greene's bench.

Afterwards, the government's lawyers used words like "disaster" and "fiasco" to describe Gerry Connell's opening argument. Actually, it hadn't been as bad as all that. The lawyers' criticism partly reflected a fear that Connell was in way over his head, and that the difference between Connell's lackluster style and George Saunders' ebullience would obscure the issues in the case. Such fears, it turned out, were unfounded.

"What is this litigation all about?" Connell asked rhetorically, after he had introduced the lawyers at his table.

And then slowly, methodically, doggedly, he answered his own question. Date by date, episode by monotonous episode, he listed the stories that made up the government's antitrust case. It was like asking someone about how they did their grocery shopping and then hearing, in response, a list of every product the person had bought in the previous five years.

"Well," Connell began, "it is about a very, very, very large company. Assets of more than $100 billion. Revenues in excess of $40 billion. Profits in excess of $7 billion, employees numbering more than a million...

"This may very well be, as some press reports have said of it, history's biggest case. I suppose that certainly in terms of the stakes in the case, it could fairly be called that....

"This case is about deliberate choices made by the Bell System at important junctures. This case is about regulation that doesn't work. This case is about... This trial is not about... But it is about... Let's talk a little bit about..." and on and on. Connell's only shining moment came when he addressed the AT&T defense constructed by George Saunders. "What about the defendant's case?" Connell asked. "What does it say, what does it argue? Well, it says a number of things, but what it says mostly... is that AT&T is really a powerless, helpless giant, totally restrained by regulation, unable to do anything.

"You kind of get the picture, if you read Bell's filings, of an enormous but friendly elephant, *Horton Hears a Who*. A slow-thinking elephant, not quite able to figure out what messages are being sent to it by its masters, the regulators. As a result, from time to time it stumbles around in a regulatory jungle, doing its best to go in the direction in which it has been pushed.

The trouble is, from time to time this big elephant might reach out and crush someone. Bell's argument—with apologies to Erich Segal, the author of *Love Story*—in a nutshell, is regulation is never having to say you are sorry."

The crowded courtroom erupted in laughter for the first time, and even the lawyers at AT&T's defense table could not resist smiling.

Finally, mercifully for both the sweating Connell and his tired audience, he concluded his opening argument shortly before noon. "This court sits to dispense justice," he said. "We ask no more than that the court do that."

In the weeks preceding the opening of *U.S.* v. *AT&T*, while Howard Trienens and other AT&T lawyers were feverishly negotiating the Crimson Sky settlement in an effort to avert a trial, George Saunders had been preparing the case as if a deal with Justice was little more than a wild pipe dream harbored by the New Realists at 195 Broadway. There were personal as well as professional reasons for Saunders' unrelenting devotion to the trial preparations. In a manner uncharacteristic of most corporate attorneys, who generally cultivate a cool detachment toward the issues they confront in their work, Saunders passionately believed that the government case was a rip-off perpetrated by Bill McGowan and some misguided liberals at Justice. He lived, breathed, and, most of all, talked about AT&T's defense as if his own urgent emotion might be enough to persuade the government to leave the phone company alone. The MCI verdict had been the most devastating event in Saunders' long professional life. Not only had he lost a case that he had worked on for some seven years, but the defeat was not even remotely ambiguous; it was a humiliating rout, the biggest antitrust loss in American history. Saunders was looking to the government trial for vindication, both of his ability as a lawyer and of AT&T's version of telephone competition history. The two things were inextricably linked. If AT&T made a deal with the government, even under the relatively benign Crimson Sky terms, both Saunders' lawyering and his beliefs about the case would be discredited. So while Saunders was aware of the negotiations being conducted by Trienens, his overriding interest was in the upcoming trial. If the executives at 195 Broadway would give him a chance, Saunders believed he would win the government case and solve the phone company's problems the best way: triumphantly.

"I hope this works," were the first words Saunders said to Judge Greene when the trial reconvened after lunch. It happened that Saunders was referring to a wireless microphone that had been rigged for him by some engineers at Bell Labs so that Saunders could wander about the courtroom, as was his style, and still be heard on the court's public address system. But if he had been talking about the personal and professional challenge ahead of him, the words would have been as true.

The stylistic contrast between Connell and Saunders was vivid. While Connell had stood rigid and perspiring for two hours behind the wooden lectern, reading from his notebook, Saunders roamed freely, drawing energy from the rapt attention of his audience. While Connell spoke flatly and occasionally stuttered or paused to search for the right word, Saunders' Alabama-accented voice rose and fell fluidly, its dramatic inflections reverberating with meaning. Connell's argument had been little more than a factual list of the government's charges against AT&T. Saunders, who spoke for six hours without notes, waxed eloquent and philosophical about the history and purposes of regulation, the background of telephone industry competition, the details of the FX and Execunet controversies at the FCC, the ambitions of Bill McGowan, and above all, the reasonableness of John deButts' responses to the challenges his company faced in the early 1970s.

Saunders began his argument by homing in quickly on Judge Greene's close personal relationship with Bobby Kennedy. "As I sat in my hotel room this week trying to figure out a plan for this opening statement, I couldn't help but recall being in this city twenty years ago during a pre-inauguration week. And in thinking about that, I was struck by the difference in the mood in this country today as compared to twenty years ago.

"Twenty years ago this country faced a lot of serious problems. We had a crisis in civil rights, we had a problem in the Middle East, many other things. At that time, however, there was a feeling in the country that we were capable of dealing with our problems. When John Kennedy said in his inaugural speech that the torch of leadership had moved from one generation to another, I believed, and I think most Americans believed, that the new generation was capable of carrying that.

"As we stand here today, this country has lost a great deal of its confidence. The economy of the country is in chaos. In 1960, we still believed that American businesses could compete effectively and vigorously with business in any other country in the world. . . . As I stand before this court today, I appear on behalf of the greatest business enterprise this world has ever produced. I say that matter-of-factly because it is a matter of fact . . . AT&T is one of the few remaining examples, as George Will recently put it, of 'conspicuous quality' left in the world.

"Let there be no mistake: the government is here to destroy that enterprise. Why? You heard the government today describe their charges. On their face, as described, many of them are trivial. There is no substantial basis in law or fact for this case, and we will prove it in court. But I couldn't help think, when I heard Mr. Connell talking, about the time I wrote a political platform for a political candidate, who can remain nameless. It wasn't long, after we got through with the platform in that negotiation, when someone said, 'That's a fine platform.' I said, and I meant it, 'Yes, it touches on every subject that is important to the people of this state, and it avoids every issue.'

"That's what happened this morning. Mr. Connell went through the subjects, but he avoided the issues. . . ."

And on Saunders went. Like most of his speeches, it seemed at times interminable. But also like most of his speeches, it was brilliantly crafted and eloquently delivered. When possible, he referred back to Connell's specific remarks.

"Mr. Connell says, quoting a sage, 'Regulation means you never have to say you are sorry.' In fact, regulation means that you always have to say you are sorry, because what we are dealing with in this case is a situation in which, starting with that decision in 1968 [*Carterfone*], the commission has evolved a set of rules that have changed on a year-to-year basis.

"I don't read Mr. Segal, but Voltaire in describing a trip across France once said, 'In crossing France, laws change about as often as you change horses.' And in crossing the decade from 1968 to 1978, regulations—which, to this company, that's [*sic*] laws, that is what we have to follow—changed more often than we were able to find horses, or elephants, and we were constantly being told by the regulators not only that they were going to change the rules but that we should have known it to start with."

The heart of Saunders' opening argument concerned the controversies over MCI's FX lines, and to a lesser extent Execunet, at the FCC. In the end, both sides would accept the view that *U.S.* v. *AT&T* was, as Saunders put it later that afternoon, "the MCI case relitigated with some trimmings." On paper, a significant part of the government's case against AT&T dealt not with MCI but with the controversies over telephone equipment competition and John deButts' PCA strategy. The terminal equipment side of the case was not trivial, but by 1981 it was largely irrelevant, both legally and economically. The goal of *U.S.* v. *AT&T*, the reason that the Justice department was willing to spend millions of dollars to bring it to trial, was relief—the breakup of the phone company. To justify such a drastic measure, the government had to prove that telephone industry competition was still being stifled by AT&T and that the only way to stop the phone company's ongoing anticompetitive behavior was to break it apart. To that end, the terminal equipment case was generally useless because the problem had already been solved. After Charlie Brown's blue team took over AT&T, they had agreed to the very equipment competition program against which John deButts had fought vigorously for nearly a decade. Beginning in 1979, a competitive equipment manufacturer had only to register his product with the FCC to ensure that it met certain technical standards. After that, he was free to sell it to consumers in whatever way he pleased. No protective coupling arrangement was required. No approval from

AT&T was needed. And thus, by the time Gerry Connell and George Saunders presented their opening arguments to Judge Greene, equipment competition was flourishing. Forcing AT&T to divest itself of all its local operating companies would do little, if anything, to make it more prolific.

Not so with the MCI part of the case—or, at least, that's what Gerry Connell argued. Bill McGowan still complained frequently and articulately that it was the structural arrangement of AT&T—the fact that the local exchanges were owned by MCI's competitor, Long Lines—that held back full long-distance competition among MCI, AT&T, Sprint, and others. Until the operating companies were divested, McGowan said, MCI and other competitors would never be treated equally. The FX controversy was important because it was the seminal example in *U.S.* v. *AT&T* of how the phone company's ownership of both Long Lines and the local exchanges had caused it to block competition. It was also the easiest story for a judge or jury to understand. If one accepted McGowan's version of the story—that FX *was* a private-line service and that AT&T deliberately refused to provide it to MCI because deButts objected to competition—then the government's relief contentions began to make sense. But if one accepted George Saunders' version of the story—that McGowan had cynically manipulated the FCC into authorizing FX lines, much as he had later done with Execunet—then *U.S.* v. *AT&T* was little more than an expensive farce, or, as Saunders liked to put it, "the biggest rip-off of the century." Of course, a jury in Chicago had been presented with the two versions of the FX story and had decided that they liked Bill McGowan's better, $1.8 billion better.

"The core issue," Saunders said that afternoon, "is, did the commission authorize MCI to provide foreign exchange and common control switching arrangements services, or did they not? That is the issue."

And if *U.S.* v. *AT&T* was to be decided in the courtroom, if Judge Greene was to make a decision about whether to break up the phone company based on Gerry Connell's and George Saunders' best arguments, the MCI story would be key. Saunders believed that this time he would persuade the court that the motives and actions of Bill McGowan and the FCC in the early 1970s were ambiguous, if not wholly dishonest, and that John deButts had tried his best to respond to them while remaining loyal to his own deep-seated notions about the phone company's public trust. Perhaps Saunders would have better luck in front of a judge than a jury. Greene was an intelligent man, and he might better appreciate Saunders' impressive oratory than a jury of nonlawyers. Greene, too, might better tolerate Saunders' occasionally wild pomposities; as a judge, Greene was accustomed to immodest lawyers. Even on the afternoon of AT&T's opening argument, Greene already seemed to like Saunders and to be impressed and engaged by him.

But the real question that Thursday afternoon was whether any of them—Connell, Saunders, or Greene—would have the opportunity to put their mark on what Connell had called "history's biggest case," or whether the Crimson Sky settlement would relegate the entire matter to the obscure annals of American antitrust law.

Chapter 16

The Sky Falls

A T 5:45 P.M. on Thursday evening, after George Saunders had agreed to resume his opening argument on Friday and the hundreds of reporters and spectators had cleared the courtroom, Judge Greene summoned Gerry Connell, Peter Kenney, and Jim Denvir from the Justice department, and Howard Trienens' assistants Robert McLean and Jim Kilpatric from AT&T, to the judge's chambers next door to the courtroom. If Greene was going to agree to recess the trial before any evidence was taken, in order to give the two sides time to work out the details of the Crimson Sky settlement he would have to act swiftly. Saunders was long-winded, but by Monday at the latest the opening arguments would be concluded and Gerry Connell would call his first witness against AT&T.

"The reason I asked to meet with you again," Greene began, slumped behind his desk, "is, of course, I have been considering the request for postponement. And while it isn't absolutely necessary, I thought it might be helpful if you could expand a little bit on how the agreement of yesterday differs from the one that was discussed on January 5. I don't particularly want to know the substantive details, because I certainly don't want you to say anything that would prejudice the case in any way if the settlement fell through and we would have to go to trial."

McLean reiterated what Trienens had told Greene the day before: The settlement was substantial, its major provisions were agreed upon by both sides, and, while the attitude of the Reagan administration was still an uncertainty, the deal had been approved by the working-level lawyers under Connell. The terms of the deal were, McLean said, "a professional recommendation" by the Justice lawyers.

"I think that's significant," Greene said.

"Just to amplify a little on the last point," said Connell, "I haven't consulted with every person on my staff, which is now very large. I have conferred with every person that either I or Peter Kenney or Jim Denvir thought ought to be consulted because of their knowledge of the issues and their responsibilities on the case. Those people support the proposal we have. Again, I am willing, if Your Honor wanted, to disclose in more detail what we have, but I won't if you don't want it."

"I am not sure it wouldn't be perfectly appropriate, but you know lawyers are always cautious, so I don't think it is necessary," Greene said. "I obviously wouldn't have asked you to come in unless I had some feeling that perhaps I should go along with this. I haven't decided yet, but obviously we don't have a great deal of time. In any event, whatever I do I will certainly let Mr. Saunders finish his opening statement."

"That should give us several days," Jim Denvir cracked.

"Yes," Greene said. "Sometime tomorrow I will let you know."

The next day, Greene issued an order recessing the trial until March 4, some six weeks away, so that AT&T and Justice could put the finishing touches on the Crimson Sky deal. Finally, everyone was on board. Greene was impressed enough by the seriousness of the negotiations and the full participation of staff-level Justice lawyers to suspend his obsession with speedy progress in the case. Brown and Trienens were willing to sacrifice a piece of Western and several operating companies to avoid a costly trial and to preserve the integrity of the nation's phone system. Litvack and the Antitrust front office hoped to prevent their Reagan administration successors from abandoning altogether Justice's prosecution of AT&T. And the division's leading staff lawyers on the case, Connell, Kenney, and Denvir, who all seriously doubted that Greene would ever successfully order the breakup of a company as large and powerful as AT&T, figured that the Crimson Sky terms represented a substantial victory for Justice; tens of billions of dollars in assets would be divested by AT&T. All in all, on Friday, January 16, Crimson Sky looked like a foolproof way to end the decade-long controversy over telephone competition. Of the major players, only George Saunders, who was convinced that he could vindicate himself and his client in court, was unhappy about the deal. And Saunders was not in a position to share his feelings with anyone but his closest confidants on the AT&T defense team.

Since the fact that settlement talks were taking place was now widely known, the negotiations between Justice and AT&T moved from the clandestine quarters at the Four Seasons Hotel to an unused office at the U.S. District Courthouse. Robert McLean, Jim Kilpatric, Luin Fitch, and Jim Denvir did the bulk of the day-to-day work at the courthouse. Trienens and Litvack talked only rarely; both were waiting to review whatever document their staffs produced. Despite plummeting morale caused by the apparent imminence of a settlement, Connell and Saunders spent most of their time urging their respective trial staffs to prepare for resumption of the case on March 4, if the negotiations broke down.

By Thursday, January 22, less than a week after Greene's recess order, Justice had drafted for discussion a complete, nineteen-page consent decree. In it, the divestiture of the three operating companies was covered in a single sentence: "Defendants are ordered and directed to dispose of all stock or other equity interest in Pacific Telephone and Telegraph Company, Southern New England Telephone Company, and Cincinnati Bell Telephone Company on or before one year from the date of entry of this Final Judgment." The provisions about the Western Electric spin-off were more complex, but they were essentially unchanged from what Trienens had personally offered to Litvack more than a month before. "Defendants are ordered to transfer to the new company assets, including cash, lines of credit, sufficient manufacturing capacity and personnel to manufacture, install, and service...equipment," the document said. The bulk of the document concerned the detailed terms of an interconnection agreement: how companies like MCI would be assured equal access to the local phone network. The draft concluded with a section labeled "Z: Statement of the Public Interest." The entire section read, "Entry of this Final Judgment is in the public interest."

To say that the deal was in the public interest was one thing, but to claim that it was in the political interest of the incoming Reagan administration was another, and by the end of January, the problem of whether Reagan would approve Crimson Sky was becoming especially sticky. One difficulty was that the two men Reagan had named to head his Justice department were legally prohibited from considering the matter. Los Angeles attorney William French Smith, long a close friend of Reagan's, had been nominated to be attorney general, but Smith had for years been on the board of directors of Pacific Telephone and thus was forced to recuse himself from any role in the AT&T case. Privately, Smith's friends and colleagues made it clear that the new attorney general thought that the case was a mistake and probably should be dismissed outright, but they also made it clear that Smith would go to great lengths to avoid even the appearance of involvement in the matter. Reagan's designated number-two man at Justice, Deputy Attorney General Edward Schmults, a conservative Wall Street attorney, was also recused because of dealings that his law firm had with AT&T. Since, in late January, Reagan had not yet named an Antitrust chief, there was not a single political appointee at Justice who was in a position to review Democrat Sandy Litvack's deal. If Litvack went ahead and approved the settlement anyway before leaving the department, he would be taking the risk that his decision might later be overturned.

Meanwhile, the teams of staff lawyers continued to refine the proposed "final judgment" of *U.S.* v. *AT&T*. Early in February, a revised draft of the document was finally sent to the Antitrust front office for Litvack's review. In just a couple of weeks, Litvack would be leaving Justice to return to his private practice at Donovan, Leisure in New York. Despite the lack of guidance from the new Republican administration, Litvack had no choice but to make his decision about the deal immediately. If the trial was to continue, if Gerry Connell was to begin presenting the government's case on March 4, the trial staff lawyers needed to redouble their preparatory work; Litvack knew that morale on the staff had slipped because of the impending settlement, and that Justice's case was not in proper shape. All along, Litvack's concern about the Crimson Sky terms had focused on the negotiations over equal interconnection for MCI and other long-distance companies. He had readily accepted AT&T's terms for divestiture, but he had also withheld judgment on the final package until the two sides had agreed on equal access rules. After all, the division's own Relief Task Force, headed by Jim Denvir, had concluded that the most important goal of the case was divestiture of all the operating companies, not just Western, because the advent of long-distance competition by MCI and others meant that Long Lines should ideally be separated from the local exchange monopolies. The equal access rules were a kind of injunctive substitute for such a radical breakup for the entire phone company. If they worked, they might achieve the goal of equal competition without forcing the subsidized operating companies to make it financially on their own.

One afternoon shortly after the drafted final judgment arrived in his office, Litvack and his deputy, Richard Favretto, set aside time to read carefully the equal-access rules that had been negotiated by the two sides. In the margins of his draft, Litvack wrote skeptical questions like "Who?", "How?", and "When?" next to the passages about equal access.

When he was finished reading, Favretto came into Litvack's office. "What do you think?" he asked.

"What do *you* think?" said Litvack.

"Forget it," was Favretto's answer. "This thing ain't never going to work."

"You're right," acknowledged Litvack. "I'm afraid you're right about that."

But despite Litvack's discouraging assessment, the decision was not yet final. When the two teams of staff lawyers had negotiated the document reviewed by Litvack, they had set aside some issues that they were unable to agree upon. Most of those issues concerned the equal access rules. The idea was that just before Judge Greene's deadline, Litvack and Trienens would personally sit down and iron out the remaining disputes. The final meeting between the two was scheduled for February 23. Trienens even flew to Washington for the session. Based on conversations with his own staff, he believed that the deal would be concluded in a matter of days.

The night before his meeting with Trienens, Sandy Litvack called Jim Denvir. "I just want to go over these issues once more before I talk to Howard," he said. "The question is, what can we live with? If he won't move on most of these rules, can we do better by going to trial?"

"I think we can do better," Denvir told him.

The next day, when Trienens called Litvack about the scheduled meeting, Litvack told him preemptively that the deal was off. Trienens was stunned and angry. After seven years and millions of dollars in expenses, AT&T was just days away from finally solving its antitrust problems. Why had Justice suddenly changed its mind?

The truth was difficult to determine, especially for Howard Trienens and Charlie Brown. Litvack had discussed his concerns about the equal access rules with some of the Justice staff lawyers, but he had not emphasized them to Trienens. And strangely, when Litvack wrote to Judge Greene that same day to inform him that the settlement talks had collapsed, he did not mention his own objections to Crimson Sky. Instead, Litvack blamed the deal's failure on the Reagan administration, and specifically its recently announced Antitrust chief nominee, Stanford University law professor William Baxter.

Litvack did write, "As of this date, no final settlement agreement has been reached . . . and, in my view, it is extremely doubtful one will be reached by March 2." But then, Litvack went on to tell Judge Greene, "However, even if such an agreement were achieved within the specified time, the fact is that the terms of any such proposal would have to be reviewed by the new assistant attorney general, who will be responsible for the decision in light of the recusal of Attorney General Smith and Deputy Attorney General Schmults.... On February 20, President Reagan announced his intention to nominate William F. Baxter to be my successor. I am advised that while Professor Baxter will consider the AT&T case as a priority matter, he has not reviewed and will not be in a position to review the terms of any proposed agreement, or to reach any view one way or the other...until after March 2."

What made the circumstances of Crimson Sky's collapse all the more confusing to Trienens and Brown was that, in the days following Litvack's unilateral announcement, Baxter let it be known that it was he, not Litvack, who had finally decided that the deal was no good. This directly contradicted Litvack's assertion to Greene that Baxter would "not be in a position to ...reach any view one way or the other" until after the judge's early March deadline. Years later, Litvack and Baxter continued to have opposite recollections about the matter. Litvack remembered that he did not discuss the case with Baxter until after a decision was made, while Baxter recalled that Litvack was ready to approve the deal until he (Baxter) decided that it was unacceptable.

To Trienens and Brown, the confusion was especially disheartening, but by no means was it an isolated example of the ways in which politics and bureaucratic infighting skewed the relationship between the phone company and the government. As had been the case with Ken Anderson's menu deal, Crimson Sky was undermined by the pending departure of Justice's main negotiator, Litvack. But also like the menu settlement, Crimson Sky probably would never have been initiated if Litvack hadn't wanted to make his mark on the AT&T case before he left the government. To AT&T, the whole thing seemed like a vicious circle. Each departing Justice lawyer offers a deal to the phone company, and then the deal is nixed by the lawyer's successor, who thinks that *he* should be the one to decide on any settlement. When the successor leaves, he offers his own deal, and the cycle begins again.

In late February 1981, when Sandy Litvack cleared out his

belongings from the Antitrust chief's cavernous office in the main Justice building, leaving behind hard feelings and the remnants of a once-promising deal, no one on either side would have guessed that his successor, William Baxter, an ideological academic who hadn't argued in a courtroom since before 1960, would be the one to break the pattern. Much to George Saunders' satisfaction, it appeared now that *U.S.* v. *AT&T* would be decided in court by Judge Harold Greene, "the man who had the answers."

Chapter 17

Litigating to the Eyeballs

THE first time that the Justice staff lawyers working on the AT&T case met Bill Baxter, their new boss, was on Friday, February 27, an unseasonably warm winter day in Washington.

The lawyers—Gerry Connell, Peter Kenney, Jim Denvir, Jeff Blumenfeld, and two or three others—walked down from their office on 12th Street to the main Justice building. The sun was bright and the air was fresh and springlike. It was a day that offered spiritual renewal, even to lawyers who had been working seventy or eighty hours a week on one case for six consecutive months.

They found Baxter in one of the deputy assistant attorney general's offices near the Antitrust chief's office on the third floor; Sandy Litvack had not yet completely moved out, so Baxter was ensconced in temporary quarters. The purpose of the meeting was purely introductory, a chance for working-level lawyers to meet the man who would dictate policy to them over the next four years. There had been some uneasy humor on the way down. None of the top lawyers running Justice's case against AT&T was an ideological conservative, and several of them had strongly held liberal views. Politics was not generally of overriding importance to the staff lawyers—Gerry Connell, for example, had worked easily with nearly a dozen

Antitrust chiefs for over two decades—but the lawyers felt some trepidation about what impact the triumphant, conservative "Reagan revolution" would have on Justice's Antitrust division. Regardless of political ideology, the staff lawyers felt strongly that the division's work was important and that it ought not to be emasculated.

As a result of some detective work, however, they did know that even if Baxter intended to reduce the division's staff by half, or if he was inclined to dismiss pending cases left and right, as had been rumored, the new Antitrust chief was unlikely to interfere with the AT&T trial team.

Baxter had been formally nominated by President Reagan the day before, Thursday, although rumors of his appointment had been floating around Washington since early February. As soon as Baxter's name had surfaced, several of the Justice staffers had rushed over to the nearest law library to look up everything that had been written by the prospective Antitrust chief in law reviews, academic journals, and the like. The trial team lawyers assumed that any Reagan nominee would take a conservative, perhaps even hostile, view of antitrust law enforcement. And since Baxter, if he was confirmed as expected by the Senate, would soon have the power to dismiss cases that he didn't like, the lawyers wanted to know if he had ever expressed any strong opinion about *U.S.* v. *AT&T*.

The search was at first disheartening, because on just about every issue of antitrust law Baxter conformed to expectations. He was a starkly ideological conservative, a free-market theoretician, a man so certain that his own economic views were right that he didn't hesitate to call the U.S. Supreme Court "wacko" and "ludicrous" when it disagreed with him. Though he was not formally trained in economics, he often described himself as an economist because his opinions about antitrust enforcement were based on his own, somewhat peculiar, notions about economic efficiency. Many practices that liberal and moderate antitrust lawyers viewed with suspicion Baxter considered acceptable, even desirable, by-products of free-market wheeling and dealing. For example, he believed that some kinds of mergers between large corporations should actually be encouraged and that some forms of price-fixing by companies benefited consumers. Too often, Baxter said, the Justice department's antitrust enforcement "penalized [big companies] for their large size." Big was not necessarily bad, Baxter believed, an opinion he shared, to the consternation of many of the Justice staff lawyers, with George Saunders and the executives of AT&T.

As for the AT&T case itself, however, the law review articles and interviews revealed a surprising quirk in Baxter's rigid conservative ideology. It seemed, at least according to his published writings, that Baxter considered *U.S.* v. *AT&T* to be, as one of the trial team lawyers put it later, "the one good thing the Antitrust division had done in the last thirty years." The reason Baxter liked the case had nothing to do with its factual merits, or with the history of John deButts, MCI, and telephone industry competition. Rather, Baxter was enamored of the government's relief theory in the case—which sought complete separation of the regulated local operating companies from relatively unregulated Western, Bell Labs, the Long Lines—because it was a flawless example of the free-market economic model Baxter believed in. Baxter argued that no one company should be able to integrate regulated and unregulated divisions of its business, because then it could use the "safe" profits from its regulated side to subsidize the prices of its unregulated products. Such "cross subsidies," Baxter wrote, skewed the otherwise pristine mechanisms of a free-market economy. Of course, the role of subsidies in the telephone industry was so complex as to be inscrutable, and in some cases the subsidies were designed to achieve social goals such as low-cost local phone service. But Baxter believed that unfettered competition was the only efficient way to achieve such social ends.

In person that afternoon, Baxter seemed to some of the AT&T trial team lawyers to be much like his writings: brilliant but academic, stridently ideological, arrogant, dispassionate. He was a severe-looking man in his early fifties, with coal-black slicked-down hair, cold, dark eyes, sunken cheeks, and a sallow complexion. He chain smoked unfiltered cigarettes, and his manner of speech was laconic and affected. Even in casual conversation, he seemed to be constantly on guard, distant, though he never hesitated to speak his mind bluntly if economics or legal theory was being discussed. Opinions about Baxter among the trial team lawyers varied, but to some he seemed like a mean-spirited Victorian schoolmaster—cold, empirical, utilitarian. Baxter was always talking about the importance of "data." He was divorced, but he had come to Washington with a Stanford University statistician with whom he lived. Once asked why he did not marry the woman, Baxter said because to do so would raise his tax bill. Some of the Justice lawyers thought Baxter's answer summed him up very nicely. Others, though, took note of Baxter's acidly dry sense of humor and the sincere enthusiasm he displayed when talking about skiing, tennis, or tournament bridge, and they chalked his impassive qualities up to the eccentricities of a sheltered university professor.

Whether or not they gave Baxter's personality the benefit of the doubt, the trial team lawyers were uniformly skeptical about his practical qualifications for his job as Antitrust chief. Historically, nearly all the political appointees who ran the division had at least some real-world experience as litigators: they knew how to try a case, how to assemble and prepare witnesses, how to evaluate judges or an opponent's litigation strategy. Sandy Litvack, for example, was a lawyer who knew little about the intricacies of economic theory but who could "prep" a cross examination as well as any trial lawyer in the division. "Fundamentally, I'm a litigator," Litvack said frequently. The AT&T trial team and its leader, Gerry Connell, were not looking to Baxter for hands-on assistance as the trial progressed, but they were concerned that without any practical understanding of how a trial was conducted, Baxter might hinder their courtroom battle against George Saunders.

As the meeting got under way that Friday, those fears were quickly borne out. "I think you understand what I think about this case," Baxter said coolly. He then reiterated his view that it was economically harmful for AT&T to own Long Lines, Western Electric, and all the operating companies. But while summarizing his opinions, Baxter never once referred to any of the

specific facts in the case—the controversies over PCAs, FX
lines, Execunet, and so on—as evidence that supported his
theory. Instead, it seemed to some of the trial lawyers that
Baxter believed that he could simply sit down with AT&T and
explain to them the theory of why it was harmful for them to
own the operating companies and they would naturally agree
to divest them.

"There's a problem with settling the case once it goes to
trial. There's a question about *estoppel*," one of the staff lawyers
said, referring to Howard Trienens' worry that once evidence
was taken, private litigants could piggyback on *U.S.* v. *AT&T*
if it was settled.

Deadly serious, Baxter replied, "Well, maybe you could
put on your bad evidence first."

The trial team lawyers stifled laughter. Afterwards, Baxter's
suggestion became a basis for them to refer to the new Antitrust
chief as a "space cadet." Sometimes, when a similarly off-the-
wall Baxter remark was reported to the trial staff, one of them
would cup his hands over his mouth and squawk, "Earth to
Baxter. Earth to Baxter. Come in."

"Trial's starting pretty soon, right?" Baxter asked. There
was an edge to that question, as if Baxter was concerned that
the career lawyers might be disappointed about the collapse of
Crimson Sky. "Are you going to prove that there's a monopoly
here, an unregulated part of the business there, and that they're
cross-subsidizing each other?"

"That's right," Gerry Connell answered. "That's the case."
Or at least, that was the part of the case pertaining to divestiture
relief—the only aspect of *U.S.* v. *AT&T* that Baxter seemed to
care about.

"That's fine," said Baxter. "Go ahead and do it. Let me
know if you need anything."

When William Baxter's nomination was announced by
President Reagan, Howard Trienens and George Saunders had
instructed AT&T's legal staff to locate and copy the same law
review articles, speeches, and interviews that had been assembled by the Justice trial team. For Trienens and Charlie Brown,

the news that Baxter regarded the government's case against AT&T as perhaps the Antitrust division's only meritorious endeavor in the last several decades was especially devastating: on the heels of Crimson Sky's unexplained collapse, it was the second major blow for the phone company in less than a week. In fact, based on statements made by Baxter, Trienens believed that it was the new Antitrust chief, not Sandy Litvack, who had unilaterally ended the Crimson Sky negotiations and ordered the government lawyers to prepare for trial on March 4. Trienens and Brown had both cautiously assumed that President Reagan would appoint an Antitrust chief who shared Regan's apparent view that *U.S.* v. *AT&T* was a mistake. When questions about the case occasionally arose during the 1980 presidential campaign, Reagan had responded by telling a story about his days in Hollywood. He recalled that the price of a first-class stamp in the 1940s was just a few cents, while a long-distance phone call was fairly expensive. Since that time, Reagan said, the price of postage had risen almost tenfold, while the cost of long-distance calls had dropped dramatically. "And, of course," the candidate said, emphasizing his theme that big government was the root of America's problems, "the government is suing the phone company." The line had garnered Reagan a few laughs on the stump, and it had heartened the executives at AT&T. Why, then, had Reagan appointed a man to run the Antitrust division who did not even consider the substantial divestiture offered by AT&T in Crimson Sky to be an adequate settlement? The answer, Trienens suspected, was that the Reagan transition team, which briefed the president about his major appointments, had never investigated Baxter's opinions about the case. They had probably assumed that since Baxter took such a generally conservative view of antitrust enforcement, he therefore had no great sympathy for the government's prosecution of the phone company.

This miscalculation about Baxter was especially frustrating to Brown and Trienens because both of them knew, based on personal conversations before and after the campaign, that several of Reagan's closest advisors—William Smith, counselor Edwin Meese, Commerce Secretary Malcolm Baldrige, Defense

Secretary Caspar Weinberger, and others—believed unequivocally that the government's case against the phone company was misguided and that it should be dismissed. Since Attorney General Smith was recused, however, Baxter was the top-ranking official at the Justice department in charge of *U.S. v. AT&T*. That meant that if the AT&T sympathizers in the Reagan inner circle were going to intervene in the case before liberal Judge Greene had a chance to rule on it at trial, they would have quickly to do an end run around Baxter and the Antitrust division.

First off the ball was Caspar Weinberger, a shrill and combative Nixon administration veteran whose personal mission under Reagan would be to restore the Pentagon to a position of bureaucratic supremacy in Washington after four years of what conservatives believed was a precipitous decline for the military—in power, prestige, and funding—under President Carter. In an early review of which specific programs, weapons systems, and policies were needed to bolster the nation's defenses, Weinberger heard from the Defense Communications Agency (DCA) that, in its opinion, dismissal of *U.S. v. AT&T* should be one of the secretary's highest priorities. The DCA worked closely with AT&T to design, maintain, and operate the strategic communications network that served military, intelligence, and other national security services. Among other things, this "defense net," as the system was sometimes called, provided for sophisticated communications between political and military officials in the event of a nuclear crisis. It was the opinion of the DCA staff, as well as of its leader, General Hillsman, that if the Justice department succeeded in breaking up AT&T, the nation's defense communications system would be severely impaired and its national security threatened. Of course, the communications experts DCA relied on in formulating this view were AT&T employees, who were not likely to offer objective analysis of *U.S. v. AT&T*. And it was also true that by relying on a centralized, large "sole supplier" such as AT&T for communications, Pentagon bureaucrats enjoyed both convenience and protection from mistakes by smaller, potentially unreliable contractors. The cozy relationship between DCA and

AT&T no doubt predisposed the defense department to defend the phone company against the Justice lawsuit. Nonetheless, it was an unavoidable fact that Pentagon officials, all the way up to Secretary Weinberger himself, agreed that if AT&T were dismantled by Justice, the national security costs would far outweigh whatever competitive benefits might accrue.

By early March, just weeks after Baxter took over, Weinberger's staff had drafted and the secretary had signed a letter to Attorney General Smith urging that *U.S.* v. *AT&T* be dismissed. A copy of the letter was sent to Smith's office at Justice.

What followed was a series of miscommunications and misunderstandings that at times resembled a bureaucratic version of a Keystone Kops movie. And when it was over, Howard Trienens and Charlie Brown would have said, the bad guys got away.

Weinberger's staff was apparently unaware that, because of his past affiliations with Pacific Telephone, Smith was recused from considering any issues affecting the phone company. So when Smith received the defense secretary's letter, there was nothing he could have done but pass it on to Baxter. Attached to Weinberger's letter, however, was another letter from the Joint Chiefs of Staff to the secretary of defense outlining some specific reasons why DCA and other Pentagon officials objected to Justice's lawsuit. This second letter contained some sensitive information about the military's defense net, and thus the whole package had been classified "secret" by the Pentagon. Because in early March Baxter had not yet been confirmed by the Senate—that wouldn't happen until March 26—the new Antitrust chief had not yet received his security clearance and thus was prohibited from reading Weinberger's communiqué. The letter was placed in the attorney general's safe. No one at Justice bothered to tell Weinberger or other Defense officials that it would be a few weeks before Baxter could respond to his request. Thus when they heard nothing from Smith, Weinberger and his staff assumed that Justice was ignoring their private approach and was, in effect, challenging them to take the issue public.

A few weeks later, on March 23, Weinberger testified in a

closed hearing before the Senate Armed Services Committee
that the AT&T case should be dropped for national security
reasons. "It seems to me essential that we keep together this
one communications network we now have and have to rely
on," Weinberger said. "None of the systems are going to be
useful if we can't tie them together into an effective communications net. The AT&T network is the most important net we
have to service our strategic systems. . . . I have written to the
attorney general and urged very strongly that the suit be dismissed."

In early April, Weinberger's secret testimony was leaked
to the *Wall Street Journal*. Baxter was at first confused and then
angry that Weinberger had gone behind the Antitrust division's
back in an attempt to sabotage the case. On the rainy morning
of April 9, the day after the *Journal* story appeared, Baxter held
a press conference in his office to respond.

"Defense department concern is not a new phenomenon,"
Baxter told the more than two dozen reporters who showed up
to hear him. "It is a position that I think has to be taken seriously. I will take it seriously, but I do not intend to fold up my
tent and go away because the department of Defense expresses
concern."

"Based on your review of the case," Baxter was asked, "are
you confident that the case that the Justice department is bringing is solid, and that you will be able to litigate in both the
liability and the relief issues?"

"Yes," he answered. "I think the case is perfectly sound.
I am sufficiently egotistical to think that if I had been here from
the beginning, I would have put together some of those evidentiary packages in a little different way so that they carried
on their face, to a greater extent than they now do, the theory
that underlies the case. But it is a good case even in its present
condition, and we have a very good chance of winning it. It
has a sound theoretical core, and I intend to litigate it to the
eyeballs."

The cameras clicked and the reporters in Baxter's office
exploded in laughter.

There are few things that journalists in Washington enjoy

more than a public feud between high-ranking government officials, and thus Baxter's remarks about Weinberger's attempted intervention in *U.S.* v. *AT&T* were widely and prominently reported. Now that the controversy was being played out in the newspapers, there was little hope that AT&T could quietly and quickly maneuver inside the Reagan administration to have the case dismissed for national security reasons. Trienens and Brown had not given up hope that Reagan would eventually step in and personally order that the case be dismissed, but clearly, it was going to take more than a letter from Cap Weinberger to do the job. In the meantime, it was up to George Saunders to hold the phone company's ground in court. In the long run, Baxter, a mere assistant attorney general, could not be expected to fight off the efforts of cabinet-level administration officials such as Weinberger, Ed Meese, and Malcolm Baldrige to drop the case. But until Baxter's authority was somehow circumvented, it was crucial that Saunders publicly present the best case possible against Gerry Connell—eyeball to eyeball.

Chapter **18**

Connell's Deception

I T did not happen because of any one thing. It was not a scintillating question, or a flourishing rhetorical speech, or a surprise witness called to the stand and brilliantly examined; such flashes of style were rarely, if ever, in evidence. Rather, it happened slowly, haltingly, in some cases grudgingly—but nonetheless inexorably. By early April, after three weeks of trial, the lawyers on both sides of Judge Greene's courtroom had come to the realization that Gerry Connell was putting on a tremendous case against AT&T.

It was the little things that began to add up, the subtle touches of experience and the nuggets of wisdom accumulated from dozens of obscure antitrust cases tried by Connell over the years in places like Tucson, Arizona, and Cincinnati, Ohio. It was the way he studied Judge Greene, day after day, scrutinizing the judge's habits, charting his moods, adjusting in tandem the presentation of the government's case. Connell noticed early on, for example, that when Greene was becoming impatient with a witness, the judge began to tap his pencil nervously and unconsciously, like a drummer. Whenever Connell saw that pencil tapping, he immediately ended his examination of the witness on the stand, or else quickly moved on to the next point. Then, too, it was Connell's self-effacing style, the way he seemed always to be apologizing to Judge

Greene or asking the court's indulgence. One day, one of the lawyers at the AT&T defense table looked over at Connell and had a flash of insight. Connell was talking to Judge Greene, and, as always, Connell's voice was mild and steady, his drooping face modestly averted. And then, as happened frequently, Connell paused in mid-sentence, eyes toward the ceiling, searching for a word that had escaped him. "Umm ... Uh ..." Connell said. And the AT&T lawyer realized: *He's doing it on purpose. He knows what word he wants to use. It's just part of his act.* Connell was like a courtroom version of the bumbling but brilliant television detective Columbo. His self-effacement was not a cynical calculation—it reflected Connell's actual personality. But it was fundamentally deceptive. And for the AT&T lawyers trying to outwit him before Judge Greene, dangerous.

All through the blustery month of March, Gerry Connell's case "went in," as the lawyers put it. Justice's presentation of its facts closely mirrored Connell's personal style: it was dogged, pedestrian, and effective. In the early weeks, there were two or three witnesses each day. Connell began with the telephone equipment part of the case, not for strategic reasons but because it was the only section that was completely ready for trial; the lull in trial preparations caused by the Crimson Sky negotiations had hampered the government more than it had AT&T. The early witnesses were the owners and executives of telephone equipment companies who had been required by AT&T in the early 1970s to purchase the phone company's protective coupling arrangements for products such as answering machines. Connell examined many of them himself, but occasionally another lawyer from the government trial team would take over. Connell boosted morale among the nearly four dozen young lawyers in his charge during the trial by promising that every attorney on the team would be allowed to examine at least one witness in court. It was a safe idea. All the direct examinations, even those presented by Connell or his senior lieutenants, were rehearsed, question by question, the night before. Connell intended to stick to an old rule of cautious trial lawyering: Never ask a question to which you don't already know the answer.

Oddly, Gerry Connell's case against AT&T was both exceedingly broad and exceedingly narrow. On the one hand, Connell intended to call dozens of witnesses to the stand over a four-month period. Some of the witnesses, such as those called in March, would testify about their attempts to sell telephone equipment in competition with Western and about the problems caused by AT&T's insistence on protective couplers. Some witnesses would testify about the procurement practices of the Bell operating companies, and about how most of AT&T's own purchasing—on behalf of its customers, to whom it leased equipment—was done internally, from Western Electric, to the exclusion of outside competitors. Other witnesses would testify that the FCC was incapable of regulating a company as large as AT&T, and that as a result the phone company priced its services and products without regard to their cost.* And finally, in the last section of his case, Connell intended to call a number of "experts" to testify about why it was necessary, given all the previous evidence presented by the government, to break apart AT&T.

This broad canvas of accusations against the phone company went all the way back to the investigations conducted by Phil Verveer in the early 1970s. Sometimes, the witnesses called by Connell testified about specific events that occurred as long ago as the 1950s and the early 1960s. There was no "smoking gun," as Judge Greene put it at one point, in the government's story about AT&T's monopolization of the telecommunications industry, although the discussion about MCI held by AT&T executives at Key Largo in May 1972 was offered as anecdotal evidence of the phone company's motives. The real purpose of

---

*This section of the government's case was especially complicated and confusing. The government did not try to prove that AT&T priced its competitive products below cost, as would be common in an antitrust case. Rather, Connell tried to show that ineffective FCC regulation and a historically haphazard system of internal cross subsidies allowed AT&T to set whatever prices it liked, depending on how much competition the phone company faced. The attempt to prove this required reams and reams of paper containing AT&T cost studies, FCC cost studies, government cost studies, and so on. When the pricing witnesses—mostly academic economists—were on the stand, the hallways outside Judge Greene's courtroom were filled with dozens of boxes containing cost studies that might be referred to in testimony. One day, Judge John J. Sirica walked down the hall and, seeing all the boxes, quipped, "I'm glad I only had Watergate."

Connell's case was to present slowly to Judge Greene a pre-
ponderance of evidence about a "pattern" of abusive behavior
by AT&T. The idea was that fact upon fact, witness upon witness, issue upon issue, the totality of AT&T's gargantuan size
and of its dominance of the phone industry would seep into
Judge Greene's mind like rain into a groundwater reservoir.
And then, during the relatively narrow part of the case that
really mattered—the MCI story, the basis for the government's
request for full operating company divestiture—this reservoir
of condemning evidence would provide the judge with context
and support for the conclusion that AT&T had wronged MCI
and should be broken up. The truth was that the MCI case
turned on a specific, disputatious, and controversial story: John
deButts' "decision to decide" and the subsequent rulings by
the FCC's Common Carrier Bureau that allowed MCI to sell FX
lines to its customers. A jury in Chicago had seen the story one
way. Judge Greene might see it another. Strategically, the best
protection for Gerry Connell's government trial team was to
hedge its reliance on the MCI story by offering Greene as much
additional evidence about AT&T's monopolistic tendencies as
possible.

Thus from its beginning, the trial of *U.S.* v. *AT&T* seemed,
to the public, a great, impenetrable muddle. It was impossible
for a casual observer to comprehend the testimony of the myriad witnesses paraded before Judge Greene by Gerry Connell.
Their stories were not related to a central theme, building toward a climax; each was a splintered tale, an anecdote about
the telephone industry in the mid-1970s. Each was confined by
its own peculiar details and the character of its teller, the witness, typically an uncharismatic businessman whose words,
stilted and riddled with technical jargon, had been rehearsed
for days by the government's lawyers. Even the newspaper and
magazine reporters who covered the trial seemed for the most
part unable to communicate any essential story to their readers:
the government's case was too complex, too fractured, and,
above all, too boring. Within weeks after Connell's presentation
began, the crushing crowds attendant at the opening arguments had thinned considerably, until the daily audience in

Greene's wood-paneled courtroom consisted almost entirely of lawyers and telephone industry executives. The case had become a private drama, played by and for the "experts" who had everything to win or lose by its outcome. So oblivious was the public and the press to this backroom legal poker game that after it was over, and the fate of AT&T had been decided, *Business Week* reported to its half million readers that the case had never gone to trial. Hardly anyone noticed the mistake.

Of course, the indifference of the public and the press suited Gerry Connell just fine. The crowds, the lights, and the attention on opening day had made him sweaty and uncomfortable. He was not a showman, like George Saunders. *U.S. v. AT&T* was by far the greatest challenge of his career—working eighty, sometimes a hundred hours a week, the case had taken him over, to the point where there was little time in his life to think about anything else. All Connell wanted was to do the job right, quietly, patiently, indefatigably, until Judge Greene finally saw things his way.

The Madison Hotel, across the street from the *Washington Post* at the corner of 15th and M Streets in northwest Washington, was George Saunders' home during most of 1981. In Chicago, the headquarters city of Sidley & Austin, Saunders had an apartment and a wife, but he rarely saw either of them. (Saunders' wife at the time, his second, was an attorney at the law firm of Jenner & Block, the main outside counsel for MCI. Saunders met her on an airplane. She did not do any telephone industry work.) During the government trial, AT&T rented several expensive suites at the Madison on a long-term basis so its top lawyers and executives could live comfortably when they were in town. Saunders' two-room suite—replete with three couches, two polished coffee tables, a large TV in a walnut cabinet, a dining table with chairs, and a refrigerator—was on the tenth floor. As Gerry Connell's presentation of the government's case got under way, the suite became the headquarters for the AT&T trial team when it was away from court. There was a kind of informal hierarchy among the Sidley and AT&T lawyers that set down who was allowed to spend how much time with George Saunders at the Madison. After a day of trial, the lawyers all drifted back to Saunders' suite for a cocktail-hour rumination of events in court led mainly by Saunders, who poured generously from pitchers of room-service martinis. If Howard Trienens was in town, he would join the group, but Trienens spent most of his time at 195 Broadway in New York with Charlie Brown. By seven-thirty or eight, the informal discussion gave way to serious planning for the next day's witnesses. Michael Yauch or John Zeglis, two of Saunders' key lieutenants from Sidley & Austin, would usher out those lawyers who were no longer needed; if everyone who wanted to be in on the action was allowed to stay, nothing productive would be accomplished. Yauch usually returned to AT&T's "litigation support center" at 499 South Capitol Street, just below Capitol Hill. There the phone company maintained voluminous files, numbering tens of millions of pages, pertaining to its various antitrust problems. AT&T employed around-the-clock shifts of paralegals, document clerks, typists, word processors, and copy clerks to help George Saunders locate and prepare the documents he needed in court. The AT&T lawyers referred to this expensive and efficient operation as "the back room," but that March, Judge Greene began to call it "the well-oiled machine."

At the Madison Hotel nerve center, the main challenge facing Saunders and his lieutenants was how to devise and implement a cross-examination strategy that would effectively counter the dogged, dispassionate presentation by Gerry Connell.

Saunders' courtroom strategy was dictated by a number of factors, not the least of which was his own passionate belief in the rightness of AT&T's defense. Over the seven years that he had worked on the case, Saunders had memorized virtually every minute detail of *U.S.* v. *AT&T*: dates, names, places, and numbers. In his mind, these particulars seemed to be organized and connected into large, sequential, coherent arguments, each related to the other. The whole of his argument—Saunders' fundamental contention that during the early 1970s, given the exigencies caused by MCI and the FCC, AT&T acted reasonably, not malevolently—was greater than the sum of its parts. Whereas Gerry Connell cut and pasted his argument together, creating a vast collage of disparate evidence, Saunders' purpose was to transform this collection of unrelated bits and parts into a mosaic, a sweeping and well-defined picture of misguided government regulation and greedy, creamskimming opportunists such as McGowan. If Saunders tried to attack the government's case on its own terms, if he responded to each of Connell's anecdotes in isolation, his cause would fail. Besides, that wasn't how Saunders saw the case. To him, U.S. v. AT&T was not confusing, or unwieldy, or even very complicated. It was a "ripoff" and an "outrage" that AT&T's competitors, and the government, had twisted the facts around to make AT&T appear the villain, when all the company was trying to do was adapt to change while continuing to serve the public and its shareholders well. The government's stories, the tales told by Gerry Connell's parade of businessman witnesses, were either trivial, or irrelevant, or explainable for any number of other reasons: sour grapes from bankrupt companies, confusing or contradictory regulations, rapid technology change, and so on. But to Saunders, that wasn't the point. The point was that U.S. v. AT&T was really a case about the relationship between the phone company MCI and the FCC—about John deButts, Bill McGowan, Bernie Strassburg, Walter Hinchman, and others. Once you boiled away the fatty stories about protective couplers, operating company procurement, and pricing, MCI was the meat that remained. Before the MCI witnesses took the stand, it was important that Saunders, and Judge Greene, not become too distracted by anything else.

In the meantime, there were all these government witnesses, unrelated to the MCI story, who had to be cross-examined. It would be impossible for Saunders to convince Greene that all these witnesses who complained day after day about AT&T's behavior were liars, frauds, or greedy opportunists. Many of them were mild-mannered, unassuming men, and, like Gerry Connell, they stuck to the facts. They talked about how, even though they had good products, they had trouble selling to the Bell operating companies because of Western Electric. They listed how long it took AT&T to provide them with PCAs back in the early 1970s. They estimated how much money they had lost because of AT&T's allegedly anticompetitive prices. And when they were done, Gerry Connell would quietly turn to Judge Greene and say, without pretension, "That's all, Your Honor."

So Saunders had to take the offensive. Instead of simply trying to impeach his opponent's case—the normal goal of cross-examination—he had to begin to present his own argument affirmatively when he questioned Connell's witnesses. He had to use cross-examination as a platform, exploit it as an opportunity to educate Judge Greene about what really happened in the telecommunications industry during the 1970s. That meant he had to take chances. He had to prod Connell's witnesses on subjects they knew little about: the FCC, the technical specifications of the phone network, public interest subsidies, the history of the telephone industry. He had to ask questions that were little more than speeches in thin disguise.

He had to ask questions to which he did not know the answers.

Early on, for example, Saunders cross-examined a somewhat unusual entrepreneur named Ronald Maxwell, who had been affiliated with Stanford University and who had been called by Connell to testify about the problems his company, called VADIC, had encountered with AT&T during the early 1970s.

"Let me sum this up..." Saunders said, for the benefit of Judge Greene. "Is it possible, in your opinion, as a philosopher/engineer, designer/inventor, that all we have here is just a good faith dispute about which way to go in a market that was evolving, one in which tariff standards were little understood by the people who were actually involved? Is that what we have here?"

"Sir," said Maxwell, "I think what we have here is the prologue of a document."

"The prologue of the document?"

Unexpectedly, Maxwell held up a paper that he had written about his company back in the early 1970s. "The prologue of the document, which characterizes VADIC as rather small and running around beating its chest. And AT&T is rather large. The practical consequence of this to us was we were deprived of a substantial market by the efforts of AT&T."

"Just so future generations won't be deprived of this, I will have you read the prologue of the document into the record," said Judge Greene.

"Do you want *me* to read it?" Maxwell asked.

"Yes," said Greene, "you are the witness."

"Do I have to read the epilogue, too?"

"I didn't see any epilogue."

"Some people say it is better yet," muttered Saunders.

" 'Hark!' " Maxwell began. " 'Do you hear? That slight patter, some timid squeaks, growing louder. Can it be what I think? Nay, they could not have. Yet, it gathers sound, sounding stronger, with determination. They must be mad. Elephants are dancing, themselves paced by mounting frenzy. Anything will be crushed beneath their supple, stamping feet. I see them. A small cloud rises from their exertions. It's a herd of mice: the VADIC mice. And they are running, why they are hurtling themselves towards the Elephant Bell! Surely they are doomed!'

"The epilogue is: 'As one can easily judge, we have not learned of fate's wish for VADIC's mice. Last seen, they were beginning to scurry up the tail of Elephant Bell, hoping, one presumes, to move faster than the giant's swishing nose and to avoid any excremental indignities. A few mice, apparently confused by physical similarities between the two beasts, migrated towards Elephant IBM, but no one knows what happened when they got near.' "

All of this was a bit more than Saunders was ready for. "Now," he recovered, having taken himself far down the path already, "in the opening statement of this case, Mr. Connell, perhaps borrowing your analogy and figure of speech, characterized the Bell System as an elephant and suggested that once in a while it reaches out and crushes someone. VADIC is not anyone who has been crushed, or they ... Mr. Maxwell, in your ten years at Stanford University, did you have occasion to make the acquaintance of the writings of George Santayana?"

"Not that I remember. I did read some of it."

"Are you familiar with his criticism of historians who write history as though they are standing in front of the crowd, waving their hands?"

"Sir, there is a crowd here."

"Your version of the story is very selective, isn't it? . . ."

And on Saunders went. Day after day that spring, he personally handled every cross-examination, and increasingly, as happened with Maxwell and his VADIC mice, his questions and speeches carried the courtroom dialogue away from the mundane particulars of Gerry Connell's accumulated facts. Many times, his larger points hit home. In other instances, Saunders seemed to get more from the witnesses than he bargained for. Overall, the government and AT&T seemed to be trying two different cases around the same set of facts. Connell's was a determined, if anecdotal, story of widespread malfeasance by the world's largest corporation; at every opportunity, Connell emphasized AT&T's almost incomprehensible size. Saunders' was a sweeping, thematic epic about regulation, politics, and the history of the telephone industry. Since he said very little and only occasionally tapped his pencil, it was impossible, yet, to guess which case Judge Greene believed in.

Both sides were confident it was theirs.

Chapter 19

Saunders and McGowan

"YOUR Honor," said Gerry Connell shortly after 4 P.M. on the gloomy afternoon of Thursday, April 9, "we are now at the end of my current direct examination of Mr. McGowan."

"All right. Mr. Saunders," said Judge Greene ironically, "do you have any cross-examination?"

Saunders smiled. Yes, he had a few questions.

The seven hours of direct testimony by William McGowan that day, the first of four exhaustive sessions the MCI chairman would endure before Judge Greene, had not been one of Gerry Connell's most effective presentations. This was not Connell's fault. For days prior to McGowan's appearance, Connell and Peter Kenney, the Justice lawyer in charge of the MCI section of the case, had worked even later than usual in the trial team's cluttered, poorly-ventilated offices on 12th Street, preparing for the testimony of the man widely considered to be the government's most important witness against AT&T. Though neither Connell nor Kenney had worked on the case from its beginning, both were aware that it was McGowan, more than any other person in or out of government, who was responsible for the existence of *U.S.* v. *AT&T*. They knew, too, that while the MCI story was by no means the only important evidence they had to present to Judge Greene, it was crucial that McGowan make a good impression on the judge, both in what the MCI chairman said and in how he said it. Without McGowan's aggressiveness and political savvy in the early 1970s, Justice probably would never have sued AT&T; without sparkling testimony from him now, the case might founder.

The trouble was that for McGowan himself, so much was different from his early, heady days as an entrepreneurial wizard and self-styled political fixer in the nation's capital. Back then, MCI was mostly just an idea with potential. It was an ambitious little company that spent its meager funds on rented office furniture and as many lawyers and lobbyists as it could buy. When he attacked the phone company in those days, McGowan seemed like an American populist, akin in spirit to the nineteenth-century family farmers who once decried the concentrated power of eastern banks and railroads. Only McGowan, in his attacks on monopolistic AT&T, was not spawning a political movement or protesting his family's livelihood. Rather, he was trying to get rich. And during the 1970s he had succeeded, in a big way. By April 1981, when Gerry Connell called him to the stand to testify about his troubles with AT&T and to urge that the phone company be broken up, William McGowan was an extraordinarily wealthy man—richer, for example, than his former nemesis John deButts, whom McGowan once attacked as an aristocrat. The annual revenues of MCI were nearing $1 billion, and its profits had risen meteorically since the mid-1970s, when Execunet was launched in competition with AT&T's regular long-distance service. McGowan's stock in the publicly-owned company was worth hundreds of millions of dollars. As he testified that April, McGowan was in the process of buying up neighboring property and building a million-dollar addition to his home in the fashionable Georgetown section of Washington, overlooking the Potomac River. Still a confirmed bachelor, he was seen at the finest restaurants about town with beautiful women clinging to his arm—he confided to friends that he almost married several times, "until common sense took over." He still worked long hours at MCI's northwest Washington headquarters, chain-smoking cigarettes and voraciously reading five newspapers a day. But with dozens of well-groomed executives and a stable of high-priced lawyers surrounding him, McGowan was no longer "a little guy," an iconoclastic cowboy capitalist. He was the fabulously rich chief executive of a sprawling, publicly-held corporation. Finally, he had become a fat cat.

And that April, he was also the chairman of a company that had recently been awarded $1.8 billion in antitrust damages by a federal jury in Chicago, an award that was like an insurance policy guaranteeing MCI's future growth and profitability. But the award was on appeal and would not be final for months, probably years. If, while testifying for Justice in the government case, McGowan contradicted any of the Chicago testimony that had led to the jury's award, he could jeopardize the outcome of his $1.8 billion appeal, and indirectly, the future of his company and his personal fortune. In conversations and meetings with the government trial teams, McGowan and his attorneys were unyielding on this issue; they protected their $1.8 billion like it was a newborn infant. Lawyers from Jenner & Block, the firm that had tried the Chicago case, poured over the questions prepared by Connell and Kenney, arguing and double-checking to be sure that McGowan's testimony was entirely consistent with all that he had said in Chicago. They spent many hours privately preparing the MCI chairman for Saunders' cross-examination—they were understandably concerned that MCI's chairman might inadvertently contradict his previous testimony. McGowan's lawyers were less interested in how Saunders' cross-examination, which was certain to challenge every aspect of MCI's history, might affect the government's case than they were in how it could jeopardize the Chicago award.

McGowan himself was certain that he could run intellectual circles around George Saunders, as he felt he had done in Chicago. In person, on the witness stand, some people described McGowan as "self-confident." Others called him "arrogant" and "obnoxious." The government lawyers were afraid that Judge Greene, a mild-mannered man who appreciated strong intellect but was intolerant of stridency or shrillness, would tend toward the latter view. This, combined with McGowan's reluctance to take risks during his testimony for fear of losing his $1.8 billion, might lead to a disastrous showing by Justice's most important witness.

The seven hours of direct testimony that Thursday morning had been workmanlike, though restricted in range and tainted by McGowan's smug bearing. Methodically, Connell had walked McGowan through the entire history of MCI: the reasons McGowan had attempted to rescue the company by investing his money in it during the late 1960s; the early, fitful interconnection negotiations with AT&T; the contentious, stage-setting meeting between McGowan and deButts in March 1973; McGowan's attempt to construct rapidly a national microwave network; the controversy over whether FX was a private-line or a regular long-distance, "MTS"-type service; deButts' decision to disconnect MCI customers during the FX controversy; and, finally, the breakthrough Execunet filing, which saved MCI from financial collapse. Apart from providing Judge Greene with a sense of the violent early relationship between the phone company and its most serious long-distance competitor, McGowan's direct testimony tried to establish three crucially important government contentions: First, that there was never any question that FX and the similar service known as CCSA were private-line offerings, which MCI was authorized to sell by the FCC; second, that knowing this, AT&T had deliberately fought with MCI over FX and over interconnection terms in order to harm irreparably its competitor; and third, that McGowan was driven to the brink of financial ruin solely by the phone company's anticompetitive behavior. If all of that was true—if Judge Greene decided that the industrial warfare carried on between McGowan and deButts in the early 1970s should be blamed on AT&T—then the government's case was close to being locked up.

"Mr. McGowan, we have discussed these matters on previous occasions, have we not?" Saunders began, pacing before the witness box to Judge Greene's left. Ever since Chicago, Saunders had been waiting for this rematch with the MCI chairman. It was a personal as well as professional challenge. Saunders believed McGowan was a manipulative liar, and this time he was going to prove it.

"It certainly depends on what matters you are talking about," said McGowan. During a decade of nonstop legal wrangling with AT&T, McGowan had become a sophisticated witness. He challenged the premise of every question, argued vigorously with his examiner, and conceded only the narrowest points.

"The matters that you discussed on your direct examination, Mr. McGowan."

"Yes, many of them."

"And there seems to be a difference in our view about the facts with respect to these matters, does there not?"

"On those occasions, I didn't realize you were testifying, Mr. Saunders. I testified to my view."

"You are aware they won't let me up there, aren't you, Mr. McGowan? . . . Jack Goeken started this company back in 1963, didn't he?"

"He started Microwave Communication, Inc., I believe . . . That company at that time had no employees and did not have them for another year or two."

"You didn't either, did you, Mr. McGowan? . . . All right. You described how MCI's application at the FCC winded its way to conclusion. The FCC's Hearing Examiner rejected the Bell System arguments against creamskimming; is that correct?"

"I am not familiar with all the details at the tip of my tongue, but the hearing examiner recommended that the application be granted, yes."

"And the commission granted the application in a four to three vote; isn't that true?"

"Yes, in August of '69, the vote was four to three."

"And the chairman of the commission said this is a 'typical creamskimming operation' and an 'outrage,' didn't he?"

"I can't paraphrase it to be that exact, but I do believe he dissented and that was one of the areas of his comments."

"That is a quote, 'typical creamskimming operation'?"

"I cannot verify that."

"But in any event, you won, and one of the key votes was cast by Kenneth Cox, wasn't it?"

"There were four commissioners voting in favor. One of them was Mr. Kenneth Cox."

"And Mr. Cox left the commission, when was it, September 30?"

"His term expired in June 1970, and the person who replaced him, I think, came on board in September 1970 and he joined . . . us as an officer in our firm to handle some regulatory matters."

"The next day? Never missed a day on anybody's payroll, came directly there on October 1 after leaving the commission on September 30?"

"He came afterwards. I do not know. I didn't count hours as to whether he came the next day. But at the time he left the government's employ, he came to work for us, yes."

"It is true, isn't it, Mr. McGowan, that in 1969, when MCI got authority to construct and operate microwave towers between Chicago and St. Louis, the thought never occurred to anyone there that you had the right to provide MTS-type, ordinary long-distance services. That's true, isn't it?"

"I do not remember any discussion of that entering into any plans. I mean, it was clear we all knew that we were building a system which had all the elements of communications that could be used for any type of service . . . but certainly I do not believe that was in the plans in 1969."

"All right. In any event, along comes 1969 and you get your application granted and the commission sets the notice of inquiry into the *Specialized Common Carriers* proceeding to define your franchise, and it asks for comments from all interested parties; is that correct?"

"Yes, they did."

"Mr. McGowan, you know very well you walked into the commission and you said, 'All we want to do is provide point-to-point private-line service,' didn't you?"

"If somebody used the term the way you are trying to define it, that is incorrect."

"All right. Let's take a look at some of the things you told the commission in those days, Mr. McGowan... Let's take a look at the comments and reply comments of MCI in the *Specialized Common Carriers* decision... Will you read the first two sentences under the heading, 'The Specialized Carriers Operations Will Not Result in Creamskimming'?"

McGowan read from the document Saunders handed him. "'There will be no creamskimming because the MCI-type applicants propose to offer only customized point-to-point services and have no intention of attempting to compete with Bell in providing local exchange or long-distance telephone service, which account for the bulk of Bell's revenues. All of these are conventional telephone switched-voice services, and none of the MCI-type carriers propose such services. The exchange services offered by the telephone company are not similar in any way to the services which the Specialized Common Carriers propose to provide. The exchange telephone services remain the dominant preserve of the Bell System, safe and secure from competition. Specialized Common Carriers will provide only specialized point-to-point private-line services.'"

"Does that accurately state your plans of that time?"

"Yes, as of that time."

"Mr. McGowan, what the commission decided in the *Specialized Common Carriers* proceeding was that the services proposed by the specialized carriers were in the public interest, didn't they?"

"No, I think that is too narrow a reading of that decision."

"This is not an easy decision to read, is it?"

"It depends on what you are trying to find in there."

"You were in court in Chicago when Judge Grady said it was an abomination, and that he couldn't understand it, weren't you?"

"Judge Grady did have some trouble at the beginning understanding it, yes."

"Did he ever understand it? Did he ever say he understood it?"

"I am sure he understood it much more at the end."

"Will you read me everything the commission says in there about FX and CCSA?"

"Where?"

"It isn't there, is it?"

"Yes, it is there. They describe private line. They say specifically, for example, even if Bell lost its entire private-line market, which includes FX and CCSA, you still would not be hurt. They could hardly have anticipated you losing your entire private-line market without losing your FX market, since that includes your FX revenues."

"Does the decision use the word 'FX' anywhere?"

"It uses it by calling it other ways."

"Does it use the word 'FX' anywhere?"

"I am not sure whether the word 'FX' is in there. It could be or not be."

"You know it's not there, Mr. McGowan."

"I have not memorized the contents of this document."

"Now, in any event, you have testified under oath that the meaning of that decision is crystal clear; isn't that right?"

"I believe it is certainly clear enough to a businessman to tell him what business this would say anyone could go into. This decision was not for MCI. This decision was for anyone who wanted to go into this business, not for us."

"You know, don't you, Mr. McGowan, that a lot of people have testified under oath that they read the decision at the time it came out and did not understand it to encompass FX and CCSA services. You know that, don't you?"

"I understand there are some people."

"Did you receive advice from any lawyer at that time, that the decision encompassed FX and CCSA services?"

"Yes, I did."

"Who was that lawyer?"

"Lawyers. I received that opinion from, certainly, Mr. Kenneth Cox."

"I don't want to trivialize this thing, Mr. McGowan, I would like to focus it. This is the major issue that separated MCI and the Bell System during this period, isn't it?"

"It was absolutely not the main issue whatsoever. The first time we ever heard this issue was after this whole thing blew up. Not once did we end up with someone saying, 'You fellows aren't entitled to it.' If AT&T thought we were not entitled to it, customers kept demanding it, and I know they would have gone to the FCC and gotten us off their back. AT&T is amply able to take care of themselves in the regulatory forum. If they didn't think we were authorized, they would have gone to the FCC and said, 'These people are bugging us, go away.' Bell thought of this idea that we weren't authorized after this whole thing blew up, not before."

"That is your testimony?"

"Yes, it is."

"That's what you are going to state here and try and convince this court?"

"That's my testimony. I believe that."

Therein lay the heart of the case: Like so many other trials, *U.S.* v. *AT&T* was going to come down to a matter of personal credibility, interpretation, and judgment. It was possible, as George Saunders believed, that McGowan was lying. It was possible, too, as the government assumed, that he was telling the truth. Saunders' strategy was to prove that MCI's story was a fraud, that McGowan's complaints about AT&T were really a smokescreen for his own manipulative and devious plan to slip into the switched phone network and make billions in long-distance competition with AT&T. Throughout his cross-examination, Saunders continually implied that McGowan was perjuring himself. And though the MCI chairman never gave in to Saunders' attack, his argumentative, defensive responses began to wear on Judge Greene. Though he recognized the importance of McGowan's cross-examination and gave both Saunders and his witness wide latitude, Greene finally was unable to contain himself and burst out angrily, "I understand, Mr. McGowan, that you want to be careful of this cross-examination. But this constant fencing of every word is kind of getting ridiculous, so would you please answer the questions?"

Greene began to ask questions of McGowan directly, focusing mainly on the relationship between MCI, Bernie Strassburg, and the FCC during the fall of 1973. McGowan treated Greene with the same contempt he directed at Saunders, and Greene snapped, "At least in answer to my questions, I wish you would answer them rather than making speeches."

For some of the government lawyers, McGowan's performance represented the low point of the entire case. Through his shrillness during cross-examination, he had called into question the integrity of the government's MCI story and he had alienated, at least temporarily, the affections of Judge Greene. McGowan's reluctance to work closely with the government lawyers in preparation for his examination seemed precisely an example of how his first and overriding priority was his own self-enrichment. This resentment did not reflect a naive view by the Antitrust division lawyers that aggressive "competitors" like McGowan should be warm, nice people; simply, it left a bad taste in the Justice staffers' mouths. They had to remind themselves that McGowan's antagonist in this drama, John deButts, was an equally unattractive personality in their minds: he, too, was arrogant, strident, dissembling. It was important, they told themselves, not to see this case as solely a clash between two men, McGowan and deButts. To some of the Justice lawyers, the end they were pursuing—the breakup of AT&T, the creation of economic pluralism in the telephone industry—justified the means, even if those means included the enrichment of a character like Bill McGowan. To others on the Justice trial team, the case was just a job, and no matter who benefited by its outcome, it was important that the job be done right.

None of them, however, could be magnanimous about the gloating faces of the AT&T lawyers who sat at the defense table across the courtroom. As Saunders scored point after point against their most important witness, the young government lawyers felt their ears burning. As much as they liked and appreciated Saunders himself, it infuriated them to see the AT&T trial team attorneys, whom they'd been fighting for years, leap to their feet to "towel Saunders off" after one of his grueling sessions with McGowan, as if George was the legal heavy-weight champion of the world, about to score another knock-out. At moments like that, the government lawyers forgot all about the merits and demerits of *U.S.* v. *AT&T* and set their hearts and minds to how it could be quickly and decisively won—with or without effective testimony from Bill McGowan.

Chapter 20

The Baldrige Proposal

WHEN the Reagan administration's commerce secretary, Malcolm Baldrige, interviewed Bernie Wunder early in 1981 for the job of assistant secretary of commerce in charge of telecommunications policy, one of the first questions Baldrige asked was, "What do you think about the AT&T case?"

"It ought to be settled," Wunder told him.

"Yeah, I think so, too," Baldrige agreed.

And so, it seemed that spring, as the trial of *U.S.* v. *AT&T* progressed, did every secretary in the Reagan cabinet. Caspar Weinberger had already taken public his view that the case should be dismissed. The new attorney general, William French Smith, was widely considered by congressional and White House insiders to support that idea, even though he was prohibited from ruling on the case because of his past affiliation with Pacific Telephone. Edwin Meese, long-time friend and counselor to President Reagan, privately told AT&T chairman Charlie Brown that he was sympathetic to the phone company's plight and would do what he could to expedite White House intervention in the case. Even cabinet-level officials who had little to do with economic or legal policy, such as Secretary of Agriculture John Block, expressed support for settlement or outright dismissal.

The question, though, was how to accomplish that goal when the administration's own Antitrust chief was boasting about litigating the case "to the eyeballs" and when the trial before Judge Greene was moving rapidly ahead.

From New York, Charlie Brown and his general counsel Howard Trienens were doing all they could to devise a workable strategy. When the brouhaha between Weinberger and Baxter hit the newspapers, Trienens called the White House and made an appointment to discuss the matter personally with Ed Meese. He flew to Washington and met with the President's counselor in his office. Trienens told him, "You all really ought to get your act together—stop this public bickering and start working on a solution." Meese agreed. But the sort of solution that Meese and Trienens wanted—dismissal of the case or favorable settlement terms forced on the Justice department by the White House—would require a direct decision by the President himself. Obviously, such a decision would have major political and policy repercussions. Meese could not simply walk into the Oval Office and ask Reagan to drop the case. A lot of groundwork would have to be laid inside the administration.

Trienens knew where to start. Malcolm Baldrige and Bernie Wunder at the Commerce department had already made it clear to AT&T that they would be willing to push a dismissal proposal to the White House. One problem was that, since February, Wunder's confirmation as assistant secretary in charge of the National Telecommunications and Information Agency had been delayed for no apparent reason. Until Wunder was confirmed, it would be impossible for Commerce to put forward a major telecommunications policy proposal such as dismissal of *U.S. v. AT&T*. During his meeting with Meese, Trienens successfully pushed the counselor to move Wunder's confirmation along quickly.

Charlie Brown, meanwhile, was spending a considerable amount of time on the telephone and in Washington talking with administration officials about why the case should be dropped. In the course of several weeks that spring, he talked with Ed Meese, White House Chief of Staff Jim Baker, Cap Weinberger, Malcolm Baldrige, and several others. The theme of Brown's presentation was that unless some direct action was quickly taken by Reagan, the telecommunications policy of the administration was going to be set, by default, by Bill Baxter and the career trial attorneys at the department of Justice.

"If that's what you want, that's what's going to happen. If that's not what you want, then something needs to be done," Brown told the members of Reagan's cabinet.

Not unwittingly, Brown was reminding the key players in the administration that Baxter was a political outsider, an obscure academic who had played no role in the 1980 presidential campaign and who had been chosen Antitrust chief because of his strongly held conservative ideology, not because of his political loyalty or experience. It was a sound tactic. Even as early as April, Baxter's blunt arrogance was beginning to alienate some of the key cabinet secretaries who wanted to dispose of the AT&T case. The political appointees at the Commerce department, for example, liked to say that Baxter thought there were two kinds of people in the world: those who agreed with him, and those who were stupid. The trouble was that because the Reagan "team players" at Justice, Bill Smith and Ed Schmults, were recused from the case, Baxter spoke for the entire department on matters concerning AT&T. Brown urged Meese, Weinberger, and Baldrige, who had direct access to the President and far more clout in the administration than Baxter could ever dream to hold, to take the problem into their own hands.

In order to seize responsibility for the decision to dismiss the biggest antitrust suit in American history, Reagan's top advisers would need expert help, and for that they turned to Bernie Wunder and the Commerce department.

Wunder was a plain-speaking, politically savvy Republican lawyer from South Carolina who, since 1975, had worked as minority counsel to the House subcommittee on telecommunications. When Baldrige offered him the stewardship at NTIA, Wunder came to his Commerce job with three objectives. First and foremost was to pass comprehensive legislation in Congress that would address the issues and problems of telephone industry competition while preserving the integrity of AT&T's national switched network.

"The sonuvabitch is working," Wunder would say when asked why he so passionately opposed breaking up the phone company. At the same time, Wunder wanted to see more competition in the industry. He felt this could be achieved without divestiture, through legislation that set down the kinds of equal access and interconnection rules that Justice and AT&T had tried to work out during the Crimson Sky negotiations. And finally, Wunder wanted to make sure that local telephone rates did not rise significantly as a result of any congressionally-mandated competitive experiments, because he feared that such rises would lead to a backlash against his program. The cross subsidies between AT&T's highly profitable long-distance service and its costly local service were politically important. Everyone paid for basic phone service, while relatively few phone users—mainly businesses—spent significant amounts of money on long distance.

Wunder also believed that the biggest obstacle to achieving these goals was the Justice case against AT&T. During six years in Congress, Wunder had worked on one comprehensive telecommunications bill after another, each designed to end uncertainty in the telephone industry while laying down rules—without divestiture—to increase competition, and each was defeated, ultimately, by congressmen and senators worried that the bills would improperly interfere with Justice's suit against AT&T. The most frustrating defeat of this kind had occurred the previous June, when—after eighteen months of intensive hearings, lobbying, and negotiating between AT&T, MCI, subcommittee members, and others—a comprehensive bill had finally cleared the House Commerce Committee, only to be killed in Peter Rodino's antitrust subcommittee. Wunder was determined, now that he was in a position of authority at NTIA, to do all he could to prevent that from happening again.

So even before the high-level lobbying by Charlie Brown and Howard Trienens stirred Ed Meese, Cap Weinberger, and others into action, Wunder had begun to prepare the data and formal policy arguments that would be needed to support any decision to dismiss the government suit. Much of the material Wunder needed was already lying around NTIA, left over from the Carter administration, whose NTIA chief, Henry Geller, had also been interested in a legislative or other out of court settlement of the Justice case. It had been under Geller's supervision that NTIA had prepared the "menu" of settlement alternatives, which led eventually to the aborted Crimson Sky deal. Geller had worked at the FCC's Common Carrier Bureau during the early 1970s, where he had helped shape the bureau's procompetition policies. After Execunet, though, Geller decided that competition policy in the phone industry was out of control, and he had come to NTIA in 1977 with goals similar to those being pursued by Bernie Wunder in 1981. (Later asked why he tried to roll back at Commerce the competition policies he had helped devise at the FCC, Geller replied, "All I can say is that I was dumb [when I was at the FCC]. I didn't have the vision to see what I was doing.") But Geller was unable to accomplish anything more than preparation of the informal menu of settlement alternatives. In the Carter White House, the Commerce department was regarded as little more than an apologist for the interests of big business, and it had little policy influence.

All that had changed with the arrival of Wunder and Baldrige in 1981. In the Reagan administration, business boosterism was a policy goal, not a political liability. So that spring, when Wunder informally presented to Malcolm Baldrige the arguments and evidence that could support a decision to dismiss *U.S. v. AT&T*, Wunder found his boss willing and able to carry the proposal directly to the President. Before he was briefed by Wunder, Baldrige knew little about the issues of telephone industry competition. A self-styled cowboy who chain-smoked Marlboro cigarettes and rode in professional rodeos—but who was also a graduate of an exclusive Connecticut prep school and Yale University—Baldrige comported himself much like his President, tending toward home-on-the range aphorisms and styles and dress from the American West. Indeed, when Reagan called Baldrige to offer him the Commerce job, the then President-elect was told by Baldrige's wife that he couldn't come to the phone because he was out riding. "That's my kind of guy," Reagan reportedly said. After a long and successful career as a corporate chief executive, Baldrige had come to Commerce intending to spearhead the private sector's role in the unfurling of Reaganomics. Getting the Justice department off AT&T's back fit nicely onto the agenda, and Baldrige listened eagerly to Wunder's presentations about why dismissing the government lawsuit was important. Wunder laid out the dismal legislative history of telecommunications policy making in Congress and explained how the government suit had thwarted the most recent attempt to pass a bill. Most impressive to Baldrige were the numbers NTIA had assembled about the rapidly growing trade imbalance in the strategically important telecommunications industry, once a sector of American dominance in the international market. According to NTIA's projections, the telecommunications trade deficit would eventually top $1 billion annually, with most of that advantage going to Japan. AT&T, particularly its Western Electric and Bell Labs subsidiaries, represented the country's best hope for righting that imbalance, Wunder said, if only because the uncertainty and debilitation caused by its antitrust entanglements could be ended. Baldrige took the NTIA numbers to heart—they turned out to be inaccurate, but only because they underestimated the size of the problem—and he decided that the international trade argument, combined with Cap Weinberger's concerns about national security, would form a solid basis for President Reagan to order publicly the dismissal of *U.S.* v. *AT&T.*

The challenge now was to orchestrate a decision before Judge Greene had a chance to rule at trial. AT&T lawyers and executives had let Commerce officials know that they believed Greene, because of his certifiably liberal background, might ultimately rule against them in court, despite the gallant efforts of George Saunders. Such speculation, calculated or not, fed the ideological prejudices of activist conservatives like Baldrige, and added a spice of partisanship to an already complex and contentious situation.

On Wednesday, May 20, a dreary spring day in the nation's capital, Baldrige met with Ed Meese in the west wing of the White House to discuss how the Commerce department's dismissal proposal should be presented to President Reagan. The

Reagan presidency was just four months old, and its decision making processes and internal centers of power were only beginning to take shape. When he was governor of California, Reagan had involved himself little in the day-to-day details of his administration; he had relied on formally structured working groups made up of his top advisers to present him with information and proposed decisions. During his first months at the White House, a similar pattern was forming; cabinet-level working groups, called cabinet councils, which were little used during the Carter administration, were looked to by Reagan as forums where top administration officials could develop and debate policy proposals before presenting them to the President once a consensus was reached. The obvious way to handle Baldrige's dismissal proposal was to carry it up through the Cabinet Council on Commerce and Trade, which Baldrige chaired. There were eleven council members, including Baldrige and Meese. If consensus support for the idea could be built within that body, then the proposal could be presented to Reagan for ratification at a formal cabinet meeting. Sherman Unger, Baldrige's politically appointed general counsel at Commerce and a veteran of Nixon administration intrigue, had suggested to Baldrige that he urge Meese to authorize the formation of a cabinet council task force on the AT&T lawsuit. That way, a working-level group made up of general counsels from some of the departments involved, including Commerce and Defense, could draft a "white paper" arguing why the lawsuit should be dismissed. Then the paper could be circulated to the cabinet secretaries who made up the council membership. Once they accepted its findings, the full cabinet council would meet with the President to seek his endorsement. If all went well, the decision to drop *U.S.* v. *AT&T* would be finalized by June 12, the date of the full cabinet council's next scheduled meeting with the President.

Meese thought Baldrige's strategy was sound, and a few days later he issued a written, internal White House order authorizing the creation of a "Task Force on Telecommunications Policy" and a working group of general counsels underneath it. The departments represented were Commerce, Defense, Agriculture, Energy, and the Federal Emergency Management Agency; Justice would have no input, even though Attorney General Smith was a member of the Cabinet Council on Commerce and Trade. The policy decision to drop the lawsuit, Baldrige and Meese agreed to argue, had nothing to do with the merits of the case, or with the progress of the trial before Judge Greene; rather, it was an issue of national security and the national interest. Thus there was no reason to include Antitrust chief Baxter in the process.

Even though his effort to drop the case was moving swiftly and smoothly, there would be a brief but no doubt intense reaction in Congress to Reagan's announcement that he had dropped a structural antitrust suit against the country's biggest corporation. After his meeting with Meese, Baldrige's staff placed calls to several key congressmen and senators, including Oregon senator Bob Packwood and the majority leader, Senator Howard Baker of Tennessee, to "get a feeling," as Baldrige put it later, about the depth of congressional support for the Justice case. Baldrige heard nothing discouraging. At the same time, he ordered Sherman Unger, Bernie Wunder, and others at Commerce who were involved in the proposal to keep contemporaneous summaries of all their meetings and telephone conversations as a precaution against a Democratic-led congressional investigation of the decision, which might try to establish politically embarrassing links between AT&T and the Reagan administration.

The cabinet task force's working group convened for its only formal meeting on Thursday, June 4, and because the arguments and data they needed had already been assembled by Wunder and the NTIA staff, it took only a couple of days to draft, type, collate, and copy the task force recommendation that *U.S.* v. *AT&T* be immediately and summarily dismissed by President Reagan. There were actually two versions of the task force report: a longer one explored in full detail the national security and international trade arguments, while a shorter one summarized the Commerce-Defense consensus. The long version contained two classified pages concerning the armed forces'

defense communications system and the geopolitical importance of the telecommunications industry; the two pages could
be removed without disrupting the paper's continuity. As soon
as the report was drafted, Baldrige personally called each of
the cabinet secretaries on the task force to be certain they supported the dismissal recommendation. Each of them said they
would back Baldrige and Weinberger when the cabinet council
met with President Reagan the following Friday. By Monday,
U.S. v. *AT&T* would be over.

When the meeting began at 10:00 A.M., no one seated around
the long, rectangular conference table in the Roosevelt Room
of the White House was certain about what, if any, consideration President Reagan had given to the proposal now before
him. Weinberger, Baldrige, and Meese knew from his statements during the 1980 campaign that Reagan's instinct about
the phone company and its antitrust problems was, "If it ain't
broke, don't fix it." They assumed that since they were presenting the President with a consensus opinion from some of
his most important and influential cabinet advisers, Reagan's
ratification of the dismissal idea would be more or less a formality. What they had underestimated, not for the first or last
time, was the tenacious vitriol of William Baxter.

Even though he had found out only a few days before
about the task force, its recommendation, and the fact that a
cabinet meeting would be held to discuss it with the President,
Baxter had arrived at the White House ready to go to the mat
with Weinberger, Baldrige, and, if need be, the rest of Reagan's
cabinet, too. A copy of the task force's paper had been sent
to Justice earlier in the week, and Baxter's Antitrust front
office staff had hurriedly drafted a stinging rebuttal, which
Baxter now carried with him. Like the task force recommendation itself, Baxter's rebuttal paid no attention to the merits
or factual details of *U.S.* v. *AT&T*; rather, it concentrated on
the theoretical arguments behind Baxter's belief that the phone
company should be broken up. It stressed that the comprehensive legislation ostensibly sought by the Commerce de-

partment was really a regulatory solution to the phone industry's competitive problems, while the full breakup of AT&T would lead to less government and less regulation, a goal that was in perfect tandem with the President's most strongly held ideological tenets.

As Baxter pressed his views, the tension around the conference table began to rise. There was something about the Antitrust chief's self-confident manner that invited irritation.

Cap Weinberger, himself testy and strident by nature, began to lose his patience. "This case should never have been brought in the first place, and it should be dropped!" he burst out at one point.

Baxter, though, continued to argue. Though he was a political amateur in his first contentious cabinet meeting with the President and his top advisers, he was not intimidated. He emphasized the shortcomings of the legislative solution that Commerce hoped to pursue, and he complained, too, about the fact that Meese and Baldrige had excluded Justice from the decision-making process. The latter point was an effective one because in the early days of the Reagan presidency, much emphasis was placed by top White House staff on the importance of unity and due process within the administration. Baxter had brought with him to the cabinet meeting Jonathan Rose, an assistant attorney general in charge of Justice's Office of Legal Policy. Rose was a Nixon White House veteran with a keen sense for intrigue and strategy inside the executive branch.

"I don't think the administration should start off by making a decision that so favors an American business," Rose told the cabinet meeting, "unless it makes clear that it listened to the contrary arguments and decided that this is best. You have to be prepared to intellectually defend your decision." What Commerce and Defense had done, Rose argued, was prepare a preset rationale that would not sell to the public or Congress. "We ought to slow down and do the job right," he said.

Baldrige, who was chair of the cabinet council and thus reluctant to adopt too adversarial a posture, mainly emphasized the arguments prepared by Bernie Wunder about the national interest and international trade. But he could not resist responding to Baxter's and Rose's political arguments.

"If we drop this case, only a handful of antitrust lawyers will care," the Commerce secretary said.

No one at the meeting wanted to pursue the political arguments too far, however. Reagan frequently said in public that he instructed his cabinet officers only to discuss the merits of an issue while in his presence, never its political consequences. In 1981, virtually all of the President's cabinet secretaries believed Reagan meant what he said.

As the debate wore on, Baxter could not tell whether he was making any headway, but he was encouraged by the fact that only he, Weinberger, and Baldrige were doing any talking. None of the other secretaries on the task force were throwing their weight behind Commerce and Defense.

Reagan himself said very little. He seemed to be listening, and occasionally he would ask a question of Baxter, Weinberger, or Baldrige. But when the vociferous back-and-forth between Justice's representatives and the task force leaders died down, and it was time for the President to indicate where he stood, Reagan had nothing substantive to add.

"I don't completely follow everything that everyone is talking about," the President said. "But I do know one thing..." And then Reagan launched into the same story he had told on the campaign trail in 1980, the one about how much it used to cost to mail a letter from Hollywood to New York in the 1940s versus how much it cost to call long distance, and about how the cost of postage had gone up while the price of the same long-distance call had fallen drastically. Only this time, Reagan left out the punchline he had used on the stump: "And of course, the government is suing the phone company." Instead, he just tailed off at the end and left the story hanging, without indicating exactly what the point was.

After the cabinet meeting broke up, some of the Commerce officials suggested that the President's story was like a "parable" that supported their position that the case be dismissed. There was some concern, however, that Justice could interpret the parable to mean the opposite, because Baxter argued that the way to drive long-distance prices further down was to force divestiture of AT&T's operating companies.

Either way, the President had ended the meeting at noon, and had gone off to eat lunch with Vice-President George Bush without resolving the issue for one side or the other. The strategy devised by Baldrige and Meese to achieve a quick dismissal of the suit had failed. To have the case dropped now, there was no point in relying on formal task forces, white papers, and cabinet councils. The issues were now clear enough, even if the President didn't "completely follow everything." Reagan had seemed to say that he was sympathetic to Baldrige's position. Despite Baxter's sharp arguments, a majority of the cabinet was still on board with Meese and the Commerce secretary. What still had to be overcome were the ensnaring machinations of political decision making inside the Reagan White House.

Chapter 21

The Disengaged Presidency

H OWARD TRIENENS was in almost daily contact with Sherman Unger and the other political appointees at the Commerce department, and so Trienens and AT&T chairman Charlie Brown learned immediately that the June 12 cabinet meeting with President Reagan had ended without resolving the Baldrige proposal to dismiss *U.S.* v. *AT&T.*

It was not clear to Trienens—nor, for that matter, was it clear to Baldrige, Unger, or Bernie Wunder—why the dismissal juggernaut inside the administration had been so suddenly derailed. Officials at Commerce and Defense, as well as Trienens, Brown, and other AT&T executives, had all been highly optimistic that Reagan would put an end to the matter when he was formally presented with his cabinet task force's recommendation.

Since the President had left the matter hanging, Baldrige's forces would have to reroute their proposal directly to the Oval Office. And that meant, for the first time, that Reagan's top White House advisor, Chief of Staff James A. Baker III, would have to be brought into the deliberations.

In the latter years of President Reagan's first term, much would be said and written about the extraordinary power wielded by Jim Baker and his so-called moderate allies—Richard Darman, Michael Deaver, David Gergen, and others—in the Reagan White House. Baker was a wealthy Texas lawyer who had managed George Bush's 1980 presidential campaign against Reagan in the Republican primaries. The staunchly ideological conservatives who supported Reagan from the beginning of his drive for the presidency were surprised when their candidate named corporate-bred, politically temperate George Bush as his vice-presidential running mate at the 1980 Republican convention in Detroit. Their surprise turned to dismay six months later when Reagan, having won a triumphant mandate for his conservative principles at the polls, chose the "pragmatist" Baker as his chief of staff. When Baker proceeded to gather around himself at the White House a coterie of like-minded traditional Republicans, some of whom had ridiculed as "voodoo" Reagan's economic proposals during the 1980 campaign, hard-line conservatives began to talk of "betrayal" and a "sellout." In the end, Baker and Bush both proved themselves to be immensely loyal to Reagan and his program, but at the same time, Baker especially demonstrated unusual savvy in his dealings with the internecine Washington world of bureaucracies, media, and Congress. Baker's ability to be simultaneously loyal and practical eventually earned him and his allies unrivaled power among the top White House staff.

Unfortunately for AT&T, none of this was apparent in May and June of 1981, when Howard Trienens and Charlie Brown had tried to woo administration support for Malcolm Baldrige's dismissal proposal. If it had been, Trienens and Brown would probably have spent more time in consultation with Jim Baker and less talking to Ed Meese and the political appointees at Commerce. Trienens said later that it was not his "beat" to read the Reagan administration "tea leaves" and that, more important, the extent of Baker's power in the White House had not yet been demonstrated. Trienens and Brown would have preferred to deal directly with Attorney General Bill Smith or Deputy Attorney General Schmults. Since that was impossible, Ed Meese, who had a keen interest in legal affairs and would in fact become attorney general in Reagan's second term, seemed a good third choice. Meese was an old friend of the President's and certainly one of his two or three most important advisers.

Trienens and Brown assumed, at least until the June 12 cabinet meeting, that their contacts with Reagan's counselor had established an effective link to the Oval Office.

That the AT&T executives were wrong became evident during the first weeks following the cabinet meeting. AT&T's sources at Commerce reported that in the aftermath of the vociferous debate between Weinberger, Baxter, and Baldrige in the Roosevelt Room, a series of meetings had been arranged to see if some kind of compromise or understanding could be reached between Commerce and Justice. Baxter, however, was unyielding in his view that telecommunications legislation, such as the comprehensive rewrite of the Communications Act being considered by the Senate that summer, was inadvisable, and that the only worthwhile solution was full divestiture of the operating companies ordered by the court. With the two sides at an impasse, the debate inside the administration shifted from the merits of dismissal—Baxter would never change his mind about that—to its political consequences for President Reagan, who was at the time battling with Congress to pass the biggest tax cut proposed by a President in almost twenty years. If dismissal was going to be forced on Justice by the White House, as Meese, Baldrige, and others were urging late that June, a serious evaluation had to be made of the political fallout from such an announcement.

"Had Bill Smith not been on the Pacific Telephone board, this case would be dropped," Baldrige lamented frequently to his top staff in the weeks after the cabinet meeting. The irony, however, was that as the debate over dismissal intensified in the last weeks of June, Smith indirectly made certain that Baldrige would have a tough time getting his proposal approved by the White House.

If Smith was privately committed to freeing AT&T from the government antitrust suit, he "could have fed Baxter to the sharks," as Jonathan Rose put it later, without creating any conflict of interest problems for himself. There was no question that Baxter lacked any real clout in the administration; he had not been selected for his job because of his political savvy or connections. If Smith stood by and did nothing that June, if he let the acerbic, academic Baxter go it alone against the likes of Weinberger, Baldrige, and Meese, the future of *U.S.* v. *AT&T* would be dim. Smith, though, for reasons having more to do with bureaucratic territorial imperatives than the merits of telephone competition issues, was unhappy about the way Justice had been summarily excluded by Baldrige and Meese from participating in the cabinet council task force that drafted the dismissal recommendation for the President. Smith felt that Justice had been stepped on by Commerce and Defense. Conservatives like Smith and Rose rejected the Carter administration notion that Justice, as a matter of principle, should "independently" enforce the law against a company such as AT&T; they felt that a President was just as entitled to make legal policy as he was to make farm or defense policy. But Smith was determined to defend his turf; as a matter of integrity and policy both, he felt it was wrong for Justice to be left out of such an important decision. So without indicating whether he supported dismissal or not, Smith strongly encouraged Rose to help Baxter navigate the treacherous political waters at the White House. Rose was an old Washington hand; his Office of Legal Policy had been created precisely for controversies such as this; and Rose was much better equipped than Baxter to consider the political, as opposed to the economic and philosophical, consequences of dismissing the case. Neither Smith nor Rose wanted Justice to be discredited as a result of the White House's decision.

So while Baxter continued to press the technical and economic arguments against dismissal to anyone at Commerce or in the White House who was still willing to listen to him, Rose began to work the political back channels of the administration. His objective was to change the nature of the debate, to inject it with political doubt. Rose knew that, to Jim Baker and other top White House staff, Baldrige's dismissal proposal was just one agenda item of many. No doubt they were sympathetic to the proposal, because to them the equation was simple: On one side were two cabinet secretaries who felt very strongly about the issue, while on the other was a mere assistant attorney general too arrogant to consider a compromise.

"We don't have time to get into the details," Rose was told by one cabinet-level supporter of Baldrige. "A powerful section of American industry wants this case dropped. Academic arguments shouldn't stand in the way. We don't think one man should stand in the way."

"This isn't what you're being asked to decide, that Cap and Baldrige are right and Baxter is wrong," Rose countered. "You're being asked to discontinue a seven-year-old antitrust case, provoke a hostile congressional antitrust committee—all to allegedly gain a legislative leg up. In fact, you'll only complicate things. You're asking the President to take on controversy in aide of an objective he won't even obtain. Hadn't you better let the string out a bit on this?"

Rose had been in the Nixon White House during the early 1970s scandal that erupted after it was learned that a Justice decision to drop an antitrust case against the multinational ITT Corporation might have been linked to illegal payoffs by the company. Rose reminded Reagan's staff that even though, so far as anyone knew, there was no smoking gun in Baldrige's proposal to drop the AT&T case, Democrats in Congress and "liberals" in the media would likely go all out searching for a way to embarrass the President over his decision. "Let's face it," Rose said. "The executives of AT&T are friendly with some administration officials."

Baxter, too, pressed the argument that if the suit was dismissed, a great hue and cry would follow, and he told Commerce officials that a number of lawyers on the Justice trial team might publicly resign in protest. Baxter also predicted to Sherman Unger, Bernie Wunder, and others that AT&T would withdraw its support from the Senate telecommunications bill so cherished by Commerce. Once the phone company got what it wanted from Reagan, Baxter said, it would have no reason to work with Congress to resolve the issues of phone industry competition.

The question, What's in it for the President? struck a responsive chord among all of Reagan's top White House aids. As Rose told Baxter, "If you're a White House staffer, you want to deliver to the President the best result, the least damage, and the best policy—sometimes in that order." The general rule at Jim Baker's White House, Rose said, was that if something was going to hurt the President, "they want to get it out of there and take it on over to Defense or Justice or OMB or wherever—just get it away from the President." In the case of Baldrige's dismissal proposal, however, there was no place to hide it, except at Justice, where Baxter wouldn't have it; if the suit was going to be dropped, the order would have to come directly from Reagan.

And where was the President himself during this intensive internal policy debate about "a major section of American industry" late in June 1981? He was utterly uninvolved. Reagan's personal administrative style, as it began to take shape in the first six months of his presidency, represented a policy of "constructive disengagement." Rarely did the President get involved in the details or even the debate about a decision such as dropping the AT&T case. His easygoing personality was better suited to detachment: he let his top aides do battle with each other over an issue until they presented him with a firm consensus. The advantage of Reagan's style was that on many issues, that consensus led to unity and strong, positive leadership within the administration. The disadvantage was that the President had a slim grasp of the questions being deliberated by his counselors and was thus unable to intervene when, as was the case early that summer, debate on a particular issue became skewed by personality clashes, turf wars, and internal White House politics.

By the July 4th weekend, Jonathan Rose had succeeded: Jim Baker had effectively taken control of the Baldrige proposal. President Reagan was not going to dismiss *U.S.* v. *AT&T* unless Baker agreed that it was a good idea. Despite Baldrige's continued insistence that neither the public nor the Congress would care if the President dropped the case, Baker had been persuaded by Rose, Baxter, and his own instincts that the decision should not be taken lightly. There were dozens of items on the President's agenda of equal or greater importance. This one could wait. At the same time, Baker had made it clear to Baxter that if the Antitrust chief could see any acceptable way to settle this dispute without forcing divestiture by AT&T, the administration expected him to pursue that settlement.

So far, though, no one had come close to changing Baxter's mind about the importance of breaking up the phone company.

Chapter 22

Escalation

O F all the arguments being pressed on President Reagan's top advisors by Bill Baxter and Jonathan Rose in their combined effort to head off a dismissal decision, the one most demonstrably true that June was the claim that Justice staff lawyers trying the AT&T case before Judge Greene would react strongly, and probably publicly, if the administration dropped the suit in mid-trial.

The gallows humor about dismissal intensified in the Justice trial staff offices on 12th Street as soon as some of the details of Baldrige's proposal leaked to the newspapers in the aftermath of the June 12 cabinet meeting with President Reagan. There was half-joking talk about government lawyers blocking traffic in the street and burning their Justice identification cards en masse. The references, even in humor, to campus protest methods of the late 1960s and early 1970s reflected both the young ages of many of the staff lawyers and their increasingly partisan view of the political forces now gathering behind a dismissal proposal. It was hard to avoid, for example, the parallels between the inclination of Reagan's Republican cabinet to drop *U.S.* v. *AT&T* and the decision twenty-five years earlier by the Eisenhower administration to settle benignly, in scandalous circumstances, a structural antitrust suit between the same two parties. Was the relationship between the government and the phone company to become a never-ending cycle of lawsuits, settlements, scandals, and resentments? Many of the Justice trial staff that June suspected it was. Led by the staff's "doom-sayer," Peter Kenney, a consensus among the trial team began to emerge. Reagan, like Eisenhower, would be loyal to his business friends and dismiss the case. Six years of preparations and four months of trial—not to mention the intense personal sacrifices and devotion by lawyers on both sides of the case—would be wasted. To the Justice staffers there was a sort of outrageous inevitability about it all.

Of course, neither the trial staffers nor their boss, Gerry Connell, was aware of the back channel lobbying effort to save the case being pressed by Baxter and Rose. Relations between the Antitrust front office and the trial team were distant and often strained. In part, that was because Baxter's cold manner precluded informal contacts with him. Also, Baxter's overall conservative philosophy about antitrust enforcement tangentially implied that the workaday lawyers in the division—who developed and prosecuted so many of the cases Baxter considered "wacko"—were misguided liberals or, worse, just plain stupid. After the chilling introductory meeting between the trial staff and their new Antitrust chief, Connell himself talked with Baxter infrequently, and then it was only to report superficially on the progress of the trial. The trial staff perceived advantages in this arms-length relationship with the division's political appointees. The last thing any of them wanted was to consult on trial strategy with Baxter or his front office assistants, none of whom had any solid litigating experience. It was better to be left alone with their case against George Saunders and AT&T, even if that case seemed increasingly to be doomed. For his part, Baxter believed that the internal deliberations of the Reagan administration were none of the trial staff's business, and he told them next to nothing about the warfare between Justice, Commerce, Defense, and the White House. "I'm doing all I can on that front," Baxter told the staff when they asked about the newspaper stories. "You are to win the case."

And day after day in Judge Greene's courtroom, thirteen blocks down Pennsylvania Avenue from the White House, Gerry

Connell and his staff were trying to do exactly that, as quickly
as possible. In May and June, after the disastrous showing by
Bill McGowan, morale on the Justice side had begun to go up
again. Other MCI executives testifying about the company's
problems with AT&T during the early 1970s had done reasonably well, particularly Larry Harris, whose relentlessly detailed
account of the early interconnection negotiations suggested that
if McGowan was arrogant and devious, he was no more so than
John deButts and other top phone-company executives. Equally
important was the testimony of executives from long-distance
companies other than MCI, who, even though they had been
mainly on the sidelines during the important battles between
McGowan and deButts, established that AT&T's behavior and
policies during the early 1970s affected more than just the personal fortune of MCI's chairman. Judge Greene's obvious interest in these witnesses—the numerous questions he asked,
his positive tone of voice, his upbeat and aggressive mood—
stirred the hopes of the Justice lawyers because it suggested
that Greene's dislike for McGowan had not tainted his view of
the crucial intercity services section of the case. Slowly, Gerry
Connell's presentation was building on itself—after sixty days
of trial, ninety-three witnesses, and more than 2,000 documents
entered into evidence, could Judge Greene fail to see that the
phone company was so large that it was beyond anyone's control? Or had George Saunders, through his aggressive cross-
examination, already convinced Greene that AT&T had been
victimized by its regulators and competitors?

The answer came at a most opportune time for the Justice
trial staff, disheartened as it was by rumors of its own imminent
demise. As soon as stories about Malcolm Baldrige's dismissal
proposal appeared in the press, George Saunders seized every
opportunity in court to remind Greene—sometimes humor-
ously, sometimes seriously—that the plaintiff in U.S. v. AT&T,
the government, seemed to be of two minds about the merits
of the case. At one point, Saunders, who was brimming over
with confidence about the progress of his defense, suggested
to Greene that he might want to change the scheduled briefings
and hearings on Saunders' "motion to dismiss." As was com-

mon in trials such as *U.S.* v. *AT&T,* Saunders had announced that as soon as Gerry Connell was finished putting on his evidence, AT&T intended to move that Greene dismiss the case, arguing that it was inadequate on its face. Although anything was possible, no one seriously expected that Greene would throw out the whole case. But the judge might decide that some sections had not been sufficiently proved by the government, thus saving Saunders the trouble of refuting them. Ordinarily, both sides filed detailed, written briefs outlining why they thought each section of the case should or should not be dismissed before the defense's case began. After that, oral arguments might be held before the judge issued his decision. What Saunders had casually suggested one day early in June was that Greene reverse the order and take oral arguments first. Saunders' idea was that since Connell would be wrapping up the government case soon, after which there would be a three-week recess, it might be useful for Greene to mull over the arguments while he was on vacation, before he saw the written briefs. But Greene interpreted the suggestion another way. He thought Saunders was implying that written briefs weren't even necessary, that the case should just be summarily dismissed on the basis of oral arguments. That idea made Greene very angry.

Harold Greene read the newspapers. He even discussed the stories about Baldrige's dismissal proposal with his law clerks. So on the scorching hot morning of Thursday, June 25, Greene knew that the proceedings in his court were under close scrutiny by the top officials of the Reagan administration, who, according to news accounts, might be just days away from a final decision to drop the AT&T case. Greene decided that Thursday morning to send those officials a message.

"Before you proceed with what you have to say," Greene announced testily as soon as he was seated at the bench, "let me proceed with what I have to say. I want to discuss briefly matters that the defendants have raised.

"Let me deal first with the suggestion that the motions to dismiss should be argued now and perhaps briefed later... The first reason, as I gather it, is that the defendants are ready to argue immediately because the issues are clear and the gov-

ernment's proof is patently inadequate. I think the case is hardly
simple by any standard. We have heard four months of testimony, many witnesses and documents... As to the question
of whether the government's case is so patently inadequate that
it can be disposed of by informal oral presentations, followed
by a more or less off-the-cuff decision from the court, let me
say this: Whatever the substantive merits of the motions and
the case generally will ultimately turn out to be, I don't believe
the government's evidence justifies such cavalier treatment.
The government has presented a respectable case that the defendants have violated the antitrust laws... Defenses have been
raised, but I certainly could not say it is self-evident that these
defenses are valid and will prevail.

"On the second point, which I think was made, that according to the press, 'The government is very concerned about
whether they are going to proceed with this case or not' and
therefore it is in the public interest for the court to decide it
now, I haven't heard from the government that they are concerned. In any event, I don't propose to act on the basis of
press reports or someone's concerns unrelated to this lawsuit.
The court has an obligation to deal with this lawsuit under
existing antitrust laws, and it will do so irrespective of speculation outside the judicial arena."

"I appreciate the things you have said," Gerry Connell told
Greené when his speech was over.

"OK," said the judge.

"I guess I better leave it there," Connell said. "There are
some things I could say, but I just think they are better left
unsaid. Thank you."

Greene, too, left something unsaid: that this would be the
first of several attempts by the judge to raise the stakes in the
Reagan administration's debate over dismissal of the AT&T case.
Until now, Greene had made no mention of how he regarded
the overall presentation by Gerry Connell and the Justice trial
team. Bernie Wunder and other Commerce officials reading the
trial transcripts every day were telling cabinet secretaries and
White House staffers that large sections of the government's

case were "a jumbled mess." Now Greene was calling the evidence "respectable" and was accusing the AT&T defense lawyers of being "cavalier." If Greene continued to speak out forcefully and frequently in support of Justice's presentation, he would make it increasingly difficult for those in the administration who argued that "only a handful of antitrust lawyers will care" if the case was dropped.

No one on either side of the courtroom doubted that this was a deliberate strategy on Greene's part. No matter what Greene was thinking about the merits of the case, no matter if he was prepared to order the breakup of the phone company or not, there was no question that he was deeply disturbed by even the specter of outside political interference in *U.S. v AT&T*. That the interference was coming from a Republican administration philosophically at odds with the judge was far from irrelevant. But the more important point was that Greene himself had been, for four years, displaying the case as an example of how federal courts could manage complex antitrust litigation. If the case was scuttled by politicians, the lesson would be lost. As long as it was in his courtroom, Greene wanted to decide the case himself, on the merits, "under the existing antitrust laws." He was not going to give it up without a fight.

For George Saunders and the AT&T trial team, Greene's outburst that Thursday was not only embarrassing, it was profoundly discouraging. Despite the research they had done into Greene's background, which suggested that the phone company faced an uphill fight in the judge's courtroom, the AT&T lawyers had convinced themselves that they were winning, that Saunders' impressive oratory and enterprising cross-examination had brought Judge Greene at least back to the middle, if not all the way over to AT&T's side. In the midst of an exhausting, full-throttle trial like *U.S. v. AT&T*, such self-confidence, even if it was deluded, was sustaining to lawyers working eighteen hours a day, seven days a week. And while Greene's speech that morning was far from a verdict, it was nonetheless deflating and demoralizing since it raised serious questions about whether the judge's mind was, to some degree, already made up. That was a thought that no litigator six or eight months from the completion of trial could afford to contemplate.

But the news only got worse for AT&T. The next Monday, in New York City, a federal jury returned its verdict in the private antitrust suit brought by Litton against the phone company. The Litton case was the largest of over two dozen private phone equipment suits filed against AT&T during the 1970s, almost all of which pertained to the protective coupling arrangements John deButts had required rival companies to buy when equipment competition was first unleashed. As it had done with the MCI case, Justice had piggybacked much of the phone equipment section of its own suit against AT&T on documents and depositions developed by Litton. After seven days of deliberations, the New York jury announced that it found AT&T guilty of anticompetitive practices, and it awarded Litton $276.6 million in damages. As much as Judge Greene's speech on Thursday, the verdict served notice to Commerce, Defense, and White House officials that a dismissal decision would have to be rigorously explained and defended before Congress and the public. Now much of the Justice case against AT&T—MCI and Litton—had been tried before juries in private antitrust suits. The results were unambiguous: two wins and more than $2 billion in damage awards. Because the verdicts and awards pertained to past conduct and not to the future of the telephone industry, they had little bearing on the relief section of Justice's case, where the government sought to break up the phone company in order to enhance future competition. But on the liability side, on the question of whether or not AT&T was guilty of violating the antitrust laws, George Saunders and his client were beginning to look extremely vulnerable.

Just before 3:00 P.M. on Wednesday afternoon, two days after the Litton verdict was announced, Gerry Connell stood at the podium before Judge Greene and said, "With that, Your Honor, I am going to say that plaintiff rests."

Outside the windowless courthouse, forty-mile-an-hour winds were buffeting the city, and lightning and thunder were crashing from a black sky. It was indeed an ominous day for the department of Justice. It had taken seven years, millions of dollars, three lead attorneys, five Antitrust chiefs, and two judges—but the deed was done. A "respectable" antitrust case seeking the breakup of the largest corporation in the world had been presented in federal court. Judge Greene, for one, was so pleased he could hardly contain himself.

"All right," he told Connell. "I think the plaintiff is entitled to rest in more ways than one.

"I should say that perhaps the four months here have been an exhausting time, particularly for the two lead counsel, Mr. Connell and Mr. Saunders, who have been here every minute of every day—and I don't know what hours they have spent outside the courtroom and I really wouldn't want to find out. Also, I am sure this has been an exhausting time for the staffs of the parties. But it was all done, and particularly so far as the government is concerned . . . I want you to know I appreciate the effort that has gone into it."

"Thank you, Your Honor," Connell said. But the judge wasn't finished.

"Despite the considerable pressure of getting the evidence in on time, the fact is it was presented, and without indicating anything at all one way or the other about the merits, I think you did manage in four months to properly present your side of the case. So I appreciate that."

"I thank you for those remarks," Connell said again.

Now Saunders stood up. "I would simply like to say that I think the graciousness and the fairness with which this court has handled this case and treated counsel for both sides is appreciated by every lawyer who has come into this court. I think we are all dedicated to making the judicial process work in a very difficult case, and I think the government is entitled to their congratulations for doing their side of it, and I hope we get ours."

Greene replied, "I have really appreciated the efforts both sides have made and the graciousness and the willingness to try to show that this process can work, which in a way is a goal of the court."

"I cannot improve on the comments of the court or of my

Brother Saunders. I will not try to, Your Honor. Thank you very much," Connell concluded.

And with that, Judge Greene recessed *U.S.* v. *AT&T* until August 3, a month away, when AT&T would begin to present its defense, assuming the Reagan administration did not dismiss the case in the interim.

The bubbly congratulations and good cheer in court that day reflected both the genuine affection that had developed between Connell, Saunders, and Greene, and also their mutual suspicion that the recess of the case might well be permanent. The two sides even held a picnic at Fort Hunt Park in Washington to celebrate the progress in court. The long, intense hours in trial had bonded the opposing lawyers in a way that their more cold-blooded superiors—Baxter, Trienens, and Charlie Brown—could never fully appreciate. The trial lawyers sometimes saw themselves as common soldiers, wedded by the culture of war even as they served the ancient enmities and prejudices of their generals. At the picnic, the Justice lawyers showed up in blue and white T-shirts that said, "Reach out, reach out and crush someone." The AT&T lawyers wore yellow shirts that bore the acronym, "TWOM," in reference to the name Judge Greene had seized on in court to describe George Saunders' AT&T trial team, "The Well-Oiled Machine." In a softball game, Saunders and Connell pitched, and the machine beat the government, 17–12. Judge Greene declined to umpire and instead played volleyball.

Chapter 23

Baxter's Finesse

O N the Wednesday following the picnic, George Saunders and Bill Baxter flew separately to Aspen, Colorado, to attend the annual conference on antitrust law sponsored by National Economic Research Associates (NERA), a prominent economics consulting firm based in New York. Saunders and Baxter were scheduled to appear on separate panels at the conference, at which prestigious antitrust lawyers from around the country traditionally gathered for three days to read technical papers, discuss issues, and play a lot of golf and tennis. That evening, Saunders and Baxter checked into The Gant, a hotel-condominium complex in the shadow of the Rocky Mountains.

Following one of the tedious panel sessions on Friday, Jules Joskow, an executive with NERA, was chatting with Baxter in one of The Gant's conference rooms. Joskow had once done some consulting work for AT&T on the Justice case and he was familiar with the trial now in recess in Washington.

Casually, Joskow suggested, "Bill, how about you and me and George sitting down and talking about the economic theory of the case?"

"That would be wonderful," Baxter said.

"I'm not calling a meeting," Joskow emphasized. "I'm not

calling a settlement conference. Let's just sit down and talk—
no promises, no suggestions."

Baxter agreed. A short time later, Joskow found Saunders
and told him about the proposition. Saunders was gleeful. He
had never spent time with Baxter before, face-to-face, and besides, there was nothing Saunders enjoyed more than a chance
to talk and argue. Saunders and other AT&T lawyers had heard
the Justice trial team refer to Baxter as a "space cadet," but few
of them doubted that the Antitrust chief was brilliant in his
own, perhaps strange, way. Since Saunders believed he could
convince Judge Greene, a certified Kennedy liberal, that *U.S.*
v. *AT&T* was a fraud, there was no reason for him to doubt that
he could also persuade the conservative Baxter.

"Look, Bill," Saunders said when he saw Baxter. "I don't
want to talk settlement. I want to convince you that this case
has no merit."

"All right," Baxter replied laconically.

That afternoon, the three met in Joskow's comfortable hotel
room. They ordered a bottle of white wine, and the debate
began.

In a virtual summation of his opening argument to Judge
Greene, Saunders went through each section of the case and
argued that the Justice department's charges were either trivial,
irrelevant, explainable because of confusing and fast-changing
regulations, or, in the case of the MCI story, part of a larger
conspiracy to skim profits from the Bell System. Saunders was
his ever-passionate self. He talked about Bell Labs and Western
Electric and their role in major technological advances during
the last century. What would be the consequences for the country if Greene ordered the divestiture of Western and Bell Labs?
Saunders asked. Would Baxter consider that to be in the national
interest?

"I would oppose that," Baxter said, as if that would make
a difference. But in fact, he was adamant on the point. According to the Antitrust chief's theoretical views about the telecommunications industry, it was important that AT&T's Long
Lines, Western, and Bell Labs subsidiaries be integrated. They
represented the part of AT&T's business that could be quickly

deregulated. The local operating companies, however, would always have to be regulated like other utilities, Baxter said. Therefore, they had to be divested. All of them. There was simply no other way.

But what about the case itself? "These are trumped up charges," Saunders said. "How can you break up the entire phone company when so many of the charges in court have already been made irrelevant by changes in the marketplace?"

"Oh, we have enough to get at you," Baxter replied.

The remark was appalling to both Joskow and Saunders. Baxter had demonstrated during the debate that he understood the broad outline of facts being contested before Judge Greene. But it was also clear that the details of the case bored him, that the only thing he was really concerned about was the economic theory behind divestiture of the operating companies. The lawsuit itself, the MCI story and the history of early 1970s phone industry competition, was little more than the means to an end for Baxter, and it was "enough." The Justice lawsuit Baxter was in charge of, though, sought not only the breakup of the operating companies but also the divestiture of Western. If Baxter "would oppose that," then was he willing to drop divestiture of Western from the suit? That, Baxter indicated, would have to be discussed with Gerry Connell and the trial staff. And Saunders knew that Connell would never go along: there was nothing for Connell to gain by dropping a major part of his case in the middle of trial. So when the bottle of wine was drained and Saunders' breath was expended, the lawyers were back at square one. Baxter was immovable.

That weekend, however, when he flew back to Washington from Colorado, it was becoming increasingly unclear whether Baxter could continue much longer to stonewall the combined forces of AT&T and the Reagan administration. It was one thing for a stubborn academic to be unrelenting about his principles. It was another for him to be just as inflexible about his political tactics. At every crucial turn thus far—the Crimson Sky deal, the spat with Weinberger, the Senate legislation he refused to support, Baldrige's dismissal proposal—Baxter had declined to cede even an inch to his adversaries. When Weinberger's call for dismissal hit the newspapers in April, for example, teams of lawyers from Justice and Defense had been organized to see if some compromise could be negotiated. A month later, Baxter broke the talks off, declaring that they had reached an impasse. Similarly, after the June 12 cabinet meeting, the White House had instructed Baldrige and Baxter to see if there was some way Justice could publicly support the telecommunications legislation, known as Senate Bill 898, that was so important to Bernie Wunder and the Commerce department. Again, Baxter had refused to budge. The bill, which was grudgingly supported by AT&T, proposed to solve the phone industry competition problem by forcing the phone company to establish separate subsidiaries for its unregulated businesses while preserving the integrity of the national network. Baxter told Commerce he could not support such a formula because it did not go far enough to prevent cross-subsidies between the "regulated monopoly" and "unregulated, competitive" sides of AT&T.

When he arrived back at his Justice office on Monday, July 13, it was apparent to Baxter that he needed to devise some new approach to his stalemate with Commerce and the White House. On Wednesday, the Cabinet Council on Commerce and Trade, chaired by Malcolm Baldrige, was scheduled to meet again for the first time since June 12 to discuss the AT&T case. It was Baxter's impression, derived mainly from his conversations with Jim Baker, that while the administration urgently wished to dispose of U.S. v. AT&T in some manner, the White House was not yet prepared to impose a solution that was unacceptable to its Antitrust chief. So far, however, Baxter had given the administration no indication that he was willing to meet them halfway. Baxter recognized that if he went to the Wednesday cabinet meeting with nothing new to offer, he would in effect be admitting to Jim Baker, Ed Meese, and Malcolm Baldrige that the debate over the case was hopelessly deadlocked. Baldrige could rightly claim that nothing had changed after more than a month of internal discussions, and he could argue that it was time now for decisive action by the President. Baxter saw, too, that his own position was weakened by his steadfast refusal to suggest changes or offer amendments that would make S.898 acceptable to him. The legislation, after all, was the most important ostensible reason behind Commerce's dismissal proposal. Everyone in the administration except Baxter, it seemed, believed that in theory it was Congress, not the courts, that should make telecommunications policy.

In bridge, a game at which Bill Baxter was exceptionally proficient, a player can "finesse" his opponents' best cards by holding back the highest card in his own hand while challenging his adversaries with cards of lesser value. The idea is to play the finesse for as long as possible in the hope that by the time the opponent reveals his strong card, it will be too late for it to do any damage. Such was the strategy Baxter unveiled at the Wednesday morning cabinet council meeting in the Roosevelt Room of the White House.

President Reagan was absent, having decided to spend his day in a series of meetings with White House staff, newly appointed ambassadors, and business leaders, and so the atmosphere in the cabinet room was far more relaxed than it had been a month earlier. There was discussion again about the merits and potential political consequences of dismissal, but Baxter preempted any heated debate by announcing that, for the first time, he would be willing to consider a nondivestiture solution to the problem of phone industry competition, and that if the proper amendments could be drafted, he would even be willing to support S.898 publicly. For the Commerce officials, so long at odds with Baxter and by now in a state of high agitation over their failure to accomplish either dismissal or unity on legislation, Baxter's announcement was a major breakthrough. Discussion shifted quickly to the details of the amendments to S.898 that Baxter wanted to propose; they were complex, technical changes to the bill. One would provide tougher standards by which to measure whether companies like MCI were being granted equal access to AT&T's local exchanges. A second outlined new regulations about how the basic operating companies could purchase phone and other equipment from outside suppliers. Together, they added a new layer of rules to S.898, which Baxter had previously criticized as too regulatory. But none of the Commerce officials minded, since even with these amendments, S.898 would still preserve the integrity of the national phone network. Intrigued, Bernie Wunder and Sherman Unger scheduled a meeting with Baxter in his Justice office at two-thirty that afternoon to begin work on the amendments immediately. The finesse play had begun.

The danger, of course, was that Baxter might be quickly trumped by the White House. Now that the Antitrust chief had admitted that there was a nondivestiture solution to phone industry competition that he might be willing to accept, Baldrige, Weinberger, and Meese could claim that there was no longer any reason to continue prosecuting *U.S.* v. *AT&T.* Baxter's willingness to compromise had gotten him past the cabinet council meeting, but it had bought him nothing more than time. Another cabinet meeting was scheduled for Tuesday, July 28. By then, the amendments to S.898, known somewhat facetiously as Baxter I and Baxter II, would be drafted. Senator Packwood, S.898's main sponsor, had announced during the second week of July that his bill was "doomed" if the Justice case against AT&T was not abandoned. If Baxter supported the bill, with his amendments, wasn't he now obligated to accept dismissal of *U.S.* v. *AT&T?*

Baxter, however, had not really changed his mind about the case. His amendments were mainly a tactical ploy, not a shift in his principles. Even during the two weeks after the July 15 cabinet council meeting, when he worked with Commerce to draft the amendments, he always qualified his support for S.898 by saying he would back the bill "if it's done right." At the same time, Baxter and Rose continued to press their argument to Jim Baker and his supporters on the White House staff that the political consequences of dismissal would be catastrophic for President Reagan. Baxter knew that the status of the Justice case was still touch and go, but his strategy was to keep pushing on every front—distracting Commerce by compromising on the amendments, but resisting dismissal in the White House. On the latter front, Malcolm Baldrige continued to oppose Baxter and Rose. He insisted to Baker and the President that there would be no great outcry if the case was dropped, and that the only losers by such a decision would be the dozens of private antitrust lawyers who hoped to piggyback on the Justice case and make handsome livings at the expense of the phone company.

The climax to all this back-channel lobbying and gamesmanship came on the hot and steamy afternoon of Monday, July 27, the day before the scheduled cabinet council meeting at which Baxter's support for S.898 was supposed to be formally ratified. At 3:30 P.M., all of the main players gathered in Ed Meese's office in the West Wing of the White House. Meese was there, as were Bill Baxter, Jonathan Rose, Malcolm Baldrige, Bernie Wunder, Sherman Unger, Jim Baker, and David Gergen, the White House's communications director and a so-called moderate ally of Baker's. The assembly was called to set the agenda for the next morning's cabinet council meeting as well as to resolve the question of whether *U.S.* v. *AT&T* had to be dismissed if S.898 was to have a reasonable chance to pass.

On dismissal, the split was an even four against four. Baxter, Rose, Baker, and Gergen argued against; Meese, Baldrige, Wunder, and Unger argued in favor.

"If I pull the plug on the case," Baxter said, "AT&T's support for the legislation would change to opposition. What I want to do is pursue parallel tracks."

That argument appealed to Baker, who the Commerce officials were by now referring to as "Mr. Caution." "I don't like the idea of sweeping the thing away," he said. For one thing, Baker said he was concerned that Peter Rodino, the fiercely partisan, Democratic chairman of the House antitrust subcommittee, would launch a major investigation into how the decision to dismiss was made, and that the President, and possibly Attorney General Smith, would have to endure a spate of bad publicity.

"But they'll be looking for a Dita Beard," Bernie Wunder countered, referring to the woman who broke the ITT antitrust scandal in the Nixon administration. "And this thing is as clean as a hound's tooth. There are no hotel keys in anybody's desk drawer." Wunder and Baldrige reminded the group that the Commerce officials had kept contemporaneous summaries of every meeting and phone call pertaining to dismissal. "Some kind of investigation is inevitable, yes. But this is not a back-room deal. It's a reasoned policy decision."

"It will interfere with the President's program," Baker said. "The priorities of the administration are the tax bill, the budget, foreign policy, et cetera. That's what we should be focusing on. All this peripheral stuff is only going to get us in trouble."

"What kind of case do you have?" Meese asked Baxter. "How good is the case?"

"I think the chances of winning are fifty-fifty," Baxter answered. "It's not the best case I've ever seen, and it's not the worst, either."

Again, the debate was at an impasse, mainly because of Baker's resistance to dismissal. Baker liked Baxter's idea about "parallel tracks," but there was no getting around the point that as long as the case was active, it would be virtually impossible to pass legislation in Congress. And legislation, everyone agreed, was the ideal way to define the future of the telecommunications industry.

Once again, it was Baxter who broke the deadlock, this time with a proposal that was as cunning as it was preposterous. Baxter insisted that if *U.S.* v. *AT&T* was dismissed, Bell would abandon its support for S.898 because it would no longer have any reason to compromise with its industry competitors. But he accepted, at least outwardly, the point that active prosecution of AT&T doomed the telecommunications bill. So why not ask Judge Greene to suspend the trial, "continue" it, in legal terminology, for a period long enough to give Congress and the administration time to pass legislation—say, about a year? With the case in a state of suspended animation, AT&T and Congress both would have incentives to pass acceptable legislation. If the bill passed, Baxter would drop the case. If it didn't pass, the trial would resume next summer.

"The case would be put on ice," Baxter explained.

"Is there any chance Judge Greene would agree to such a proposal?" Baxter was asked.

"We've got a good chance. There's a real shot at it," he said.

The proposal served Baxter's strategy in three important

ways. First, on the surface at least, it appeared that the Antitrust chief was once again offering a major compromise. Just a few months earlier, he had talked of litigating "to the eyeballs," and now, for the sake of unity in the administration, he was willing to suspend the case for a year and possibly abandon it altogether. Second—and Baxter did not admit this to his rivals from Commerce—the continuance request itself would serve as a kind of political trial balloon testing Baldrige's assertion that the public would react indifferently if the case was dismissed. How Congress and the press responded to Justice's attempt to suspend the AT&T case would provide an accurate reading of the public's attitude. Baxter suspected, as he had said all along, that there would be a great commotion about it, so great that Baker and the President would decide once and for all that dismissal was a politically flawed idea. And finally, if Judge Greene turned down the request, Baxter would be in a position to say to Baker, Meese, and the Commerce officials, "Look, I've stretched a long way. Dismissal just isn't tenable. Let's go back to my amendments and pursue the parallel tracks."

Of course, the proposal was a red herring. Baxter and Rose were the only two people in Meese's office that afternoon who understood just how unlikely it was that Greene would grant a year-long continuance of the case. Some of the Commerce officials read the daily trial transcripts, but they did not understand that since 1978, when he took over the case, Greene had said repeatedly that *U.S.* v. *AT&T* was going to be a model of efficiency for the federal court system. Yes, it was technically possible that Greene would agree to a suspension—a continuance was legally permissible. But realistically, Baxter knew well that barring some bizarre turn of events, the chances were almost nil that Greene would accede to such a request, especially when it was coming from the Reagan administration at a time when rumors about an imminent dismissal decision were still rife in Washington. For Greene, granting a continuance would be giving the administration an easy way out of its dilemma, and in his courtroom speech a few weeks earlier, the judge had already made it plain that he was going to do all he could to raise the stakes for the President should he choose to drop the suit. Nonetheless, in the context of the internal administration debate among Commerce, Justice, and the White House (Weinberger and his Defense staff had stayed out of the detailed talks once their focus shifted from outright dismissal to a compromise on legislation), Baxter's proposal was attractive. The consensus was that it was at least worth a try.

On that note, the meeting in Meese's office broke up. The next morning at the White House, the Cabinet Council on Commerce and Trade ratified Baxter's proposal and authorized him, on behalf of the administration and the President, to seek an eleven-month continuance of *U.S.* v. *AT&T* from Judge Greene. If granted, the case would be suspended until June 1982. By then, the cabinet council hoped, S.898 would be passed by Congress and signed by President Reagan. Then the antitrust case would be formally dropped.

When Baxter got word that afternoon that the cabinet had signed off on his proposal, he called Howard Trienens at AT&T headquarters in New York to see if Trienens would be willing to seek the continuance jointly with the Justice department.

AT&T's general counsel thought that Baxter's proposal was absurd. To Trienens, it was yet another example of what he described as the administration's "failure of will." But there was no reason for Trienens to oppose the request: perhaps this proposal was really just a last ditch effort by Baxter to stave off dismissal. Perhaps, if the request was denied, the administration would act to drop the case immediately. Trienens did not ask Baxter where the continuance proposal had come from. He assumed that Baxter had been ordered by the administration to present it to Greene.

"Judge Greene will kick you in the teeth," Trienens told Baxter.

"I have strong teeth," Baxter replied.

Baxter then called Judge Greene's chambers and made an appointment to see him the next day, Wednesday, at noon.

On Wednesday morning, Baxter called Gerry Connell at the Justice trial staff offices on 12th Street. "I've been told to go over and ask for a postponement of the trial from Judge

Greene," Baxter said. He explained the details of the continuance request. "Do you want to go along?"

"If you don't care, I'd just as soon not," Connell said. He explained to Baxter that since the trial was in recess and the air conditioning in the trial staff offices was erratic, he had not worn a suit to work that day. Baxter accepted this explanation. In fact, Connell thought the continuance proposal was doomed and he had no desire to sully his reputation with Greene by being an active party to it. When Baxter hung up, Connell told the Justice trial staff about the call. The consensus among the staff was that Baxter had resorted to this desperate move because it was his only chance to prevent outright dismissal. They expected that once Greene turned him down, the case would be dropped. Baxter had said nothing to Connell to contradict that impression. If the trial staff was outraged by the request and its implications, it would only help prove his point that the political consequences of dismissal would be severe.

At the appointed hour, Trienens and Baxter arrived at Greene's chambers on the second floor of the U.S. District Courthouse. Trienens had persuaded George Saunders to accompany him: it might help the cause if Greene saw a united front from AT&T. But Saunders, like Connell, and for that matter Trienens himself, thought the continuance request was preposterous. During the discussion with the judge, Saunders sat off to one side, as if to distance himself physically from the proposal. Trienens and Baxter sat in the chairs directly in front of Judge Greene's desk.

"Your Honor, we are here to ask you to continue the case until June 30th, 1982," Baxter began abruptly. "I am urging the motion on you. I can assure you that I am speaking not just for the Antitrust Division of the Department of Justice, but for the administration and the President.

"The administration has concluded that there is no realistic possibility of moving the legislation, which is now usually known as S.898—a very comprehensive reshaping of the telecommunications industry—through the Congress unless, in some sense, this case is put on ice.

"I was, myself, rather difficult to convince of that point, not because I have any particular expertise about Congress, which I certainly do not, but because I did not view S.898 as an adequate substitute for the relief we are seeking in the case.

"In the last several weeks, we have worked out an amendment to S.898, which addresses itself to what I viewed as a primary weakness in that legislation. We have checked it out with the Bell company, and the administration is wholly in support of it. That enabled us to come to you today with complete agreement, I think, throughout the administration and ask you to do that."

"I am not sure I understand that," Greene said, visibily agitated. "What does all of that mean? You mean the legislation is going to be passed before then? Then the case will not go forward, or the case will go forward in June, or..."

"If the legislation passes with the amendments that have been worked out, it would be the administration's intention to discontinue the litigation," Baxter explained.

"Is there anything more you wish to add to that rather summary-cryptic communication?" Greene asked, annoyed.

"There is really nothing else I would like to add, Your Honor, although I would be happy to make it less summary and less cryptic at any particular point you would care to explore," Baxter said.

"Well," Greene replied, "I obviously have to think about it, but the case has been pending for seven years. We have heard the government's evidence. We are ready to proceed to hear the defendant's evidence starting next Monday. If the Congress passes legislation that moots the case in some way or other, that is one thing, but the mere fact that legislation may be pending, that may or may not be enacted, doesn't seem to be a very good basis for truncating a case and recessing it for, what are you talking about, a year?"

"Eleven months."

"Well, I have to think about it. But I can tell you right now that my immediate reaction is that it is not a good idea."

"It is an unusual motion," Baxter conceded.

"While I am not opposed to either unusual or innovative

matters, this . . . well . . . I don't regard it as a very constructive proposal. Mr. Trienens?" Greene asked, looking to AT&T's counsel for some explanation.

"The pendancy of this case does, in fact, as Mr. Ba .ter said, get in the way of resolving the structure of this industry through legislation. . . . Everything is hung up with no answer."

"I don't understand the Congress," Greene said. "If you think legislation is the appropriate way to go, why can't Congress pass legislation regardless of what happens here?"

"Your logic is impeccable," Trienens conceded. "There is no question about it. The tensions, the jurisdictions between the two committees, the Judiciary Committee, and the Commerce Committee—it is just a complication that gets in the way of getting anything done. It shouldn't be. I agree, thoroughly, but it does get in the way."

"Well, I am sorry the judicial process is a complication," Greene answered facetiously. "But I can say, just like Mr. Saunders, 'I am just a simple country boy.' I don't know about these kinds of high political matters. . . . All I can do is sit here. I didn't file the lawsuit. I didn't pursue the lawsuit since September or November, whenever it was, 1974. I wasn't even on this court at that time.

"The case came here. The case was pursued by the department of Justice. The department of Justice and the administration have seen fit not to dismiss it. It is here.

"Now, I am also ready to have the parties settle it. Don't misunderstand me: I am not eager to take this masochistic punishment of being here every day and absorbing a great deal of technical, economic, and legal information, day after day, even as much as I like the lawyers in the case."

"I thought you were enjoying it, Judge," George Saunders said.

"To an extent. To an extent . . ."

"I certainly understand your reaction," Baxter said. And a few minutes later, the Antitrust chief ended the conference with Judge Greene.

A few hours later, Greene issued a terse order denying the continuance request.

Late in the afternoon, the administration players involved in the case met again in Ed Meese's West Wing office. The question was, "Where do we go from here?"

Dismissal was not an option, at least for the time being. Baxter's "compromise" continuance proposal had decided that question for Jim Baker on Monday. Besides, press and congressional reaction to the request was already lending credence to Baxter's and Rose's thesis that the political consequences of dropping the case were unacceptable. Reporters were deluging Justice with phone calls about the meeting that day with Greene; on Thursday, headlines across the country would trumpet news about a possible dismissal of the AT&T case. The Republican-controlled Senate Judiciary Committee was planning hearings for the next Wednesday to investigate the origins and circumstances of Malcolm Baldrige's original proposal to dismiss. The political trial balloon, it seemed, had been blasted out of the sky.

But the Commerce officials had one last proposal, an idea that had been inadvertently suggested by Baxter's finesse strategy. If the Antitrust chief was willing to support S.898, as amended by Baxter I and Baxter II, then shouldn't he also accept a negotiated settlement of the antitrust case if it mirrored the Senate legislation? By compromising on the bill, Baxter had acknowledged that it was possible, in his view, to solve the problems of phone industry competition without any divestiture by AT&T. Clearly, it was the view of the President and his top advisers that any settlement acceptable to Baxter should be pursued. Would the Antitrust chief be willing to negotiate with AT&T a consent decree, identical to S.898, that would settle *U.S.* v. *AT&T* out of court?

Baxter agreed that the idea was logical. While he still believed that divestiture of the operating companies was by far the most attractive solution, he really had no choice but to accept the Commerce proposal. Sherman Unger said that he would contact Howard Trienens as soon as possible to arrange the initial negotiations, which would soon be dubbed by AT&T "Quagmire II," the sequel to the phone company's nickname for the Crimson Sky deal. Baxter told Unger that he would assign two of his Antitrust front office assistants, Richard Levine and Ron Carr, to handle the day-to-day talks with AT&T.

Since Quagmire II would be a nondivestiture, immensely complex injunctive settlement, there was no reason to hope that it could be concluded in a few weeks, or even a few months. But from Baxter's tactical vantage, there was no harm in opening negotiations between Justice and AT&T: the talks would be an element of the "parallel tracks" idea that Baxter had so effectively sold to the administration.

And meanwhile, on Monday, August 3, the trial would resume before Judge Greene, where the lawyers would again pore over the history of telephone competition in the early 1970s in an effort to decide the industry's future. As Peter Kenney of the Justice trial team was heard to remark in the weeks following Baxter's continuance request, "We on the trial staffs are like the grunts in Vietnam. We do the other guys' dirty work."

Chapter 24

A Judicial Temperament

ON Monday, August 3, when Gerry Connell and George Saunders returned to Judge Greene's courtroom to resume the five-month-old trial of *U.S.* v. *AT&T,* only a handful of people in and out of the Reagan administration knew that dismissal of the case by the President was now highly unlikely. And for various reasons, those few people were keeping the information to themselves.

Over at Malcolm Baldrige's Commerce department, for instance, the compromise forged with Baxter during the last days of July was not being loudly lauded as a victory. True, since the Antitrust chief now publicly supported S.898 there was a better chance than before that Congress, and not the federal courts, would decide the future of the telecommunications industry. But the widespread public perception that Baxter had been forced against his will to offer amendments and back the legislation undermined the value of his support. There was some hope among Commerce's political appointees that the Quagmire II negotiations might lead to a nondivestiture settlement even if S.898 failed in Congress, but after Sherman Unger explained the Quagmire II idea to Howard Trienens, there was no role for Commerce in those discussions; any deal would have to be made solely between Justice and AT&T. Baldrige himself was disappointed by the way things had turned out.

Among other reasons, the cowboy cabinet secretary felt that he had personally failed to achieve the relatively simple objective he had laid out the previous spring: dismissal of a bothersome and destructive antitrust case. So distraught was Baldrige that on Thursday, July 30, he made a personal appointment to see President Reagan to try to persuade him one last time that outright dismissal was the only sensible course for the administration, even though by now the compromise with Baxter seemed impossible to change.

"The President would say, 'If it ain't broke, don't fix it,'" Baldrige told one of his aides before he met with Reagan. "He has common sense."

But Reagan also had an acute sense about politics. The President told Baldrige that for him, a deciding factor was what effect dismissal would have on his friend and attorney general, William French Smith. Reagan said he was worried that if the case was dropped, Congress and the press might think that Smith had a hand in the decision, even though Smith was recused from the case for conflict-of-interest reasons. The previous March, when Cap Weinberger had ignited a furor by saying that the AT&T case should be dropped, a rumor had circulated in the media and on Capitol Hill that it was really Bill Smith who had put Weinberger up to it. Although precautions had been taken by Baldrige in anticipation of a congressional investigation, Reagan was concerned that they would not be enough to protect Smith.

Despite this seemingly final decision by Reagan, neither Baldrige nor his subordinates were ready yet to advertise that dismissal had been ruled out by the administration. The continuance request by Baxter and widespread rumors that the case might still be dropped served as a kind of threat to Congress, urging it to move legislation along quickly. Besides, there was still the chance that Reagan might change his mind; nothing would be gained for Commerce or AT&T by a public surrender to Baxter. The Antitrust chief, too, was tight-lipped about the success of his finesse play. The Quagmire II negotiations had to be conducted in secret, and there was no reason for him to stop "pushing on all fronts," as he put it. The victory in the administration might only be temporary. Anyway, the taciturn Antitrust chief shared the details of his battles with Commerce with only one or two of his front office aides. For the most part, Gerry Connell and the Justice trial team were kept uninformed.

And so, of course, was Judge Harold Greene, with whom the fate of AT&T once again rested as George Saunders began to present his defense in early August. Before Saunders called his first witness on Monday, August 3, Greene announced to the courtroom, "All I know about the government's position in this case is what Mr. Connell and his colleagues tell me in this courtroom. What other people may say in other places, either to the Congress or to the newspapers or anybody else, is not my concern. The government's position is stated right here by the attorneys representing the government."

Privately, however, Greene was far from uninterested in the reports about the Reagan administration's deliberations. He had been appalled and angered by the continuance request from Baxter. When the Antitrust chief had called to set up the appointment, Greene and his clerks had assumed that they were about to be presented with a settlement or dismissal proposal, and they had discussed whether Greene could exert any control over the case if Justice tried to drop it outright. There was a law known as the Tunney Act, which provided for judicial review of government antitrust settlements under certain conditions. Greene wanted to know if he could invoke the Act, which was designed to protect the public interest in settlement deals, even if the prosecution was dropped and no consent decree was entered with the court. The clerks had discussed with him various tactics he might employ. One idea they agreed on was that if Baxter tried to dismiss the case, Greene would refuse to accept the dismissal filing, at least until he held a hearing to investigate whether the Tunney Act applied. When Baxter had instead requested an eleven-month continuance, Greene was incredulous. How could the government even contemplate such a proposal? Greene asked his clerks. None of them could understand it.

And despite his pronouncements that he didn't care what the newspapers said, Greene immediately made plain in court his attitude about the administration's meddling in the AT&T case, his case, about which he was already delivering didactic lectures at prestigious bar association and antitrust conferences around the country. During the first week of his defense case, George Saunders offered for admission into evidence a package of documents that included a Defense department position paper outlining why Secretary Weinberger thought the AT&T case should be dropped. The paper had been written earlier in the summer during the debate over Baldrige's dismissal proposal. Saunders offered it as "an admission by the plaintiff," the executive branch of the government. It was one of a number of documents that Saunders hoped would persuade Greene that there was a sharp disagreement inside the administration about the case. While Greene was reading the paper, a story broke in the *Washington Star* alleging that AT&T executives involved with the country's defense communications systems had helped draft Weinberger's brief. Greene was furious: he thought such collusion between the phone company and the government augured a repeat of the 1956 settlement scandal, and he was determined to investigate. Two weeks into Saunders' defense presentation, Greene suspended the trial and called for evidentiary hearings about the document's origins. Half a dozen Defense officials were called to the stand and grilled about their contacts with AT&T employees during the time the paper was written. It turned out that the phone company had indeed contributed technical information to the paper, but it was unclear whether the information had influenced Secretary Weinberger's conclusions, which reflected the longstanding views of career Defense department officials. Crystal clear to both the Justice and AT&T attorneys, however, was that the fanfare about the document was intended to demonstrate Greene's own powerful indignation over the Reagan administration's ongoing interference in the AT&T case. In courtroom speeches, the judge made plain his cynicism about the motives of both the Pentagon and the Bell System in the internal Reagan administration debate about the lawsuit.

Before the trial, lawyers on both sides of *U.S.* v. *AT&T* had heard through the Washington legal grapevine that Judge Greene tended to make up his mind about a case before all the evidence was in, and that once his mind was made up, it was difficult, if not impossible, to change his opinion. Even before they had called a dozen witnesses for the defense, the phone company's lawyers were beginning to wonder seriously if the trial was now just a formality, a doomed charade. It wasn't just Greene's outburst about the Defense document, or his remarks before recess about how "respectable" the Justice case was, that gave rise to these doubts. It was the judge's full demeanor in court that August, his mood, the questions he asked and didn't ask of witnesses, the irritation he now increasingly displayed toward representatives of the Bell System. During Gerry Connell's case, Greene had been mostly silent, reticent, attentive but uninvolved in the daily questioning. But as soon as the AT&T witnesses were called by Saunders, the judge seemed suddenly active, skeptical, at times almost a substitute cross-examiner for the government. Greene said later that this was because early in the case, during Connell's presentation, he was not yet well acquainted with the complex facts and issues in *U.S.* v. *AT&T* and so he had held his tongue. By the time Saunders began to call his witnesses, Greene felt well schooled enough to take a more active role in court. The AT&T lawyers had considered this explanation, but they did not accept it. It seemed to them that there was something openly hostile about the judge's attitude toward their defense case.

The example constantly remarked on by Saunders and his partners late that summer was Greene's unsettling outburst during the testimony of Marvin Wooten, a relatively innocuous state utility commissioner from North Carolina. Wooten was called early in the defense case, on Wednesday, August 26, to testify about the relationship between AT&T's state regulators and its federal regulators at the FCC. During the early 1970s, the states had far less contentious dealings with Bell than did the FCC, mainly because of AT&T's system of local service subsidies, which made it possible for the politically appointed or elected state regulators to keep local phone rates low. The state commissioners did not want to see that subsidy system disrupted, and so they joined with AT&T in opposing the FCC's decisions authorizing phone equipment and long-distance competition. Wooten testified about how in 1973 the North Carolina commissioners had decided to challenge the FCC's *Carterfone* decision by banning phone equipment interconnection in their state.

"We didn't think we had the legal authority to do it," Wooten explained, "but it was ... designed to do away with interconnection of all kinds and was as broad as we could possibly structure it. We wanted to give notice to the world that we were studying this entire matter, and we wanted all comers, everywhere, to take us on about this rule, so that we could come to some conclusions [in court] as to what was a reasonable route."

Suddenly, Greene interrupted the examination. "This was after the FCC had decided that there could be interconnection?" he asked.

"Yes, sir. This was in 1973, sir."

"You were going to overrule the FCC?"

"No, sir. That was not our intent."

"Somewhat like Governor Wallace and Governor Barnett, who decided at the same time to overrule the civil rights laws of this country?"

"No, sir. That was not our intent. Our intent, sir, was to notice the public. What we were really doing was trying to develop a record on which we could convince the FCC that these things needed to be gone into, because as we perceived it, we had pleaded with them to go into it, and they declined to do so."

But Greene would not let up. "I noticed on page four of your written testimony, you talk about the North Carolina commission putting pressure on Bell to assure that Bell would not knuckle under to the FCC."

"Yes, sir."

"Is it your understanding ... that when an entity follows proper regulatory decisions, that it is 'knuckling under'?"

"No, sir. That's not the intent of what I meant ..."

When the shaken North Carolina regulator stepped down, Saunders and the rest of the AT&T attorneys were in a lather. They felt that Greene had cross-examined their witness with personal vindictiveness. No matter what his role in the civil rights revolution, it was an "outrage" that Greene would compare Marvin Wooten, whom he had never met and about whom he knew very little, to the reactionary Alabama governor George Wallace. Telephone industry competition was not a racial issue. The conflict between state regulators and the FCC was not a social policy battle disguised as a dispute over "states' rights" versus federal authority. It was a legal matter, a debate over economic and regulatory policy. Greene's declarations had shaken Saunders' abiding faith in the judge's essential, personal fairness. And it was with more than a little vengeful self-satisfaction that, immediately after Wooten's testimony, the AT&T lawyers called to the stand, as planned, a state regulator from Illinois who would testify on the same subject as Wooten. The Illinois commissioner happened to be black.

The Wooten episode was only a symptom, the AT&T lawyers feared. Perhaps, they told themselves at their nightly caucuses in George Saunders' Madison Hotel suite, the basic problem was that Greene could never be comfortable with the phone company's gargantuan size. Perhaps the judge's jokes about "the well-oiled machine" genially masked a deeply held suspicion about huge, centrally managed organizations. Although he never dwelled on it, Greene had seen during his childhood in Nazi Germany the extreme consequences of manipulated, concentrated power, and perhaps the experience, understandably, had left an indelible impression. Or maybe the judge's changed attitude more reflected the personal game of "chicken" that Greene had decided to play with the Reagan administration. The more questions Greene raised about AT&T's defense and the more enthusiasm he expressed for Gerry Connell's Justice case, the higher he raised the stakes. Both of these explanations for Greene's behavior were plausible to the AT&T attorneys. That Greene might have preemptively decided that the weight of the evidence favored Justice was a possibility the phone company's lawyers preferred not to contemplate.

Judge Greene, however, was not going to allow them even that dubious luxury for long.

Chapter 25

Judgment Day

B Y the end of that sultry Washington summer of 1981, it was not only AT&T's trial lawyers ensconced nightly in the Madison Hotel who had begun to dissect and analyze the moods and prejudices of Judge Harold Greene. Two hundred and fifty miles to the north, at the phone company's 195 Broadway headquarters, Charlie Brown and Howard Trienens were engaged in a similar exercise. Both had been closely involved in the drafting of AT&T's 535-page motion to dismiss *U.S.* v. *AT&T*, which was now pending before Greene. In consultation with Saunders, Brown and Trienens had deliberately chosen to submit an unusually long and detailed motion to the judge in expectation that a definitive opinion from Greene would provide a guide not only for Saunders' defense but also for the larger political and business strategy being devised by AT&T's leaders.

The various threads of Charlie Brown's dilemma were becoming increasingly intertwined. In Congress, where Brown personally directed most of his hope and energy, S.898 was moving slowly through the Senate. A floor vote there could be expected by early October. On the House side, Colorado Democrat Tim Wirth, chairman of the renamed House Telecommunications Subcommittee, had made it clear that he would await a Senate telephone competition bill before making any move of his own. Brown and Trienens regarded Wirth as a powerful and hostile opponent; when news of Baldrige's dismissal proposal had broken in the newspapers earlier that summer, Wirth had written a strong letter to the White House urging that the case against AT&T not be dropped. But if a comprehensive bill, supported by AT&T, its competitors, the Reagan administration, and Baxter, could be passed in the Senate, Wirth would be under pressure to cooperate.

Meanwhile, at the Justice department offices ten blocks from Capitol Hill, AT&T attorneys Bob McLean and Jim Kilpatric were negotiating almost daily the Quagmire II deal with Baxter's Antitrust front office assistants. The document was months from completion, and it grew thicker every time it was shipped to 195 Broadway for review by Brown and Trienens. Greene's opinion on the motion to dismiss, whenever it came, could affect progress on both the legislative and settlement fronts. If the judge threw out large portions of the Justice case, the pressure on AT&T to negotiate would ease, and Saunders could aggressively pursue a vindicating courtroom victory. On the other hand, if he was so inclined, Greene was in a position now to tighten drastically the political vise grip on the phone company by writing an opinion that supported the views of AT&T's opponents in Congress and the Reagan administration.

The day awaited by the phone company arrived, without warning or fanfare, on Friday, September 11, a sunny and steamy Friday in Washington. Saunders was now six weeks into his defense presentation before Greene; he intended to call dozens more witnesses than had Gerry Connell during the government's case, and he expected the trial would last until early 1982. Aside from the judge's temperamental displays, the big event in August had been the testimony of former AT&T chairman John deButts, which each side thought had gone reasonably well. Now the case had settled into a predictable rhythm and routine. Saunders examined few of the AT&T witnesses himself, though he was in court every day supervising the work of his partners and subordinates. Except for big witnesses like deButts, whom he personally cross-examined, Connell, too, had settled back into a supervisory role. Friday was to be a thoroughly ordinary trial day, dominated by the testimony of Jacob Schaefer, a Bell Labs executive called to discuss the history of two obscure pieces of AT&T phone equipment known as the Com Key 718 and the Com Key 1434.

Before Schaefer took the stand, Saunders and Connell stepped to the matching wooden podiums facing Judge Greene to discuss, as usual, witness scheduling and other preliminary matters. After a brief and friendly talk, Greene interjected casually, "I have, for your enjoyment or edification, an opinion on the motion to dismiss."

"Thank you, sir," said Connell.

"Can we go home, Judge?" Saunders asked, taking the document.

"No."

Saunders began to flip through the thick opinion. "While I read this, I think I should call Mr. Schaefer to the witness stand."

Jacob Schaefer's testimony passed by in a blur as the lawyers at both the government and defense tables read voraciously through Greene's seventy-four-page opinion. The trick to reading any legal document is to begin at the back, and so the lawyers quickly turned to page seventy-three and the start of a section labeled "Conclusion." The first two sentences said it all: "The motion to dismiss is denied. The testimony and the documentary evidence adduced by the government demonstrate that the Bell System has violated the antitrust laws in a number of ways over a lengthy period of time." AT&T, Judge Greene seemed to be saying, was already guilty. The next sentence said, "The evidence sustains the government's basic contentions, and the burden is on the defendants to refute the factual showings made in the government's case."

The body of the opinion was not so starkly conclusive, but to Saunders and his cohorts it was just as depressing. In guarded, detailed, and intelligent language, Greene marched through each important section of the government's case and declared that "the evidence sustains the allegation." On the question of phone equipment competition and John deButts' PCA strategy, Greene wrote, "The Court concludes ... that defendants have used their local exchange monopolies to foreclose competition in the... equipment market." About the MCI story and the controversies over FX lines and Execunet, the judge said, "The Court finds that... AT&T has monopolized the intercity services market by frustrating the efforts of other companies to compete with it." On whether the Bell operating companies bought too much phone equipment from Western and not enough from outside suppliers, Greene also firmly supported the government's contentions. The judge's only concessions to AT&T came on the relatively minor issues concerning legal and economic definitions of markets, equipment pricing, and a disputed legal theory concerning AT&T's filings before the FCC during the early 1970s.

When Jacob Schaefer's testimony was over, Judge Greene called for a brief recess. George Saunders stood up.

"Before you go, I have had a chance to glance over your opinion, and on page seventy-three of this opinion, in the conclusion, it says, 'The testimony and documentary evidence adduced by the government demonstrate that the Bell System has violated the antitrust laws in a number of ways over a lengthy period of time.' I don't think this is what your opinion says, but I think that sentence will be read and reported in the press as saying you have made up your mind and it is all over. Am I wrong?"

"That's obviously not what it means," Greene answered. "If you will read the next sentence, it says that the government has satisfied its burden, and the burden is now on the defendants to disprove what the government has done."

"I say, I have not digested this weighty opinion yet," Saunders said cautiously. He did not want to make Greene angry. "But I have glanced at it, and that's what I understood the opinion to be saying, until I got to that sentence. I wanted to make sure...."

"It is absolutely clear," Greene snapped. "The American way is you have your chance, and you can disprove it. I think the opinion says in at least fifteen different places..."

"Absolutely."

" . . . that you have the burden and you may disprove, and you may well succeed in disproving everything."

"We are confident that we will, Your Honor."

Some of the government lawyers, pink with excitement over the unexpectedly laudatory opinion, joked outside the courtroom that Saunders' challenge to Greene had only served to call the newspaper reporters' attention to an especially quotable passage that might otherwise have been ignored. But they understood Saunders' distress. Unstated in Saunders' exchange with the judge was the obvious fact that Greene's opinion was as much a political salvo as it was a legal document. The Justice lawyers understood that, as did their discouraged opponents at the defense table. The opinion was far more conclusive than it needed to be, and it was unusually long and detailed. In scope and tone, it was much like the hefty, passionate advocacy motions on dismissal filed by the two sides after Gerry Connell rested the government's case in July. Because the trial lawyers, like Greene, were then unaware of Baxter's finesse strategy against Baldrige's proposal, they had all assumed that the motion to dismiss would most likely be their last opportunity to argue the facts in *U.S.* v. *AT&T* before the case was dropped. Thus they had thrown themselves into the project like condemned men devouring their last meals. Greene had done the same: this opinion might well be his only chance to state his views about the evidence he had listened to, day after day, for the past six months. At the same time, if he used the opinion to affirm zealously the government's case, he would raise the political price of dismissal for Reagan to an intolerable level. Neither Greene nor the majority of attorneys trying the case was aware on that September morning that a nearly irrevocable decision not to drop *U.S.* v. *AT&T* had already been made by the White House. Greene's strong opinion could not change Reagan's course; it simply confirmed the cautious reasoning and political instincts of the President's chief of staff, Jim Baker.

When a copy of the opinion was sent over to Bill Baxter's Antitrust front office later that afternoon, it was not received with unanimous enthusiasm. Ron Carr, Baxter's chief deputy,

was a former U.S. Supreme Court clerk and a self-described
ideological purist on the issue of judicial activism. While Carr
supported Baxter's efforts to save *U.S.* v. *AT&T* from dismissal
by Reagan's cabinet, he thought Greene's opinion went much
too far: he thought it was as if the judge wanted to preserve
the dispute over phone industry competition, rather than resolve it.

"I think the opinion is irresponsible," Carr told Baxter when
both had read it.

Baxter smiled indulgently. In the last few months, he had
learned a few things about the peculiar blend of ideological self-
righteousness and ruthless political pragmatism necessary for
success in Washington. "It's a clever maneuver," he replied.

Greene maintained for years afterwards that it was nothing
of the sort. He said that if the opinion was unusually strong
and detailed, it only reflected AT&T's repeated requests for an
expansive answer to their motion to dismiss, and certainly it
was true that Charlie Brown and Howard Trienens wanted to
know as much as possible about where Greene stood that September. Greene also said, as he told Saunders in court, that his
harsh language in the conclusion was not meant as a verdict
but rather as "the American way . . . that you have the burden
and you may disprove, and you may well succeed in disproving
everything."

In fact, however, there had been a protracted debate in
Greene's chambers during the week before the judge released
his opinion about whether the language in the conclusion was
too strong. The argument among Greene and some of his clerks
centered on phrases such as "the testimony and the documentary evidence . . . demonstrate" and "there has been proof of
anticompetitive conduct." Some of the clerks who had helped
research and draft the opinion felt that Greene had over-
extended his reach, that he was implying in his conclusion that
the defense could not disprove the government's case, which
was precisely George Saunders' initial reaction. It was a se-
mantic question with legal implications, and at one point the
judge and his clerks even looked up words in the dictionary
and read aloud their precise definitions. In the end, Greene

rejected the objections to his wording, and he told his clerks that the meaning of his conclusion was clear enough. The judge was not going to back off on his political message to Reagan, Congress, and the public about how important he felt it was to try *U.S.* v. *AT&T* to its end in federal court—to make the system work.

On the twenty-sixth floor of 195 Broadway that hot Friday afternoon in September, Charlie Brown and Howard Trienens received Greene's message sullenly but stoically; the opinion was yet another disappointment in a year of unrelenting disillusionment. Distant and unemotional, AT&T's two top strategists had neither the capacity nor the inclination to let loose their giowing personal frustration with Washington's "system," which seemed on the one hand not to work at all and at the same time to be perfectly designed to drive them and their company into chaos and disfunction. It seemed to Brown that all of AT&T's executive talent, and a good deal of its money, had now been diverted into an endless and unwinnable war with Washington. Perhaps Brown would have felt better if he had smashed an ashtray against his office wall or pounded his desk with his fist. Instead, he reacted impassively: he believed that reliability, stability, and consistency of manner and style were among the most important qualities of a corporate chief executive, and he had spent decades cultivating those attributes. "What you see is what you get with me," he liked to say.

Much of the time, however, what there was to see was spiritless and inscrutable. And that was why only a handful of top executives at 195 Broadway who were close to AT&T's chairman could appreciate that Charlie Brown might soon do something very drastic.

Chapter 26

The Inter-Intra Split

O N October 14, 1981, the leading executives of Charlie Brown's corporate management team gathered in a conference room at 195 Broadway to talk about Charles Hugel's blackboard.

Brown himself was absent, but Howard Trienens attended. Hugel, the former president of Ohio Bell who had championed, with Brown, the blue team competitive strategy during the 1970s, was present. Hugel had been brought to New York by Brown soon after John deButts retired. Also at the meeting were Morris Tanenbaum, a diminutive, soft-spoken scientist and engineer who had begun his career at Bell Labs in the early 1950s and who was now Brown's executive vice-president for corporate affairs and planning, and Ian Ross, the president of Bell Labs.

The history of Hugel's blackboard was no secret within the upper reaches of AT&T's management, although information about what was being drawn on it was disseminated to executives outside corporate headquarters only on a need-to-know basis. The blackboard dated back to the summer of 1980, a demoralizing season for the newly ascendant blue team. In June of that year had come the $1.8 billion verdict in the MCI case. In July, the comprehensive telephone competition bill, to which Charlie Brown had devoted so much personal attention, was

killed by House Antitrust Subcommittee chairman Peter Rodino, who feared it would interfere with the Justice antitrust
suit, which Judge Greene was then aggressively pushing to
trial. Earlier that same year, the "menu" settlement deal with
Ken Anderson had been nixed by Sandy Litvack.

In August, on the heels of these successive disappoint-
ments, Brown had called in Howard Trienens to pose him the
obvious, and forbidden, question.

"Why are we fighting this case?" the chairman asked. "Why
are we fighting so hard to keep the local exchange bottleneck?"

The most important answer was that the question had never
been asked before, at least not by anyone in a position of leadership at AT&T. Over the course of a century, the men who ran
the Bell System had grown up inside the company, their "bell-
shaped heads" drilled with the values of stability and the ethic
of public service. Proposing to divest the local operating companies—the foundation of the American telephone system—
was akin to "loose talk about breaking up the Holy Roman
Empire," as a congressional staffer once put it. It could be
argued that in August 1980, when Charlie Brown first seriously
broached the topic, the strategic inviability of AT&T's mono-
lithic structure had been obvious for at least a decade. John
deButts and his contemporaries in Bell's corporate management
had been unable to accept that idea—unable, even, to examine
it critically. But while deButts derived his strategic vision from
the phone company's long and glorious past, which he had
hoped to preserve, Charlie Brown was a futurist, an engineer
fascinated with the advance of technology, a man who thought
he saw scattered light on the business horizon—the dawning
of the information age. In the summer of 1980, he was not yet
convinced that AT&T would have to destroy and recreate itself
in order to realize this future, but he was willing to contemplate
the possibilities.

The idea became known on the twenty-sixth floor as the
"inter-intra split." Brown first discussed it openly with his board
of directors in the fall of 1980, after he, Trienens, Hugel, and
some others had informally explored the concept. It was an
alternative to be fully considered, nothing more or less, Brown

said. In its purest form, the inter-intra split described a complete separation of AT&T's "interexchange" and "intraexchange" facilities, its long distance lines and local loops. The basic local telephone infrastructure would be separated from its intercity support network; there would be no shared facilities. This was a far different idea from the menu and Crimson Sky settlement terms that Trienens had begun to discuss with Justice in 1980. Those deals involved divestiture of only one wholly-owned operating company, troubled Pacific Telephone. The inter-intra split would require AT&T to reinvent the American telephone network. It was, of course, exactly what the Justice department wanted.

Late in 1980, Charles Hugel set up a blackboard in his 195 Broadway office to investigate, with chalk and eraser, how it might be done. He worked with Al Partoll, an up-and-coming Brown protégé, Paul Villieres, and occasionally others. The first question was whether it was economically feasible to make a "pure" split, with absolutely no shared facilities, within five years. They tried to put a price tag on that set of assumptions, but it turned out to be absurdly expensive. So many new buildings and other facilities would have to be constructed that not even Bell, the bastion of investment capital in corporate America, could afford it. So they swept over that idea with an eraser and drew up alternative plans. During the Crimson Sky negotiations late in 1980 and early in 1981, Hugel's office became suddenly busy with engineers and executives who were trying to determine how, precisely, to cut loose Pacific, Cincinnati Bell, and Southern New England Telephone, if a final deal was consummated with Justice. That work provided the inter-intra team with new ideas and approaches. During the spring and summer of 1981, after Crimson Sky fell apart and while Trienens and Brown were largely preoccupied with intrigue in Congress, at the White House, and in Judge Greene's courtroom, Hugel refined the plan for total operating company divestiture.

By the fall of 1981, it was near final form. The conceptual issues—how the intraexchanges could be defined, how they would be technically and economically separated from long-distance facilities, how long it would take to complete such a

Draconian divestiture, and so on—had been resolved by Hugel and his team of managers and engineers. What remained were the larger strategic and political questions, such as the one that Hugel, Trienens, Tanenbaum, and Ian Ross convened to discuss on October 10: namely, national security.

In Hugel's mind, this was the last major issue that had to be resolved before he could recommend the split to chairman Brown as a viable, ready alternative. On October 1, Brown had promoted Hugel to a new post in charge of reorganizing Western Electric and Bell Labs for the new age of competition, and so Hugel was about to turn over the inter-intra planning to Tanenbaum.

Tanenbaum told the group that the split could probably not be accomplished without destroying the integrated national security communications network, which depended on central management and facilities. That, the Bell executives were aware, was what Caspar Weinberger had unsuccessfully argued the previous summer during the White House debate over dismissal of *U.S.* v. *AT&T.* Tanenbaum felt that the Defense department was probably right, and that AT&T's management was obligated to consider the impact of its actions on national security.

Ian Ross, the Bell Labs president, agreed with Tanenbaum's assessment, and he argued loud and long against the inter-intra split that Hugel had devised. There had long been a tension in Bell System management between executives like Tanenbaum and Ross on the one hand, who were scientists committed to the purity and independence of Bell Labs' research, and executives like Hugel on the other, who felt that the Labs ought to be more closely integrated with Western Electric in a traditional "product development" relationship. Hugel felt that in the precompetitive era, it had been fine for the Labs to be unusually independent, almost like a university science center. The country as a whole derived obvious benefits from that structure, since Bell Labs was required by law to license to competitors the many patents it developed. But now that the competitive era had arrived, this "ivory tower" system would cripple Western's attempt to compete against the likes of IBM, Xerox, Wang, and other large, sophisticated computer and communications equipment companies. It was Hugel's view that divestiture of the operating companies was an acceptable trade-off for the opportunity to transform Western and the Labs into a "lean and mean" product-oriented, competitive organization. Such a transformation was precisely what Ross, particularly, dreaded; he was determined to argue at every opportunity against divestiture. But the long-standing antagonism between Western and Bell Labs colored his opposition to Hugel's plan.

"There are ways to overcome the defense communications problem," Hugel said. For example, AT&T could create a central services organization for the Pentagon that would pool the resources of all the newly created companies. Tanenbaum wondered if that would be enough, but he agreed to work on it as he fleshed out Hugel's skeleton plan in the weeks ahead.

When the meeting was over, Hugel felt that a turning point had been reached. During the 1970s, as he had risen through AT&T's management ranks to the elite corps around Charlie Brown, Hugel had been frustrated by his company's seeming inability to shake off its past. For example, Hugel believed that Bell had wasted an opportunity in the late 1960s and early 1970s to "trade off" politically the possibility of unlimited phone equipment competition for the right to preserve its national network. But instead of accepting equipment competition, deButts had pursued his PCA strategy.

"The old telephone people didn't recognize terminal equipment for what it was—not an integral part of the network," Hugel said later. "There was the PCA argument, and the studies about harm to the network were legitimate, but that really wasn't seeing the forest for the trees." After the Bell Bill debacle in 1976, such a trade-off became unrealistic, and the frustration of Hugel and his like-minded colleagues in AT&T's high management grew. By the time they came to New York after Charlie Brown's ascendance in 1979, Hugel and other blue team executives felt that 195 Broadway had been virtually swallowed up by antitrust litigation and the fitful efforts to pass legislation in Congress. Brown, Trienens, and other company leaders spent nearly all their time strategizing about and responding to events in Washington. Now, more than two years later, the whole mess only seemed worse. And there was no end in sight.

Except for the inter-intra split. That was the best solution, Hugel thought, the only way to cut the phone company's Gordian knot.

When contemplating such a radical strategy, which by its nature contravened the precepts of Bell System culture, it was helpful for executives like Hugel to address the bottom line: the interests of AT&T's three million shareholders. This was not simply an obligation of corporate officers, who serve at the pleasure of a company's shareholders. It was a matter of self-interest and even survival. No matter what course they chose in October 1981 or later, Charlie Brown and his senior managers had to be certain they protected themselves and their board of directors from shareholder lawsuits, which at the least would be embarrassing and distracting, and at the worst could cost them millions of dollars and their jobs and reputations. The only way to prevent litigation that challenged their management decisions was to pursue a strategy that could be justified purely as a matter of profit and loss. To each of the alternatives facing AT&T's senior executives that fall—the Quagmire II deal with Justice, congressional legislation along the lines of S.898, continued litigation against the Justice department, the inter-intra split—a price tag had to be attached.

And from that narrow yet essential perspective, the numbers on Charles Hugel's blackboard were again compelling.

The essence of John deButts' "public interest" arguments to Congress and the FCC during the early 1970s was that competition in the telephone industry would destroy AT&T's system of pricing subsidies. If competition flourished, deButts said, the price of phone equipment and service would no longer be determined by regulation, which was really a form of systematic political compromise between AT&T, the government, and the public. Over the years, those three parties had agreed, for purely political reasons, to keep the price of basic local phone service artificially low—at or below its cost. What outraged deButts and his red team generation of AT&T executives was that the FCC had decided in a piecemeal fashion to disrupt this political accommodation without ever considering, or taking responsibility for, the consequences. Charlie Brown and his generation of Bell executives agreed entirely with deButts' assessment, and they shared his outrage. But by the fall of 1981 they had accepted, as deButts never could, that a fundamental shift from regulated pricing to cost-based, free-market pricing was inevitable. The reasons why this radical and fundamental shift had occurred—again, purely political—did not alter the fact. And the fact, once accepted, demanded an equally radical rethinking of AT&T's structure and business strategy.

Charlie Brown's question in August 1980, "Why are we fighting to keep our local monopoly?" preceded an obvious conclusion. If profit and loss in the phone industry now depended on costs, not regulatory accommodation, then the smart thing to do would be to jettison AT&T's most costly, least profitable subsidiaries, the local operating companies, and retain its high technology profit centers, Western Electric, Long Lines, and Bell Labs. *The inter-intra split.* It was true that this restructuring was a major goal of the Justice case, but it was not that lawsuit's only goal. The government was also trying to break off Western and Bell Labs. Losing both the operating companies and AT&T's manufacturing arm would be an intolerable blow, Brown thought, because in a deregulated, cost-based phone industry, Western would become a major player in the phone equipment and computer markets. Or so it had to be, if AT&T was going to realize Brown's vision of an emerging information age.

There was something else. The clarity of the inter-intra split strategy, its appositeness in a fundamentally changing industry, was complemented by the sweet revenge it would wreak on Bill McGowan, the man so singularly responsible for the excruciating dilemma faced by Charlie Brown in the fall of 1981.

The billion-dollar success of MCI and the vast personal fortune McGowan had made at Bell's expense sometimes drove even AT&T's most staid executives into a nearly apoplectic rage. Not only had McGowan built his company through legal skulduggery and deceitful lobbying, Bell's leaders felt, he was now reaping the immense profits of his malfeasance without anyone calling him to account. Though it was in some aspects self-destructive, a pure inter-intra split was a way to hurry MCI toward its day of reckoning. Simply put, the divestiture of all the local operating companies would give McGowan everything he had ever asked for, and by doing so, it might well destroy him.

Neither Charlie Brown, Howard Trienens, nor any of the other cautious and solemn top executives at 195 Broadway ever thought of this happy, coincidental consequence of the inter-intra split in such vengeful terms. But they understood it well enough.

In 1978, in the aftermath of the U.S. Appeals Court decision that sanctified full long-distance competition by approving MCI's Execunet service, MCI and AT&T had negotiated something called the ENFIA agreement. The agreement, in effect, specified the amount of rent MCI would have to pay the Bell operating companies for access to their local exchanges. The rent was $235 per line, per month. The "line" actually rented was a connection between a local MCI office and an operating company central switching station. An MCI customer's long-distance call from, say, Washington, would travel by microwave to the MCI office in, say, Chicago. Then it would be routed over the line rented from the operating company to Bell's central switching station for the Chicago area. From there it would travel through the local exchange to the telephone designated by the MCI customer when he dialed the call. The line between the MCI office and the central switching station could only carry one call at a time. If, at the peak of a business day, for example, MCI had 100 customers calling long distance from Washington to Chicago at the same time, it would need 100 rented access lines in order to route all the calls through the Chicago exchange. If it had not rented 100 lines, some of the callers in Washington would get a busy signal, and, presumably, they would then consider using AT&T's long-distance service. So it was important for MCI to rent the correct number of lines in each market it served, and those at a low price. If it rented too few, MCI customers would get a lot of busy signals. If it rented too many or paid too much for access, the company would not make a profit.

The $235 figure, then, was a key to MCI's profitability in 1981. It represented a substantial percentage—more than one-fourth, and perhaps as much as one-half—of the actual cost of an MCI customer's call. If the rent went too much higher, MCI's cost advantage over AT&T—and its profits—would disappear.

And the inter-intra split offered a way to raise MCI's rent dramatically.

In two ways, the monthly ENFIA (Exchange Network Facilities for Interstate Access) rent of $235 was a tremendous bargain for MCI. First of all, when the amount had been negotiated in 1979, it had been based on a hypothetical number of minutes that MCI was expected to use the line—approximately 4,500 minutes per month. Soon after the deal was made, MCI introduced some new, more sophisticated switching equipment that allowed it to use its rented lines about 7,500 minutes a month, over 50 percent more than had been anticipated. Already, then, MCI had achieved more than a 50 percent saving on its rent, a discount that would evaporate when the deal was renegotiated to reflect MCI's actual usage. Secondly, the $235 price, even without figuring for the extra minutes, was about half what MCI could expect to pay eventually if the operating companies were divested in an inter-intra split. Because MCI's Execunet long-distance service had been put together under such strange circumstances back in the mid-1970s, it was not really comparable in quality to AT&T's. The system consisted of inverted FX lines combined in such a way that MCI customers could call freely from all the phones in one city to all the phones in another. But among other differences, MCI customers had to dial more numbers to make a call than did AT&T customers. So the $235 figure, it was agreed by both sides, represented a substantial discount from what MCI would pay if it ever had "equal access" with AT&T to the local exchanges. Such equal access would only be possible, as McGowan had said all along, if the operating companies were separated from his competitor,

Long Lines. Once independent, the operating companies could extract the same rent from MCI as they did from AT&T.

And there was nothing Charlie Brown would have liked more than to compete with MCI on level ground, with each company paying the same rent for access to the local exchanges. Brown's main complaint about the S.898 bill and the Quagmire II deal being negotiated with Justice that fall was that neither provided for competition on equal terms. Through the complex system of local service subsidies, called "separations payments," AT&T's Long Lines was already paying a higher "rent" to the operating companies than MCI's $235 fee, although Bell's payment system was put together much differently than MCI's. Because of its market share and the size of its system, AT&T could afford to pay $500, even $600 in rent if the operating companies were divested in an inter-intra split. And because the whole idea of such divestiture, at least as McGowan and the Justice department had always stated it, was unmitigated equal access, MCI and the other competitors would eventually have to pay the same amount. When that happened, the competitors' cost and pricing advantage would disappear, their profits would come under tremendous pressure, and they would probably all be facing insolvency within a decade, if not sooner. If the cost of doing business was the same for everyone, there simply wasn't much room in the long-distance market. It was, as George Saunders was so desperately trying to convince Judge Greene, a natural monopoly. Or so believed the executives of AT&T. Certainly, none of them was reluctant to test their belief against the likes of Bill McGowan. Long Lines was never going to go out of business. MCI very well might.

The question was, at what price for AT&T?

In the fall of 1981, key headquarters executives such as Charles Hugel looked to Howard Trienens for leadership in the increasingly intense debate over the phone company's future. There was no doubt that Charlie Brown was in charge, that he would take final responsibility for any decision about the inter-intra split. But the Bell chairman was a solitary figure on the twenty-sixth floor, a loner, genial but distant. He was not a man with whom one might share a cab uptown to the East 60s and then shoot the breeze over drinks in a hotel bar. In the evenings, he returned to his home in Princeton, New Jersey. In the mornings, he exercised, often alone. Trienens, on the other hand, was more accessible. Though he was a faithful ally of Brown's, he bridged the generation gap in the company's senior management. He was able both to synthesize and to separate the legal and business aspects of AT&T's sundry problems in Washington, and he sponsored an atmosphere of frank but noncombative debate on the executive floors. And it was clear that he had the trust of both Brown and the board of directors.

Trienens himself saw his job as a matter of analysis, not leadership. In the aftermath of Judge Greene's September 11 opinion, as the Quagmire II negotiations and the now heavily amended S.898 bill slogged onward, Trienens began to develop for Brown a series of scenarios about AT&T's legal entanglements. In October, George Saunders told him that he now believed Greene would decide against AT&T on liability and would order the divestiture of some or all of Western Electric, but probably not the operating companies. At the same time, Trienens quietly hired an independent law firm in Washington to conduct a "peer review" of the trial and to analyze its likely outcome. The idea was to bring a fresh set of eyes to a case about which neither Trienens, Saunders, nor any other AT&T lawyer could honestly claim to be objective anymore. The review tended to confirm what Saunders and Trienens had already concluded. Greene would find against the phone company on liability, and there was a serious danger that he would try to break off Western.

Though he spent considerable time psychoanalyzing Judge Greene with Brown and the trial lawyers in Washington, Trienens knew that it would be a monstrous error to rely on his or anyone else's predictions about Greene while developing a business strategy for AT&T. Confident though he was about where Greene was going to come out, it was impossible to forecast precisely another man's actions, especially a man as subtle and complex as Harold Greene. Instead, Trienens developed that fall what he called "best case" and "worst case" scenarios about the Justice trial. In the best case, AT&T would win everything and the government would be forced to appeal. In the worst case, AT&T would lose and Greene would order the divestiture of all the operating companies, as the government was seeking. The odd thing about it was, as Trienens and Brown pored over the scenarios, the worst case seemed closer to being "good" than did the scenarios in between. That was because, as Trienens advised Brown, the more radical Greene's verdict, the more likely it would be that the Supreme Court would hear the case and reject the divestiture. The idea that Greene himself would decide against AT&T was not a major concern for Trienens. Assuming the case was not settled or dropped, *U.S.* v. *AT&T* was ultimately going to be decided on appeal, not by Greene. What troubled Trienens was the possibility that Greene might leave the operating companies alone and divest some or all of Western. Trienens felt that Western was especially vulnerable because it had a long history in the litigation, dating even beyond the still-lingering 1956 settlement scandal. A decision by the judge to split off the equipment side of AT&T's business might be very difficult to reverse on appeal. Such a decision would be easier for appeals judges to understand than if Greene ordered the breakup of the operating companies. There was more precedent for divesting the manufacturing arm of a monopoly whose primary business was not manufacturing. And viewed in the context of seven decades of litigation between the U.S. government and the phone company, during which so many ill-fated attempts had been made to break off Western, its divestiture by Greene might seem politically acceptable to an appeals court—even logical.

But as their hopes for a victory before Judge Greene were deteriorating in October, Trienens and Brown had reason to be optimistic that they might yet extricate themselves from their debilitating morass without having to sacrifice the operating companies in an inter-intra split. After all, though they were heavily capitalized and relatively unprofitable, the local operating companies nonetheless represented more than $80 billion in assets, $50 billion in annual revenues, and $5 billion in profits. No sane man would give them up unnecessarily.

On October 7, the Senate had finally pushed S.898 to the floor, where it had passed 90–4. Privately, Trienens and Brown thought the bill was a mess—complex, ineffective, and unfair—but they continued to back it publicly in the hope that new compromises could be reached in the House or in conference. There was nothing to be gained by preemptively sabotaging the first telephone competition bill to clear a house of Congress in over a decade. One problem was that Bill Baxter had not been similarly reserved about expressing his opinion on S.898. The day after the bill cleared the Senate, the Antitrust chief had announced that if the House passed the bill in its present form, he would not drop U.S. v. AT&T—as he had promised the previous summer—because the Senate and the administration had tinkered with his amendments, the renowned Baxter I and Baxter II. Until the amendments were fixed, Baxter would withold his support.

Despite the Antitrust chief's tirade, Brown and Trienens were confident that once Representative Tim Wirth began to work on S.898 in November, serious bargaining would begin anew. Wirth was awaiting the results of a sweeping study on telephone industry competition that was being prepared by his staff. Once the study was complete, he would draft a companion to the Senate bill. Wirth was no friend of the phone company, but he had now been thrust into a position of leadership on an issue in which he had always taken a deep interest: telecommunications regulation. Brown and Trienens assumed that if nothing else, Wirth would want to take credit for authoring the first major telephone reform act passed by Congress since 1934 and would thus be in a deal-making mood. As the two AT&T executives liked to say when discussing the problems faced by their company that fall, "Congress sets the policy. That's what they teach you in civics class."

And for the time being, Brown and Trienens were content to sit, and wait, and learn. No matter what Wirth did with the reform legislation in the House, they knew that they could always go back to Charles Hugel's blackboard.

"Perhaps I was naive," Charlie Brown said later, "but my basic thought was that policy was being made in the wrong place. I wanted to give every opportunity for the right place to be making the decision, and the Congress seemed the right place. Theoretically, everybody agreed about that; the problem was how to do it. . . . I was still optimistic about Wirth taking a leadership role."

Chapter 27

Court of Last Resort

JUDGE Greene's face was contorted in agitation. Before him was a list of nearly 100 new witnesses, including several present and former cabinet secretaries, senators, famous business executives, the president of the National Association for the Advancement of Colored People, and assorted other public policy celebrities, all of whom George Saunders intended to call before AT&T rested its defense case. The judge had received the list earlier in the morning, and the rage it had produced in him was only now boiling to the surface.

"And some of these people," Greene was exclaiming to Saunders and Connell, who stood before the judge's wooden bench on a cloudy November morning, "I don't know what they are going to testify about, but it looks to me, at first glance, that they are more here for—I use my words carefully—for publicity value than for contributions to this case. I have tried very hard to not have this case deteriorate, and I am not going to have it conclude on a circus-like note!"

"I do have somewhat the same perception," said Connell self-effacingly. Connell and the government lawyers seated behind him were clearly enjoying Saunders' predicament. Ever since the September 11 opinion, AT&T's defense had become an increasingly hopeless affair, they thought, and this was the pinnacle of Saunders' desperation—a moment to be savored. "I can't figure out what Alexander Haig is going to contribute to this lawsuit, or Senator McGovern."

"I didn't even see Senator McGovern," Greene said, consulting the offensive list again.

"In December," Connell said helpfully. "I can't understand why these people have to be called."

"I am telling you right now, Mr. Saunders," Greene continued angrily, "there had better be some very good reasons for these, because whatever lobbying, whatever publicity campaigns are going to be made, they will have to be made in congresses or in other forums.

"In this court, the issues are going to be tried according to the facts. And this court isn't going to be impressed with big names. If these people are being brought in here simply to get publicity for the defendant's case, it is not going to be a very favorable development as far as I am concerned."

"Well, Your Honor, I must express my disappointment that the court would suggest that that is my motivation," said Saunders, attempting a recovery. "I am trying to try this case as best I know how. I am trying it as a lawsuit. Every witness who is on that schedule has a hard fact or opinion for which he has, I think, a suitable role in this case. I am trying to get across what I consider to be some very fundamental facts that, as I sense the proceedings in this case, have not been easy to get across."

That was a vast understatement. The AT&T trial lawyers had concluded that Greene might well be intractable about the case. It was impossible, however, to throw in the towel.

"For example," Saunders went on, "last summer we presented Your Honor with a document signed, adopted, and sent to the President of the United States by the secretary of defense, and you will notice I have a lot of witnesses on here from the department of Defense in an effort to prove the facts set forth in that document. Now, I believe those facts are true; they have been held as opinions by the people most knowledgeable in that part of the government for a long time, and I think the document has not been given the attention it deserves.

"Now, with respect to the other people, take Senator McGovern, for example..."

But Greene had taken enough. "I am not going to go into all of that right now," he interrupted. "You are going to have to show good cause. For most of the more exotic people, who don't know anything about telecommunications or the network, you will have to have some showing why they are necessary. Otherwise, I am not going to let them testify. I don't care how high up they are or who they are."

"Now, all I can say is, I am trying to do my best, Judge," Saunders said. "I am not trying to turn this case into a circus. I am trying as best I can to lay out all the facts that I think are relevant to this decision, because I fervently believe if this court sees all the facts, the answer to this case is easy."

Saunders meant what he said. He had never stopped believing in the righteousness of his defense, even after the September 11 opinion, and even as his client was initiating plans to surrender his cause. At the same time, his posturing about simply trying to "lay out all the facts" was somewhat disingenuous. The "parade of stars," as it came to be known, was a calculated and indeed desperate ploy, though not of the sort Judge Greene assumed. It was not publicity Saunders was after, it was ideological credibility. As the defense presentation had worn on that fall, Saunders and his trial team had become increasingly despondent about the seemingly immutable suspicion Greene expressed about the motives and character of AT&T's executives, past and present. In October, they had tried to combat the judge's attitude with sheer numbers of witnesses: at one point, Saunders proposed to call the presidents of every Bell operating company to testify to their benign attitude toward phone equipment competition and MCI during the 1970s. The idea was, as one of the AT&T lawyers put it later, "If Judge Greene thinks these AT&T people are liars, he's going to have to see and listen to all of them. We've got a million employees and he's going to see all of them." A tangential benefit of this strategy, which was called "Octoberfest" by the phone company trial team, was that it would build a record of pro-AT&T testimony that might be useful when Greene's verdict was appealed.

But Greene rebelled against this festival of witnesses. "I would think that these operating company presidents have better things to do than sit here and give this essentially repetitious testimony, day after day, and I have something better to do, too." The judge was careful not to prevent the presidents' testimony arbitrarily—such action could come back to haunt him on appeal, since the views of ranking AT&T executives were clearly relevant to the case. But the vehement "guidance" he offered on the matter caused Saunders to rethink his plans, and the vast majority of the presidents were never called.

Bitten, the AT&T trial team retreated to its caucus suite at the Madison Hotel. "What can we do to convince this guy?" Saunders asked, referring to Greene. "What haven't we tried?" It was then that Saunders seized on the "parade of stars" idea. The plan was, as one of the AT&T lawyers put it later, to tell Judge Greene, in effect, "Look, you dumb son of a bitch, this is not a liberal-conservative thing. Good, honest people who you respect share our opinion on this thing." One Sunday morning, the senior trial team convened in Saunders' suite to discuss what kinds of witnesses might be able to soften Greene's harsh attitude toward the phone company.

"If you could have anybody in the world come in and talk to Greene—anybody in the whole world—who would it be?" Saunders asked his partners.

They made a list on a blackboard and tried, once again, to work up the judge's psychological profile. George McGovern was an obvious candidate. Maybe a Kennedy. Benjamin Hooks, NAACP president and a former FCC commissioner, seemed a good choice. They tried to narrow the profile even further. What about someone who shared Greene's most fundamental life experience, his escape from Nazi Germany? Someone suggested a man named Frederick Heig, a scientist from Austria who had escaped the Nazis. One of the trial team lawyers finally tracked him down, but it turned out that Heig was a little hard of hearing and was not terribly distraught about the potential breakup of the Bell System. Later, an AT&T executive named

Saul Buchsbaum suggested for the list Arno Penzias, the Nobel Prize–winning Bell Labs scientist who had published the "big bang" theory most scientists believe was behind the creation of the universe. Saunders was excited by the idea. One of his partners called Penzias' house in the New York area. Penzias' wife explained that the celebrated scientist was in Germany, giving a speech honoring the fiftieth anniversary of a synagogue that survived the Nazi holocaust. "Perfect!" the AT&T lawyers exclaimed. They reached Penzias in Germany, and he agreed to fly straight to New York from Munich. An AT&T lawyer met him at the airport and flew him down to Washington in a corporate jet.

Of all the stars paraded before Judge Greene that fall, Dr. Penzias was easily the most engaging, though whether he was at all effective was another question. Saunders conducted the examination himself, and Penzias spoke articulately and delightfully about the spirit of the Bell System, his breakthrough scientific work at Bell Labs, and the importance of preserving AT&T as it had existed for a century. Greene clearly was fascinated by his honored guest, and he even asked some entirely digressive questions about the big bang theory. Later, when Penzias addressed the merits of U.S. v. AT&T, Greene asked gently if it wouldn't be possible to preserve the benefits of Bell Labs even if some or all of the operating companies were divested.

"The kind of relationship we have, talking to people, the fact that we work for the same company, I think makes a big difference," Penzias answered thoughtfully. "A Nobel Prize–winner has a lot of advantages. One of the disadvantages is that almost everybody calls me 'sir'; it is very hard to get through that kind of barrier. But as telephone people working for the same company, I have an easier time getting through it. People are willing to talk. Down in Mississippi, talking to somebody about the kinds of problems they have—poverty, not much money, a lot of rural problems—it helps that we work for the same place, we are interested in the same problems. There is really a connection."

Gerry Connell's cross-examination strategy when Saunders' star witnesses appeared was mainly to ignore or discount them. Often, he conducted no cross at all. When he did stand to ask a few, brief questions, it was to say, in effect, "You're a nice, honest man, but you don't really know anything about the phone industry, do you?"

Penzias, for example, had said that Bell Labs without the operating companies would be like a "sinking ship," because the luxury of long-term research it currently enjoyed would be replaced by short-term pressures for product development. So Connell simply asked him, "Do you understand what we are talking about is leaving Bell Labs, Western Electric, and AT&T Long Lines in one piece?"

"Yes, sir," Penzias said.

"And that's a sinking ship?"

"Absolutely."

"All right, sir," said Connell, quietly sardonic. "No further questions, Your Honor."

Saunders recognized that Connell's taciturn questioning was very effective, but he hoped his celebrities would none- theless have a subtle, transforming effect on Greene.

"I came to the FCC as a so-called consumer activist," Ben- jamin Hooks testified. "And I had the know-it-all opinion that all business was bad. I mean, there's no question about where I stood on the telephone system. It had to be bad. And I came there determined to hit them pretty hard. But unfortunately I came in contact with facts that sort of changed my opinion about a lot of things."

See, Saunders was saying to Greene, *here is a black man, a liberal, a man with whom you presumably share a certain instinct and ideology about the world. And he is telling you that it is OK to like the Bell System, to appreciate it as a monopoly that serves consumers well.*

It didn't work, of course. Greene allowed many of the star witnesses to testify, but he grew increasingly impatient with them. And since the celebrities seemed to have no effect on the judge, their presence only spoke to the stark desperation of AT&T's defense team. "We were sitting around with our feet up on the desk, smoking cigars," one of the government lawyers described it later. "We were in the driver's seat, and they were going crazy. We were sure we had won on liability. The only question was divestiture."

On that crucial issue, too, which was now driving the business strategy debate at 195 Broadway, Saunders hoped the celebrity witnesses would have some effect on Greene. Throughout the fall, the judge had repeatedly displayed sharp skepticism on the need to keep Western Electric and its companion research arm, Bell Labs, integrated with the Bell System. Even though the Justice lawyers had since 1974 shifted the emphasis of their relief contentions from divestiture of Western to divestiture of the operating companies—a shift that coincided with Bill Baxter's passionate views about the case—Greene concentrated his courtroom questions and remarks about relief on Western. When AT&T witnesses talked about the benefits of the "vertical" integration of Western and the operating companies, Greene jumped into the testimony with active and skeptical cross-examination. It was clear to lawyers on both sides, as it had been to the "peer review" analysts hired by Howard Trienens, that the judge did not believe any great harm would ensue if some or all of Western was broken off. It seemed to the lawyers that Greene was less strident about operating company divestiture, which was the Justice department's overriding goal in the case.

The irony of this development was not lost on the lawyers from either camp. A year earlier, before trial began, the Justice attorneys preparing *U.S.* v. *AT&T* had been immensely skeptical about the relief side of their case, especially in the areas of phone equipment competition and procurement, where Western was vulnerable. The government lawyers had been reasonably confident that they could establish in court that John deButts' PCA strategy was anticompetitive and had been conducted in bad faith. But unlike the MCI part of the case, which both sides regarded as the key to *U.S.* v. *AT&T,* proving liability on the equipment competition issues did not suggest, ipso facto, that divestiture or even injunctive relief was necessary. The FCC's 1979 phone equipment registration program had rendered moot the issue of "harm to the network," and perhaps even the entire equipment case. An effective and open system for equipment competition was now in place. Western Electric's market share had diminished drastically. New equipment products, mainly Japanese but some American, were sprouting like mushrooms in a rain forest. By contrast, the allegations in the MCI part of the case were based on a situation that, despite MCI's explosive growth after Execunet, had not really changed: competitive Long Lines and the monopolistic operating companies were still owned by the same corporation. If one believed that long-distance competition could succeed over time, and if one accepted MCI's version of the history of telecommunications regulation in the early 1970s, then divestiture of the operating companies was a logical, if no less radical, idea.

That just wasn't true of the divestiture of Western. Even if the judge was convinced, as the government contended, that deButts' PCA strategy had been nothing more than a cynical attempt to postpone equipment competition until AT&T was better prepared to meet it, Greene could not order Western's divestiture as a means to punish the phone company for its behavior. Punitive divestiture was not allowed in a government antitrust suit. Structural relief could only be ordered if it addressed ongoing or future competitive problems, not those in the past. If a company had been harmed in the past by deButts' PCA strategy, it had the right to sue AT&T for monetary damages. Many had, and some had won. But such awards had no direct relevance to the relief aspects of Justice's phone equipment competition allegations.

To compound the irony, Greene seemed willing to justify the divestiture of Western on the basis of the relatively ineffective "procurement" section of the government's case, a section that the Justice lawyers had considered their weakest going into trial. Saunders and his trial team had assumed, too, that the procurement allegations would be relatively easy to defeat. The government contended that Bell's operating companies deliberately and systematically ignored outside suppliers when they purchased phones and other equipment to lease to consumers, and that the operating companies had a "pro-Western bias or in-house bias" that inhibited competition. The trouble with the government's evidence in this section was that it was almost entirely anecdotal. Even some of the government lawyers conceded that the stories they had to tell about procurement did not add up to much of a grand conspiracy.

Nonetheless, Greene had detected and zeroed in on a contradiction in AT&T's defense. Saunders argued that the operating companies made their procurement decisions solely on the basis of quality; there was no pro-Western bias. At the same time, Saunders contended that Western's products were far superior to its competitors', and he introduced evidence to prove the point. But logically, if Western's products were superior because the Bell manufacturer better understood the workings of the phone system and the needs of the operating companies, as Saunders said, then the operating companies should have a pro-Western bias. It would have made far more sense for AT&T to argue, as one of the government lawyers put it later, "You're damn right we have a pro-Western bias. That's the only way we can get the job done." The trouble was that during the 1970s, AT&T had repeatedly assured the FCC that its operating companies had no such prejudices; such assurances had been necessary to buy peace with the company's federal regulators. When the AT&T lawyers talked with their government opponents outside the courtroom about their self-contradictory procurement defense, they only sighed, "We had to try the facts as we found them."

By November, it was clear that the issue had become a major theme with Judge Greene. In his opinion on the motion to dismiss, he had written about how Western was like a "counselor" to the operating companies and that the "familial attitude" of Bell employees stifled competition by prejudicing procurement decisions. To testifying Bell executives and Saunders' celebrity witnesses alike, he reiterated his skepticism about the capacity of Bell employees to treat outside suppliers fairly. And each time he did so, he added more credence to Howard Trienens' and Charlie Brown's growing fear that the ultimate price of U.S. v. AT&T would be divestiture of some or all of Western Electric and Bell Labs, the twin jewels of the high technology future AT&T's chairman envisioned.

Chapter 28

Fence with a One-Way Hole

T HE internal office line on Ed Block's phone was ringing, and Block punched the button. It was his boss,
Charlie Brown. "Come see me, please," Brown said impassively.

Block, whose Texas accent and natural candor had not been
entirely diluted by three decades as a corporate public relations
executive, was just a few steps down the hall from the chairman's office. It was not unusual for Brown to summon his
senior vice-president for public relations for consultations, and
there was no reason to assume on this chill December day that
the chairman's call was anything but routine.

Brown was behind his desk in the small and modest executive bay that he had retained as his office since the days
before becoming leader of the world's largest and richest corporation. To one side, a window opened on an unobstructed
view of the Brooklyn Bridge. Across from Brown's desk there
was a rarely used conference table for six, now piled high with
assorted memoranda, legal briefs, and other papers. Adjacent
to the office was a small meeting room with a couch, three
chairs, a television, and a video recorder. The chairman had
his coat off, as usual when he was in his office. Though he
sometimes seemed a stiff and exceedingly sober man, Brown
relaxed somewhat in meetings with his trusted executives. He

walked about his office while talking, perching occasionally on a window ledge or on the edge of his desk. But he did not prop his shoes on its polished surface or roll up the sleeves of his shirt.

Howard Trienens had already arrived and was seated in one of the two chairs facing Brown's desk. Block sat down in the other. There was no sly grin on either Brown's or Trienens' face, no look of pain or weariness or relief or joy. They were utterly, even defiantly unemotional.

And then Charlie Brown asked, "Ed, I want to know if we could satisfactorily and plausibly explain ourselves if I should decide to accept the government's terms for a consent decree settlement—complete divestiture of the operating companies?"

Block kept his balance. He knew that some of his colleagues had been working that fall on the concept of a full inter-intra split, but he had no idea that such a radical decision was being seriously contemplated by the chairman. Brown's question was shocking. A year earlier, during the Crimson Sky negotiations, Block had done some thinking and some work on how a settlement with Justice could best be sold to AT&T's one million employees, three million shareholders, and the public. But that deal—three operating companies and a piece of Western in exchange for a clear and certain industry future and an end to the phone company's legal entanglements—would have been an easy sell. A deal that sacrificed two-thirds of AT&T's assets and resulted in the total dissolution of the national phone network would be quite a different challenge.

Block began to think on his feet. The key, it seemed to him, was that when the announcement was made, the story had to be told one time, one way—AT&T's way.

"It's very important to simultaneously announce it with the Justice department," Block said. He envisioned a "sword surrendering" ceremony with Baxter and Brown both present. Otherwise, in the media frenzy that would inevitably erupt after the announcement, reporters would bounce back and forth between sources at Justice and sources at the phone company. The story would become muddled, contradictory. Whatever message AT&T hoped to convey would be lost.

And precisely what message did Brown hope to sell? That would be Block's job, in consultation, of course, with Trienens and the chairman.

"Obviously, we cannot make the decision until I am convinced that it can be explained," Brown said.

In just fifteen minutes, Block had received his instructions. He was to breathe word of this to no one—not a soul. He would have to work alone, at home, at night, and on weekends. He would even have to do his own typing. His assignment was to devise and prepare a full-scale public relations strategy that would successfully sell the breakup of AT&T, so long decried by the phone company as a kind of industrial Armageddon, as a reasoned, even savvy decision of benefit to the company's shareholders and the public. Time was of the essence. On Friday, December 11, Trienens was flying to Washington to meet with Baxter and determine whether an immediate inter-intra split would be acceptable to the Antitrust chief. The following Wednesday, the 16th, AT&T's board of directors was convening for its monthly meeting. At that meeting, Brown wanted to present them with the inter-intra divestiture proposal for ratification. Block agreed to begin immediately, and the meeting broke up.

Suddenly, it had come to this.

There was no moment of revelation, Charlie Brown said later, no instant of clarity or will that led him to decide affirmatively to break up the American Telephone & Telegraph Company. The decision was a continuum, he said. Throughout November and December of 1981, when he discussed the inter-intra split informally, or "off line," with various members of his board of directors, Brown emphasized a kind of strategic fatalism about the idea. Regulation of the telephone industry had become like "a fence with a one-way hole," he said, designed to let myriad competitors in while holding AT&T out. The 1956 consent decree with Justice, under which the phone company still operated, severely restricted AT&T's ability to develop new kinds of business products that could blend emerging computer technologies with the phone network. Such products, melding voice and data communications, were at the center of Brown's vision of an emerging "information age," when businessmen would communicate with computers as routinely as they now talked on the telephone. The essence of Brown's plan for AT&T, which had invented the old form of communication, the telephone, was to arrive in this new age of digital data transmission, satellites, and computer networks in the best possible strategic position. Until now, "best" had meant "in one piece." At the FCC and in Congress, Brown had been working for more than two years to devise a regulatory formula that would allow AT&T, through Western or some other subsidiary, to sell computers and data communications products while at the same time retaining control over the national telephone network. That was the goal of S.898. It had been the goal of the telephone industry competition bill killed by Peter Rodino in 1980. It was the goal of a long and exceedingly complex regulatory proceeding at the FCC known as "Computer Inquiry II." In each case, the problem of "cross subsidies" between the phone company's local telephone monopoly and its new, competitive computer products—the same issue that was at the core of the Justice antitrust case—had been solved by regulation, not divestiture. AT&T would establish a "fully separated subsidiary" for its competitive computer products. The local telephone monopolies, as well as the newly competitive long-distance and phone equipment markets, would be governed by detailed federal rules enforced by the FCC. AT&T would arrive in the information age intact. Telephone service would continue to be provided by the company that did it best.

That was Charlie Brown's best-laid plan: the "A" plan. The one, he thought, that made the most sense for the phone company and the public. And the one that, on November 5, 1981, had been rendered seemingly impossible.

On that day, the staff of Congressman Tim Wirth released a 435-page report titled "Telecommunications in Transition: The Status of Competition in the Telecommunications Industry." The report was the long-awaited precursor to Wirth's S.898 companion bill. It was a statement of Wirth's policy and legislative priorities. And to Charlie Brown and Howard Trienens the report said, simply, that there was no longer any hope that an acceptable solution to the company's problems could be forged in Congress; that, in fact, whatever happened on Capitol Hill was likely to compound the already dismal situation in Judge Greene's courtroom.

More than any other single event, Brown and Trienens said later, the Wirth report led them to pursue affirmatively the inter-intra split strategy that had been drawn and redrawn on Charles Hugel's blackboard during the previous year. While its stated purpose was to lay a "firm foundation of fact" about phone industry competition, so that Wirth could better draft an S.898 companion, the report was actually more like a legal brief assembled to argue that unless new and more pervasive restrictions were placed on AT&T, competition in the phone industry would be just a pipe dream. More stringent protections for AT&T competitors than were contained in S.898 were needed, Wirth and his staff said. Rather than tearing down the fence with the one-way hole, Wirth intended to build it higher. Trienens had met with the staff, which was led by a lawyer named David Aylward, but he had left with the impression that Wirth considered AT&T immune to regulatory pain, that the congressman thought the phone company could overcome any obstacle thrown in its path. Indeed, so it had been for many years of the long and contentious relationship between AT&T and the U.S. government. Not this time, however. Trienens could see that AT&T's myriad competitors were "buzzing around the Wirth staff, and they all wanted their little ornament on the bill." By the time legislation was drafted, Trienens thought, it would be so debilitating that even another "Quagmire" sequel title probably wouldn't do it justice.

"The separate subsidiary by itself isn't adequate protection for competitors, so other protections have to be built in," Wirth told reporters while attacking S.898 early in November. "And you can't entirely depend on the 'expert agency,' the FCC, because the expert agency isn't very expert."

The Wirth bill, finally released on Thursday, December 10, confirmed Trienens' worst fears. It required AT&T to develop new subsidiary configurations, legislated tougher equal-access rules than even Baxter I and Baxter II, instituted procurement quotas for the operating companies, and generally attacked AT&T from all sides. By making unrealistic demands, Wirth had abandoned his brief leadership role in telecommunications policy making. In the course of just a few months, the mercurial subcommittee chairman had publicly declared his opposition to operating company divestiture—during his attempt at re-writing the Communications Act—then had written a letter to President Reagan urging that the Justice suit, which sought what Wirth opposed, not be dismissed, and finally had issued a report that scuttled the chances for a legislative solution to the whole mess. His contribution to the breakup of AT&T would not soon be forgotten by Charlie Brown or Howard Trienens.

After it was all over, one of the AT&T executives who was informed early on of Brown's decision to pursue the inter-intra split sat down at his typewriter and rapped out a stream-of-consciousness account of why his boss had done it. The document was meant to be a private primer about the decision for interested outsiders. But it had a peculiar, almost confessional tone about it, as if the author were still trying, years afterward, to make sense of his dizzying December experience.

"Who can AT&T deal with to get a way out of the quag-mire?" the executive wrote. "One person proposes a coherent antitrust theory, can make a deal and have it stick: Baxter. The omnibus 'break it all up' approach of Justice has gradually been replaced by a workable scheme, the dimensions of which offer AT&T a valuable commodity—reasonable certainty as to the future.

"The shareowners can be protected, the Bell companies can survive it, and so can AT&T. Significantly, the court has now become by far the best option for a final resolution of issues that simply can't wait any longer. Brown sees this as the best of a series of hard alternatives—one of the worst being to do nothing but continue to slug it out on all fronts. The Bell orga-nization says we'll do it and we'll make it work and we'll leave the philosophizing till later. Besides which, we're not wimps. We want to compete and we want to demonstrate that we can. Offense is more fun than defense. This is a workable solution. Let's take the initiative and put the destiny of the business back in the hands of management. Let's get on with it. The monopoly was shattered a decade ago and whatever its merits—and shortcomings—our business is management, not politics, not industrial theology. Hooray for Charlie Brown..."

And so it was that on Friday, December 11, a cold, overcast, and blustery autumn morning, Howard Trienens found himself winging to the nation's capital to discuss the inter-intra split with Bill Baxter.

Trienens had told Baxter nothing about his agenda when he called to arrange the appointment. His pretext for a visit was the ongoing Quagmire II settlement negotiations, which still showed no signs of nearing a conclusion.* The document outlining the Quagmire deal continued to grow longer and more complex. But as far as Baxter knew, it was the only deal AT&T was interested in making. So the Antitrust chief had continued to supervise the talks, and from time to time he and Trienens met to discuss their progress. At those meetings, Baxter would frequently joke, "You know, there are a lot easier ways to do this, Howard." But Trienens generally ignored Baxter's overtures about divestiture. He told the Antitrust chief that AT&T was still interested in trying to work out an injunctive settlement along the lines of S.898.

The scene at Baxter's office in the main Justice building when Trienens arrived that Friday morning was chaotic. The phones were ringing and secretaries and lawyers were running in and out. Trienens and Baxter tried to talk, but after a while Trienens suggested that they move over to the Madison Hotel for lunch. While the Justice trial was in progress, AT&T had rented an executive suite directly above George Saunders', on the eleventh floor, its height an unintended symbol of the phone company's legal hierarchy. Baxter agreed to go. It was the first time he and Trienens had ever talked about the AT&T case outside a Justice department office.

At the Madison suite, which was as comfortable and well-

*Some lawyers on the Justice trial team said later that they suspected during the fall that Baxter was deliberately stalling the Quagmire negotiations so that Greene could deliver his verdict at trial. Baxter denied that, though he admitted that he was never convinced at any time in 1981 that a nondivestiture deal could work.

appointed as Saunders' below, the two aging and idiosyncratic lawyers both ordered club sandwiches from room service.

Still, Trienens did not reveal the purpose of his trip to Washington. He had come to gather information, not make a deal with Baxter. Until Charlie Brown went to the board of directors the next Wednesday, there could be no negotiations. Trienens and Brown were both confident that the board would approve the inter-intra split plan. The board had been kept well-informed about the internal discussions, and, unlike at some large corporations, the AT&T directors almost routinely supported the judgment of their chief executive. Nonetheless, until the board passed on the matter, there was no point engaging Baxter in formal talks.

So for nearly the entire meeting, Trienens talked with Baxter about how a settlement—the Quagmire II deal, he meant—could be filed with the court so as to lift the computer restrictions of the 1956 consent decree. This was a crucial issue for Brown and Trienens if they were going to pursue an inter-intra settlement. The 1956 decree had been filed in federal court, but not in the same district as the 1974 case now being tried before Judge Greene in Washington. The 1956 decree was in New Jersey, under the control of a federal judge named Vincent Biunno. Trienens proposed that instead of actually settling the 1974 case, Justice and AT&T would file the Quagmire II deal as a "modification" to the 1956 consent decree. Simultaneously, Baxter would dismiss the case pending before Judge Greene in Washington. Then, Biunno would be asked to transfer the 1956 case down to Greene for review. These Byzantine legal manuevers would fold the 1956 decree into the current settlement and eliminate the computer prohibitions. Trienens made it clear that this was essential. One of Brown's first priorities in any deal was to clear AT&T's path to the information age. There was no reason for him to settle the 1974 case if the 1956 restrictions remained in place. Another potential attraction of the lawyers' plan was that since the 1974 case would be technically dismissed, not settled, Justice and AT&T might avoid submitting their deal to the close judicial scrutiny provided for by the Tunney Act, which empowered a judge to reject a settlement if it wasn't in the public interest. Out of political necessity, AT&T and Justice would probably have to accept "Tunney-like" proceedings before Greene, but perhaps they could avoid the sort of contentious inquiry, involving all of AT&T's competitors, that might sabotage a deal. This was an issue that would have to be explored more fully later. But on the first point, Baxter was agreeable. As long as the settlement effectively prevented cross subsidies by AT&T, Baxter, unlike some AT&T competitors and members of Congress, was happy to let the phone company into the computer business.

Trienens' purpose in this discussion, of course, was to lay the groundwork with Baxter for the legal procedures that he hoped to employ in just a few weeks' time, when the inter-intra split settlement was ready to be filed. Satisfied that Baxter was flexible on the issue, Trienens wound up the discussion. Then, just as Baxter was ready to leave, he casually dropped his bombshell.

"I know the hundred-pager isn't your way of doing it," Trienens said, referring again to Quagmire II. "You'd prefer the two-page, clean, surgical chop."

"I sure would," Baxter replied.

That was not an offer, Trienens intimated, only a possibility. But Baxter sensed that something was afoot. When they parted, Trienens told the Antitrust chief he would be in touch next week.

Trienens flew back to New York and met with Brown. He told him that the board of directors could be informed that Baxter would go along with an inter-intra settlement. The entire deal could be finalized in just a few weeks.

Brown had so carefully prepared his directors—many of whom were "old telephone men" themselves—for the proposal he intended to unveil that the Wednesday board meeting was something of an anticlimax. It commenced at 10:30 A.M., and Brown began by reminding the directors of the tangled history that had brought them to this morning. Formally and informally, the directors had already heard Howard Trienens' legal analysis about the possibility that Greene would divest Western and that successful appeal might be difficult. They knew, of course, that the Wirth bill had closed off a legislated regulatory solution, which, like Brown, the directors would have preferred. They were ready to hear their chairman's proposal.

"We are left with three alternatives," Brown said, and he listed them.

First, they could continue to fight—in Congress, in court, and at the FCC. No surrender. Obviously, there would always be a chance that they would somehow be vindicated. But in Congress, they had already taken their best shot, and even with the support of much of the Reagan cabinet, they had failed. In court, Greene was obviously against them. Even if they prevailed on appeal, the price was at least five, perhaps as many as seven years of continued uncertainty, during which time Wirth and other AT&T enemies in Congress would renew their legislative coddling of the phone company's competitors.

Second, there was Quagmire II. The previous summer, the S.898 regulatory formula had seemed an attractive alternative to continued litigation against Justice. But once Baxter had escaped the administration's threat to drop the lawsuit, he had achieved the upper hand in the negotiations. As the document became more and more complex, AT&T had no leverage with Baxter to pare it down. The deal had been born as a tactical compromise in the midst of a political and policy dispute among Reagan's cabinet; now that the dispute had withered away and Baxter had won, his heart seemed to have gone out of the negotiations, if indeed he had ever been sincere about them. There was a reasonable chance that some kind of injunctive settlement could be worked out in the next year or so. But there was at least an equal chance that Brown and his board would find the terms too debilitating to accept, causing Quagmire II eventually to be scrapped.

Finally, there was the inter-intra split. A clean break. An opportunity to regain control of AT&T's destiny, to compete on equal terms with McGowan, to abandon the rites of "industrial theology" and return triumphant to the competitive, secular world of profit and loss. Yes, to the Bell System's "family" of one million, many of whom would find no place in the restructured industry, the costs would be tremendous. But for the company's shareholders, there would be no pain. In the short term, the equity value of the entire Bell System would not be devalued by its breakup. In the long term, the new AT&T would retain its most profitable, cash-rich subsidiaries while divesting the relatively less profitable operating companies. The operating companies would survive because regulators would force local phone users and AT&T's competitors to pay the subsidies once doled out by 195 Broadway. The cost of local phone service would rise dramatically, but that would be Congress' political problem, not AT&T's. The phone company had said all along that higher local rates would be the most obvious price of phone industry competition.

When Brown concluded his presentation, the board's first decision was to drop the first alternative—continuing to fight on all fronts—from consideration. A brief discussion ensued about whether it made sense to pursue Quagmire II to its conclusion before offering the inter-intra split to Justice, and about how the split would actually be made. The atmosphere of the meeting was calm and reasoned and unemotional. A clear majority agreed with Brown that there was nothing to be gained by postponing the inter-intra decision. After the Christmas holiday, a new phase of George Saunders' defense presentation would begin, and Brown was scheduled to testify. The chairman was not looking forward to that event. No doubt there would be media coverage, and the Justice lawyers would pull out the notes from the May 1972 Presidents' Conference in Key Largo and ask Brown what he had meant by "choking off" competition and "hitting the nails on the head." Brown considered that Key Largo meeting to be an honest discussion about how to respond to new competition, given AT&T's "nationwide average" pricing, and he thought that the notes of the meeting, first introduced during the MCI trial in Chicago, were nothing but a cheap ploy designed to feed the media's appetite for sensationalism in a lawsuit that was too complex for most reporters to explain. Nonetheless, Brown's very appearance at the trial in Washington would not be good publicity for AT&T, and it would be unpleasant for him personally. If for other reasons the board agreed with Brown that the inter-intra split strategy was the best available, then the chairman was anxious to close the deal as quickly as possible.

A resolution was presented authorizing Brown to begin negotiations with Justice immediately. A voice vote was called. The resolution passed overwhelmingly. Shortly before 12:30 P.M. and less than two hours after the meeting had begun, the AT&T directors filed out of the board room having decided to destroy their own company.

Outside the panoramic windows of 195 Broadway, a light snow had fallen on Manhattan. Christmas lights were strung across the city's avenues, and everywhere was visible the red and green and gold of holiday decorations. The snow had begun melting in the streets, churning under tires into foul brown slush, but on the buildings and trees and parked cars it lay unblemished and bright.

Whether Charlie Brown returned to his office from the board room to gaze at this sweet and melancholy scene, whether it made him feel misty or indifferent or just relieved, is something he decided he would always keep to himself.

Chapter 29

The Two-Pager

THERE was snow on the ground in Washington, too, and Christmas decorations were hanging over Pennsylvania and Constitution Avenues. Between those two broad thoroughfares, the main Justice building was alive with holiday cheer. Around five o'clock, just as the twilight vanished from the western skies across the Potomac, the department's annual Christmas party had gathered form in the fifth-floor hallway outside the attorney general's conference room.

Two floors directly below the party, Bill Baxter, not a sociable man, was still at his desk. His telephone rang, and he picked it up. It was Howard Trienens calling from New York.

"I've talked to Chairman Brown," Trienens said, "and we'd like to see what a two-page decree would look like." One trait Trienens shared with Baxter was an exceedingly dry sense of humor.

Baxter said he thought that could be arranged.

In a rare moment of introspection, Baxter once remarked, "One of my great faults as a person is that I don't get too excited." Trienens' phone call, however, tickled him so much that he hurriedly climbed two flights of stairs to search for his Antitrust front office deputy, Ron Carr, to tell him the astounding news.

In the crowded corridor, the bearded Carr was nowhere

in sight. Pushing through the reveling lawyers, Baxter bumped into Richard Levine, the Justice attorney principally in charge of the Quagmire II negotiations.

"Is Ron Carr around?" Baxter asked.

Levine said that he had seen Carr at the party earlier, but didn't know where he was now. Baxter, uncharacteristically urgent, moved off to look.

Curiosity began to gnaw at Levine, a rotund, moon-faced man renowned in the Justice department and among AT&T lawyers for his strange characteristics, which included a stuttering style of speech reminiscent of a sheep's bleat, and an affection for the arcane details of law and regulation; it was said of Levine that he subscribed to the *Federal Register*, the inscrutable government publication where new rules and regulations are published, when he was ten years old. The fact that Baxter had appointed Levine to handle the Quagmire II negotiations was one reason some Justice lawyers suspected those settlement talks were really just a filibuster designed to force AT&T's hand; the growing size and complexity of the Quagmire II document was mainly a result of Levine's insistent tinkering and revisions. In some ways, though, Levine was much like his boss, Baxter. Both were brilliant theoreticians who seemed instinctively to resist being pragmatic, and both were outsiders to the institutional culture of Justice's aggressive, workaday trial lawyers.

In any event, Levine knew Baxter well enough to suspect that it was not Christmas spirit that was the cause of the Antitrust chief's animated expression, so a few minutes later he wandered down to the third floor to see what was up. Baxter and Carr were in the Antitrust chief's expansive office, and when Levine stuck his head in the door, they waved him in. There was something conspiratorial about the looks on their faces.

"What's going on?" Levine asked.

"Well," Baxter replied, "Howard suggested that we go ahead with the two-pager. And what I told Howard is that I want to do it short and clean. Just short and clean."

Levine, stunned, said he had some ideas about how to do

that, and he ran up the four flights of stairs to his office. He sat down at his typewriter, quickly tapped out a document, and then carried it back down to Baxter and Carr.

"This is only one page long," Baxter remarked when the breathless Levine handed him his draft.

"That's not the decree, Bill, that's just the prospectus."

Baxter read it over. "OK. Write up the decree."

On Thursday and Friday and over the weekend, Levine and Carr worked together to compose the first draft of a document entitled "Modification of Final Judgment." It turned out to be longer than two pages. The first draft of the decree itself, which provided, not very eloquently, for "the transfer from AT&T and its affiliates to the basic operating companies of sufficient personnel, facilities, and rights to technical information to permit the BOCs independently to engage in procurement for, and engineering, management, and marketing of, retained functions," took three pages. Two appendixes, one concerned with definitions and another having to do with "transitional" rules by which the divested operating companies would provide "equal access" to AT&T's long distance competitors, took another twelve pages.

The equal-access appendix, Levine and Carr knew, was going to cause problems once AT&T saw the draft. The question of precisely how AT&T would divest two-thirds of its assets, where the lines would be drawn, was of course crucially important to the phone company, since it would dictate the future profitability of the new AT&T as well as the new operating companies. How many new operating companies should there be? What assets and services should they be allowed to keep? The Justice lawyers had decided to let AT&T work all that out for itself and then submit a "plan of reorganization" to the court for approval. But the question of how the new companies would treat MCI and other long-distance competitors was something they could not leave to AT&T. So the two lawyers drafted a series of detailed rules designed to enforce pure equality between all long-distance companies. Among other things, the operating companies would have to convert the phone system to allow MCI customers to dial the same number of digits that

AT&T customers did. But the appendix did not specify how much "rent" MCI would have to pay for this improved service, or whether that rent would be the same as AT&T's. All the draft said was that "the charges for each type of exchange access shall be cost justified on the basis of differences in services provided." In other words, the important matter of access fees would have to be negotiated after the phone company was dismantled. In truth, there was no other feasible way to do it "short and clean."

The collaboration of Levine and Carr was not without its difficulties. Levine would draft a paragraph, and Carr would rewrite it, and then they would argue, Levine insisting that Carr "would never understand the issues" as well as he did, and Carr trying to transform Levine's writing "into something near English." By Monday, however, they had a roughly typed document ready to be sent to Trienens in New York.

The circle of secrecy surrounding the "December 21st draft," as it was called, was extremely tight. Trienens had been vehement on this point when he called Baxter, and he used every available opportunity to remind the government lawyers that if its confidentiality was violated, the deal would be off. At Justice, only Baxter, Levine, and Carr were aware of the negotiations. And since the two AT&T lawyers in Washington who were in charge of Quagmire II, Jim Kilpatric and Bob McLean, were not yet aware of the decision made at 195 Broadway, Levine had to carry on with the injunctive settlement talks as if nothing had happened.

In New York, knowledge about the board of directors' decision the previous Wednesday had been closely controlled. There were less than ten executives on the twenty-sixth floor who knew what had happened. The plan was that once Trienens received the Justice draft, he would take Christmas week—while most AT&T executives were away from the office—to review and revise it. Then the December 21 draft would be returned to Baxter. If Justice accepted the changes, or if it appeared that the outstanding differences could be easily resolved, then more executives would be brought into the discussions to prepare for the devastating announcement.

Prior to the Wednesday board meeting, for example, Ed Block had drafted what he later described as the "rhetoric" by which the inter-intra split could be sold to AT&T's employees, shareholders, and the public.

At home, feeling shocked, dismayed, and abandoned, Block had typed, "It is your right to know how we reached this decision. And why. And what the effects of it will be. We did not come to this decision easily. What we and all the other parties sought was to balance the interests of tens of millions of consumers, three million shareowners, one million employees, and the national defense. The issues have been debated for over a decade in the executive, legislative, and judicial branches of government; in the industry; in the marketplace; in the company; and in the press. There has been no referendum, but the verdict is plain enough. We agreed to the consent order because we believe it expresses the consensus that, in the main, has been reached on the framework for a new national telecommunications policy."

The core idea, which Block had discussed with Brown, was to try to persuade the public that the inter-intra split, while it was on the one hand a "deal" between Justice and AT&T, also represented a "consensus," perhaps by default, about how the country wanted its phone system to be run. That way the burden of justifying this radical act would be shifted away from the phone company, while at the same time AT&T would appear accommodating. To be sure this strategy would work, Block had secretly hired Lou Harris, who was told nothing of the impending settlement, to conduct a poll about how consumers and shareholders would react to the announcement of an inter-intra split. The Harris interviewers were able to ask hypothetical questions about breaking up the Bell System by using an interview with Bill Baxter recently published by a telephone industry newspaper. There was enough information in that interview about how the breakup of AT&T might actually be accomplished for the Harris surveyors to construct a hypothetical questionnaire. The results of that poll had convinced Block that the breakup could be explained and would be accepted by the public, and he had communicated this belief to

Brown before the Wednesday board meeting. When Trienens received the December 21 draft from Baxter, Block was instructed to await a "go" signal from Brown before beginning to prepare the full array of public relations materials that would be needed for an announcement; that preparation required that a number of public relations and media relations executives be informed of the settlement decision. Brown was not going to risk widening the circle of knowledge about the deal until after Trienens had revised and approved Baxter's draft. And that, said Brown, a deeply religious Christian, could wait until after Christmas.

And with no further ado, the AT&T chairman flew off to Florida with his wife for the holiday. That Brown could vacation in the sunny citrus state while the very terms of his company's dismantlement were being drawn up struck Block as compelling evidence that his boss was a "pretty cool customer."

Indeed, none of the principals in the negotiations allowed the impending breakup of the world's largest corporation to interfere with his Christmas vacation plans. On Monday, as soon as the December 21 draft arrived by special courier from Washington, Howard Trienens flew home to Chicago. On Thursday, the 24th, Ron Carr was flying to California to spend the holiday with his wife and her parents. Baxter planned to stay in Washington for Christmas, but he confirmed the reservations he and his live-in companion had made to fly to Utah on New Year's Eve for a week of skiing.

Monday evening in Chicago, Trienens came from the airport to the headquarters office of Sidley & Austin to attend his firm's annual Christmas party. George Saunders, too, had flown back from Washington for the festivities. When Trienens saw Saunders, he cornered him and said, "I've got something I want you to look at."

The two lawyers stepped into an empty office. Trienens took out the typed draft from Washington and handed it to Saunders. The trial lawyer, who had spent the last eight years of his life fighting against the very eventuality that was now laid before him, was astonished. He couldn't believe it; he had never thought the Bell System would do something like this.

Trienens went on to brief his partner about the deliberations at 195 Broadway and explained that he had taken the draft to Chicago to work on it over Christmas.

"We've been saying all along that it was crazy," Saunders remarked. "It doesn't look any better on paper." He shook his head. For once, Saunders had nothing to say.

On Sunday, two days after Christmas, Trienens finally called Baxter at his home in Washington to say that in principle, he and Charlie Brown found the December 21 draft acceptable. He had one suggestion: Justice should allow AT&T to create a "central services organization" for the new operating companies, in which some of Bell's vast managerial and technical resources could be pooled after the breakup. Baxter said he had no problem with that idea. Trienens also had some clarifying questions about the ownership of all the "embedded" phone equipment in the country, which was owned by AT&T and leased to residential and business customers. The value of this embedded base of equipment was somewhere between $9 and $14 billion and Trienens wanted to be sure that Baxter agreed AT&T would retain ownership of all of it after the breakup. That, too, was fine with Baxter—the operating companies would be prohibited from entering the phone equipment business after divestiture, and Western could then sell or continue to lease the phones already present in American homes and offices. The franchise of the divested operating companies would be to provide local phone service only, Baxter said; everything else belonged to AT&T. When Trienens hung up, the only substantive aspect of the deal that remained to be negotiated was the consent decree's "equal access" appendix. The two lawyers arranged to meet in Baxter's office on Wednesday to discuss again the broad principles of the settlement. Charlie Brown would fly up from Florida, Trienens added, to participate.

Baxter then called Ron Carr at his in-laws' house in California. "They want to do it. Come back as soon as possible," he instructed. Carr agreed to cut short his vacation and catch a plane to Washington the next morning.

* * *

There were several reasons why George Saunders was in a disagreeable mood when he answered the ringing telephone beside his Madison Hotel bed at seven o'clock on the cold and sunny morning of Wednesday, December 30.

For one thing, Saunders was rarely his effusive and articulate self so early in the day. He typically stayed awake until two or three in the morning, keeping company with his trial team staff and perhaps a pitcher of room service martinis. But in the morning, it was often a struggle to reignite the engines that drove his enthusiastic personality. For another, Saunders had hoped by now to be golfing in Florida on a short winter vacation. The trial was in recess until January 15, and even Judge Greene had fled town for a Caribbean holiday. But Saunders had been forced to return to Washington to manage the details of his recently escalated battle with Greene over how many more witnesses AT&T would be allowed to call in its defense. About two weeks earlier, just as the last of the celebrity witnesses had finished testifying, Saunders had submitted to Greene a list of yet another 100 witnesses that he had intended to call. The judge had erupted in a fit of temper previously unmatched in his, or perhaps any, courtroom. A few days later, he had ordered Saunders to prepare a detailed brief justifying why each of the witnesses on his list was necessary to the AT&T defense. Saunders had known that his witness list would provoke Greene to anger, but he had decided to prolong his defense until either Greene changed his mind about the case or he told Saunders to shut up and sit down. So Saunders had canceled his golf and returned to town to write his justifications, like a schoolboy on detention. Finally, there was the lingering memory of the document Trienens had shown him in Chicago. Saunders still did not believe that AT&T was serious about the deal, but the very idea had shadowed his mood over the last week.

Saunders answered the phone gruffly. It was Howard Trienens, who had spent the night in AT&T's eleventh-floor suite. "Come up here, George. I want you to look at something."

After pulling himself out of bed, Saunders dressed, staggered out of his suite, and rode the hotel elevator one floor up.

When he entered Trienens' suite, his partner handed him a copy of the working draft of the inter-intra settlement decree. Saunders still didn't understand why AT&T would do something like this, but instead of saying anything to Trienens, he ordered some coffee and read the document.

With some caffeine in his system, Saunders was about to announce to Trienens that the Bell System would never allow this to happen when his words were stifled by the sound of a key turning in Trienens' door. The door pushed open and Charlie Brown stepped inside, carrying the bags he had taken on the flight from Florida that morning.

"Have you got it?" Brown asked Trienens.

"Here it is," Trienens said, handing the chairman a copy of the draft that Saunders was holding. As Trienens and Brown talked, it finally dawned on Saunders that in just a matter of days, *U.S.* v. *AT&T* would be over, and the Bell System would be no more.

"Charlie, if you do this, what are you going to say about all the sworn testimony we entered that says this is crazy?" Saunders inquired.

"Well, I know we put in some testimony criticizing the government's remedy, but I think we can handle that."

"But Charlie, the other day we had a guy on the stand from the Italian phone company. He testified about the government's remedy. And he spoke in Italian, so I couldn't understand everything he was saying, but he kept saying over and over, '*Pazzo! Pazzo!* (Crazy! Crazy!)'"

Brown only laughed. But in the days ahead, in meetings with Justice department lawyers or Reagan administration officials, Brown and Saunders would occasionally catch each other's eye, and one of them would say, savoring the irony, "*Pazzo! Pazzo!*"

Chapter 30

Après Ski

"I can't understand how you are letting something like this hang up the whole thing," Charlie Brown was saying. "You're jeopardizing the whole deal."

"Well, so be it," Bill Baxter replied.

Brown hung up the phone; the deal was off, he thought. It was Friday, New Year's Day. Brown was back in Florida. Baxter was in a Park City, Utah, ski chalet, negotiating the inter-intra split between runs down the Rocky Mountain slopes. Two days earlier, at the meeting in the Antitrust chief's Washington office, Brown and Baxter had reviewed together the main sections of the proposed decree: the reorganization of the Bell System, the responsibilities of the newly divested operating companies, and the rules governing equal access to the local exchanges by AT&T, MCI, and other long distance companies.

"All right," Brown had said when the review was complete. "We agree in principle to these terms. Now let's go through and flyspeck it."

Brown had departed and later that afternoon Howard Trienens had arrived at Justice to work on the details with Ron Carr and Richard Levine. Quickly a snag had arisen in the negotiations. In Appendix B, the section of the decree that described the new rules governing equal access between AT&T and MCI, Baxter had insisted that the new operating companies be required to construct their switching stations in a way that ensured that AT&T would not obtain a technical and pricing advantage over MCI by virtue of the phone company's pre-existing, ubiquitous long-distance network, which contained many more switches than did MCI's. It was a relatively minor technical issue, but the provision outraged Trienens and Brown because Baxter was actually trying to dictate the detailed engineering of AT&T's physical plant—something the Bell executives thought no government official had a right to do. Brown could understand Baxter's concern, but he thought the Antitrust chief's approach to the problem was plainly "ridiculous." But when Baxter would not give in to Trienens at the Wednesday negotiating session, Brown had decided that he would personally call the Antitrust chief in Utah on New Year's Day. That, too, had failed, and now the entire deal was in jeopardy.

Ed Block didn't know that. At 195 Broadway on New Year's Day, he had begun feverish preparations to shape and control how the breakup of AT&T would be perceived by news media, shareowners, employees, and Wall Street. After the Wednesday meeting with Baxter, Brown had given him the "go" signal. On Thursday morning, Block told several of his key underlings about the impending settlement. One of them, Bill Mullane, an assistant vice-president for media relations, reacted first with shock and dismay, and then said, "It'll be a helluva news story." Now Mullane, Block, and several other assistant vice-presidents were in Block's office mapping a strategy. The television set was tuned to the college bowl games, but the sound was off.

There were nine separate elements of the massive information control plan that Block had in mind. They would have to finalize the ad copy previously drafted by Block. Not only would that copy become a national newspaper advertisement addressed to shareholders and employees, it would also be the basis for Charlie Brown's statement at the unveiling press conference. They would have to prepare elaborate "briefing materials" for the press, statements from Bell executives and other documents selling the idea that divesting two-thirds of the phone company's assets was a sound and rational idea. Similar press material would have to be prepared for all of the local operating companies, whose executives would not be informed of their fate until the last possible moment. The operating company presidents, soon to be on their own, would need a private briefing package delivered to them on the morning of the announcement. Less sophisticated material would have to be prepared for the rest of AT&T's one million employees so that the first information they received about the breakup came from the company, not outsiders. Perhaps most important, a series of "shareowner and key constituency" letters had to be written—hundreds of letters addressed to the company's regulators, creditors, and equity holders—which were designed to "get to them immediately with our side of the story," as Block put it. Then there was the physical advertising mock-up and media schedule that had to be prepared. Block decided to bring into his confidence some executives at AT&T's Madison Avenue advertising agency, N. W. Ayer. Ayer secretly sent the ad copy to a trusted typesetter in Philadelphia, who had his employees set and proofread the ads in different pieces, so none of them understood what the announcement was about. Finally, "talk-from" outlines and other general background materials would have to be prepared for AT&T account executives, who would have to explain the breakup to the company's large business customers.

In each of these separate publicity campaigns, Block wrote in an early planning document, the overall objective was "to assure, to the extent that we can, that our business emerges from the public clamor that is almost certain to attend such an event undiminished as an investment prospect; undiminished as a place to work...; and undiminished in its reputation as a well-managed business." At the same time, Block conceded, "It has to be acknowledged that the price is high and that it will be the subject of considerable criticism and debate. Our information materials must affirm the prudence of the management judgment that the advantages of the new decree warrant its costs and its risks.... Our objective should be to gain broad public acceptance of the change as being in the best interests of the nation as a whole. In achieving an effective balance of interests, the proposed decree maintains local service capabilities; retains ability to plan and operate unified nation- wide intercity network; assures that critical national defense responsibilities can be met; provides for growing co~apetition in every aspect of telecommunications, in line with emerging public policy directions; is positive in terms of preserving and enhancing U.S. industry leadership in world markets."

In the weeks ahead, Block's "thematic" objectives would become like a repetitive hit song crooned by Bell executives and, eventually, by Wall Street analysts and the news media. Block was aware that his sales campaign was more than a little disingenuous—the breakup of AT&T was a cataclysmic event for the phone company and the nation, he believed—but like Chairman Brown, Block thought that the worst thing that could happen would be if Congress decided to interfere with this historic decision after it was made. If AT&T could not break itself up on its own terms, if it failed to tell the story "one way, our way," then the inter-intra split might turn out to be one of the greatest business fiascos in American history. The prospect of Congressman Tim Wirth attempting to "fix" the breakup was almost too chilling for AT&T's top executives to contemplate. A week was not much time to prevent such a catastrophe, but Block and his public-relations cohorts began that Friday to at- tempt the feat.

And over the weekend, by the miracle of modern teleph- ony, the deal that had been dead on Friday was slowly being brought back to life. The negotations conducted that Saturday and Sunday were like an advertisement for the importance of quality, universal phone service. Trienens had returned to his home in Chicago, Richard Levine and Ron Carr remained in Washington, Brown was still in Florida, and most of Baxter's days were spent skiing in Utah. Trienens discussed the sticky paragraph by phone with Levine and Carr. When they reached an agreement on some point, Trienens would call Brown while the Antitrust front office lawyers would try to reach Baxter. Sometimes Baxter returned their calls from a pay phone in a warming hut halfway down the Park City ski slopes. By the end of the day on Saturday, Baxter had backed down from his insistence on engineering the operating companies' physical plant, and by Sunday a compromise pricing formula had been devised to address his equal-access concerns. That day, when it was clear that the settlement deal was on again, Trienens and Brown discussed setting a date for an announcement and the commencement of Block's publicity campaign. They wanted to make the announcement on a Friday—a weekend would help to moderate the first wave of public reaction.

In one of his telephone conversations with Levine on Sunday afternoon, Trienens asked, "Richard, could you do us a favor?"

"Sure."

"We have a situation here where we've got to tell a lot of people about this decision—the operating company presidents and other people—but once we get that done, we really can't hold it. We've got to get it out. So we're structuring some things that we'd really like to do. What I'm asking is whether we could announce the settlement on the morning of January 8, Friday."

"I'm sure we could do that, Howard," Levine replied without hesitating.

In fact, Levine was ecstatic. Trienens' proposal coincided perfectly with a secret plan now in the final stages of preparation in the Antitrust front office, a plan that had nothing to do with the AT&T case. Before he flew off to Utah, Baxter had made the final decision to dismiss the pending Justice antitrust suit against computer giant IBM. Baxter had been reviewing the long-entangled IBM case ever since he had come to Justice the previous April, and he had found little in the case to recommend it. Not only was the 1968 suit an "embarrassment" because it was so bogged down procedurally, it was precisely the sort of antitrust case that offended Baxter's conservative ideology. The case adhered not to the "bottleneck" theory of *U.S.* v. *AT&T* but rather to allegations deriving from IBM's market share in the computer industry. One firm tenet of Baxter's theoretical views about antitrust law was that neither huge size nor large market share was by itself a violation of the antitrust laws. The only thing that really mattered to Baxter was economic efficiency. If IBM had become a huge corporation because it was more efficient than its competitors, then it deserved its riches. During the summer, Baxter had held a series of secret private "hearings" in his office, in which Justice lawyers had debated the issues in the IBM case against the computer corporation's own trial counsel. Baxter had asked the Justice attorneys to justify why they should be allowed to continue prosecuting the case, and, similarly, he had challenged the IBM lawyers to argue why it should be dismissed. Now he had made his decision, and as soon as the attorney general approved it, he wanted to make an announcement. The trouble was that on Saturday, January 9, Baxter was flying off to Europe for an international antitrust conference. Since he would be skiing until Thursday, the only "window of opportunity," as Levine put it, was Friday, the same day AT&T wanted to announce the inter-intra deal.

On Monday, Levine and Carr worked quickly, in consultation with Trienens and one or two other AT&T executives, to finalize the language of the AT&T consent decree. They also polished up the "fact memo" that would recommend the IBM dismissal to Attorney General William French Smith. Both documents would have to be reviewed personally by Baxter as soon as possible. Carr and Levine decided to recruit a front office attorney named Loren Hershey to fly to Utah with the documents. They told him about the AT&T settlement, but not about the decision to dismiss the IBM case. On Monday night in the main Justice building, they presented Hershey with two sealed manila envelopes and instructed him to fly to Park City the next morning.

At dawn Tuesday, Hershey drove from his home in suburban Virginia to Washington National Airport to catch a 7:00 A.M. Western Airlines flight to Salt Lake City, via Chicago and Minneapolis. Fortunately, he locked the two sealed envelopes inside his briefcase and carried them on the plane; somewhere between Washington and Salt Lake City, Western lost Hershey's checked baggage.

It was snowing when Hershey's plane touched down at the Salt Lake City airport. Inside the terminal, he called back to Ron Carr at the Justice offices in Washington.

"Get those papers to Bill and tell him that Charlie and the boys are standing by in New Jersey," said Carr, who was by now well amused by the cloak-and-dagger secrecy surrounding the AT&T deal. Carr's humor, like Baxter's, was so dry as to be often indecipherable, and Hershey wasn't sure what Carr was talking about. So he hung up and dialed the Antitrust chief's Park City resort condo to pass on the message.

The son of Baxter's statistician girlfriend answered the phone. "Is Bill Baxter there?" Hershey asked.

"He is out skiing. He said I should expect your call. He said to come on up here and leave the papers."

"If he calls or comes back, tell him I'll be up there in an hour."

Hershey rented a car and began the forty-five-minute drive to Park City. The snow had let up and the well-traveled roads were clear. Around 1:00 P.M., he arrived in the snow-covered, pine-forested resort town and followed the directions he had been provided to Baxter's condominium.

But Baxter was still out skiing. He had called down while Hershey was en route, and he had repeated his request for Hershey to just leave the papers and return for them later. But Hershey was determined to turn the envelopes over to Baxter personally. And since the Antitrust chief had left further instructions that Hershey was to be offered something to eat if he was hungry, the Justice lawyer devoured a ham sandwich and waited.

A little after two, Baxter called again. "I'm up here on the mountain," he told Hershey. "I'll be down in an hour."

"I have the papers and a message from Ron. He said to tell you that Charlie and the boys are standing by in New Jersey."

Baxter was characteristically distant. "Fine. Fine. I'll be down."

Still, though, the Antitrust chief did not return. Hershey decided to go for a walk; in his cashmere overcoat and business suit, he felt ridiculous traipsing through the resort town. When he returned to the condo, Baxter still wasn't back.

Finally, just as the sun was setting behind the Rocky Mountains, Baxter appeared carrying his skis and brushing the snow from his clothing. His ordinarily pale complexion had been reddened by the wind and cold.

"How was the skiing?" Hershey inquired.

"It was mystical," the Antitrust chief replied, seemingly serious.

Hershey handed him the papers. "Why do you think they did it?"

"Well, I think they had to consider their options. And I think they considered their self-interest as well as ours."

And with that inscrutable summation to mull over, Hershey soon found himself winging back to Washington with the documents, now signed and approved by Baxter.

Meanwhile, "Charlie in New Jersey" had been informed that a Friday announcement was now definite. A final draft of the consent decree had been approved by both sides. The "boys" also referred to by Carr were the presidents of AT&T's twenty-two local operating companies from around the country, who had been instructed to assemble at the parent company's campus-style office complex in upscale Basking Ridge, New Jersey, for an 8:00 A.M. Tuesday meeting. The presidents were not told what was on the agenda, but it was not unusual for a Presidents' Conference to be called on short notice or without explanation. The New Jersey site, where 4,500 employees of AT&T's "general departments" worked, was chosen because its conference room facilities were considerably larger than those at 195 Broadway. That morning, the two dozen presidents gathered in a tiered, theater-style room in Basking Ridge's executive office building. Before each row of chairs was a single, seamless desk, or, in the vernacular of modern corporations, "work space." Before the audience of quizzical executives stood Charlie Brown, Howard Trienens, and Ed Block.

AT&T's chairman began the meeting by announcing that in a matter of days, the phone company would likely agree to a consent decree ordering the divestiture of all the operating companies run by the men now seated in this room. It was not clear, Brown said, how many new operating companies would be formed—that was a question AT&T's top executives would answer together. Brown explained the franchise of the new operating companies: local service only. The new companies would not be permitted to sell phone equipment or long distance or any other "enhanced" service. All of that would be the franchise of the new AT&T, made up of Long Lines, Bell Labs, and Western Electric.

"What are the chances that the agreement will go through?" one of the presidents asked.

"Eighty percent," Brown answered. By the end of the day, after Hershey had reported Baxter's approval of the documents back to Ron Carr, that estimation had moved close to one hundred percent.

It was, typically for AT&T, a somber group of executives who began to absorb the devastating implications of Brown's words even as they were spoken. The operating company presidents were all white males in their forties and fifties. Like Brown, they had almost all worked for AT&T since their early twenties, and most had never been employed by another company. Gradually they had risen through the Bell System's management ranks, moving from job to job, city to city, back and forth between Long Lines, Western, corporate headquarters, Bell Labs, and the various operating companies. Now, without warning, their careers were being presented to them as a game of musical chairs in which the record had just been turned off. Suddenly, their jobs at the operating companies were no longer just a rung on the Bell promotion ladder. This was it. This was the end of the line. This was the future—regulated local service, utility functions, nothing more.

It was a shock that AT&T would agree to such a settlement, but it was not so shocking that the operating company presidents did not immediately see that they might be getting the raw end of a major business deal. As soon as Block and Trienens were finished with their respective short briefings about the upcoming publicity campaign and the legal background of the settlement, the questions began.

"I really see a problem, looking ahead," one of them said. "I mean, we're out of the equipment business, we're out of the long distance business, we're out of a lot of other things..."

They wanted more detail. Would they have the opportunity to negotiate? Yes, they would, both internally and before Judge Greene. Would it be possible to expand the operating companies' franchise to make them more viable, more diverse? Possible, but not likely, was the answer. Almost uniformly the presidents' questions reflected their fear and concern they had been been abandoned to the low technology end the phone business while 195 Broadway, plump and ready with Bell Labs, Western, and Long Lines, raced off into the information age. As the discussion flowed, it became clear that was a plausible interpretation of the deal with Justice but it was even more clear that the details of the local companies' franchise were yet to be negotiated and were, in effect, up for grabs. Anything was possible. By the end of the day-long meeting, one or two of the operating company presidents had even begun to joke, "Free at last!"

Watching the meeting progress, Ed Block, the philosophical public relations man, was astonished by one aspect of the presidents' reactions. Even after their initial agitation over the future viability of the operating companies had been quelled by answers to their many questions, the presidents did not wax nostalgical about the end of the century-old Bell System. There were no tears shed or fists pounded on the desks or even any wistful remarks about what might have been if it weren't for Bill McGowan, or Bill Baxter, or Jim Baker, or Tim Wirth, or Harold Greene, or the fact that Attorney General Bill Smith once sat on the board of Pacific Telephone. The presidents were engineers, by and large, very task-oriented and disciplined. Instead of pausing to reflect about the breakup of their company, they moved immediately to the challenge of completing the job ahead in the time allotted. In some way, then, the most compelling tribute to the service-driven, centenarian Bell System culture—which was hopelessly inappropriate in the new age of competition—was the lack of any tribute at all.

The next morning, Charlie Brown flew to Washington to pay tribute to those Reagan administration officials who had gallantly supported the phone company during the political intrigue of the previous summer. He met with Caspar Wein-

ber at the Pentagon and explained the terms of the settle-
mer emphasizing that steps had been taken by AT&T to ensure
that Defense Communications Agency would experience
as li disruption as possible. Weinberger was not asked to
inter e in any way; it was too late for politics. Brown's visit
was nly a courtesy call, as were his meetings the next day
at the ite House with Ed Meese and counselor Fred Fielding.
All th meetings were brief, and Brown did most of the talking.

In dition, the Commerce department officials who had
develo the dismissal proposal and had fought against Baxter
and his lies were informed about the terms of the inter-intra
settlem deal. They, especially, expressed regret that it had
come to is.

Ger Connell's courtesy call came on Wednesday afternoon fro Ron Carr. "Can you drop over later this afternoon?"
he asked

Neith r Connell nor his Justice trial staff, who had given
up vacatis to work on the case over the Christmas holiday,
had been formed about the negotiations between AT&T and
the Antitr t front office. In part, that reflected the tight secrecy
about the eal insisted upon by Howard Trienens. In part, too,
it was due o the ever-widening gulf between the trial staff and
Baxter and his front office lieutenants. On New Year's Eve, the
front office had released a cryptic statement saying that settlement talks between the two parties had resumed, but hinting
at no details about the terms. The statement had also expressed
pessimism about the prospects for an early agreement. The
Justice trial staff had assumed that the talks referred to in the
statement were the ongoing S.898 injunctive negotiations being
handled by Richard Levine. The trial lawyers regarded that
nondivestiture solution as a sellout of major proportions, and
after the front office statement was released, they had become
gloomy once again about the future of their case.

At 5:30 P.M., Connell arrived at Carr's office over in the
main Justice building. Carr showed him the consent decree
documents and asked for his comments. He also asked if Con-

nell would be willing to sign the final decree, which ald
serve as evidence that the trial staff supported the settlent,
but the request was also a courtesy to Connell, the ma ho
had carried out Justice's triumphant case in court.

But Connell refused to sign the decree. He told C that
without consulting with his trial staff colleagues, he co not
satisfy himself before Friday as to whether the decr had
been done right." Ever cautious, Connell did not wa to be
affiliated with a potential political disaster not of his o making. Also, he was loyal first to his staff, not Baxter's fro ffice.
Even though he was immediately pleased by the reli Baxter
had obtained, it was possible that the decree itself l been
improvidently drafted. But Connell acceded to Carr equest
that he present the deal to Judge Greene in court o Friday.
Carr told Connell that he should be at Baxter's offi Friday
morning at 8:00 A.M. for the signing ceremony.

When he left Carr's office, Gerry Connell walke o his car
and drove straight home to Virginia, even though ere was
plenty of work left to do at the now-illuminated trial aff headquarters up on 12th Street. Connell knew himself w l enough
to fear that if he returned to work, he might not be a e to keep
from his colleagues the secret that, after seven ye s of hard
work, the Justice department's humble trial lawy s had defeated George Saunders, Sidley & Austin, and all th resources
of the American Telephone & Telegraph Company.

Chaer 31

Jnuary 8

FDAY morning dawned clear and cold, and once again Grry Connell was driving north along the George Washingtn Parkway toward Washington, his Plymouth Horizon weang among the homogeneous capital commuters, his car radio ned to the comic disk jockeys on WMAL. The icy Potomac Rver to his right glistened in the sunlight; beyond it, the familia monuments on the Mall appeared conspicuous in the early gare. Almost exactly one year before, Connell had traveled ths route through confounding fog and snow to begin the trial of U.S. v. AT&T, a case whose outcome had seemed as dubious as the weather. Today Connell's twelve-month courtroom triumph would be clearly revealed, if not universally acknowledged, and the pensive satisfaction of that event could perhaps only be appreciated by someone of Connell's redemptive maturity, someone who had tackled the biggest challenge of his life at age fifty, who understood even as he met it that nothing could be so sweet again.

Indeed, as he drove to the consent decree signing ceremony, Connell had already decided that his two-decade-long career as a government lawyer was over. After winning the biggest antitrust case in American history, it would be impossible to return to the routine investigations and obscure trials of everyday Justice department work. Jim Denvir, the young lawyer on Connell's trial team who was in charge of the relief section of the case, was the obvious person to succeed Connell during the Tunney Act proceedings, wherein the exact terms of the inter-intra split would be approved by Judge Greene. After such a long, communal, and invigorating ordeal as the trial of *U.S.* v. *AT&T*, Connell faced an inevitable period of postpartum adjustment. Perhaps he would spend some time skiing, a passion he had developed only recently, almost as a complement to the renewed energy he devoted to his work. And later, of course, he could enter private practice, where his new reputation would command a lucrative partnership.

At 8:00 A.M. in Baxter's cavernous office, the mood was also reflective, but for reasons as various as the crowd gathered there. For Justice, there was Baxter, Levine, Carr, Connell, and one or two other front office lawyers. That morning, Howard Trienens and George Saunders had come over from the Madison. Morris Tanenbaum, the corporate planning executive at 195 Broadway who had worked out the final details of the inter-intra split, was also there, as were Bob McLean and Jim Kilpatric, the AT&T lawyers who had been negotiating the S.898 injunctive settlement with Levine—the pair had recently been informed that their client had cut a rather different sort of deal with Justice. Once assembled, the group gathered around Baxter's desk. Some stood attentively; others, like George Saunders, seemed numb or distracted, as if they did not believe such a portentous event was about to occur before their eyes, and they sat casually on the red leather chairs scattered about Baxter's office, remote from the group. Tanenbaum was crying gently, and by the look on Charlie Brown's face it seemed that even he might break his cool veneer with a tear of mourning for the once proud, glorious, and unified Bell System.

The consent decree document was laid out on Baxter's desk, and the Antitrust chief, feeling that somehow this was all too good to be true, signed it. There were no speeches or jokes, not even from the normally gregarious Saunders. As Baxter moved aside, Trienens stepped behind the desk and signed the deal for AT&T. And with that, everyone shook hands. If the executives and lawyers had been generals at the Appomattox courthouse, the room would have been no more still or solemn.

But there was still business to be conducted, and the sober ambiance was soon disrupted by a general discussion about strategy for the day's events. The mechanics of how the decree would actually be filed with the court were complex and required precise coordination. The plan was for Ron Carr and Bob McLean to fly immediately to Newark, New Jersey, on an AT&T corporate jet. The pair would then travel to the Newark courthouse, where the 1956 consent decree was filed. At the same time, Gerry Connell and another Antitrust front office attorney would drive over to the district courthouse at 3rd and Constitution, where the case before Judge Greene was being tried. Another attorney would take the Metroliner train to Philadelphia, where a Justice department appeal of an FCC decision about the phone company's right to sell computers was pending. At exactly ten-thirty, the lawyers at all three courthouses would call back to the main Justice building in Washington. Then, at the same moment, Carr and McLean would file the inter-intra split as a modification to the 1956 decree while Connell in Washington and the other lawyer in Philadelphia dismissed the cases pending in those districts. In Newark, Carr and McLean would also file a request that Judge Biunno, who was in charge of the 1956 decree, transfer his case immediately to Judge Greene in Washington. There was a certain amount of lawyerly paranoia from Justice about making sure that everything was filed at the same time. The way things had been arranged, if Connell dismissed the case in Washington before the inter-intra modification was filed in New Jersey, it would be technically possible for AT&T to back out of the settlement at the last minute and claim that the case before Judge Greene was over because Justice had dismissed it. That no one involved in the settlement considered such a nefarious move by AT&T to be even a remote likelihood did not lessen the Justice attorneys' concern that all the papers be filed simultaneously. After all, there were lawyers involved.

A more realistic concern was how Judge Greene was going to react to the unusual filing procedure. It was Trienens who had insisted on this fire drill, because, as Charlie Brown saw it, one of the main selling points of the inter-intra split was that it eliminated the computer-selling restrictions of the 1956 settlement. But once the procedure had been proposed, Justice agreed to it not only to make AT&T happy but also because Carr and Baxter wanted to establish a peculiar legal precedent having to do with the Tunney Act, the law that required a judge presiding over an antitrust case to determine whether a settlement was in the public interest before he approved it. It was Carr's belief that the Tunney Act only applied to ongoing antitrust cases, not to modifications of previously existing consent degrees. This was an important point because modifying consent decrees was a routine method by which the Justice department enforced the antitrust laws, and Carr was concerned that if Greene applied the Tunney Act to this modification, a precedent would be set for all others. Carr thought such a precedent would severely restrict Justice's ability to make deals in minor or routine antitrust cases, because any modification would have to be approved by a judge. In a case as far-reaching and controversial as *U.S.* v. *AT&T*, where the public's stake in the outcome was obvious, some "Tunney-like" proceedings before Judge Greene were necessary, Carr and Trienens agreed. But while they were willing to abide by the "spirit" of the Tunney Act, Carr wanted to avoid submitting the modification to the letter of the law. Trienens went along. It was a trade-off: AT&T got rid of the 1956 decree, while Justice avoided setting a restrictive precedent.

The danger, of course, was that Judge Greene would not appreciate the subtlety of Carr's and Trienens' thinking. To him, it might very well appear that the whole charade had been designed to circumvent his own and the public's role in the outcome of *U.S.* v. *AT&T*. And that would hardly be an unreasonable conclusion. While Justice's willingness to abide by the "spirit" of the law sounded noble, it was a little like a burglar arguing that in the "spirit" of justice, it was all right to steal as long as the pilfered goods were distributed to needy folks such as himself.

To avoid such a misunderstanding, Gerry Connell and George Saunders were supposed to arrive at the courthouse early and explain to Judge Greene exactly what was about to happen and why. Greene clearly liked and trusted the two trial lawyers, so perhaps the judge would be at least temporarily mollified by their assurances.

So around ten, Connell and Saunders rode over to the courthouse and walked up to Greene's chambers on the second floor. They asked a secretary if the judge was in.

"Judge Greene is on vacation in the Caribbean and won't be back until Monday," they were told.

A few minutes later, Connell called over to Baxter's office and relayed the bad news. There was nothing they could do, everyone agreed, but go ahead with the plan and wait to explain it to the judge on Monday.

At ten-thirty-eight, with lawyers in three cities on the line, Richard Levine instructed, "OK, do it."

Connell walked down to the clerk's room on the ground floor of the courthouse. He stepped up to the filing clerk and handed over a piece of paper dismissing *U.S.* v. *AT&T*. "We've got something to file here," Connell said.

The clerk took the document, looked it over, and said, "Oh, yeah, we've been waiting for you."

"You have?"

The clerk smiled, stamped several copies, and handed one back to Connell. In the place where it was supposed to say, "Filed with the clerk of the court, January 8, 1982," it instead read, "Lodged..."

"Lodged? What the hell does that mean?"

That was the question on the lips of the lawyers back at the main Justice building as soon as Connell called. What was Judge Greene up to? Where was he? Apparently, Connell had determined, the judge had left instructions with the clerk of the court not to accept any dismissal filing of *U.S.* v. *AT&T* while he was on vacation. The judge's apparent interpretation was that if a dismissal was "filed," then it might be irrevocable, but if it was "lodged," then Greene could later decide whether he would allow it to be filed. At noon, less than two hours away, a press conference announcing the settlement was to begin at the National Press Club on 14th Street. Did this mean the settlement was in doubt?

The man with the answers was at the same moment in his hotel room on the French portion of St. Martin in the Caribbean trying to hear through a crackling telephone connection what Jean Vita, his clerk in Washington, was saying about the settlement of *U.S.* v. *AT&T.* Vita had just called, and the connection was so bad that Greene wasn't sure what had happened. The case had been settled, he thought she said, and the parties had tried to file something with the court in Washington.

"Don't let them file anything until I get back there," Greene tried to tell her forcefully. But the connection was deteriorating. Greene yelled to Vita that he would call her back immediately.

He dialed the hotel operator and asked for a line to Washington, preferably one that was audible. But Greene couldn't get through, and the long-distance operator, who was French, was not in a mood to cooperate with a demanding American tourist. She told him to try some other time.

His frustration at a peak, Greene charged down to the hotel lobby, briefly explained his dilemma to the desk clerk, and said, "I'm going to change hotels if you don't get me connected to Washington."

A few minutes later, Greene had his line. Vita reassured him that as per his instructions, the clerk of the court had stamped the dismissal "lodged," not "filed." This was something the judge had actually discussed with the filing clerk the previous summer, when word of Malcolm Baldrige's proposal to dismiss the case had leaked to the newspapers. Just before Greene left for St. Martin on New Year's Eve, Justice had issued its cryptic press release about the resumption of settlement talks, and he had reminded the filing room clerks of his original instructions. Greene felt that he was just being cautious. Normally, if a judge was absent when something was filed on one of his cases, a designated "motions judge" was free to rule on the filing. Greene did not want a motions judge ruling on something as important as the dismissal of history's biggest antitrust case, so he had devised his "lodged" strategy and passed the instructions on to the clerk.

Now the judge told Vita that he wanted a hearing on the settlement scheduled for as soon as he returned to Washington, and he dictated a court order over the phone reiterating that dismissal of *U.S.* v. *AT&T* was not yet official.

It didn't seem that way at the National Press Club, where shortly before noon scores of reporters and a half dozen television crews began to arrive for a "major" press conference called by the department of Justice. The filings in court and some advance publicity material from Justice and AT&T had already made clear what the announcement would be, although until that morning no one in the media had been able to break through the secrecy surrounding the inter-intra split negotations—nor, for that matter, had there been any reporting about the S.898 injunctive settlement talks that had been taking place all through the fall.

Outside the National Press Building entrance, across from the crumbling, historic Willard Hotel, Bill Baxter pulled up in his Justice department staff car. As the driver was letting Baxter and Richard Levine out, Charlie Brown arrived in a Buick from AT&T's Washington motor pool. Baxter and Brown shook hands and rode the elevator together to the press club on the top floor. A draped table had been set up on a platform at the front of the room, and there were three chairs behind it for Baxter, Brown, and Howard Trienens. As soon as they were seated, photographers began crouching in front of them, their cameras snapping and whining. Baxter's face, as always, was sallow and expressionless, and his eyes wandered aimlessly around the room. Brown and Trienens struck serious poses and tried to ignore the unrelenting photographers.

"They always manage to catch you while you're licking your lips," Brown joked to Trienens, who laughed. It was one of the few times all day that Brown and Trienens smiled.

Gerry Connell and George Saunders had arrived at the club by the time the conference began, and so had most of the lawyers on the Justice and AT&T trial teams. It was a strange encounter for all of them. As Justice lawyer Peter Kenney had put it before, they were the soldiers whose entire lives had been consumed by fighting someone else's war. Now that the war had been abandoned—for reasons none of them would ever fully understand—the lawyers mingled uneasily, cautiously. When Connell had called his team from the courthouse to inform them that the deal was done and that the terms were "relief plan A," everything they had wanted in court, he had let the cheering subside before saying sternly, "Now, when you see them, you should be gracious to the AT&T lawyers. Your exuberance will be matched by their lack of it. Do justice to yourselves, and don't rub it in." Certainly, after all the years of posturing and arguing, that was a temptation. But the young Justice lawyers knew that Connell was right, and they resisted. Saunders and the AT&T team were numb, befuddled, and somber, but some of them were also gracious toward their victorious Justice opponents. Saunders, particularly, was unequivocal in the admiration and respect he expressed for the case presented by Connell, Kenney, Denvir, Blumenfeld, and the others, although later he would occasionally annoy the Justice lawyers with goading compliments such as, "You should be exceptionally proud—it's one thing to win a case, but to win a case you shouldn't win is really quite an achievement for a lawyer."

When the reporters had been seated and the television cameras focused, a Justice press spokesman introduced the stone-faced men at the head table. Baxter was the first to step to the podium. His frumpy brown suit and unfashionably long sideburns emphasized his social awkwardness, as did his high-pitched voice. He spoke slowly and very deliberately, pausing often, as if each phrase was a crucially important choice.

"Ladies and gentlemen... the Justice Department... and AT&T... have reached an agreement... which will enable them to terminate... the various pieces of litigation... in which they are currently engaged. In substance... the agreement... calls for reorganization of the AT&T company... over the next eighteen months. It will have the consequence... of separating from the rest of the AT&T company... the several operating companies that provide local telephone service... exchange access

...around the United States. The agreement...I think...is a very good one. It completely fulfills the objectives... which the Antitrust division has been pursuing in this litigation. It of course is not my place to say... but I think it is also very much in the best interest of the AT&T company and its shareholders. ...The agreement...of course...is complex...as it would necessarily have to be in a controversy as complex and multi-faceted as this one is...."

For many of the reporters in the room, it was their first encounter with the Reagan administration's bloodless Antitrust chief, and one effect of Baxter's stilted and dispassionate speech was to convey the impression that the Justice department hadn't really won at all—if they had, wouldn't Baxter seem just a little bit pleased about it? This suspicion was reinforced by Charlie Brown's statement, which had been carefully prepared by Ed Block as the linchpin of AT&T's ambitious public relations strategy.

"Today's action clears the way for a new order in the telephone industry," Brown said. "It will encourage competition, and it will do so without sacrificing the American consumer's need for economical, dependable, and readily available telephone service. It also does not sacrifice any part of the country's leadership in communications research and development, and manufacturing. . . . Today's action also disposes of a matter of importance to the AT&T company. It gets rid of restrictions which are contained in the 1956 consent decree. No one contemplated twenty-five years ago that a revolution in modern technology would largely erase the difference between computers and communications. As a consequence, the Bell System has been effectively prohibited from using the fruits of its own technology. And this new decree will wipe out those restrictions completely. . . ."

But by the end of his statement, Brown had lost his salesman's enthusiasm. As he talked about the Bell System's long relationship with American consumers, its traditions of quality and reliability, its service to the country, the AT&T chairman momentarily lost his grip. When he spoke the words, "We have served the public very well since the Bell System began," his voice cracked, his mouth twitched, and he seemed ready to cry. As he went on, ". . . and we are going to continue to do that service job," he focused his eyes on the paper resting on the podium, gathered himself, and forced a firm tone in his voice. "I speak for all of us in the Bell System when I tell you that we look forward to getting out of court and back to business."

The mixed signals from the podium—Baxter's cold inscrutability, Brown's simultaneous enthusiasm and despair—left the reporters in the room, some of whom didn't know the difference between AT&T and ITT, understandably puzzled. Their questions reflected their befuddlement. Over and over they asked Brown and Baxter why AT&T had agreed to divest two-thirds of its assets, especially when Brown insisted that the case before Judge Greene was going fine and that AT&T expected to win on appeal. Brown could only insistently repeat the rhetoric prepared by Ed Block about how, given the history of the telecommunications industry over the last decade, there now appeared to be a "consensus" on a "new national telecommunications policy" that required the breakup of the AT&T phone monopoly. Baxter compounded the ambiguity when he was asked how the settlement compared to what Justice was seeking in court. Instead of answering emphatically that it was precisely what Justice wanted, he hesitated and lifted his eyes upward to consider his words, as if about to deliver a qualified answer.

In the silence, Brown stepped back to the microphone and said, "I'll answer that for Mr. Baxter. It's exactly what the government wanted. He's too modest to say so." The remark brought loud laughter, but it also left the impression that AT&T was putting words in the Justice department's mouth, confirming many reporters' natural suspicion that the largest corporation in the world had somehow gotten its way with the Reagan administration. Since only a handful of trade press and Justice department "beat" reporters had a clear understanding of the issues and recent history of *U.S.* v. *AT&T*, the notion that Ma Bell had won again seeped in quickly. For the first time in a decade of political manuevering, the widespread distrust of the

phone company's motives was working to AT&T's advantage.
Instead of wondering whether the settlement was one of the
great fiascos of American industrial history, as many reporters
later decided that it was, the press began to conclude that divestiture of the low technology operating companies in exchange for the end of the 1956 computer restrictions was a deal
that Charlie Brown had probably wanted all along.

And as the questioning wore on, Baxter's strange demeanor continued to frustrate the reporters. At one point, the
Antitrust chief was asked how long he had been negotiating
the settlement with AT&T. Baxter responded, "That's a very
difficult question to answer. Mr. Trienens and I have been seeing
a great deal of one another for quite some time now. Things
are said explicitly and things are said implicitly. I could answer
your question by saying, 'Since last April.' I could answer your
question by saying, 'Only for the last few weeks.' Both would
be accurate."

In fact, Baxter was being honest, but his presentation was
so typically abstruse and abstract that the reporters thought he
was joking, and they laughed convulsively. The Antitrust chief
never smiled, and he appeared confused by their reaction. When
the reporter who had asked the question repeated it more forcefully, Baxter only said, "If you really mean the pieces of paper
you have in front of you this morning, the answer is, 'A week
or ten days.'"

Forty-five minutes after it had begun, the "historic announcement," as Brown had called it, was over. The reporters
bundled up again in their scarfs and overcoats and prepared
to head out into the chill winter sunshine. But before they had
left, Tom DeCair, the Justice press spokesman, announced, "Just
to save us a lot of phone calls, I'd like to say that we'll have
another significant announcement at the Justice department
this afternoon at four o'clock. Another one in the area of antitrust."

Amid the murmuring that followed a reporter called out,
"That sounds like the IBM case," and he was right. By the end
of the day, two of the biggest antitrust cases in American history
would be over.

On the network news that evening, the stories emphasized both AT&T's astronomical legal expenses—$360 million, Brown had said—and the many benefits that would accrue to the phone company by its act of self-destruction. Bill Greenwood of ABC News reported, "There are some big pluses for AT&T. It loses its most heavily regulated subsidiaries. It loses eighty percent of its costly physical plant, while retaining its most profitable operations. It's nothing for AT&T stockholders or employees to worry about. They are not expected to suffer any losses, but it could spell trouble for IBM, since the agreement would let AT&T compete in data processing. . . ."

On the twenty-sixth floor of 195 Broadway in New York, Ed Block was fielding the first of several thousand press calls his department would receive over the weekend, and he was too busy to congratulate himself on a job well done. Later, however, he would remark to his colleagues, "What a shame that the finest performance the PR department ever put on was associated with the destruction of the company."

Chapter 32

"This Case Is History"

W HAT happened in New Jersey on Monday morning made Judge Greene very angry, mainly because he didn't understand it, and his anger was not quelled by assurances that no one else understood it, either.

If it hadn't been for the eccentricities of Vincent Biunno, a wiry, white-haired federal judge in Newark, the whole mess might have been avoided. As it was, the public's first impression of the settlement of *U.S.* v. *AT&T*, already somewhat distorted by the Friday press conference, had been thrown completely out of whack by the middle of the following week. By then, Judge Greene was talking publicly about resuming the trial and rejecting the settlement altogether, and a loud clamor was rising about whether the Reagan administration's Justice department was trying to subvert the law by avoiding altogether public scrutiny of its deal with AT&T.

Ron Carr, the Justice lawyer who had principally masterminded the plan that caused so much trouble, believed as he flew to Newark on Monday morning that it was all going to turn out fine. Gerry Connell had not been able to warn Judge Greene about all the complex legal maneuvering on Friday, but Carr expected that by the time the judge returned to Washington from the Caribbean on Tuesday, everything would be in order for him. The proposed inter-intra settlement, now attached as a proposed modification to the 1956 consent decree in New Jersey, would be transferred by Judge Biunno down to Judge Greene. Greene would then be free to devise and enforce whatever Tunney Act–like "public interest" hearings and procedures he thought appropriate. At the same time, the Antitrust front office would avoid setting a precedent about whether the Tunney Act applied to consent decree modifications. Everyone would be happy.

The purpose of Carr's trip to Newark Monday morning was to attend a hearing called by Judge Biunno to consider whether he should do as Justice and AT&T were asking and transfer the 1956 decree, with the proposed settlement attached, down to Washington. It had occurred to Carr and other Justice and AT&T lawyers that out of ego or resentment or caprice, Biunno might not want to give up so prestigious a matter as determining whether the breakup of the world's biggest company was in the public interest. In case Biunno refused a transfer and decided to hold the Tunney proceedings himself, Justice and AT&T had already prepared a joint petition to appeal his decision immediately to the U.S. Appeals Court, and if necessary, the U.S. Supreme Court.

And there was some reason to be concerned about what Biunno might do. Though he was not very well-known among the Justice and AT&T lawyers in Washington, Biunno did not enjoy a favorable reputation. Some described him as "a little eccentric" or "difficult"; others said outright that he was not one of the federal bench's better judges. About one thing there was no question: Biunno loved to talk. In a hearing he would ramble on and on about any subject that was remotely relevant, and even on some that weren't. Before he left for Newark on Monday, Carr asked Jim Denvir, who had once appeared before Biunno for Justice, what the most effective strategy was in the judge's courtroom. Denvir advised that Carr say as little as possible and try not to antagonize Biunno, who sometimes ranted at lawyers. Carr was also warned about the judge's tendency to talk on and on. When Denvir had appeared before Biunno, he said, the judge had begun a two-hour-long diatribe about the state of modern communications by saying, "It all started with the smoke signal..."

So Carr arrived in Biunno's court prepared for an unusual morning. But he did not anticipate the disaster that was about to unfurl.

The bearded Justice lawyer began by explaining that the settlement he filed with the New Jersey court on Friday was a proposed modification of the 1956 consent decree. He was about to say that both parties intended for the whole matter to be transferred to Greene when Biunno interrupted.

"This modification is the equivalent in the legislative field of the technique of receiving a bill. Let's say a bill originates in the Senate and goes to the House. The House may choose not to amend the Senate bill. It may introduce a House substitute."

"Substitute, correct," said Carr. It was impossible to determine what Biunno was talking about.

"Which replaces, but it's still the same bill."

"That's correct." Carr was along for the ride now.

"It's this concept."

"Yes."

"Or, you can take the common example of long-term leases, where problems arise. Long-term leases may have provisions that didn't take into account things that happen in the future. Long-term leases, by their definition, run for long periods of time..."

On Biunno went. Unprompted, he talked about leases, and about the concept of local service subsidies, and about his career as a lawyer in private practice, and about the fact that there were independent telephone companies in New Jersey, and about "peak load demand" in the phone industry, and about how a small business's phone system is put together, and about a photocomposition plant in Newark that he recently visited, and about how a small microwave dish can reduce business communications costs, and about a case that he tried in 1980, and about a few other things, too. Occasionally Biunno would pause and Carr would say, "Of course...." But as soon as the lawyer opened his mouth, Biunno caught his breath and jumped back in again. After talking virtually nonstop for about half an hour, the judge finally asked "What do the defendants wish to add to what has been said?"

Bob McLean, the Sidley & Austin lawyer who had accompanied Carr to Newark, didn't have much to add.

"I take it," Biunno said, "the parties feel the day-to-day detail that Judge Greene has been exposed to will equip him to deal with the proposal with great facility, as against someone, no matter how familiar with the subject"—a veiled reference to the judge himself, whose windy ramble had seemed largely designed to establish his own expertise in telecommunications matters—"who has not been so exposed."

"That's part of it, Your Honor," Carr answered, stepping carefully around the judge's ego. "Quite frankly, it's just much simpler for us to deal with the District Court in the District of Columbia on matters involving day-to-day appearances.... "

"Would you agree with the impression I have that the decision, the business decision of the parent company to turn loose the twenty-two operating companies, in effect eliminates, takes out of the picture, so to speak, the basic ground for controversy that underlay the antitrust case?"

"That is very much our view," said Carr.

"That is our view, Your Honor, also," added McLean.

"And this is a business decision. This could have been done regardless of the antitrust suit, I suppose."

McLean tried to answer. "As a lawyer, Your Honor, I've always been trained to try to stay out of business decisions. I think Mr. Brown, the chairman of the board..."

But Biunno didn't want to hear it, and he cut in. "I say it could have been done as a business decision even if there were no antitrust suit."

"It certainly could have been done, yes," McLean said, giving up.

And with that, Biunno told the two lawyers that he would issue a decision on their request for transfer as soon as possible. The hearing was adjourned.

Later that afternoon, the judge was scheduled to enter the hospital for a minor operation, and so before he left to prepare for the surgery, he issued his decision. Carr and McLean were dumbfounded. Biunno had agreed to their request and ordered the transfer of the 1956 consent decree to Judge Greene, but

he had also approved the inter-intra settlement as being in the
public interest—without any public comments or hearings. It
was an open question as to whether Biunno's decision was even
legal, but, more important, it was a political disaster. It was
bad enough that Judge Greene had not been informed about
the reasons for the parties' circuitous maneuverings. Now the
judge was going to return to Washington and find that the very
thing he had tried to prevent with his "lodged" strategy—
settlement of the case without judicial review—had occurred
in spite of his efforts. Carr had never imagined that Biunno
would approve such a massive antitrust deal without any examination of its terms, its impact on the public, or its impact
on competition in the telephone industry. Even after the deed
was done, no one was able to suggest a satisfactory reason for
Biunno's decision.

But since the judge was about to go under the knife, there
was neither time nor opportunity to urge him to change his
mind. Gerry Connell and George Saunders in Washington would
have to straighten things out the next day, when Greene returned from his Caribbean holiday.

The judge, looking tanned and fit when he arrived in his
courtroom just after two on Tuesday afternoon, was livid, although he was also quite confused about just what had happened to his landmark case while he was out of the country.

"We are here to find out what goes on, and why," he said
perfunctorily to Connell and Saunders. "And the parties are
invited to tell me what goes on, and why."

Connell tried to explain what Justice was attempting to
accomplish by its legal sleight of hand. It was perfectly willing
to submit the inter-intra deal to the "functional equivalent" of
Tunney Act public interest proceedings, but it did not believe
that the Act technically applied. Connell also told Greene that
none of them expected Biunno to approve the deal, that they
had not asked him to do so.

"It is certainly a peculiar procedural posture, is it not?"
Greene asked.

"I am not going to deny it is a little peculiar, Your Honor.

It was not the way the road had been mapped out, and it just took a small turn."

"Did it occur to anybody that this was not the way to proceed? We have a suit that has been ongoing for eleven months here. It is being settled, and it is being settled in a place and proceeding that is twenty-five years old, and where the Tunney Act doesn't apply, and where the public interest doesn't need to be considered. Did anybody think about those things?"

"I think everybody thought about them, Your Honor," Connell answered. "The fact is that the 1956 decree has always been one of the very significant elements of ongoing dispute between the parties. . . . The parties felt there needed to be a single package."

"It also avoided the Tunney Act."

"It is not our desire to avoid the Tunney Act as such. Again, I would like to assure Your Honor that it is our intention to proceed and comply entirely with the spirit of the Tunney Act."

"There is something I am missing," Greene said a minute later, "and it must be my fault, having been away, and I don't understand these arguments. I take it everybody is eager to have the Tunney Act apply and give the public a chance to comment and have the court pass on the public interest and so on?"

"Absolutely," Saunders confirmed.

"If everybody is so eager to do it, wouldn't that have been the simple thing to do, to file the settlement in the court where the Tunney Act applies, namely this court?"

"No," Saunders answered, "because this is not a settlement of this case. In no sense is it a settlement of this case. If you pardon my use of tense, this case was dismissed last Friday. It doesn't exist anymore."

"No, it is only dismissed when the court orders the dismissal filed, and the court has not done that." Greene was heated.

But Saunders came back even stronger. "I cannot mince words on this one. This court has no power to restrain the filing of the dismissal filed last Friday. This case is history, Your Honor.

"Now, let me explain why this case is not a settlement, what has happened. I think I told Your Honor, and if you look at page 240 of the transcript of my opening statement you will see it, the biggest concern of the telephone company was the consent decree of 1956. We cannot live with that decree.... As I understand what happened, and my understanding is based on personal conversations with Mr. Brown as well as Mr. Trienens, the company came to the realization that if it was going to be permitted to exist as a free enterprise, this was the price—a considerable price, a price that wrenches the heart of the Bell System's employees, and candidly, its lawyers. It is not what we sought. As a matter of fact, it is precisely what Mr. Connell sought in this court—precisely. But what is the choice? The choice is to keep the Bell System as an integrated enterprise with regulations that will strain it, or satisfy the national consensus, which says that in order for the Bell System to be free, it must be much smaller. And that was the decision that was made....

"I told Your Honor last January that this case raised a truly fundamental issue. It is a broad, profound, philosophical, almost legal issue. What is the relationship between a public utility and the antitrust laws? How do you put those two things together? What are the obligations? And Your Honor has expressed it yourself: 'Hey, you are just a big corporation, go out and make money, quit pretending that you are really concerned with the public interest.' That tone.

"You know, the company...it may be hard for a lot of people to believe it, but for a hundred years this company has been based on the notion of public service. A lot of Bell System people cried this morning, and not because they are not going to make any more money.... We can live with this as a money-making institution. The problem is, what does it do to the public? What does it do to the concept of universal service? And the message that has been coming out from Congress, and from this court, is, 'That is none of your business. The market protects the public interest. You are being arrogant in thinking you even have a responsibility to consider it.'"

"If there is a lack of certainty in regard to the consent decree or settlement, or whatever you wish to call it," Greene said, "it is because it was filed in a court where there is some doubt about the jurisdiction and the application of the statute. I don't understand—it certainly can't be blamed on me. I was not even in the country. You did that one by yourself."

"I am not blaming it on you," Saunders answered. "We tried our best, and things have not gone the way we wanted. We will have to deal with the problem. I do say, the problem can only be exacerbated by failing to give effect to papers that have been filed in this court on Friday . . . you know, the Tunney Act was essentially passed to prevent the government from giving up its antitrust position too cheaply. It's pretty hard to say that is what happened here. The very people who are screaming in the newspapers that this is contrary to the public interest . . . I can't help but think, 'Where were you?'"

"Some of them were here, were your witnesses," Greene said, smiling.

"You are not kidding, Judge. 'Where were you?' Judge, I can only end by saying this was a great case, we all had a lot of fun, you handled the case magnificently, but the case is over, and we must face the fact."

Appearing far more relaxed than he had an hour earlier, Greene called for a brief recess so that he could make up his mind about what to do next. When he returned, he began a long, uninterrupted speech by ladling out sweet praise to both the government and AT&T lawyers. About Connell's team, he said, "Unlike the usual case where the United States is the party, it appears that in this particular instance the balance of resources may have favored the government's opponents. Also, judging from some of the remarks that were made at the trial, not all the departments of the government necessarily supported what the litigators were trying to do. Yet a small group led by Mr. Connell did an outstanding public service in presenting this important case." About the defense lawyers, he said, "They fought with vigor and imagination and determination. Never in sixteen years on the bench have I seen anyone fight so ably and well to present their case. The well-oiled machine was really well-oiled and tremendously effective. I never felt they tried to do anything other than to win the case on the merits. . . . And there was Mr. Saunders, whose ability to recall every detail of the case and relate it to the whole and make a convincing presentation of both the evidence and the law is truly astounding."

Greene then went on to say that since Justice and AT&T had created this mess over the Tunney Act in New Jersey, it was up to them to solve it—and quickly. Greene wanted the case out of Biunno's hands and back in his courtroom. He intended to take control and to make his own determination of whether the inter-intra deal was in the public interest. By the next Monday, he expected the parties to straighten everything out. Then, Greene would vacate Biunno's order approving the settlement, and the Tunney Act proceedings would begin under his supervision. If Justice and AT&T refused to cooperate, Greene would reassess his options and consider resuming the trial of *U.S.* v. *AT&T*.

Neither Connell nor Saunders could permit that to happen. Baxter had flown off to Europe for his international antitrust conference; Charlie Brown was busy explaining his decision on television news programs and at Wall Street luncheons. Clamor on Capitol Hill about the deal was cresting and the politicians had to be placated. There was no choice but to give Greene precisely what he wanted—the right to make his own decision about the settlement.

When the two lawyers stepped out of the district courthouse onto Constitution Avenue that Tuesday afternoon, January 12, 1982, a frigid wind from the north was whistling through the capital city, and only a few huddled passersby hurried along the street. Across the way, the barren oaks and elms lining the open Mall rustled stiffly. To one side stood the west façade of the Capitol, its once bright sandstone faded and crumbling from the seasons.

Before that chilly and majestic scene, it was possible, just possible, for a sentimental lawyer to feel that something important had passed beyond his grasp and into history.

Aftermath

Chapter 33

Congress Awakens

AN obvious but unanticipated consequence of Ed Block's public relations strategy for AT&T was that if the phone company was somehow going to be a "winner" by giving Bill Baxter all the divestment he wanted, then inevitably there would have to be some perceived "losers" in the Bell breakup. Rather quickly after the deal with Justice was announced, the victims were identified: the divested operating companies, and by extension, the tens of millions of local telephone consumers they served. No sooner were Wall Street and the business press done praising Charlie Brown for his "brilliant" act of capitulation and corporate self-destruction than howls of outrage about the suddenly clouded future of the "best phone service in the world" began to echo in the unctuous halls of Congress.

It was not enough for Charlie Brown and Howard Trienens to ask bitterly, as George Saunders had, "Where were you?" At all costs, congressional intervention in the settlement had to be prevented. For Brown and AT&T, the strategic advantages of the inter-intra split, and there were a number of them, all derived from the radical purity of full divestiture. Legislative tinkering could only pollute the deal.

By sacrificing two-thirds of his company's assets, Brown hoped to gain in return quick and sweeping deregulation of the "surviving" AT&T. It turned out, as it had so many times during the 1970s when the phone company meddled in politics, that AT&T's assessment of the mood in Washington was naive. But during the first weeks and months of 1982, there was no time to worry about whether the new AT&T would be rapidly deregulated in reward for its sacrifice. A far more pressing task was to hold the rabble rousers in Congress at bay. What Brown, Trienens, and Block considered "the worst of all possible worlds" was the prospect that Congress might respond to the breakup by finally enacting the heavily regulatory legislation it had failed to pass for so many frustrating years. If that happened, the "fence with a one-way hole" would be resurrected around AT&T, and Brown would have succeeded only in shrinking the size of his captive company.

Ed Block had not drafted any plans for how AT&T should respond to outrage about the impact of Charlie Brown's "masterstroke," as the chairman of the FCC was calling it, on the divested operating companies and local consumers. If he had thought such a reaction was possible, Block would have planned for it. But in the weeks before the deal with Justice was announced, the public relations department had been working under the logical assumption that most people would consider the breakup of the century-old Bell System to be an overall "negative" for AT&T. Brown had instructed Block to do what he could to soften the impact of that negative reaction.

It was not simply that Block had done his job too well. There was good reason for congressmen and consumer activists to be concerned about the viability of the operating companies and the future of cheap, high-quality, local phone service after divestiture. If it was true, as AT&T had been saying for more than a decade, that revenues from profitable long-distance service subsidized the high cost of the local telephone infrastructure, then wouldn't divestiture of the operating companies inevitably result in higher local rates to make up for the local subsidies? And wouldn't the quality of local service suffer because the now cash-poor operating companies would be unable to invest sufficiently in their local plant? Obviously, these were not new issues. For one thing, they had been the foundations of George Saunders' relief defense in the trial before Judge Greene. At the Friday press conference, Brown and Baxter had both answered questions about higher local rates with the same answer: It was competition in the phone industry generally, not the breakup of the Bell System, that was the culprit.

"The introduction of competition into the telephone business, as I think is well known by most of you, has had the effect over the years of driving prices toward costs," Brown said. "I don't see that this decree has any great significance from that standpoint. The main reason for that is the introduction of competition itself." A few minutes later, Baxter chimed in, "The local operating companies have a very powerful position ... but as Mr. Brown has said, competition will tend to bring prices in line with costs."

There were three reasons why this sales job by the two settlement architects did not hold up in the first weeks and months after the inter-intra split was unveiled to the public. The most obvious problem was that the history of *U.S.* v. *AT&T* and of the politics of telephone industry competition was simply not "well known by most" of Congress and the media, as Brown seemed to assume. The fact that the inter-intra breakup was the culmination of a long and sordid history of industrial intrigue, ideological conflict, and political cowardice was not widely appreciated. Since it was impossible to understand Brown's deal with Justice in isolation from its historical context, most reporters and politicians looked at the division of the Bell System's spoils and pronounced AT&T the victor, even though the phone company had just surrendered a costly and profoundly demoralizing war against its competitors and the government. On the one hand, the reporters and politicians did not know enough about the phone industry's recent history to assess independently whether Brown and Baxter were right about the inevitability of higher local rates, regardless of divestiture. On the other hand, since they wrongly assumed that Brown had gotten exactly what he wanted from Baxter, they were suspicious about any explanation offered jointly by Ma Bell and the Reagan administration.

And immediately, this atmosphere of skepticism was exacerbated by the presidents of the operating companies themselves, who were at once shocked by Brown's decision and anxious to position themselves as favorably as possible for the post-divestiture world, now that they were "free at last." After the announcement was made on Friday, January 8, a number of operating company presidents predicted to reporters that local phone rates would rise dramatically because of the settlement. Delbert Stanley, president of New York Telephone, told the *Wall Street Journal* that the price of local service would "at least double" in the next five years. Others bemoaned the loss of AT&T's efficient vertical structure, its "end-to-end" service responsibility, and the promotional opportunities formerly available to operating company executives. The presidents' predictions about drastic rate hikes and deteriorating service, while sincerely made and ultimately accurate, were also self-serving. An important part of a local operating company president's job was to convince his state regulators that proposed local rate hikes were necessary and justifiable. It was not an easy task, since no politically appointed state regulator liked to be known for routinely passing on higher phone prices to consumers. By predicting that the Bell breakup would accelerate the rising cost of local service, the presidents were already laying the political groundwork for their independence: if regulators, politicians, and the public thought the local operating companies were worse off because of the breakup, it would be easier for the companies, once on their own, to win rate hikes from their state utility commissioners.

Brown and other top managers at 195 Broadway were sufficiently alarmed by the operating company presidents' predictions of drastic local rate hikes that, during the weekend after the deal was announced, they dashed off a memo urging the presidents to keep their mouths shut about rising local phone rates. "News accounts in the national as well as local media are conveying the impression that the consent decree signed Friday in Washington will give rise to substantial increases in local exchange rates," the memo said. "It is important that you promptly take whatever measures may be effective in correcting this misunderstanding. As you know, there is nothing in the consent decree that changes local rates."

Of course, the presidents had heard that line on Tuesday at the secret meeting in Basking Ridge, New Jersey, and on Friday morning; they had even been provided with a "fill in the blanks" press release about local rates from one of Ed Block's PR men. Nonetheless, some of them had chosen to speak their minds about the settlement. After the weekend memo, the presidents stopped talking about local rates until after the deal with Justice was finalized. On Capitol Hill, the sudden silence was met with charges that the local presidents had been "muzzled" by AT&T's corporate headquarters, and while 195 Broadway executives told congressmen the accusation was "a myth and an insult," the presidents' first statements had already made an indelible impression.

Finally, the contention by Charlie Brown himself that the deal with Justice would have no "significant" effect on local phone rates was increasingly exposed as flawed. Brown and Baxter were technically correct when they said that local rates would have gone up anyway because competition was driving prices to reflect actual costs in the industry. But very early in 1982 it became obvious to regulators, industry analysts, and even Congress that divestiture would dramatically·accelerate the trend. In a speech to Wall Street analysts in March 1982, Brown predicted that local rates would rise only 8 to 10 percent over the next four to five years; less than a year after the deal with Justice was approved, Southwestern Bell, which was still under Brown's stewardship, applied to its regulators for a $1.2 billion, 26 percent rate increase to make up for revenues lost because of the impending breakup. Brown and other AT&T executives tried to play down the linkage between divestiture and dramatically higher local phone bills—by 1985 the cost of local phone service had nearly doubled in many states—because they were afraid that rate hikes would provide Congress an excuse to meddle with the Justice settlement. In Brown's view, the danger was that the breakup itself would be blamed for changes in the phone industry that had actually been initiated by the FCC in the early 1970s, blessed by a decade of inaction in Congress, and relentlessly pursued by the U.S. Department of Justice. The chairman's fear was well-founded; no matter how many times he declared, "This is clearly not our choice—our choice was the way we had the place organized," AT&T still found itself on the defensive about the settlement.

With the operating company presidents silenced, state regulators stepped in as their proxies to press for the best possible deal for local companies from Congress and Judge Greene. The California Public Utility Commission formally declared that the settlement was not in the public interest because Pacific Telephone could not survive without the help it received from AT&T. A New York utility commissioner told the press, "This thing is an abomination. The stockholders will be better off and AT&T competitors will be better off, but the customer is the forgotten man."

Such declarations provoked Congress to apoplexy. Hearing after hearing was called by committees in both the House and Senate, and a swarm of bills was introduced aimed at preserving "universal" and "lifeline" telephone service; establishing a national "consumer board" to protect telephone users from rising local rates; forcing AT&T to dismantle itself further by separating its Long Lines department from Western and Bell Labs; allowing the local companies to sell telephone equipment in competition with the new AT&T; restricting AT&T's use of its patents; regulating control of the Yellow Pages; creating a national fund to assist elderly and poor phone users; and a host of others.

Charlie Brown spent so much time in Washington during 1982 testifying about the breakup and fighting against restrictive legislation that some executives at 195 Broadway felt there was a void in leadership at AT&T. In July 1982, Charles Hugel, one of the original blue team executives and a leading candidate to inherit Brown's chairmanship, resigned unexpectedly from AT&T to become chairman of Combustion Engineering. Hugel said later, "By April, there was so much that had to be done and you couldn't get senior management to focus on it. . . . It was difficult to get anyone to make a decision. You wouldn't believe how many committees there were by then. You'd go out to Basking Ridge, New Jersey, and the cars would be lined up and down the driveways and adjoining roads because there were so many people at committee meetings. It just kept rolling around and around. Charlie and Howard were up to their necks in Washington appointments—only the chairman could do that. But there was no chief operating officer. There was no one in charge."

Congress, similarly, was in a state of such outrage and confusion that it was effectively paralyzed. When the deal with Justice was announced, Senator Barry Goldwater, a communications subcommittee chairman and ostensibly a leader on telephone issues, declared that breaking up the phone company was "one of the best decisions ever made." Some months later, he pronounced, "If there was any way we could legislate to put AT&T back together again, I'd be in favor of that."

The back-flipping by Goldwater and others pushed Brown into the position of one day defending the settlement against charges that it was a "rip-off of the consumer," while the next explaining that he was as sorry as Congress that the Bell System had been destroyed. At one point, while fighting legislation designed to reconfigure the post-divestiture phone industry, the AT&T chairman wrote a letter to every member of Congress that said, "It is too late for Congress to have second thoughts about whether or not, and at what pace, competition should be encouraged—or whether the Bell System should have been broken up to begin with. Please do not, at this juncture, disrupt the . . . restructuring of the telephone industry."

AT&T's most daunting nemesis in Congress, Tim Wirth, returned with a vengeance to fight the phone company after the settlement was announced. In March 1982, he introduced a bill known as H.R. 5158 that provided for separation and partial outside ownership of Long Lines, rules preventing AT&T from competing with the divested operating companies, and the transfer of some lucrative lines of business from AT&T to the new operating companies. The confusion surrounding the lobbying and debate over the bill was overwhelming. MCI, ITT, and other AT&T competitors quietly bankrolled a Ralph Nader

campaign to generate "grass roots" consumer concern over issues raised by the Justice deal—MCI wanted to be sure that
AT&T was not too quickly deregulated. But after the Nader
group sent out 150,000 direct-mail pieces urging consumers to
express their opinions to Congress about rising costs and declining service, McGowan changed his mind and attacked the
Wirth bill as "legislation that's so backward-looking it simply
cannot pass." So just as 30,000 letters expressing consumer
outrage, generated in part by MCI, arrived in Congress and
propelled 5158 out of committee, McGowan began publicly to
oppose the same legislation because he had decided it was not
too favorable for the operating companies and consumers—it
allowed the operating companies to compete at MCI's expense.
Fifteen AT&T competitors also spent part of a $300,000 joint
fund to hire Washington superlobbyist Robert Beckel, who had
headed the Carter administration's successful effort to pass the
Panama Canal treaty in the Senate, to lobby for the Wirth bill.
Meanwhile, AT&T was dumping more than $1.5 million into
its Washington lobbying operation in a blitzkrieg effort to defeat
the same legislation. At one point, Beckel remarked that the
Panama Canal treaty was "a piece of cake compared to this."
Bill Baxter even jumped into the fight, telling a congressional
committee that separating Long Lines from Western and Bell
Labs "would be like going after a cockroach with a twelve-gauge
shotgun," and prompting a congressman's response, "It's the
largest cockroach I've ever seen."

Battered from all sides, Wirth finally threw in the towel in
July, declaring at an emotional House Commerce Committee
meeting, "In my eight years in this body, I have seen nothing
like the campaign of fear and distortion that AT&T has waged
to fight this bill. In the short run, AT&T has won a tactical
victory. But AT&T's victory is a major setback for the American
people. . . . AT&T is preventing Congress from making the decisions that are ours to make. Let me make it very clear that
our commitment to these issues remains as strong as ever. We
recognize our responsibility to make telecommunications policy. . . . From the day the settlement was announced, everyone
knew it was a great deal for AT&T and that it would increase

local rates. Until the settlement, AT&T was the leader in advocating that Congress—not the FCC, and not the courts—should set telecommunications policy. What followed the settlement is an unprecedented attempt by AT&T to block Congress from setting that policy. After all, Bell got a very good deal from the Justice Department."

William Baxter, the man responsible for this "very good deal," was at the same time being bashed around by various House and Senate committees, but unlike Brown, Baxter had nothing to lose in Congress and by nature he was unaffected by attacks on his person or character. Jonathan Rose, the assistant attorney general who had helped Baxter defeat Malcolm Baldrige's dismissal proposal in the summer of 1981, said later, "To Baxter, life should be decided on its economic merits. He never had any trouble dealing with these congressional hearings—he just went up there and told them what he thought. His attitude was, 'Why should anyone be troubled by these congressmen?' Cross subsidies and deregulation were the only things that mattered to him."

So when the Antitrust chief found himself before the Senate Commerce Committee in early 1982 answering pointed questions about why he had seen fit to take a skiing vacation in the midst of the inter-intra negotations, Baxter deflected the attacks as if they were harmless toy arrows.

"Defense Secretary Weinberger said that divestiture would be disastrous. . . . Could you tell us how long the Defense department had to study the actual proposed decree?" Senator Harrison Schmitt of New Mexico demanded of Baxter angrily.

"I really can't," Baxter replied. "I was out of the city. And Mr. Brown, the chairman of the AT&T Company, took the decree, I believe, to Secretary Weinberger."

"You left it to Mr. Brown to discuss this with the secretary of defense? It seems to me that might have been the responsibility of the Justice department."

"I understand. I left it with Mr. Brown."

"I am incredulous!" Schmitt bellowed. "I can't think of another thing to say."

But Baxter had nothing to add, either, no apology to make.

He sat expressionless at the witness table, chain-smoking his unfiltered cigarettes, waiting to field the next question.

In the end, both Justice and AT&T escaped unscathed from Congress' season of outrage. By April 1982, Baxter had endured questioning at nearly a dozen different Capitol Hill hearings, and if his reputation for candor was not unblemished, his anti-trust policies—the AT&T settlement, dismissal of the IBM case, his lax attitude toward corporate mergers—remained unaltered. For Brown, on the other hand, 1982 was a long and demanding year of travel, speeches, congressional testimony, and eleventh-hour legislative negotiations. The excruciating demands on the chairman were perhaps mitigated by the decision of AT&T's board of directors in 1982 to raise Brown's annual salary 17 percent to $661,667 and to hike his overall compensation, including incentive and savings plans, insurance and personal benefits, and director's fees, to $1.3 million, a 30 percent increase. Whether for that or other reasons, the chairman responded with extraordinary energy and determination, and at every crucial moment in the phone company's battles with Congress during 1982, AT&T prevailed. No legislation affecting the terms of the inter-intra deal with Justice was passed by the nation's preeminent body of lawmakers.

When Congress' last hope for a role in telecommunications policy making, Tim Wirth's H.R. 5158, was abandoned in July, former FCC chairman Richard Wiley remarked, "Judge Greene has now become the man of the hour. His decision in the Tunney Act proceedings will chart the future of the telecommunications industry like nothing else—because there will be nothing else."

Once more, the answer man. It was a role to which Harold Greene was growing well accustomed.

Chapter 34

The Telecommunications Czar

"THERE are two ways to explain what Judge Greene did," the Justice department's Ron Carr said when it was all over, a trace of bitterness in his voice. "One is the ego theory, that he wanted to become a miniature FCC and that he likes the power and attention. The other, more generous theory is that if you look at everything he did, there is no principle running through it but one: How do you avoid a political reversal of this judgment? How do you avoid congressional interference? I think that is the unifying principle. Actually, the two theories can complement each other—Greene was protecting his turf from Congress while simultaneously creating a kingdom for himself."

It was, of course, Judge Greene's prerogative, even his duty, to consider whether the settlement of *U.S.* v. *AT&T* was in the public interest. Given the judge's comments and demeanor during the year-long trial, neither Justice nor the phone company doubted that Greene would look favorably on the basic decision to divest all the operating companies, and, indeed, even during the first angry hearing after the judge returned from the Caribbean, Greene remarked that at first glance he thought the deal between Justice and AT&T appeared to be a good one. Greene said later that he had felt for some time that divestiture was the most sensible solution. In a 1985 interview, Greene insisted that he had not decided during the trial how he would finally rule on *U.S.* v. *AT&T*, but he also observed, "I have no doubt about the correctness of deregulation. The basic fact of the phone industry is it grew up when it was a natural monopoly: wooden poles and copper wires. Once it became possible to bypass this network through microwaves, AT&T's monopoly could not survive. What the Bell System did was illegal. It abused its monopoly in local service to keep out competitors in other areas. Competition will give this country the most advanced, best, cheapest telephone network."

So the question was not whether Greene would find the breakup of AT&T to be in the public interest—both parties in the lawsuit assumed he would—but whether the judge would tinker with the terms of the consent decree before approving it. It was not clear whether Greene was legally empowered to change unilaterally the terms of the deal, but there was no question the judge could refuse to approve the settlement until the changes he wanted were agreed upon by Justice and AT&T. If the parties refused to go along, Greene might force the resumption of the antitrust case.

In Congress, AT&T was spending millions to prevent precisely the sort of meddling that Judge Greene might indulge in. But the irony was that during the Tunney Act proceedings before the judge, it was Justice lawyers like Ron Carr and Bill Baxter who most vehemently objected to Greene's increasingly autocratic role. What Charlie Brown and Howard Trienens wanted more than anything was to get the deal approved and over with so that AT&T could get on with the gargantuan task of reorganizing itself to prepare for final divestiture. Thus the phone company was in a mood to compromise in court. AT&T's lawyers and executives generally felt that while Judge Greene had been a hostile opponent during the trial, he was also a fundamentally reasonable, hard-working, and intelligent man, and he was not likely to concoct something "nutty," the word Howard Trienens often used to describe provisions of congressional legislation. More importantly, Greene was the one man in Washington now empowered to strike a final deal and make it stick. And unlike Congress, he was of one mind, he was well-informed about the issues, and his decisions could be appealed. The Justice Antitrust front office, on the other hand, was anxious that Greene's role be restricted as much as possible. To Baxter and Carr, the inter-intra deal was an agreement of nearly transcendent ideological purity, since it cleanly separated the competitive part of AT&T from the regulated monopoly part. The conservative, free-market principles underlying the settlement were of paramount importance to Baxter and Carr, and they wanted to make certain that those principles were not violated during the proceedings before Judge Greene.

Their hopes were frustrated: Greene retained firm control over the terms of the settlement for the next four years, dictating numerous changes, and, by 1986, there was still no reason to believe that he would ever let go of *U.S. v. AT&T.*

Under the Tunney Act, Greene's first job was to receive public comment and then approve or reject the actual document negotiated between Justice and AT&T during the three weeks prior to the January 8, 1982, announcement. (Although the document was called by the parties the "Modified Final Judgment," or "MFJ," Greene refused to refer to it that way because the name was derived from the maneuverings before Judge Biunno in New Jersey, which Greene never accepted as legal.) The process, which lasted more than seven months, was laborious and contentious. Present and potential competitors in the equipment and long-distance markets, state regulators, the FCC, consumer activists, corporate-sponsored "telecommunications users" groups, newspaper publishers, and assorted other specially interested parties all filed voluminous comments, mainly in the form of legal briefs, with Judge Greene. It was a field day for Washington communications lawyers; any attorney of passing acquaintance with the 1934 Communications Act and the history of *U.S. v. AT&T* could hang out a shingle and find a client who wanted to put his two cents in to Judge Greene, and of course the lawyers themselves made off with more than loose change. Once the comments had been filed, Justice and AT&T were given an opportunity to respond, and they each weighed in with hefty briefs urging the judge to abide by the

original terms of the deal. There were hearings, and letters back
and forth between the parties, and by summer Judge Greene's
snug chambers on the second floor of the district courthouse
were overflowing with the paper residue of legal pandemon-
ium.

Like the surviving AT&T itself, those who filed comments
objecting to this or that portion of the inter-intra settlement
were simply out to obtain from the Bell System's misfortune
the best deal possible for themselves. Phone equipment and
long-distance companies wanted guarantees that the newly lib-
erated AT&T would not crush them in the free market. State
regulators argued that the divested operating companies should
not be confined to the provision of unprofitable, monopolized
local phone service, but rather should be free to compete with
the new AT&T in phone equipment and other competitive markets; if the operating companies could make money in such
ways, the regulators would not have to raise local phone rates
precipitously. Consumer activists, similarly, were concerned
about the financial health of the local companies, and they also
sought assurances that universal telephone service to the poor
and elderly would be preserved in the newly cutthroat and
competitive communications industry. Corporate telecommunications users were worried that in the coming subsidy-free
world of cost-based pricing, the burden of maintaining the expensive telephone infrastructure would be shifted to business,
and there was threatening talk of corporations "bypassing" the
phone network with their own private microwave and satellite
communications systems if the cost of local business phone
service became too high.

But amid all this self-interested clamor, there was one voice
whose shrill and demanding tone rose clearly above the rest—
the American Newspaper Publishers Association (ANPA). Perhaps because of its members' long exposure to the rhetoric of
politicians, the ANPA was surpassingly adept at couching its
patently selfish demands in the appealing language of the public interest. The publishers were scared stiff by the prospect of
a deregulated AT&T. It was their opinion that the future of the
newspaper industry lay in what they called "electronic pub-

lishing"—videotext services, links between newspapers and cable television, computerized information banks, and so on. AT&T was anxious to enter these markets, and it had been working for some time to develop prototype services. But the ANPA argued that because AT&T owned some of the means of transmission of electronic publications—the long-distance phone lines—it would be unfair to allow it also to sell electronic services. Then AT&T would own both the product and some means by which publishers would transmit competitive services. Justice argued vigorously in its reply comments that the "essential facilities bottleneck" had been broken by the proposed divestiture of the operating companies and that the new AT&T should be allowed to compete freely with the publishers. It was essentially an issue about whether Greene should intervene in the terms of future competition between some of the country's largest corporations—AT&T, Gannett, Post-News-week, Knight-Ridder, and others. But the publishers never condescended to debate the competitive issues; instead, they tried with long-winded speeches to elevate the dispute to the lofty province of constitutional law. The First Amendment was imperiled, they said, because AT&T might begin to monopolize the electronic publishing industry and thus restrict the diversity of information available to all Americans. It was a dishonest, even cynical argument, the Justice department believed, but since the publishers had direct, daily access to tens of millions of readers, it was pressed effectively.

And over the objections of both Justice and AT&T, Greene gave in. In August 1982, he imposed a seven-year ban on electronic publishing by AT&T over its own transmission facilities. The unexpected decision deeply angered the Antitrust front office, which regarded it as a blatantly political maneuver by the judge that unnecessarily restricted the new AT&T. As a government lawyer put it later, "That prohibition on information services was an important stroke for Greene. That decision had the consequence of gaining for the divestiture almost complete editorial support in the United States. Almost every newspaper in the country came out in favor of the deal, despite the fact that there was no real popular support for it."

Indeed, with the newspapers well appeased by the summer of 1982, the breakup of the phone company proceeded without much fanfare or discord until divestiture was finally implemented on January 1, 1984. Concern about the financial health of the new operating companies was dissipated when, after the months of comments and hearings, Greene ordered some changes to the terms of the Modified Final Judgment. He proposed that the operating companies retain possession of the Yellow Pages, which accounted for $2 billion in annual revenues, and he also suggested that they be allowed to sell, though not manufacture, telephone equipment in competition with AT&T. Justice and AT&T agreed to Greene's changes just two weeks after they were proposed. Ever since the deal was announced, AT&T had endured much criticism that it was "selling out" the operating companies by not allowing them to keep the Yellow Pages or sell equipment, but actually it was Baxter who, for ideological reasons, was adamant about restricting the local companies' franchises as much as possible. When Greene suggested his changes, Baxter said, "Basically, we came out where I wanted to come out. Regulated utilities shouldn't be fooling around in competitive markets. But the judge gave us 99 percent—perhaps that's overstating it—he gave us a great preponderance of what we wanted." A few days later, Baxter met with Trienens in Washington and the two wrote Greene's changes into the consent decree. On August 24, 1982, the revised decree was filed with Greene and approved, and *U.S.* v. *AT&T* was finally dismissed.

In December, after nearly a year of committee meetings at its Basking Ridge, New Jersey, facility, AT&T filed its plan of reorganization with Greene for approval. The company had decided to consolidate its twenty-two local operating companies into seven "basic operating companies," which would take with them about 75 percent of the Bell System's assets, between 60 and 70 percent of its employees, and about half of its revenues. The new companies were organized by geographical region and were roughly equal in size. After many more months of speeches, public comment filings, and hearings, Greene approved the AT&T divestiture plan with only one major change—

AT&T would have to give up use of its familiar Bell name to the new companies. AT&T accepted this final indignity without appealing Greene's decision.

When the judge's restructuring by fiat of the telephone industry had reached the peak of its activity, the *Wall Street Journal* editorialized, "Judges in our republic were not meant to make decisions like this. Courts are not equipped to be administrators, nor are they supposed to make policy decisions that are the responsibility of executives and legislatures subject to electoral accountability.... Judge Greene's decisions add an unfortunate precedent for judicial intrusion into industrial structure: even if his changes are by and large intelligent, some judges might not be as sensible as he." Some months earlier, Charlie Brown and Howard Trienens might have chuckled sorely at the irony of the editorial, especially the part about "the responsibility of executives and legislatures subject to electoral accountability," but in the midst of such an all-consuming task as breaking apart a company with over $150 billion in assets, the AT&T executives allowed little time for sour grapes.

Not so at the Commerce department, where Malcolm Baldrige's staff could only watch bitterly as Judge Greene stepped forcefully into the policy-making vacuum left by Congress, the Reagan administration, and the FCC. And the more Greene did, the more resentment of him took on a personal tone. Ken Robinson, the NTIA lawyer who had developed the "menu" settlement in 1979 and had worked on the ill-fated Baldrige dismissal proposal during the summer of 1981, said in 1984, "The case became a real ego-builder for Greene. Look at the average menu of district court judges—you'll get a lot of ambulance chasers and half-wit public defenders. The AT&T case fills up your courtroom with people who make half a million dollars a year and up. You get to hobnob with Charlie Brown, you get lawyers flying down from New York in the corporate jet. Important people are hanging on your every remark. You get invited to all these prestigious antitrust conferences. It's very ego gratifying. I mean, geez, he gets his picture in *Fortune* magazine. How many of the other 772 federal district judges get their pictures in *Fortune*? Only the ones that get locked up."

Confronted by such criticism, the diminutive, mild-mannered Greene only shrugged, offered one of his affectionate and self-effacing smiles, and began his familiar speech about how *he* didn't file the case, *he* didn't settle it. He was only an arbiter—parties brought disputes before him, he examined them and ruled according to his own best judgment and the law. FCC officials said they couldn't regulate the phone company. Reagan and other presidents chose to prosecute *U.S.* v. *AT&T* to its end. Congress never passed a law about phone competition. What was a judge supposed to do, other than his job?

Indeed, ostensible public humility such as Judge Greene's was to be a prevailing ethic in the post-divestiture telephone industry. On May 17, 1983, AT&T announced that it was selling its twenty-six-story corporate headquarters at 195 Broadway, the "temple to the god of the telephone," in favor of a new $200 million postmodern high-rise in midtown Manhattan.

The company said that it would take down the gold "Genius of Electricity" statue from the top of 195 Broadway and put it in the lobby of its new building as a kind of museum piece. For sentimental reasons, AT&T also decided to keep the two eight-foot bronze medallions that were laid in the floor of its old headquarters lobby, which depicted Mercury bearing the messages of the gods with the motto, "Universal Service."

Chapter 35

An Imperfect World

WHETHER the breakup of American Telephone & Telegraph Company will be remembered decades from now as one of the more spectacular fiascoes of American industrial history, or whether it will be recalled as a seminal event in the emergence of a great, global "information age," or whether it will be forgotten altogether, is a matter that was impossible to predict intelligently in 1985—which is not to say that politicians, journalists, authors, Wall Street analysts, and other salaried pundits nobly refrained from offering their forecasts on the question. Indeed, during the first year or two after the breakup, the rapidly changing communications industry provoked a furious commerce in the marketplace of ideas, or "analysis," as it is described in the current corporate vernacular. So urgent was the discourse that a virtually brand new profession, the "telecommunications consultant," was born to accommodate it, to explain what had happened and what was likely to follow. Naturally, the most sought after of these consultants— Walter Hinchman, the former FCC Common Carrier Bureau chief; Richard Wiley, former FCC chairman; Richard Levine, of Bill Baxter's Antitrust front office; and numerous others—were the very people who created the chaos in the industry that gave rise to the need for their analysis. Similarly, Washington, D.C.'s, "telecommunications bar" boomed like a Nevada silver town as thousands of attorneys young and old flocked to practice a rapidly expanding discipline of law that had not been substantial enough five years before the breakup to have its own "division" at the D.C. Bar Association, but which by 1984 was doubling in size almost every year. As in war, the only clear winners during the first months after divestiture were those who possessed the means to turn carnage into profit.

Also, as in war, the clear losers early on were those in whose name the battle was fought—ordinary American telephone users. In nearly every state between 1982 and 1985, the price of basic residential telephone service increased significantly, while the quality of service declined. The cost of installing and repairing telephone equipment also rose dramatically—as much as tenfold in some areas—and the higher prices were compounded by widespread confusion over which of the newly formed telephone companies was responsible for phone equipment. For a century, consumers had enjoyed the convenience of "one-stop shopping" for nearly all telephone services; suddenly they were confronted by a pluralistic new industry in which even the largest companies seemed confused about which role they were supposed to play. The newly formed "basic operating companies" could "provide" phone equipment, but they did not lease or repair the phones already in consumers' homes; that was the province of the surviving AT&T, which retained title to the nation's "embedded" phone equipment base. When a consumer's phone service broke down his instinct was to call the local operating company for help, as he had always done. But if it turned out that the problem was in the phone equipment, not the local telephone lines, then the operating company would not make repairs, though it would charge a plumber's ransom for the house call. The consumer would then have either to buy a new phone or take his broken one to AT&T for expensive servicing. There was even more aggravating confusion about telephone bills. In many areas, the new operating companies provided AT&T with a billing service for long-distance calls, but not for phone equipment leasing. Charges for long-distance calls made over AT&T lines showed up on the monthly bill from the basic operating company, but fees for phone leasing, which used to appear on the same bill, now arrived separately. So, of course, did bills from alternative long-distance carriers such as MCI and Sprint.

Widespread disillusionment among consumers during what Justice lawyers liked to call the "transitional" period from a monopolistic to a competitive phone industry was entirely predictable. Before the breakup, a *New York Times* poll found that more than 80 percent of American telephone customers were happy with their service—according to the Commerce department, that was the highest customer satisfaction rate of any business in the country. Justice lawyers anticipated that there would be some confusion during the first months after divestiture was announced, but no one was prepared for the deep and sustained negative reaction that lasted through 1985. A poll taken by Lou Harris and Associates three years after the January 8, 1982, press conference found that 64 percent of Americans still thought the breakup was a bad idea, 25 percent thought it was a good idea, and 11 percent were not sure. Less empirical but more affecting evidence of disenchantment arrived almost daily at Judge Greene's chambers and at the Justice and Commerce departments' offices in Washington in the form of sometimes vile and threatening hate mail from angry consumers around the country; the letters were not offset by any expressing enthusiasm for the decision to destroy the Bell System.

It may yet be, as liberal and conservative deregulation enthusiasts continue to insist, that the long-run benefits of phone industry competition, such as lower long-distance prices and faster introduction of technological innovation, will quell consumers' anger and that the currently profound confusion about telephone service will dissipate as the industry begins to stabilize. But long-distance prices have yet to drop significantly amid tepid competition, and besides, well over half of all long-distance revenues are generated by businesses, not residential consumers. And while confusion may tend to dissolve with time, the quality of service cannot and will never be restored to what it was during the now fondly-remembered days of matriarchal Ma Bell's reign.

There would be something corrupt yet poetically inevitable, something reassuringly symmetrical, about the raw deal handed to consumers in the breakup if it was also true that in the first years following divestiture, *Fortune* 500 corporate giants such as AT&T and MCI were the clear "winners." Certainly both remain, for the time being, profitable companies with optimistic outlooks. Yet in the circumstances of the deal between Justice and AT&T, and in the long, tangled history of corporate warfare that preceded it, there lies a haunting specter. And yet almost everything that has happened in the telephone industry since January 8, 1982, has contributed to its growing plausibility. Simply stated, the specter is this: that in the uncompromising battle that began between William McGowan and John deButts at their meeting on March 2, 1973, each man planted the seeds of his company's final destruction.

To be sure, the "surviving" AT&T will never go belly up, and probably will never fail to pay its shareholders a healthy dividend, at least not in any business future imaginable in 1985. The company's intercity phone network and dominant position in the long-distance market will generate billions in annual revenues for the rest of this century and well into the next. But Charlie Brown's entrancing vision of an unbridled AT&T racing into the technology-driven "information age," competing with the likes of IBM and Wang and Data General and others for dominance of the "global information village" imagined by popular academic futurists such as Marshall McLuhan, John Naisbitt, and Alvin Toffler, has already been clouded by muddled realities, and there is much evidence that his company's boundaries will continue to shrink, rather than grow, in the decades ahead. McGowan and MCI, on the other hand, lacking any guarantee of long-term profitability, once again face the possibility of financial difficulty, and while the vista is familiar to McGowan, this time there will be nothing to grab onto if he falls. It is quite possible—some would argue it is more than likely—that the final landscape of the Bell System breakup will include a bankrupted MCI and an AT&T returned to its original state as a regulated, albeit smaller and less effective, telephone monopoly.

The source of this specter lies not in anyone's crystal ball but in the history of *U.S.* v. *AT&T*. Precious little in that history—the birth of MCI, the development of phone industry competition, the filing of the Justice lawsuit, McGowan's deceptive entry into regular long-distance service, the prolonged inaction of Congress, the aborted compromise deals between Justice and AT&T, the Reagan administration's tortured passivity, the final inter-intra settlement itself—was the product of a single, coherent philosophy, or a genuine, reasoned consensus, or a farsighted public policy strategy. Rather, the crucial decisions made in the telecommunications industry during the 1970s and early 1980s were driven by opportunism, short-term politics, ego, desperation, miscalculation, happenstance, greed, conflicting ideologies and personalities, and finally, when Charlie Brown thought that there was nothing left, a perceived necessity. The point is, if anyone had emerged triumphant from that embarrassing history in how *not* to make public policy, it would have been a phenomenal accident. And no one did. Not telephone consumers, not AT&T, not MCI.

Consider, for example, the plight of William McGowan in 1985. Fifteen years earlier, the MCI chairman could not have dreamed that his legal and political guerrilla war against the phone company would go so far, would actually lead to the complete breakup of the world's biggest corporation. If he had dreamed it, he might have awoken in a cold sweat. Before the breakup, MCI was paying $235 per line, per month for access to AT&T's local exchanges. That was the price negotiated under the so-called ENFIA agreement of 1979. The cost to AT&T for the same access was well over $600; the difference supposedly reflected the superior access enjoyed by AT&T. After the breakup, as the first step of a process that was to lead to fully equal access, and more significantly, equal payments by MCI and AT&T, MCI's per-line, per-month price rose to $330. When it did, the company's profits fell precipitously for the first time since McGowan won the right to sell Execunet service. MCI's stock, which had been selling at well over $20 per share, fell to under $7 per share. From the beginning, MCI's profits, its discount prices, indeed its very reason for being, derived from its cost advantage over AT&T—an advantage that was marketed to consumers in the form of lower long-distance prices. But McGowan's cost advantage was not the result of superior technology or innovative processes. It was artificial. It resulted from government regulation, not free market forces. Once the operating companies were separated from AT&T's long lines, the rationale for MCI's so-called deep discount evaporated. In theory, MCI and AT&T would both pay the same price for access to local exchanges by the year 2000—somewhere in the neighborhood of $500 per line, per month, or more than twice what MCI had paid in the early 1980's, when it blossomed into a billion-dollar corporation. If the move toward equal access proceeded on schedule, MCI would most certainly face difficulties. In 1984, there were 96 million long distance subscribers in the United States. Ninety million of them were AT&T customers; MCI had 1.7 million, good for second place. Given the immense costs of constructing, financing, and maintaining a nationwide communications network, it would be simply impossible for MCI or any "other common carrier" to survive equal access with so paltry a market share. McGowan's hope was that once customers were offered a truly equal choice among long-distance carriers—a chance to vote for ten digit, "dial one" service from MCI, AT&T, Sprint, or whomever the customer pleased— AT&T's immense market power would dissipate. That process will not be complete until 1990 or beyond, but so far, AT&T is holding steady with more than 80 percent of long-distance revenues, even in those areas where "elections" have been held so that customers could freely choose their long-distance carrier. The fact is that unless Congress intervenes and decides for political reasons to prolong the other common carriers' artificial deep discount, AT&T will find itself alone in the basic long-distance market by the end of the century. These days, McGowan and his lawyers and lobbyists are once again swarming around the FCC and the Capitol, this time urging lawmakers and legislators to delay the very thing that MCI publicly sought throughout the 1970s: equal and fair competition with AT&T. And they have a potent argument. If Congress allows equal long-distance competition, it risks putting a group of companies with $6 billion in plant and 350,000 employees out of business.

Bill McGowan is nearing the end of the tightrope he has walked since MCI was first authorized by the FCC to sell private line service in 1969. According to attorneys close to MCI, McGowan hoped to survive the cash crunch engendered by the rising cost of equal access by using the $1.8 billion antitrust judgment he won from AT&T in 1980 to expand his network and finance an aggressive marketing campaign to win new long-distance customers. As it turned out, though, the $1.8 billion was reversed on appeal, and in 1985 a new trial was held to reconsider the damages MCI was entitled to because of the FX and other controversies during the early 1970s. At the new trial, MCI sought over $15 billion, but a Chicago federal jury awarded the company less than $300 million—a major victory for AT&T. Immediately after that verdict, McGowan approached computer giant IBM and offered to sell out 30 percent of his company for cash. IBM agreed, although its vice-chairman emphasized that it would not provide "deep pockets" for McGowan over the long run. The "strategic alliance" between MCI and IBM, as well as mounting political pressure in 1985 on the FCC and Congress to preserve artificially the other common carriers' deep discounts, has probably guaranteed that MCI will remain solvent until at least 1995. But there are few in the telecommunications industry who doubt that McGowan's day of reckoning is rapidly approaching.

AT&T, too, has been rocked by one crisis after another in the post-divestiture world, although, unlike MCI, it faces no danger of financial difficulty. In 1985, the price of access to the divested operating companies' local exchanges was draining away 60 percent of AT&T's revenues. Regulation by the FCC, which was supposed to begin to disappear after the breakup, was more pervasive than ever. Western Electric, renamed AT&T Technologies, Inc., was still desperately struggling to adjust to a competitive world, and its telephone equipment market share, which had been steadily eroding before the breakup, took a nose dive. The company's overall profits in 1984 ran a full $1 billion short of projections, and its annual rate of return was substantially below the 12.75 percent allowed by the FCC. Fourteen thousand employees were laid off or asked to retire early as part of a breakneck plan to pare costs. And the company showed no signs of racing off into the profitable information age with the Bell System's family jewels, Western and Bell Labs. AT&T's much ballyhooed new computer products, introduced in 1984 and 1985, were plagued by technical problems and flopped in the marketplace. To gear up for a second try, the company decided to shut down four factories and cut its production costs by 25 percent. But as its position in the computer and equipment markets continued to deteriorate, Wall Street analysts began to question loudly whether a century-old monopoly could learn to compete before it was too late.

"AT&T did not get anything that they bargained for," says one government lawyer prominently involved in the breakup. "If they thought they were going to get peace in their time, they got a worse war. If they thought they were going to get deregulated, they were stupid and naive. Now they've got these operating companies out there draining their capital and they don't have sufficient money to do all the things they want to do."

By contrast, the divested operating companies, declared by so many in 1982 to be facing a bleak and unprofitable future, flourished in the first years after the breakup. Fear that the companies would founder without unlimited long-distance subsidies allowed them to raise prices for local service, while at the same time AT&T and its long-distance competitors continued to pay billions for access to local exchanges. Protected by state regulators and boosted by the favorable decisions made by Judge Greene in the summer of 1982, profits for each of the seven basic operating companies exceeded projections in 1984 and continued to grow in 1985. Whether that unexpected success reflected the benefits of a temporary overreaction by regulators and politicians concerned about the operating companies' future, or whether it was a true indication of the companies' financial health, is a question that will not be answered for decades.

Irving Kristol, the former socialist turned neoconservative editor of *The Public Interest*, once commented that *U.S. v. AT&T* was less a conventional antitrust case than a "modern day variant on classical Marxist class warfare theories," because it was fundamentally a struggle for power between a class of bureaucrats in the government—lawyers and technocrats in the Justice department, the FCC's common carrier bureau, and in Congress—and the class of bureaucrats who ran the nation's phone system, the one million employees of AT&T. Certainly it is true that the government lawyers and bureaucrats at Justice and the FCC were not driven to break up the phone company by any clear, coherent vision about how a decentralized telecommunications system would work better than the existing one. The Justice lawyers, for example, never seriously believed that the operating companies would ever be divested, and until it became a necessity as the case was about to go to trial, they spent very little time drawing up plans for how the nation's phone network would be managed if they won their case. Instead, the government lawyers were driven by the conviction that AT&T was "unregulatable," as Walter Hinchman, the former common carrier chief, always put it. With McGowan playing every angle, MCI was unleashed, nurtured, protected, and defended by the FCC and Justice because, in the words of Hinchman's predecessor, Bernie Strassburg, "AT&T was getting so big, so fast." Competition was a means for the government lawyers and bureaucrats to wrest power away from AT&T, to regain control over the phone company. Judge Greene, a former government lawyer himself, indicated clearly, from his jokes about "the well-oiled machine" to the harsh language of his September 11 opinion, that it was AT&T's size and power that troubled him above all.

Thus it should come as no surprise, as Ken Robinson and Dr. Paul MacAvoy, dean of Rochester University's graduate school of management, have pointed out, that the "result of the settlement was not to facilitate deregulation," as the academic ideologue Bill Baxter said it would be, "but was rather to reduce AT&T to more regulatable dimensions." Baxter believed that *U.S.* v. *AT&T* was fundamentally a case about ideology and economic theory. But events in the telephone industry since the 1982 settlement announcement have made it plain that Kristol's view of the case as "class conscious" war between rival bureaucracies is a far more accurate description. Broken into eight pieces, the political power of AT&T's one-million-strong telephone bureaucracy, so disastrously overplayed by John deButts during the 1976 Bell Bill fight with Congress, has faded. Whereas AT&T was once able to present its resources and power in a unified front against the government, it has now been broken into two factions with separate and often conflicting interests: the local operating companies and the "surviving" AT&T. Judge Greene, for one, has accumulated great autonomy and influence by mediating disputes between the two rival factions, who only a few years earlier were pooling their immense capital resources to thwart his will in court. The FCC, similarly, will wield far more control over AT&T's fortunes during the late 1980s and early 1990s, as it decides the crucial issues of long-distance equal-access payments, than it ever did during the 1960s and 1970s. In those days, there was little the commission could do to affect the phone company's profits but impose an ever-higher limit on AT&T's rate of return. In stark contrast to that era of Bell dominance, AT&T was forced in 1984 to file an "emergency petition" with the FCC asking for relief from certain regulations for fear that its annual rate of return would fall below 5 percent and jeopardize the company's standing in the financial community. The FCC granted the request, but the point was made. AT&T, so long despised by commission staffers for its high-handed arrogance, was on its knees at last.

Chapter 36

Epilogue

THERE were moments in the first months after the settlement of *U.S.* v. *AT&T* was announced when it seemed that the breakup of the Bell System would be paralleled by the demise of George Saunders' ebullient personality. After a decade of relentless hard work, passionate oratory, desperate connivance, and uninterrupted dedication, Saunders had come away with nothing—or less than nothing, since his efforts had resulted in the destruction of his client. Some trial lawyers, imagining themselves as mercenary professionals emotionally unattached to the fortunes of their clients, might have accepted that the settlement was beyond their control. But Saunders was not like most lawyers. It seemed to his partners and colleagues that Saunders' very soul was inexorably linked to the spirit of the Bell System. There were times after the settlement when he seemed moody, sentimental, angry, devastated, as if he was mourning the loss of a close companion.

But there was more to it than that. After the $1.8 billion defeat in the MCI trial, Saunders had approached *U.S.* v. *AT&T* seeking vindication for himself as well as his client. When Charlie Brown made his fateful decision to surrender to Justice, he snatched that vindication from Saunders in the most categorical manner imaginable. Some felt that after the trial before Judge Greene, Saunders began to tire of the great telephone litigation wars, as if the demonic flame that had driven him to fight and scratch and claw on AT&T's behalf since the early 1970s had dimmed or been snuffed out. Perhaps it was simpler than that: perhaps after so much work and frustration, he had had enough of it all. But he could not let go of it, either, and that turned out to be a fortunate thing.

During the second week of May 1982, five months after the settlement announcement, the trial of *Southern Pacific* v. *AT&T* got under way before Judge Charles Richey in U.S. District Court in Washington. Southern Pacific was the parent of Sprint, the discount long-distance company that had cautiously followed McGowan and MCI into the intercity services market. The case was nearly an exact duplicate of the MCI lawsuit that had resulted in the $1.8 billion trial verdict, which in turn closely mirrored Justice's suit against the phone company—many of the same documents were entered and many of the same witnesses testified in all three trials. Saunders had thrown himself into preparations for the Southern Pacific case almost as soon as the settlement with Justice was announced, and the work had provided an important distraction for him. By the time the trial began, Saunders seemed restored to his old self, at least in the courtroom, railing in his hours-long opening statement about how there was no doubt Sprint "was a creamskimming operation."

The six-month trial was held in a courtroom very near to Judge Greene's in the district court building on Constitution Avenue. From the beginning, Richey seemed more sympathetic to Saunders' arguments than had either Greene or Judge Grady from the MCI trial in Chicago. Saunders pressed the same arguments he had made in the MCI and government cases. He cross-examined the same witnesses in more or less the same way. He entered the same documents. And when it was over, he had won, for the first time, a stunning victory.

"The FCC's introduction of competition in the long-distance market has been and will be shown to be contrary to the best interests of millions of Americans," Judge Richey wrote in his December 1982 opinion dismissing the entire case. "Every action complained of in this case could have or should have been handled by the appropriate regulatory bodies. ... The court believes that the antitrust laws were never intended to destroy an essential public utility such as we have here."

Beyond offering some vindication to Saunders and AT&T, Richey's decision provided compelling evidence to many observers that the judiciary ought not to become involved in economic policy making. Here were two judges in the same court building, Greene and Richey, whose opinions about the telecommunications industry were diametrically opposed. Greene, by virtue of the case he drew, reshaped the entire telecommunications industry; Richey, by the lot of the same draw, was able merely to dismiss a private antitrust suit while sniping at Greene's decision in his final opinion.

For Saunders, victory begat victory. The $1.8 billion MCI verdict was set aside by a federal appeals court, and a new trial for damages, in which Saunders was not directly involved, resulted in a much smaller award. Saunders continued to try private antitrust cases for AT&T, though his breakneck pace eased somewhat. To preserve his health, he gave up cigars and occasionally checked himself in for six weeks at a Santa Monica, California, health camp, where he would quit drinking, eat nutritious food, and jog serenely along the shores of the Pacific Ocean. Once released from camp, Saunders seemed to return to many of his former vices, but when he ran himself down, he returned to California to be reinvigorated.

The Justice trial lawyers, unable to afford retreats to paradisiacal health farms and without any new litigation to absorb their energies immediately, languished for months after the settlement in what many of them described as a "void." Some stayed with the government for several years to work on the Tunney Act proceedings and other cases, but most of the prominent members of the Antitrust front office and the original trial team—Jim Denvir, Peter Kenney, Ron Carr, Jeff Blumenfeld—eventually followed Gerry Connell into private practice in Washington.

Bill Baxter's tenure as Antitrust chief became even more controversial after the AT&T settlement. After the *Wall Street Journal* revealed that Baxter had done consulting work for IBM while he was a law professor at Stanford and that he owned stock in computer companies affected by his decision to dismiss the government case against IBM, the Justice department's Office of Professional Responsibility launched an investigation into the possible conflict of interest. Baxter was eventually exonerated. However, no sooner had his name been cleared than new controversies arose. Newspapers reported that morale had "plummeted" in the Antitrust division during Baxter's reign, and that the Antitrust chief was perceived by government lawyers as "aloof and contemptuous" of the division's employees. After dramatically loosening the Justice department's "merger guidelines," Baxter set off an unprecedented wave of corporate mergers and hostile takeover attempts, prompting a fresh round of criticism from Congress.

Still, on December 8, 1983, when Baxter resigned his position as assistant attorney general for Antitrust and returned to teach law at Stanford University, he left behind a profound legacy in the Antitrust division—a legacy that must have pleased him.

After he retired as chairman of AT&T, John deButts, the man who embodied for so many Washington lawyers and politicians the unchecked power and stark arrogance of the unified Bell System, built a mansion for himself and his wife, Trudie, on eighty sprawling acres in the somber Virginia hunt country, fifty miles west of the nation's capital.

Though he was an immensely wealthy man, he found the pace of retirement in the countryside difficult to accommodate after so many years of living in Manhattan and traveling the globe as the distinguished leader of the largest corporation in the world. After moving into his new estate, a circulation problem led to the amputation of one of his legs. So it was that after the settlement of *U.S.* v. *AT&T*, deButts spent much of his time sitting in a wheelchair in the glass-enclosed porch behind his house. There he commanded a melancholy view of unbroken pasture, maples, and oaks stretching west to the Blue Ridge Mountains.

DeButts never publicly criticized the decision taken by his

successor to dismantle the Bell System, although there were many in the company who remained convinced that deButts himself would never have given in to the government, no matter what the cost. In December 1981, in the midst of the inter-intra negotiations, Brown called deButts in Virginia to tell him about the deal that was under way. At the end of their conversation, deButts said, "You have no choice."

But the destruction of AT&T shook deButts deeply. One autumn afternoon in 1984, sitting with a visitor in his glass-enclosed porch, chain-smoking Merit cigarettes, deButts spoke eloquently about the impact of the breakup on the last years of his life. During the monologue, he paused occasionally to fight back tears.

"I hear about it every single day from my friends," he said. "Friends from business, neighbors, even my family. I have a cousin around here who couldn't get phone service installed in his barn. Nobody could make up his mind about who was going to do what. He wanted service in several barns, with all the wires underground. He just wasn't getting to first base. So I finally called somebody at AT&T headquarters in New York and said, 'Why don't you get somebody down here who can take care of these problems?' And they did. But my cousin got a bill for over $5,000. We never used to charge anybody that much for installation. It's unheard of. I even made them go back and check it to make sure it was right. It was.

"It pains me. It hurts me a lot. I've been used to saying, 'OK, Mr. Customer, if that's what you want, then that's what you're going to get.' What bothers me the most is that I see a deterioration of the service concept in the operating companies themselves. Profits are beginning to come first.

"I used to get questions when I first became chairman. 'Which do you want, profits or service?' And I said, 'I want both. But service comes first. Profits will come right along with it.' And they finally stopped asking me that because they knew I meant it. People won't think about what it costs if the service is good, as long as the cost is within reason.

"It's a tragedy, I think. During the 1976 fight with Congress, I was disappointed that I didn't get a better reaction from stockholders and customers. They never thought we were in trouble. As a guy at the FCC told me once, 'John, don't worry about it. No matter what we do to you, you always come out all right.'

"And we did. But we couldn't survive this."

October 8, 1986
En route from Tokyo

Notes and Sources

The preceding narrative is the product of approximately 100 interviews and a review of tens of thousands of pages of documentary evidence—including trial transcripts, settlement conference transcripts, court pleadings, depositions, exhibits, congressional hearings, internal Justice department documents produced under a Freedom of Information Act request, corporate filings with the Securities and Exchange Commission, calendar and diary entries, expense reports, letters, and handwritten notes. Nothing in the book has been invented or disguised by the author. References to weather conditions are derived from the federal government publication *Climatological Data*. Descriptions of meeting rooms, hotel rooms, and other locations are based in most cases on personal visits by the author, but also on brochures, books, maps, and the recollections of persons interviewed.

Much of the dialogue in the book is taken from transcribed proceedings in open court or from closed chambers conferences where a court reporter was present. In rare instances, a word or two has been changed for grammatical reasons or to clarify meaning. In a few cases, conversations were condensed without the constant use of ellipses. Such condensation is usually referred to in the narrative. In any event, the author took extreme care to be sure that these few changes did not alter the context of the dialogue or its meaning.

Other dialogue is based on the recollections of persons interviewed. In most cases, the substance of these conversations was confirmed by two or more sources, though occasionally dialogue is based on the recollection of only one source. The reader should not assume that the direct source of any recollected conversation is one of its participants; in some cases dialogue was repeated to third parties and then confirmed by the author, while in other cases conversations are based on handwritten notes later made public or available to the author against the wishes of the participants.

INTERVIEWS

Approximately half of the persons interviewed for this book requested anonymity. Most often, their reasons reflected concern about damaging existing professional relationships. Despite such legitimate fears, many of these sources gave generously of their time in an attempt to make the book fair and accurate.

Other sources, equally generous with their time, allowed their names to appear on a list of persons interviewed by the author. Among them: Ken Anderson, Bill Barrett, Bill Baxter, Lewis Bernstein, Ed Block, Charles Brown, Ron Carr, Tom Casey, Keith Clearwaters, Gerry Connell, Ken Cox, John deButts, Bob Eckhardt, Richard Favretto, Charles Ferris, Joseph Fogarty, Jules Fried, Henry Geller, David Gergen, James Graf, Harold Greene, Vance Hartke, Walter Hinchman, Gregory Hovendon, Charles Hugel, Jules Joskow, Thomas Kauper, Richard Levine, William Lindholm, Sanford Litvack, Thomas Mauro, Archie McGill, Nick Miller, Hugh Morrison, Bernie Nash, Stuart Newberger, Alexander Pires, Martha Roadstrum, Kenneth Robinson, Romano Romani, Teno Roncalio, Jonathan Rose, William Saxbe, Lee Selwyn, Harry Shooshan, Bernie Strassburg, Morris Tannenbaum, Howard Trienens, Lionel Van Deerlin, Philip Verveer, Bernie Wunder, and John Zeglis.

DOCUMENTS AND SECONDARY SOURCES

The author employed voluminous primary and secondary documents in the course of his research. The following list is not intended as a comprehensive bibliography. Rather, it is a citation of certain key documents, many of them publicly available, that interested readers may examine to explore the events chronicled in the book.

Chapter 1: U.S. v. *AT&T,* civil no. 74–1698. Plaintiffs' Third Statement of Contentions and Proof, 451 ff.; 679–696. Defendants' Third Statement of Contentions and Proof, 612–625. Testimony of John deButts, trial transcript, 13, 986–14,135. Testimony of William McGowan, trial transcript, 4,023 ff.

Chapter 2: U.S. v. *AT&T,* testimony of William McGowan, trial transcript, 3,638–4,057. Testimony of Larry Harris, 4,165 ff. January 9, 1973, handwritten notes of Kenneth Cox. March 2, 1973, notes of George Cook and William McGowan. Plaintiffs' Third Statement of Contentions and Proof, 543–560. Defendants' Third Statement of Contentions and Proof, 645 ff.

Chapter 3: Justice department log of contacts during Civil Investigative Demand investigation of AT&T. United States Judiciary Committee, Subcommittee on Antitrust, hearings July 1973; hearings July 9, 30, and 31, 1974. *U.S.* v. *AT&T,* Testimony of William McGowan, trial transcript, 3,684 ff.

Chapter 4: U.S. v. *AT&T,* testimony of Walter Hinchman, trial transcript, 10,692 ff. Testimony of William McGowan, 3,684–4,023. Confidential MCI financial statement dated December 1973. Memorandum by Larry Harris dated October 2, 1973. Letter to Bernie Strassburg dated October 1, 1973. Memo from Walter Hinchman to Federal Communications Commission dated December 4, 1973. Plaintiffs' Third Statement of Contentions and Proof, 388 ff.; 560–621. Defendants' Third Statement of Contentions and Proof, 645–700. Testimony of John deButts, trial transcript, 13,995 ff. Testimony of Bernie Strassburg, 23,357–23,398. *Electronic News,* November 12, 1973.

Chapters 5–7: Justice department log of contacts during Civil Investigative Demand investigation of AT&T. Original *U.S.* v. *AT&T* complaint filed November 20, 1974. Transcript of proceedings before Judge Joseph Waddy, February 20, 1975. *Washington Post,* November 21, 1974. *Business Week,* November 30, 1974. *Electronic News,* December 25, 1974.

Chapter 8: U.S. v. *AT&T,* testimony of Walter Hinchman, trial transcript, 10,302 ff. Direct and cross examination of Bert C. Roberts, April 27, 1981. Testimony of William McGowan, trial transcript, 3,895 ff. Internal MCI business plan and Execunet proposal dated June 3, 1974. MCI stock prospectus dated November 1975. Defendants' Third Statement of Contentions and Proof, 692–700.

Chapter 9: "Agenda for Oversight," staff report of the House Communications Subcommittee, April 1976. Hearings on CCRA, House Communications Subcommittee, September 27–30, 1976. *Business Week,* March 15, 1976. *Electronic News,* April 12, 1976; April 26, 1976; May 10, 1976; May 31, 1976. *Wall Street Journal,* November 4, 1983.

Chapters 10–12: U.S. v. *AT&T,* transcripts of status hearings before Judge Harold Greene, August 21, 1978; January 12, 1979; November 7, 1979; September 17, 1980.

Chapters 13–16: Transcripts of settlement conferences in the chambers of Judge Harold Greene, January 5 and January 14, 1981.

Order of Judge Greene dated January 7, 1981. *U.S.* v. *AT&T,* trial transcript, 3–246. Transcript of settlement conference, January 15, 1981. Letter from Howard Trienens to Judge Greene, January 29, 1981. Letter from Charles Renfrew to Judge Greene, January 29, 1981. Letter from Howard Trienens to Judge Greene, February 23, 1981. Letter from Sanford Litvack to Judge Greene, February 23, 1981.

Chapters 17–18: Senate Armed Services Committee hearing on S.694, March 23, 1981, testimony of Caspar Weinberger. *U.S.* v. *AT&T,* Defendants' Memorandum Concerning Defendants' Exhibit D–1–141. Letter from Frank Carlucci to William Baxter, April 8, 1981. *U.S.* v. *AT&T,* Defendants' Chronology of Events Concerning Exhibit D–1–141. "Department of Defense Analysis of the Effects of AT&T Divestiture Upon National Defense & Security and Emergency Preparedness," June 30, 1981. Letter from William Taft to William Baxter, July 2, 1981. Transcript of Press Conference of William Baxter, Department of Justice Office of Public Affairs, April 9, 1981. "Confirmation Hearing of William F. Baxter," Senate Judiciary Committee, March 19, 1981.

Chapter 19: U.S. v. *AT&T,* Testimony of William McGowan, April 9, 1981; April 10, 1981; April; 13, 1981; May 1, 1981.

Chapters 20–21: "Telecommunications Competition and Deregulation Act of 1981," Senate Commerce Committee hearings, June 2, 1981; June 11, 1981; June 15, 1981; June 16, 1981; June 19, 1981. "DOJ Oversight: *U.S.* v. *AT&T,*" Senate Judiciary Committee hearing August 6, 1981. See testimony of Malcolm Baldrige, Sherman Unger, Bernard Wunder, William Baxter, William Taft.

Chapter 22: U.S. v. *AT&T,* trial transcript, 6,803–6,814; 11,233–11,242; 11,380–11,411. *Telecommunications,* July 20, 1981.

Chapter 23: Transcript of chambers conference before Judge Greene, July 29, 1981. Order of Judge Greene, July 29, 1981. Department of Justice, Office of Public Affairs, "Press Guidance," July 29, 1981.

Chapter 24: U.S. v. *AT&T,* trial transcript, 12,974–13,149; 13,796–13,834; 14,687–14,700.

Chapter 25: U.S. v. *AT&T,* trial transcript, 14,844–14,1910. Opinion of Judge Greene, September 11, 1981.

Chapter 26: All interviews.

Chapter 27: U.S. v. *AT&T,* trial transcript, 15,889–15,911; 16,101–16,152; 16,645–16,651; 16,994–17,008; 17,458–17,544; 19,529–19,637; 19,958–19,970; 23,320–24,711.

Chapters 28–30: "A Public Relations Case History of the Biggest Business Story of the Decade," keynote address by Edward Block to the PRSA Regional Conference, Chicago, June 9, 1983. "Telecommunications in Transition: The Status of Competition in the Telecommunications Industry. A Report by the Majority Staff of the Subcommittee on Telecommunications . . . House of Representatives," November 3, 1981. Also see *Wall Street Journal's* excellent article of January 19, 1982.

Chapter 31: Unedited network videotape of January 8, 1982, press conference. Transcripts of CBS and ABC evening news, January 8, 1982.

Chapter 32: Transcript of hearing before Judge Biunno, Newark, New Jersey, January 11, 1982. Transcript of hearing before Judge Greene, January 12, 1982.

Chapter 33: "DOJ Oversight: *U.S.* v. *AT&T*," Senate Judiciary Committee hearing January 25, 1982. "Proposed Antitrust Settlement of AT&T," joint hearings of House Telecommunications Subcommittee and House Subcommittee on Monopolies and Commercial Law, January 26 and January 28, 1982. "DOJ Oversight: *U.S.* v. *AT&T* (The Effect on Local Rates)," Senate Judiciary Committee hearing, March 25, 1982.

Chapters 34–35: "Losing by Losing: Market Response to Judicial Policymaking in the First Year of the AT&T Divestiture," draft paper by Paul W. MacAvoy and Kenneth Robinson, 1985. "The Judge Who's Reshaping the Phone Business," *Fortune*, April 1, 1985. *Business Week*, December 3, 1984. AT&T Annual Reports to Shareholders, 1981–1984.

Index

Agriculture Department, U.S., 217–218
American Newspaper Publishers Association (ANPA), 360–361
American Telephone & Telegraph Company (AT&T):
board of directors of, 111–112, 299–302, 306–308
Brown's changes at, 135–136
"central services organization" of, 309
competitive pressures on, 10–15; see also competition
computer entry of, 372
decline in quality of "pots" at, 7–8, 10, 11, 46
Eisenhower administration and, 230–231
future of, 368–372
"government relations" office of, 9
headquarters building of, 22, 364
jokes and satire about, 7–8
Justice department investigations of, see Justice department, U.S.; U.S. v. AT&T; U.S. v. AT&T trial
Litton antitrust suit against, 131, 236
lobbying efforts of, 83–85, 93–102, 110–111
Long Lines department off, see Long Lines department

manufacturing subsidiary of, see Western Electric Company
marketing department organized by, 107–109, 111
MCI and, see MCI
as natural monopoly, 45–46, 85, 277, 358
new realism of, 135–146, 160
1956 consent decree and, 59, 60, 77, 142, 149, 293–294, 298, 327, 337–340
operating costs of, 8, 107–108
political clout of, 90–100
political naïveté of, 348
Presidents' Conferences of, 5–15, 22, 39, 103, 192, 301, 319–321
profits of, 8, 11, 13, 85–86, 107–108, 368
public relations of, 291–293, 307, 313–316, 332, 333, 335, 347, 348
as public trust, 6, 10, 40–41
red team vs. blue team at, 102–112, 122, 135–137, 169, 272–274
reorganization plan of, 362–363
research and development of, see Bell Laboratories
size of, 6, 42, 48, 78, 193, 373
stock of, 69, 71, 152, 368
see also local operating companies; specific companies
Anderson, Kenneth, 114–122, 136–146, 150

Anderson, Kenneth (*cont.*)
  background and personality of,
    114–116, 121–122
  Connell compared to, 162–163
  Greene and, 129, 130–131
  Levy's visits to, 119–122
  Otter Tail case and, 115, 116, 129,
    131
  resignation of, 138, 149, 162
  secret settlement attempted by,
    138–146, 269
  Trienens' meetings with, 121, 136,
    140–146
  Verveer compared to, 115–117,
    121
ANPA (American Newspaper
  Publishers Association), 360–
  361
answering machines, 11, 92
antitrust law, 20–21, 23, 25, 27–35,
    56–82, 106
  Baxter's views on, 316–317
  "essential facilities" doctrine in,
    20–21
  IBM case and, 116, 117, 128, 131,
    316–317, 334
  Litton case and, 131, 236
  Otter Tail case and, 23, 115, 116,
    131
  Southern Pacific v. *AT&T* and, 376–
    377
  see also *U.S.* v. *AT&T*; *U.S.* v.
    AT&T trial
Appeals Court, U.S., 337
AT&T, *see* American Telephone &
  Telegraph Company
AT&T Technologies, Inc., 371–372
N. W. Ayer, 314
Aylward, David, 295

Baker, Howard, 218
Baker, James A., III, 212, 223–224,
    226, 228, 242
  at cabinet council meeting (July
    27), 245–246
Baldrige, Malcolm, 185–186, 189,
    211–222, 242
  background and personality of,
    215–216
  dismissal proposal of, 216–228,
    230, 232, 254–255

Meese and, 216–218
  Senate Bill 898 and, 244–245
Barrett, Bill, 113–114, 119
Basking Ridge Presidents'
  Conference (1982), 319–321
Baxter, William F., 177–189, 213,
    225–231, 239–253, 308, 344
  in aftermath of settlement, 349,
    355–356, 362
  appointed to succeed Litvack,
    177–179, 184–185
  Cabinet Council and, 219–222,
    242–248
  conservatism of, 181–182, 185
  finesse strategy of, 243, 252, 255,
    265
  Greene's dismissal opinion and,
    265–266
  IBM case and, 316–317
  inter-intra split and, 297–299,
    303–305, 312, 315–323, 325,
    330–334, 349, 358–359
  Levine compared to, 304
  at NERA conference, 239–241
  personality of, 182–183
  post-settlement career of, 377–378
  Quagmire II and, 252–253, 297,
    298
  Senate Bill 898 and, 242–246, 252,
    254, 280
  Trienens and, 184–186, 297–299,
    303, 309
  Weinberger's letter to, 187, 212
Beard, Dita, 245
Beckel, Robert, 354
Bell Bill (Consumer
  Communications Reform Act;
  CCRA), 92–102, 240
  consequences of, 101–102
  provisions of, 92
  terminal equipment and, 109–
    111, 272
Bell Laboratories, 9, 10, 12, 216,
    288, 290, 372
  controversy over role of, 271–272
  inter-intra split and, 274, 320–321
  Penzias and, 286, 287
bellwether approach, 142–144, 151
bills, telephone, 366–367
Biunno, Vincent, 298, 326, 336–340,
    359
"Black Friday," 148
Block, Edward:

at Basking Ridge Presidents'
  Conference, 319–321
inter-intra split and, 291–293,
  307–308, 313–316, 332, 333,
  335, 347, 348
Block, John, 211
Blumenfeld, Jeff, 164, 180–181, 331,
  377
bond issue, 67, 70
bottleneck monopoly, 55–56, 67,
  316
Brown, Ann, 103, 308
Brown, Charles L., 344, 369
  aftermath of settlement and, 347–
    353, 356
  AT&T changes under, 135–136
  background and personality of,
    103–104
  at Basking Ridge Presidents'
    Conference, 319–321
  Baxter and, 184–186
  Block's meetings with, 291–293
  as blue team head, 103–104, 109–
    112, 135–137
  at board of directors' meetings,
    299–302
  Crimson Sky and, 173, 177, 178
  deButts compared to, 103–104
  as deButts' successor, 112
  decision continuum of, 293
  Greene's dismissal opinion and,
    266, 267
  Hugel promoted by, 271
  inter-intra split and, 268–270,
    274, 275, 279–280, 292–293,
    296–302, 307–308, 309, 311,
    312–313, 319–322, 325, 327,
    330, 332–334
  at Key Largo Presidents'
    Conference, 14, 103, 301
  leadership style of, 135, 277–278
  Ma Bell moniker hated by, 123
  Meese and, 211
  new realism of, 135–137, 140,
    144, 145, 160
  as president of Illinois Bell, 14,
    103, 121
  quick solution to *U.S.* vs. *AT&T*
    sought by, 122, 129, 136, 140,
    144, 173, 212
  Reagan administration and, 212–
    213, 223–225
  salary of, 356

Senate Bill 898 and, 261–262, 280,
  294
testimony of, 301–302
Trienens and, 140, 144, 145, 147–
  149, 195
at *U.S.* v. *AT&T* trial, 163, 301–
  302
Wirth report and, 294–295
Brownell, Herbert, Jr., 58–59
Buchsbaum, Saul, 286
Bush, George, 222, 224
Business Week, 194

Cabinet Council on Commerce and
  Trade, 217–223, 242–248
California Public Utility
  Commission, 352
capital contribution plan, 19–20
Carr, Ronald, 253, 265–266, 336–
  340, 357, 377
  inter-intra split and, 303–306,
    308, 309, 312, 315, 317–320,
    322–323, 325–327, 358–359
Carter, Jimmy, 127, 128, 145, 148,
  186
Carter administration, Commerce
  department in, 215
Carterfone, 10–11, 44, 92, 104–105,
  136
  North Carolina's challenging of,
    259
Casey, Tom, 113–114, 119
CCRA (Consumer Communications
  Reform Act), *see* Bell Bill
Chesapeake & Potomac Telephone
  Co. of Virginia, 9
Cincinnati Bell Telephone Co., 143,
  144, 150, 151, 174, 270
Civiletti, Benjamin, 146
civil rights, 53, 125–128
Clark, Ramsey, 126
Clayton, Henry, 30–31
Clayton Act (1914), 30, 151–152
Clearwaters, Keith, 60–61, 65–70
Commerce department, U.S., 211–
  228
  in Carter administration, 215
  inter-intra split and, 322
  National Telecommunications and
    Information Agency of, 141,
    212–216

Commerce department, U.S. (*cont.*)
Senate Bill 898 and, 243–246
common carrier principle, 41
Communications Act (1934), 28, 149, 225
Communications Workers of America, 90
competition, 10–15, 30
AT&T disadvantages in, 107–108, 122
Baxter's views on, 182
Brown's views on, 277
Carterfone decision and, 10–11, 44, 92, 104–105, 136, 259
deButts' views on, 34, 41–44, 85, 89–90, 96, 105–111, 122, 169, 170, 272, 273–274
intercity services, 11–15, 22–24, 89–90, 264; *see also* MCI
public opinion and, 79
Strassburg's views on, 46
terminal equipment, 10–11, 15, 23–24, 104–111, 122, 135–136, 144, 169–170, 272, 288–290
Computer Inquiry II, 294
computers, 105, 144, 326, 327
AT&T's entry into, 372
1956 consent decree and, 59, 60, 293–294
Congress, U.S., 126, 315, 347–356
AT&T lobbying of, 93–102, 110–111
Bell Bill and, 93–100, 109–111
corporate lobbying strategies in, 94–95
deregulation trend in, 95–96
Execunet and, 90–91
MCI lobbying of, 28–35, 152, 370–371
telephone regulatory functions of, 28
Wunder in, 214, 216
see also House of Representatives, U.S.; Senate, U.S.
Connell, Gerald, 161–174, 189–203, 231–238, 241, 336
Anderson compared to, 162–163
background and personality of, 162
Baxter and, 180–181
at consent decree signing ceremony, 324–326
continuance request and, 248–249

cross-examination strategy of, 286–287
inter-intra split and, 322–323, 324–326, 328, 330–331, 340–344
McGowan's testimony and, 200–203
opening arguments of, 163–166
Quagmire II and, 256
retirement from government service of, 324–325, 377
Saunders compared to, 162, 165, 167, 194, 195, 196, 262
Saunders' witness list and, 282–284
self-effacing style of, 190–191
consent decree (1956), 77, 142, 149, 298, 327, 337–340
computers and, 59, 60, 293–294
consultants, telecommunications, 365
Consumer Communications Reform Act (CCRA), *see* Bell Bill
"consumer revolution," 31
consumers, effects of AT&T breakup on, 366–368
Cook, George, 23, 25, 26
copper wire technology, 12
Court of General Sessions (District of Columbia), 126–127
Cox, Archibald, 61
Cox, Kenneth, 29, 48, 51, 205, 207
Verveer's conversations with, 55–56
Crimson Sky (Justice-AT&T negotiations), 152–158, 164, 166, 171–179
collapse of, 177–179, 184, 185
revision of, 174–175
crown jewel divestiture, 142–144, 151
CSSA service, 47, 203, 207
customer premises equipment, *see* terminal equipment

Darman, Richard, 223–224
DCA (Defense Communications Agency), 186–187, 322
Deaver, Michael, 223–224
deButts, John Dulany, 6–15, 70–71, 92–112, 170–171, 267
AT&T accomplishments of, 111

AT&T breakup and, 378–380
background and personality of, 9
Bell Bill and, 92–102
Brown compared to, 103–104
competition as viewed by, 34, 41–
44, 85, 89–90, 96, 105–111, 122,
169, 170, 272, 273–274
"decision to decide" of, 39–43,
193
FX lines and, 24, 49–52, 90
Hi/Lo pricing announced by, 22
at Key Largo meeting, 6–15, 39
McGowan's meeting with, 21–27,
49–50, 368
political agenda of, 90–100
retirement of, 103, 111–112, 135,
378
Saunders and, 77, 78
Strassburg and, 43–44, 46–47, 48,
52
testimony of, 262
U.S. v. *AT&T* and, 77, 262
deButts, Trudie, 378
DeCair, Tom, 334
"December 21st draft," *see*
"Modification of Final
Judgment"
Defense Communications Agency
(DCA), 186–187, 322
Defense department, U.S., 186–187,
217–219, 226
Denvir, Jim, 164, 172–174, 176, 177,
331, 337, 377
Baxter and, 180–181
as Connell's successor, 324–325
deregulation, national trend
toward, 95–96
Dewey, Ballantine, Bushby, Palmer
& Wood, 77
divestiture, 288
Baxter's views on, 240–241, 252
crown jewel, 142–144, 151
Greene and, 278, 279
price effects of, 349–351
punitive, 289
Robinson plan for, 141–144, 150–
151
see also inter-intra split

Eisenhower, Dwight D., 58
Reagan compared to, 230–231
electronic publishing, 360–361

Energy Department, U.S., 218
Ervin, Sam, 64
"essential facilities" doctrine, 20–21
Exchange Network Facilities for
Interstate Access (ENFIA)
agreement, 275–276, 369–370
Execunet, 83–91, 93, 96, 109, 129,
203, 276
FCC and, 83–90, 95
in Saunders' opening argument,
169–170

Favretto, Richard, 176
Federal Communications
Commission (FCC), 10–14, 24,
371
AT&T breakup and, 373, 374
Carterfone decision of, 10–11, 44,
92, 104–105, 136, 259
Common Carrier Bureau of, 44–
48, 50–52, 83–85, 87–89, 193,
215
Computer Inquiry II at, 294
deButts' criticism of, 42, 44, 48
Execunet controversy and, 83–90,
95
FX controversy and, 47–52
MCI and, 12, 13, 17–19, 48–52
MCI antitrust suit and, 21, 28–29
MCI created by, 11, 19, 25, 38, 78,
89
Specialized Common Carriers of, 50,
205–206
state regulators' rivalry with, 41,
258–260
telephone network regulated by,
28, 37, 78
U.S. v. *AT&T* and, 78–82
Western Electric investigated by,
60
Federal Emergency Management
Agency, 218
Federal Rules of Civil Procedure,
130
Fielding, Fred, 322
First Amendment, 361
Fitch, Luin, 152, 174
Flexner, Don, 139, 145
Ford, Gerald, 61, 64, 65, 71
Fox, John, 110
FX service, 24, 47–52, 83, 88, 129,
193, 203, 207, 276

FX service (*cont.*)
  description of, 48–49
  Hinchman's views on, 83–84
  in Saunders' opening argument,
    169–170

Garlinghouse, Mark, 65–68, 70, 77,
    136–137, 140
  in MCI-AT&T negotiations, 19–20
  Strassburg and, 48
Geller, Henry, 215
Gergen, David, 223–224, 245
Gifford, Walter, 40, 41
Goeken, Jack, 20, 21, 204
Goldwater, Barry, 353
Grady, Judge, 206–207
Greene, Harold H., 123–131, 136,
    153–160
  Anderson and, 129, 130–131
  AT&T reorganization plan and,
    362–363
  background of, 124–127, 216, 260
  celebrity witnesses and, 282–287,
    312
  continuance request and, 246–
    251, 256
  Crimson Sky and, 153–158, 172–
    173, 177
  cross-examination by, 258–260,
    288
  dismissal proposals and, 232–234,
    262, 263–264
  inter-intra split and, 325, 326–
    330, 336–344
  as "liberal activist judge," 127–
    128, 216, 240
  "lodged" strategy of, 328–330
  opinion on motion to dismiss of,
    262–265, 290
  Richey compared to, 376, 377
  Robinson's criticism of, 363
  Saunders and, 128–131, 171, 179,
    216, 232–233, 235, 237, 240,
    256–260, 277, 282–290, 340–344
  Saunders' challenge to, 264–265,
    266
  Saunders' witness list and, 282–
    285, 312
  Tunney Act proceedings and,
    356, 358–364
  U.S. v. *AT&T* settlement and,
    356–364

U.S. v. *AT&T* trial and, 139, 149,
    155–159, 163–174, 190–210,
    216, 231–238, 246–251, 256–
    265, 278–279, 282–290, 300
  Wooten testimony and, 258–260
Greenwood, Bill, 335

Haig, Alexander, 64, 283
Harris, Larry, 232
  in MCI-AT&T negotiations, 19–
    20, 36–39
  Verveer's conversations with, 55–
    56
Harris, Lou, 307, 367
Hart, Philip A., 29–35, 42, 60
Hart-Scott-Rodino antitrust law, 30
Heig, Frederick, 285
Hellerman, Gerald, 34
Hershey, Loren, 317–320
Hi/Lo pricing, 22–24
Hilsman, William J., 186
Hinchman, Walter, 83–85, 89, 144,
    365, 373
Hooks, Benjamin, 285, 287
Hough, Richard, 11, 12
House of Representatives, U.S., 93,
    110, 352
  Antitrust Subcommittee of, 59
  Commerce Committee of, 354
  Communications Subcommittee
    of, 97–99, 101, 102, 149
  Judiciary Committee of, 128
  Telecommunications
    Subcommittee of, 261–262
H.R. 5158, 353–354, 356
Hugel, Charles, 352–353
  Bell Labs as viewed by, 271–272
  blackboard of, 268–273, 281, 295
  promotion of, 271

IBM, 108
  Baxter's connection to, 377–378
  Justice suit against, 116, 117, 128,
    131, 316–317, 334
  MCI's strategic alliance with, 371
Illinois Bell Telephone Co., 9, 14,
    142
Industrial Reorganization Act, 30–
    32
intercity services, competition of,
    11–15, 22–24, 89–90, 264; *see*

also MCI
interconnection agreements:
Crimson Sky and, 176–177
ENFIA, 275–276, 369–370
MCI-AT&T interim, 36–39
U.S. v. *AT&T* and, 150–151
inter-intra split, 268–281, 292–293,
296–344
aftermath of, 347–380
announcement of, 329–335
AT&T board of directors and,
300–302
Block's publicity campaign and,
291–293, 307–308, 313–316,
332, 333, 335, 347, 348
compromise in, 315–316
Congress and, 347–356
deButts' views on, 378–380
economics of, 270, 273–274
future views of, 365
Harris poll on, 308
"lodging" of document in, 328–
330
national security and, 271–272
origin and description of, 269–
270
settlement decree of, *see*
"Modification of Final
Judgment"; "Modified Final
Judgment"
Tunney Act proceedings and,
356, 358–364

Jackson, C. W., 36–39
Japan, 216
as competitor of Western Electric,
111, 122, 289
Jenner & Block, 194, 202
Joint Chiefs of Staff, 187
Jones, James K., 31
Joskow, Jules, 239–241
judges, motions, 329–330
Justice department, U.S., 54–82
Antitrust division of, 21, 30, 54–
62, 65–71, 73–82; *see also U.S.*
v. *AT&T*; *U.S.* v. *AT&T* trial
Civil Rights division of, 53, 125–
127
Clearwaters' investigation in, 60–
61, 65–70
generational clash in, 54

IBM suit of, 116, 117, 128, 131,
316–317, 334
Office of Professional
Responsibility of, 378
Relief Task Force in, 139, 145,
151, 176
Verveer investigation in, 56, 59–
61, 67, 79, 113–114, 117, 192

Kauper, Thomas, 59–61, 65–70, 77
Kennedy, Edward M., 31
Kennedy, John F., 168
Kennedy, Robert F., 125–126, 127,
167
Kenney, Peter, 140–141, 164, 172–
174, 200, 231, 253, 331, 377
Baxter and, 180–181
Verveer compared to, 140
Key Largo Presidents' Conference
(1972), 5–15, 22, 39, 103, 192,
301
Kilpatric, Jim, 172, 174, 262, 306,
325
King, Martin Luther, 126
Kingsbury Commitment, 58
Kissinger, Henry, 64
Kristol, Irving, 373, 374
Kroll, Leon, 68

Levine, Richard, 253, 365
inter-intra split and, 304–306,
312, 315–317, 322, 325, 330
Levy, Harold, 119–122
Litton Industries, 131, 236
Litvack, Sanford, 145–158, 269
Anderson's successor chosen by,
162–163
Crimson Sky and, 152–158, 173–
179, 185
litigation experience of, 183
in return to private practice, 175,
178–179
Trienens' meetings with, 150–
157, 177
Trienens' phone calls to, 146,
147–148, 149, 177
local operating companies, 10, 24–
25
Baxter's views on, 182–184
corporate management vs., 7, 14
Crimson Sky and, 174, 176–177

local operating companies (*cont.*)
divestiture of, 274, 288–289, 292,
296, 309, 319–321, 349–352,
372–373
inter-intra split and, 274, 319–
321, 349–352
local service franchise of, 320–321
McGowan's recommendations for,
34, 56, 143, 276–277
MCI antitrust suit against, 21
post-breakup, 366–367, 372–373
procurement decisions of, 289–
290
profits of, 372–373
state regulators and, 37–38
U.S. v. *AT&T* and, 142–143, 144,
176
see also specific companies
local service:
increase in price of, 349–351, 366
long distance as subsidy for, 13
state regulation of, 37–39
tariffs, 37–39
long distance, 150–151
AT&T pricing of, 13, 22–24
Bell Bill and, 92–100
local service subsidized by, 13
MCI and, 11–15, 83–91
number of subscribers to, 370
post-breakup prices of, 367
tariffs, 28, 37
Long Lines department, 9, 10,
24–25, 34, 170, 176, 277
Baxter's views on, 182, 183
H.R. 5158 and, 353–354
inter-intra split and, 274, 320–321

MacAvoy, Paul, 373–374
McGill, Archie, 108
McGovern, George, 283, 284, 285
McGowan, William, 16–36, 47–52,
71–72, 148, 170
Anderson secret settlement
attempt and, 143–144
antitrust suit considered by, 20–
21
background of, 17
Bell Bill and, 93–94
credibility problem of, 89–91, 93,
109
deButts compared to, 43

deButts meeting memo of, 25–26
deButts' meeting with, 21–27,
49–50, 368
Execunet and, 83–91, 109
Goeken's relationship with, 20, 21
H.R. 5158 attacked by, 354
inter-intra split and, 274–275
local operating companies as
viewed by, 34, 56, 143, 276–277
Otter Tail case and, 23, 115
Saunders and, 200–210
Strassburg's correspondence with,
51–52
success of, 201–202, 274–275
testimony and cross-examination
of, 200–210, 232
Verveer's conversations with, 55–
56
McLean, Robert, 172–174, 262, 306,
325–326, 339
McLuhan, Marshall, 368
McNeely, Michael, 164
marketing, 107–109, 111, 371
Mauro, Tom, 81
Maxwell, Ronald, 197–199
MCI, 11–39, 47–52, 367
annual revenues of, 201
artificial cost advantage of, 369–
370
AT&T antitrust suit of, 20–21,
27–35, 52, 56, 77, 131, 148–149,
169–171, 202, 371
AT&T negotiations with, 18–25,
34, 36–39, 48
AT&T views on survival of, 89–90
cost of AT&T interconnection
with, 19–20, 275–276, 369–370
CSSA service of, 47, 203, 207
description of AT&T
interconnection with, 18–19
economic problems of, 34–35, 47,
48, 86–87, 89–90, 368, 371
ENFIA agreement and, 275–276,
369–370
Execunet service of, *see* Execunet
FCC and, *see* Federal
Communications Commission
future of, 368–371
FX service of, *see* FX service
IBM's strategic alliance with, 371
interim interconnection contract
of, 36–39
inter-intra split and, 274–275,

276, 353–354
lobbying of, 28–35, 152, 370–371
McGowan's vision of, 27
marketing campaign of, 371
microwave towers of, 12, 15, 18, 27, 34–35, 87, 89
Nader campaign funded by, 353–354
operating costs of, 12, 369–370
"prayer breakfasts" of, 29
stock of, 370
U.S. v. AT&T and, 148–149, 169–171, 196, 200–210, 288–289
Meese, Edwin, 185–186, 189, 211, 242, 322
Baldrige and, 216–218
at cabinet council meeting (July 27), 245–247
Trienes' meetings with, 212, 224–225
message toll service (MTS), 49, 86
migration strategy, 108
Mitchell, John, 57
"Modification of Final Judgment," 305–306, 308–311
"equal access" appendix of, 305, 309
final draft of, 317–319
signing ceremony for, 324–326
snag in negotiations on, 312–315
"Modified Final Judgment," 359, 362
monopoly:
bottleneck, 55–56, 67, 316
likelihood of AT&T's return to, 369
natural, 45–46, 85, 277, 358
Morrison, Hugh, 65–67, 118, 120, 163
U.S. v. AT&T supervised by, 74, 75, 114
motions judges, 329–330
MTS (message toll service), 49, 86
Mullane, Bill, 313

Nader, Ralph, 31, 353–354
Naisbitt, John, 368
National Association of Regulatory Commissioners, 40
National Economic Research Associates (NERA), 239–241

National Press Club, U.S. v. AT&T settlement announced at, 329–334
national security, 186–188, 216
inter-intra split and, 271–272
National Telecommunications and Information Agency (NTIA), 141, 212–216
NERA (National Economic Research Associates), 239–241
New Deal, 45, 58
New York City, AT&T quality problems in, 7, 12, 46
New York Telephone Co., 142
New York Times, 367
Nixon, Richard M., 6, 57, 61, 64
North Carolina, state utility commissioners in, 258–260
Northwestern Bell Telephone Co., 14
NTIA (National Telecommunications and Information Agency), 212–216
Nurnberger, T. S., 14

"Octoberfest" strategy, 284–285
Otter Tail utility case, 23, 115, 116, 131

Pacific Telephone & Telegraph Co., 144, 150, 151, 174, 270
crown jewel divestiture and, 142–143
inter-intra settlement and, 352
poor performance of, 143
Smith's affiliations with, 175, 187, 211, 225
Packwood, Bob, 218, 244
Partoll, Al, 270
Penzias, Arno, 286–287
Pires, Alexander, 140–141
Pope, Bayard, 59
"pots" ("plain old telephone service"):
deButts' emphasis on, 8, 10
decline in quality of, 7–8, 10, 11, 46
MCI required to pay for, 19–20
Powertron Corporation, 17
Presidents' Conferences:
Basking Ridge, 319–321

Presidents' Conferences (*cont.*)
  Key Largo, 5–15, 22, 39, 103, 192, 301
pricing of telephone services, *see* tariffs
private lines, 85–86
  AT&T, 12, 13
  FX as, 84, 88
  inadequacy of MCI reliance on, 27–28, 89–90
  MCI entry into, 11–13
protective coupling arrangements (PCAs), 106–107, 109, 131, 137, 169
  Greene's views on, 263–264
  Hugel's views on, 272
  U.S. v. *AT&T* trial and, 191–192, 263–264
public relations, inter-intra split and, 291–293, 307, 313–316, 332, 333, 335, 347, 348
publishing, electronic, 360–361

Quagmire II, 252–256, 262, 277, 297–301
  AT&T board of directors and, 300, 301
  Levine's handling of, 304

Reagan, Ronald, 148, 150, 160, 175, 244, 248
  Baldrige and, 215, 216
  Baldrige dismissal proposal and, 219
  Baxter appointed by, 177–178, 181, 184–185
  cabinet councils and, 213, 219–222, 223, 243
  dismissal of case rejected by, 254–255
  Eisenhower compared to, 230–231
  Greene's dismissal opinion and, 263, 265
  Meese and, 211, 212
  tax cuts of, 225
  Wirth's letter to, 296
  working style of, 217
Reagan administration:
  business boosterism in, 215
  cabinet councils in, 217–222

Crimson Sky and, 155–158, 173, 175, 177, 185
disengaged presidency in, 223–229
  U.S. v. *AT&T* and, 148, 150, 155–158, 160, 173, 175, 177–178, 184–189, 211–230
regulation, *see* Federal Communications Commission; state regulation
Relief Task Force, 139, 145, 151, 176
Richardson, Eliot, 61
Richey, Charles, 376–377
Robinson, Kenneth, 141–144, 373–374
  divestiture plan of, 141–144, 150–151
  Greene criticized by, 363
Rockefeller, John D., 58
Rodino, Peter, 30, 149, 214, 245, 269, 294
Romnes, H. I., 10, 12, 105
Roncalio, Teno, 98
Roosevelt, Franklin D., 58
Roosevelt, Theodore, 31
Rose, Jonathan, 220–221, 225–228, 230, 247, 355
  Senate Bill 898 and, 244–245
Ross, Ian, 268, 271–272

Saunders, George L., Jr., 75–82, 113, 119, 182, 194–210
  Anderson's meetings with, 121–122
  background and personality of, 75–76, 375–376
  Connell compared to, 162, 165, 167, 194, 195, 196, 262
  continuance request and, 249–251
  courtroom strategy of, 195–199
  Crimson Sky and, 174
  cross-examination conducted by, 196–199, 204–210, 235
  demise of, 375–376
  Greene and, 128–131, 171, 179, 216, 232–233, 235, 237, 240, 256–260, 277, 282–290, 312, 340–344
  Greene challenged by, 264–265, 266
  inter-intra split and, 308–311, 325, 328, 330–331, 340–344

McGowan and, 200–210
MCI antitrust suit and, 148, 149
at NERA conference, 239–241
opening argument of, 159, 166–173
in *Southern Pacific* v. *AT&T*, 376–377
Waddy as viewed by, 123–124
witness list of, 282–285, 312
Saxbe, William, 61–71, 77, 164
Schaefer, Jacob, 263–264
Schmitt, Harrison, 355
Schmults, Edward, 175, 178, 213, 224
Securities and Exchange Commission (SEC), 68–69
Segal, Erich, 166
Senate, U.S., 110, 149, 187, 352
Armed Services Committee of, 188
Commerce Committee of, 251, 355–356
Communications Subcommittee of, 98
Judiciary Committee of, 128, 251, 252
Subcommittee on Antitrust and Monopoly of, 29–35, 42, 60
Weinberger's secret testimony to, 187–188
Senate Bill 898, 242–250, 252, 254, 261–262, 277
Baxter's amendments to, 243–244, 252, 280
passage of, 280
Wirth report and, 295
Shenefield, John, 116, 118, 128, 139
Sherman, John, 30–31
Sherman Act (1890), 30
Sidley & Austin, 59–60, 75–82, 308
judges researched by, 124–127
Silverstein, Alan, 164
Simms, Joe, 118
Simon, William, 70–71
Sirica, John J., 127, 192*n*
Smith, William French, 185–186, 213, 224, 225–226, 245, 317
Baldrige dismissal proposal and, 255
nominated attorney general, 175
Pacific Telephone affiliation of, 175, 187, 211, 225
Southern Bell Telephone &

Telegraph Co., 142
Southern New England Bell Telephone Co., 143, 144, 150, 151, 174, 270
Southern Pacific Corporation, 50–51
Southern Pacific v. *AT&T*, 376–377
Southwestern Bell Telephone Co., 142
price increases of, 351
Specialized Common Carriers, 50, 205–206
Sporkin, Stanley, 69
Sprint, 170, 367, 376
Stanley, Delbert, 350
state regulation, 37–39, 41, 78
FCC rivalry with, 41, 258–260
inter-intra split and, 352
in North Carolina, 258–260
stock:
AT&T, 69, 71, 152, 368
MCI, 370
Strassburg, Bernard, 43–48, 83, 373
background of, 45
FX lines and, 50–52, 86–87
subsidies, 104–105, 258–259, 273
Baxter's views on, 182, 242
cross, 182, 184, 192*n*, 242, 294, 299
long distance as, 13
separations payments, 277
Supreme Court, U.S., 23, 121, 126, 181, 279, 337
Swift, Jonathan, 93
switched telephone network, 11, 24, 56
equipment competition and, 105–107
MCI duplication of, 85–90
Swope, Bill, 118

Tanenbaum, Morris, 268, 271, 325
tariffs:
AT&T, 28, 37–39, 192
costs and, 192, 349
local, 37–39
long-distance, 28, 37
MCI, 85, 87–89
modular, 87–89
telephone competition and, 349–351
Task Force on Telecommunications Policy, 217–219

telecommunications bar, 365–366
telecommunications consultants,
    365
"Telecommunications in Transition"
    (Wirth), 294–295
telephone bills, 366–367
telephone industry:
    economies of scale in, 90
    rates in, see tariffs
    regulation of, see Federal
        Communications Commission;
        state regulation
    transitional period in, 367
    see also American Telephone &
        Telegraph; local operating
        companies; MCI
telephones, see terminal equipment
television, 45, 101
terminal equipment (customer
        premises equipment), 10–11,
        15, 23–24, 104–111
    Bell Bill and, 109–111, 272
    deButts' concern about
        competition in, 105–111
    embedded, 309, 366
    FCC registration proposal and,
        106
    leasing of, 108
    Litton suit over, 131, 236
    protective coupling arrangements
        and, 106–107, 109, 131, 137,
        169, 191–192
    United Fruit approach and, 144
    U.S. v. AT&T and, 169–170, 191–
        192
Toffler, Alvin, 368
Tomlin, Lily, 7–8
Trienens, Howard, 59–60, 76–79,
        140–160, 195, 223, 261–262,
        277–281
    Anderson's meetings with, 121,
        136, 140–146
    at Basking Ridge Presidents'
        Conference, 319–321
    Baxter and, 184–186, 297–299,
        303, 309
    continuance request and, 248–251
    Crimson Sky and, 152–158, 166,
        173, 174, 177, 178
    Greene's dismissal opinion and,
        266, 267
    inter-intra split and, 268–271,
        275, 279–280, 292–293, 297–

        299, 303, 306, 308–313, 315–
        317, 319–321, 325, 327, 330, 348
    leadership style of, 277–278
    Litvack's meetings with, 150–157,
        177
    Litvack's phone calls to, 146, 147–
        148, 149, 177
    Meese's meetings with, 212, 224–
        225
    Quagmire II and, 254, 297, 298
    Senate Bill 898 and, 280
    Wirth report and, 294–295
Truman, Harry S., 58
Tunney, John, 31
Tunney Act, 256, 299, 325, 327, 337,
        341
    AT&T settlement and, 356, 358–
        364

Unger, Sherman, 217, 218, 223, 245
    Quagmire II and, 252–253, 254
United Fruit approach, 142, 144, 151
U.S. v. AT&T, 74–82, 107, 113–131
    Anderson approach to, 117–119,
        121, 122, 130
    Anderson's secretive settlement
        attempt in, 138–146, 269
    as antitrust case vs. regulatory
        dispute, 78, 81–82, 114, 121
    appeal of, 279, 300, 337
    AT&T attempts at settlement of,
        119–122, 140–159, 266–267
    Baxter's views on, 374
    Brown's attempt to find quick
        solution to, 122, 129, 136, 140,
        144, 173, 212
    class warfare in, 373, 374
    cost of legal expenses in, 335
    Crimson Sky and, 152–158, 164,
        166
    defense issues in, 186–188
    deregulation vs. regulation in
        breakup of, 373–374
    inter-intra split and, see inter-intra
        split
    Kristol's views on, 373, 374
    leaks and, 152, 188–189, 230
    MCI suit as influence on, 148–
        149, 169–171
    piggybacking in, 152, 184
    pretrial discovery in, 130–131
    public's views of, 193–194

reactivation of, 114, 122
Reagan administration and, 148, 150, 155–158, 160, 173, 175, 177–178, 184–189, 211–230
Robinson settlement plan in, 141–142, 150–151
Saunders' sabotaging of, 76–82, 113
Senate Bill 898 and, 242–250
settlement of, 324–344; *see also* inter-intra split
settlement requirements in, 142, 150–151
Supreme Court's view of, 121
terminal equipment and, 169–170, 191–192
Verveer approach to, 114, 117–118
Verveer's views on, 74
U.S. v. *AT&T* trial, 123–124, 139, 144, 149, 151–152, 163–174, 190–210, 230–238
Baldrige dismissal proposal and, 216–228, 230
as bench trial, 164
best case vs. worst case scenario for, 279
Brown's testimony in, 301–302
celebrity witnesses in, 282–287, 312
Connell's cross-examination strategy in, 286–287
Connell's opening arguments in, 163–166
continuance request and, 246–251
deButts' testimony in, 262
Greene's cross-examination in, 258–260, 288
Greene's "lodged" strategy in, 328–330
McGowan's testimony in, 200–210, 232
MCI case and, 169–171, 196, 200–210, 288–289
"Octoberfest" strategy in, 284–285
opening of, 159, 163–173
peer review of, 278, 288
postponement request and, 155–159
protective coupling arrangements and, 191–192, 263–264
recesses of, 173, 238

Saunders' courtroom strategy in, 195–199
Saunders' cross-examination in, 196–199, 204–210, 235
Saunders' witness list in, 282–285, 312
start of Saunders' defense case in, 256–260
Wooten testimony in, 258–260

VADIC (company), 197–199
Vail, Theodore, 58
Van Deerlin, Lionel, 99
Van Sinderen, A. W., 14
Verveer, Philip, 53–63, 66, 73–76, 113–119
Anderson compared to, 115–117, 121
AT&T investigated by, 56, 59–61, 67, 79, 113–114, 117, 192
Kenney compared to, 140
legal experience of, 73–74
morality of, 53–54, 74, 115–117, 121
replacement and resignation of, 118–119
Saunders as viewed by, 75, 76
Saunders' views on, 78
U.S. v. *AT&T* and, 74–76, 78–82, 107, 192
Villieres, Paul, 270
Vita, Jean, 329–330
Voltaire, 169

Waddy, Joseph C., 79–82, 114, 123–124, 127
Wallace, George, 259, 260
Wall Street Journal, 188, 350, 363, 377–378
Washington, D.C. Bar Association, 366
Washington *Star*, 257
Watergate, 57, 61
WATS, 13
Weinberger, Caspar, 186–189, 211, 216, 241–242
AT&T position paper of, 257–258
Cabinet council and, 219, 220
inter-intra split and, 321–322, 355
secret testimony of, 187–188
Western Electric Company, 9, 10,

Western Electric Company (*cont.*)
56, 149, 216, 240, 279, 288–290,
299–300
Baxter's views on, 182, 183
Bell Labs' relationship with, 271–
272
competition and, 105, 111, 120,
122, 192, 264, 271–272, 289
Crimson Sky and, 174–175
FCC investigation of, 60
Greene's views on, 288, 290, 299–
300
inter-intra split and, 271–272,
274, 320–321
Justice suits to force divestiture
of, 58–59, 60, 65–67
operating companies' bias
toward, 289–290
post-breakup, 371–372
renaming of, 371
U.S. v. *AT&T* and, 142, 144, 150,
151, 176
White House, Office of
Telecommunications Policy, 60
Wiley, Richard, 356, 365

Wilkes-Barre, Penn., 17, 22
Will, George, 168
Wilson, Woodrow, 58
Wirth, Timothy, 97, 99–102, 261–
262, 280–281, 294–296, 300, 315
H.R. 5158 introduced by, 353–
354, 356
inter-intra split settlement and,
353–355
"Telecommunications in
Transition" of, 294–295
Wood, John, 68
Wooten, Marvin, 258–260
Wright, Skelly, 111
Wunder, Bernard, 211–216, 218,
220, 223, 234–235
Senate Bill 898 and, 244, 245

Yauch, Michael, 195
Yellow Pages, 362

Zeglis, John, 195

Steve Coll was born in Washington, D.C., and is a
Phi Beta Kappa graduate of Occidental College in Los
Angeles. He has worked as a contributing editor for
California and *Inc.* magazines and was most recently
a staff writer for the *Washington Post*. His writing has
appeared in several anthologies and in dozens of
newspapers and magazines in the United States and
abroad. Coll, who lives with his wife and daughter
in Gaithersburg, Maryland, is currently at work on
his next book, an account of the battle for control of
Getty Oil.